P9-DVS-930

Mistakes and Miracles

CONGREGATIONS ON THE ROAD TO MULTICULTURALISM

Nancy Palmer Jones and Karin Lin

Skinner House Books
BOSTON

Copyright © 2019 by Nancy Palmer Jones and Karin Lin. All rights reserved.

Published by Skinner House Books, an imprint of the Unitarian Universalist Association, a liberal religious organization with more than 1,000 congregations in the U.S. and Canada, 24 Farnsworth St., Boston, MA 02210-1409.

www.skinnerhouse.org

Printed in the United States

Cover design by Kathryn Sky-Peck
Text design by Jeff Miller
Nancy Palmer Jones photo by Dana Grover
Karin Lin author photo by Suzi Grossman

print ISBN: 978-1-55896-841-7
eBook ISBN: 978-1-55896-842-4

6 5 4 3 2 1
23 22 21 20 19

CIP data is on file with the Library of Congress

"Prayer for Living in Tension" reprinted with permission of Joseph M. Cherry.
"Call of Something More" reprinted with permission of Marta I. Valentín.

PRAYER FOR LIVING IN TENSION

If we have any hope of transforming the world and changing
* ourselves,*
we must be
bold enough to move into our discomfort,
brave enough to be clumsy there,
loving enough to forgive ourselves and others.

May we, as a people of faith, be granted the strength to be
so bold,
so brave,
and so loving.

—Rev. Joseph M. Cherry

DEDICATION

For all congregations everywhere who embark
and who stay on the journey,
and especially for the members and friends
of the First Unitarian Church of San José
and First Parish in Cambridge (Unitarian Universalist),
the congregations where we make our spiritual home—
for they teach us what it means to be fully human
in community:
vulnerable and curious,
stumbling, falling, and rising again,
loving and learning to love.
They give us the brave space, the time, and the trust
in which we can do this work
and learn how to do it better.
They inspire us, always, to grow alongside them.

Contents

Foreword

Janice Marie Johnson

FROM TIME TO TIME, *I ask myself, how might I meet a longing for the kind of intentional engagement that will transform my faith, deepen my faith, and enrich my soul?*

How refreshing it is that Karin Lin and Nancy Palmer Jones have taken the time to write a book that addresses my questions with intention, love, and respect.

My life experience has afforded me an understanding of multiculturalism *writ large*. I have spent much time living in cultures other than my own. I move comfortably in the world as an internationalist, a Jamaican of the Caribbean Diaspora, and surprising to me, as a New Yorker.

As a culture builder, I fervently believe that that there is a force greater than our individual selves telling us that we *need* to act in spite of any discomfort.

This force beckons us into the brave space that author and activist Micky ScottBey Jones invites us into—this realistic place, as opposed to a privileged, safe space.

We know, instinctively, how to be of help to others. But we humans are very good at resisting our instincts, especially when they are telling us to do something that takes us out of our comfort zone.

This volume invites us into careful inquiry of the bumpy journey toward building Beloved Community. In addition to lifting up the mistakes *and* the miracles along the way, the authors offer us powerful, reflective questions to deepen our understanding of what is at stake. We get clear about what we give up—as well as what we gain—in the journey.

Lin and Jones have taken quality time to focus on five congregations being intentional about building the Beloved Community. They have carefully studied the identities, cultures, and ethos of these respective congregations. They have examined how they deal with race, racial equity, and racialized resistance.

THE STORIES IN THIS BOOK are made up of moments large and small that emerge in hindsight as defining moments. They are the moments that shape a community's identity, its history, and its vision for the future. I know from my own lived experience that the personal and historical impacts of such moments are intertwined. In 1962, I witnessed the birth of a nation exemplified by the Union Jack being lowered and *my* Jamaican flag being raised at the birth of a nation—*my* nation, Jamaica. This moment left an indelible mark on my heart. I had witnessed the power of self-determination that my ancestors, my parents, and their peers had strived for.

During my lifetime, I witnessed the first man and woman landing on the moon. I witnessed carbon copies give rise to laser copies and telephones give rise to cellphones. I witnessed the rise to stardom of Marian Anderson, Paul Robeson, Nina Simone, Prince, Luther Vandross, India.Arie, and Beyoncé.

I also witnessed the following:

On September 22, 1973, Billie Jean King beat Bobby Riggs during a tennis match dubbed the "Battle of the Sexes." Riggs had boldly asserted that a woman could never beat a man at tennis. King proved him wrong by defeating him as part of her fight for equal pay for women's tennis.

Back in the day, I took a strong political stand against injustice. For example, I vowed never to visit South Africa until it became free of the plague of apartheid. In 1990, after twenty-seven years in confinement, Comrade Nelson Mandela was released from prison. Four short years later, in 1994, he was inaugurated as South Africa's first black president, leading with an unfathomable spirit of forgiveness for those who had stolen those many years of his life from him.

I wryly note that some of my defining moments have been centered around presidents. In 2009, I could hardly believe that a black man became the forty-fourth president of the United States. During his inauguration speech, President Barack Obama said, "We, the people, declare today that the most evident of truths— that all of us are created equal—is the star that guides us still, just as it guided our forebears through Seneca Falls and Selma and Stonewall. . . . " That this First Family sustained this presidency without assassination is to me, indeed, a miracle.

I applaud Martha McSally, the first woman in the Air Force to fly in combat. After becoming a senator, she had the courage to testify in front of the Senate Armed Services Sub-Committee about being sexually assaulted in the military by a superior and officer. Following her compelling testimony, the Sexual Assault Accountability and Investigation Task Force was formed. This is reminiscent of the development of the Unitarian Universalist Association's Safe Congregations program.

During my Unitarian Universalist lifetime, I can't help but notice that presidents continue to factor into my picture. In 2001 I celebrated the election of the first minister of African descent to become president of the UUA, Rev. Bill Sinkford. In 2009, I celebrated the election of the first Latino minister to be elected as president of the UUA, Rev. Peter Morales. Two years ago, in 2017, I celebrated the election of the first woman to be elected as president of the UUA, Rev. Dr. Susan Frederick-Gray.

I also celebrated the first trio to be appointed as interim co-presidents of the UUA: Rev. Bill Sinkford, Rev. Dr. Sofía Betancourt, and Dr. Leon Spencer. All three are black and one is also Latinx. Two are ministers and one is a lay leader. All of this, in *my* UUA lifetime!

We are in yet another moment in time that defies imagination: Unitarian Universalists are daring to "get right" with the fight against white supremacy culture. We have committed ourselves to a no-turning-back journey to build new ways to express, to live into, and to *be* our cherished faith. We are demanding for ourselves that we concretize our aspirations and ensure that they are centered in *our* story.

Today, we dare to invite equity and transparency to the fore. Demanding it of others has been easy. Demanding it of ourselves as religious professionals, UUA staff, lay leaders, and as congregations and communities has been hard for us. We are moving toward being the people whom we seek to be—*no matter what.*

Unitarian Universalists need to disrupt the workings of racism to transform, truly transform, how we relate across racial, ethnic, and cultural differences in our congregations and beyond.

We need to articulate and embrace individual and community practices vital for sustaining our living faith now and into the future.

Karin Lin and Nancy Palmer Jones have chosen to risk being vulnerable with their respective stories and with those of others who have entrusted their stories to these courageous authors. They have taken a keen look at tumultuous challenges and difficult choices. Thankfully, they have chosen to center *relationship* as core to their work and ministry. They invite us to listen deeply and listen deeper still. The stories that they lift up are real, raw, and revealing. They invite us to face them without flinching and without denying the truth that we are invited to be privy to.

This volume invites us to notice when and how we lift up the voices of diverse populations of people and our partnerships with them as we, with intention, break down our congregational walls to create robust, vibrant community centers. And there's more. We need to make room among ourselves to step back, ensuring venues for our partners to speak to us, knowing that their voices must be heard by us.

Karin Lin and Nancy Palmer Jones are helping us to develop our antiracist, antioppressive, and multicultural habits and skills in order to prepare us to do our part to collectively nurture multiculturally competent, actively antiracist congregations into being. They are memorializing the kinds of moments that form our identity, our history, and our vision for the future. For this, I give thanks.

Introduction:
The Power of Stories at a Crucial Time

> For transformation to occur, we all need stories of people who
> are working to dismantle this culture of white supremacy,
> stories that reveal what it takes to go against the grain. We
> need stories of people who are striving to create new ways of
> being together, ways that truly merit the name "Beloved
> Community."

EARLY ON THE FIRST FULL DAY of the Unitarian Universalist
Association's Justice General Assembly in June 2017, the three
interim co-presidents take their places, along with the conversation's facilitator, in black overstuffed chairs set stage right on the
convention center stage. For a gathering of thousands of Unitarian
Universalists accustomed to prepared reports presented at a central podium, the tone and setting are striking.

Prompted by facilitator Jesse King, Rev. Sofía Betancourt,
Rev. Bill Sinkford, and Dr. Leon Spencer engage in thirty-five
minutes of informal reflection on their brief time in office. They
speak from their hearts about what this moment means for the
faith. And in a religion that is still predominantly white, it is also
striking that—as they themselves point out—all four of the people onstage are people of color.

Everything about this break in business as usual at the religion's annual assembly communicates that Unitarian Universal-

ism sits at a crucial juncture. It is not the first of such crossroads and no doubt not the last, but it is certainly a make-or-break moment. Three months ago, in March 2017, the UUA's then-president, Rev. Peter Morales, has resigned amid charges that the Association's hiring practices for lead roles in the association favor white, male, cisgender, ordained Unitarian Universalist ministers—symptoms of the white supremacy culture that still holds the United States in its grip.[1]

The widely publicized charges of institutional racism, followed by Morales's resignation and that of other key leaders, have caused a disruption in this faith movement that shocks many Unitarian Universalists, especially some who are white. But as Rev. Sofía says at that General Assembly, "most UU people of color were not surprised—only surprised that it had been called out." That difference—between those who are surprised and those who are not—points to the painful, healing work of truth telling, understanding, accountability, relationship building, and structural change that Unitarian Universalists need to do.

Onstage in the big black chairs at General Assembly, the interim co-presidents frame the disruptions in Unitarian Universalism as an opportunity—an opportunity, Rev. Bill says, to "chart a different, more inclusive, more grounded course forward." If we "focus not on the *persons* but the *patterns*," he urges, then we can discover ways to "embody this fabulous faith and make some changes so that we can live into a hopeful future."

The work of dismantling white supremacy culture and creating a faith that lives up to its promise of Beloved Community "is an inside job," Dr. Spencer emphasizes. This moment, then, is an "opportunity for us to do the inside work in our fellowships and congregations. There is *lots* of inside work to be done, and it's

---

[1] Please read "Some Words about Language," which follows this introduction, to learn about our language choices.

rich." His smile at the prospect adds a few hundred watts to the powerful stage lights.

Rev. Sofía reminds us that what makes it possible to view this moment as one of "*incredible* opportunity" are the many Unitarian Universalist groups who have come together to respond in new and different ways. Religious educators Aisha Hauser, Christina Rivera, and Kenny Wiley have created curricula and webinars so that more than seven hundred congregations could hold "UU White Supremacy Teach-ins" that spring. Equally important, the decades-long struggles and gifts of Unitarian Universalists of color, as well as those of white allies and accomplices, provide a foundation that makes this moment one of opportunity rather than discouragement and despair.

A moment of opportunity built on a history of engagement. A new turning point in a long journey. When we co-authors arrive at General Assembly 2017, we have been wrestling with such images for months. By this time, we are already three years into the research for and writing of this book. We have examined history, visited congregations, and mined our own experiences of struggle and growth on the road to creating multicultural, anti-racist Beloved Community. The disruptions of the spring have shaken us; will our perspectives still be relevant?

The interim co-presidents' words affirm our approach and renew our determination. The events of the spring have laid bare the raw pain that white supremacy culture causes so many people of color in our congregations and our movement. In truth, white supremacy culture diminishes and dehumanizes white lives too, even though (and maybe because) being part of any "dominant" group can make these losses harder to see.

For transformation to occur, we all need stories of people who are working to dismantle this culture, stories that reveal what it takes to go against the grain. We need stories of people who are striving to create new ways of being together, ways that truly merit the name "Beloved Community." These stories of works in progress won't go out of date, at least not any time soon.

The road to building multicultural, antiracist Beloved Community is long, and the work never ends. A brief look at Unitarian Universalism's history in this area over the past two decades illustrates these core truths.

THE ROAD IS LONG

Twenty-five years before the interim co-presidents come onto the convention center stage for that informal conversation, Unitarian Universalists at the 1992 General Assembly call on the UUA's then-president, along with the moderator, Board of Trustees, staff, and all the congregations, to turn the "vision of a racially diverse and multicultural Unitarian Universalism" into a "substantive reality" (Responsive Resolution, 1992). In 1997, this call becomes a Business Resolution, "Toward an Antiracist Unitarian Universalist Association," which includes specific suggestions for next steps on the journey.

Unitarian Universalism has wrestled, off and on, with issues of race and culture, implicit bias, and sometimes life-destroying exclusion since the establishment of its parent religions in the United States more than two hundred years ago. With these votes in the 1990s, the movement for antiracism and multiculturalism in the institution of the UUA and in our congregations gains intentionality and renewed focus.

Over the next two decades, the UUA creates teams, including the Journey Toward Wholeness Transformation Committee, to assess its progress. The UUA and other Unitarian Universalists develop an ever-evolving series of antiracism and multicultural-competency trainings. Some congregations dive in, examining systemic racism in themselves and their surroundings and setting up their own Transformation Teams to help keep them on the road. Unitarian Universalists of color form powerful organizations of support, including the Diverse Revolutionary Unitarian Universalist Multicultural Ministries (DRUUMM), the Latino/a Unitarian Universalists Networking Association (LUUNA), the Asian/Pacific Islander Caucus (A/PIC) of DRUUMM, and in 2015, Black Lives of Unitarian Universalism (BLUU). White Unitarian Universalists create Allies for Racial Equity (ARE), a group that holds itself accountable to these communities of color.

These are crucial stages in a much longer journey. Those who plunge in at this point, or who have already been engaged for years, experience the joys and the frustrations of striving to reverse centuries-long habits around multiculturalism and white supremacy. They note the slow pace of progress, and they celebrate the gains. They lay down a strong foundation on which Unitarian Universalism can build.

Still, it's hard to estimate what percentage of Unitarian Universalists participate in the trainings, the caucuses, the support groups, and the intentional changes of those two decades. As the disruptions of the spring of 2017 make clear, these changes haven't yet been thoroughly institutionalized. They haven't yet created the deep structural changes that Bill Sinkford refers to when he mentions the need to focus "not on the *persons* but the *patterns.*" Both on the national level and at the grassroots, in the majority of congregations themselves, there is still so much work to be done.

WHY THE FOCUS ON CONGREGATIONS NOW?

In the first two decades of the twenty-first century, many brick-and-mortar religious communities have seen membership and attendance drop. People have lots of choices now for how they spend their weekends, and many demands on their time.

They have some new choices too, for how and where they go to strengthen their values, make meaning of their lives, and build community—the gifts that faith communities have traditionally offered. Opportunities to build relationships across differences show up in many areas of twenty-first-century life. Identity-based groups, entrepreneurial ministries, online and virtual gatherings, social justice coalitions, and interfaith work offer exciting possibilities for multiracial, multicultural interaction and relationship building.

Even so, physically gathering together in a congregation remains a primary method of engagement, growth, and learning for many faithful people. This is perhaps especially true for Unitarian Universalists, whose congregational polity identifies the source of each community's authority as the local congregation itself. Christina Rivera, in an April 2017 episode of *The VUU*, the Church of the Larger Fellowship's weekly podcast, reminds listeners that the Unitarian Universalist Association is in fact an "association *of congregations*."

"So the congregations and the communities are really where the structure and a lot of the power of the UUA lies," Christina goes on. "Power—I say that both in the framework of strength and also of change." This is why Christina, Aisha Hauser, and Kenny Wiley choose to hold the "UU White Supremacy Teach-ins" in congregational settings.

Rev. Susan Frederick-Gray, elected president of the UUA at Justice General Assembly 2017, underscores the importance of congregations in her President's Report a year later. She begins, "What a time this is! A time when we are all being called into a deeper practice of our theology—living into the call at the heart of Unitarian Universalism for Beloved Community—a community that practices a radically inclusive and compassionate, antiracist, antioppressive, multicultural, multigenerational faith within, and acts powerfully in partnership and solidarity for justice and liberation beyond." The work to create such Beloved Community, she goes on, "takes deepest root within our congregations—where we live into the fullness of the calling."

We co-authors believe in the power and potential of congregations and of communities like them. Our own experiences show us that when a diverse group of people hang in there together—mindfully, humbly trying to embody their faith in all they say and do, while learning how to be in right relationship with each other—miracles of transformation take place both in the congregation's individual members and in the institution itself.

Congregations are living, breathing human organisms. They are messy, constantly in flux, and prone to make mistakes. Yet they also can be sources of inspiration, comfort, action, and joy. They are not where the fastest change happens on an issue, but they can be where some of the most important and enduring change happens.

"We are a covenantal faith where we call each other into the work," Christina Rivera reminds us. On the one hand, when congregations and their congregants fail to live up to this covenant, they can harm the people who have trusted them. Too often those harmed come from traditionally marginalized groups. Too often these people are barred from the center of our congregations or pushed out entirely.

On the other hand, when we Unitarian Universalists live up to our covenant—when we build radically inclusive, compassionate, antiracist, antioppressive, multicultural, multigenerational communities that act in partnership and solidarity for justice and liberation, as Rev. Susan describes—then we revitalize the whole project of congregational life. Then our congregational stories can serve as inspiration points, cautionary tales, and launching pads for both traditional brick-and-mortar congregations and newer, twenty-first-century forms of community building.

THE CONGREGATIONS WE STUDY

By the time we begin this project, quite a few Unitarian Universalist congregations are participating in the work of creating multicultural, antiracist Beloved Community. How do we choose just a few of them to study?

We start with these criteria: We want to pluck out a handful of congregations that sit in different parts of the country, serve different demographics, are different sizes, and are at different stages of their journey toward multiculturalism. We want to lift up the famous and the not-so-famous.

We also want to honor the work of congregations that take part in the Unitarian Universalist Association's Mosaic Makers consultation, convened by the UUA's Office of Multicultural Growth and Witness, led by Taquiena Boston. Mosaic Makers: Leading Vital Multicultural Congregations is a group of about twenty congregations whose leaders gather every two or three years to share their challenges and successes and to deepen their multicultural skills through workshops and training sessions.

In 2012, for a book tentatively titled *Mosaic*, some of the Mosaic Makers produce draft chapters about a portion of their journey. Each chapter is written by a multiracial team. The full manuscript is never completed, but the draft chapters become a crucial source for our own work and discernment.

We finally settle on five congregations that meet our criteria and that greet us with remarkable openness and generosity as we dive into our research:

- Unitarian Universalist Church of Annapolis, Maryland
- Unitarian Universalist Congregation of Phoenix, Arizona
- All Souls Unitarian Church, Tulsa, Oklahoma
- First Parish in Cambridge, Massachusetts
- First Unitarian Church of San José, California

Supported by two grants from the Fund for Unitarian Universalism, we visit each of these congregations over the course of several years. We drive around the cities where they are located, because a congregation's specific context makes a difference in how it approaches the work. We read congregational histories to catch a glimpse of what's in each congregation's DNA. We absorb mission and vision statements. We look at how these congregations structure their work on multicultural competencies and antiracism. We worship with each congregation, and we pay attention to what moves us. We notice whether one of us feels more comfortable or welcome than the other.

Most of all, we speak by phone and in person with laypeople and clergy members, passionate champions of the work alongside some doubters and a few naysayers. We call all of these folks our "conversation partners," and we focus on building accountable, trustworthy relationships with them so that a full range of truths can be told.

THE STRUCTURE OF THIS BOOK

The first chapter of this book takes up a key question: Since Unitarian Universalism is a noncreedal faith, what in our theology demands that we do the work of building multicultural, antiracist Beloved Community? Chapter 1, "The Call of Our Faith," invites a range of voices to help us express the core message of Unitarian Universalism that makes this work essential to who we are.

Chapter 2, "Common Threads," looks at themes that run through every congregational story. In this chapter, we draw on the wisdom of beloved colleagues and other researchers to suggest habits that can help create a new way of being together.

In describing our Common Threads, we are inspired by, but not limited to, the core principles that earlier researchers have discovered, most of them studying Christian communities. Our Common Threads, though, are not a roadmap or a to-do list. That approach would just reinscribe the either/or, "expert"-driven practices of the culture we want to change. Rather, these Common Threads offer multiple points of entry for congregations that want to launch or deepen their journey toward multicultural, antiracist Beloved Community.

Chapters 3 through 7—the congregational chapters—offer the complex stories of our five chosen communities. These are human stories of conflict and redemption, of setbacks and transformations, of mistakes, misgivings, and the hard-won miracles that make this work worthwhile.

Because we each participate wholeheartedly in our own congregations' journey toward multiculturalism, we risk telling the stories of our two communities in the first person—Karin for First Parish in Cambridge and Nancy for the First Unitarian Church of San José. We offer a glimpse of what it feels like to be us in our roles as lay leader and senior minister. What does it feel like to be this particular person of color, Karin, and this particular white minister, Nancy, in congregations striving to create multicultural, antiracist Beloved Community? In chapters 6 and 7, we tell you our stories of longing, love, discouragement, hope, and transformation.

Finally, chapter 8, "The Journey Continues," sums up our own experiences in writing this book and describes how the project has changed us.

At the end of the book, we include a list of additional resources—books, videos, podcasts, websites, and more that we find helpful. We refer to many of these resources throughout our chapters. We hope our readers will develop an ongoing practice of searching for emerging, contemporary resources, as well as timeless ones, to fuel their journey toward building Beloved Community.

RELATIONAL, ACCOUNTABLE, AND INEVITABLY PARTIAL

This book has come to life *in relationship*. Rather than asking people to describe their experiences in their own essays, we have invited them into conversation and asked them to trust us with their stories. In our interviews, we have asked questions and listened deeply, but we have chimed in too. We haven't pretended to be neutral observers or set ourselves up as trained sociologists or scholars. Our conversation partners have gotten to know us, at least a little, just as we have gotten to know them. We have met them as colleagues and potential friends, all of us caring deeply about our faith.

As each chapter neared completion, we sent it for review to everyone mentioned. We then worked with our partners' requests for revisions, returned to dialogue with them when we had questions about how a story should be framed, and tried to be transparent about why and how we reached our decisions.

We honor everyone who has contributed to this project, and we are profoundly grateful for their generosity and trust. We are responsible for the final versions of each chapter and thus for any mistakes we have made. Our commitment to the relationships created in this process will outlast the years we have given to this particular book.

We also know how *partial* our work is, in many senses of that word. In the first place, every congregation featured here deserves a whole book of its own. Even our meaty chapters can capture only a fraction of their stories.

Second, although deep institutional change can take a long time in congregational life, which makes some of our themes timeless, still there's a constant ebb and flow in community. Ministers change locations or retire. Some of our conversation partners move, and some die over the course of our writing. What's more, because each of these five congregations is deeply committed to the journey toward multicultural, antiracist Beloved Community, they keep trying new ways of moving forward, and they keep reaching new stages of the journey.

We have had to focus on just a few aspects of each congregation's story, simplifying some details and limiting ourselves to a relatively narrow time frame. The nuances we include are rich and telling, but the stories are partial, indeed.

This work is partial in other senses too. We have chosen to focus this project on race and ethnicity, but we are deeply aware of the pressing need for attention to other areas of oppression, such as ableism, heterosexism, sexism, and transphobia, to name just a few. We know that our readers bring an intersection of complex identities to their encounter with this book, just as we do, and that they will want to see their own struggles represented.

But we also know that trying to focus on all oppressions at once dilutes our work on any one of them. At Justice General Assembly 2017, Rev. Sofía Betancourt says about the interim co-presidents' work, "We have an intersectional approach and it centers on race, and this is how we become more whole."

Earlier that week, speaking to members of the Unitarian Universalist Ministers Association about intersectionality, she stresses that "there's no getting away from the importance of race in establishing systems of dominance. There's an interconnected narrative of systems of dominance. We chip away at our humanity," she exclaims, when we ignore either the centrality of the social construct of race in white supremacy culture or the way that the racial system of dominance influences all others.

We co-authors are partial to this view. Our life experiences and our experiences in Unitarian Universalism teach us that Rev. Sofía's words hold truth.

We are partial in another way too. Our experiences as Unitarian Universalists have brought us into community with just a portion of the great interconnected web of people working to build multicultural, antiracist Beloved Community. We call on our longtime mentors and friends for this project; at the same time, we have strived to expand our own web of connections.

For instance, reading *Centering: Navigating Race, Authenticity, and Power in Ministry*, edited by Rev. Mitra Rahnema, adds crucial voices to our own learning. And, of course, our visits to our five chosen congregations introduce us to whole villages of folks we wouldn't have known otherwise. We hope that this partialness both reassures our readers and inspires them to honor their current relationships, to deepen them, and to stretch to connect with more people.

Finally, we bring our own lives and identities to this work. Although we include the voices of many other people in this book, we use our own voices to string theirs together. In the sheer act of writing down others' words, in our descriptions of people, events, and contexts, we inevitably interpret and shape these stories under the influence of who we are, all that we have learned and been taught, where we are now on our own journeys toward multiculturalism, and how much of our own biases, our own partiality, we are able to perceive and address right now.

Throughout this book, we strive for transparency and mindfulness about our interpretations. But our own particular stories create the lenses through which we tell the stories of others. So, before we move further along, we want to share parts of our stories too.

WHO ARE WE?

KARIN LIN: I grow up in the late 1970s and '80s in Manhattan, Kansas, as the only child of Taiwanese immigrants. I do not remember a time when I did not know I was different: I look xxviii | MISTAKES AND MIRACLES

different, my parents speak a different language, I bring food for lunch that is unfamiliar to my peers. In sixth grade, a girl I consider a friend tells me that I "don't really belong here," and I nod in agreement. That is, after all, the message I have heard throughout my eleven years of life.

Studious and academically ambitious, I know that my race affects how people see me, but I assimilate to the best of my ability. In college, when my white boyfriend tells his mother about me, she grumbles, "Well, at least she's not Black." My only response is relief—relief that, yes, I am close enough to "white" to be acceptable.

As a physics major at the Massachusetts Institute of Technology in the early nineties, I notice the multitude of Asian religious and cultural groups around campus, but I have no use for them and am somewhat baffled by their existence. Throughout my college years and during my doctoral program at the University of California, Berkeley, sexism is a far more salient issue for me than racism.

Shortly after 9/11, my white husband and I step into our first Unitarian Universalist congregation. The intellectual sermons and our highly educated fellow congregants make us comfortable, and we rise quickly into leadership. We feel like part of a family and appreciate the community even more after the birth of our two daughters. In 2006, I am elected to the Board of Directors.

As president-elect, I begin to focus on a question that has always puzzled me: Why, at the gateway to Silicon Valley in one of the most diverse areas of the nation, is our congregation, which has so much to offer, still over 90 percent white? I am completely unaware of the conversation that has been happening elsewhere in our religion for over a decade. I have never heard the terms *white privilege* or *institutionalized racism*. In my naïveté, I think this is simply a matter of outreach, a project that needs a leader. I have no idea that this will begin a process of deep awakening, tremendous pain, and all-encompassing love that will completely transform my life and my understanding of my faith.

Over the next two years, I begin to understand what it means to claim my racial identity and ethnic heritage. Conversations on race begin; the energy grows, but so does the resistance. "I'm the last white person in my neighborhood," says a white congregant. "I like coming to a place where I can just be with other white people." I am confused and hurt, particularly by anti-Asian comments spoken directly to my face by people I have happily worked with for years. Do they not realize I'm Asian? Do they want me to agree with them?

Utterly inexperienced, unsettled by my own transformation, I am unable to hear these comments as anything other than personal. I feel alone, confused, and no longer at home in my congregation. After completing my term as Board president, I resign my membership from the only faith community I have ever known.

For many months I float around, trying different congregations, doubting more and more that there is a place for me in Unitarian Universalism. In the spring of 2009, I learn of First Parish in Cambridge, Massachusetts, their strong desire to create a congregation that reflects the diversity of their community, and their commitment to hiring an associate minister of color. Two months later, by luck or divine intervention, I am recruited for a job in Boston, and in the fall I move back to the East Coast.

At First Parish, I find fertile soil for the antiracism and multiculturalism work that has become my calling. I find a congregation that embraces me in my entirety, honoring my gifts and loving me in my brokenness. Within two weeks, I am recruited to the newly created Transformation Team, which I will later chair for more than three years. Pain, loss, and despair give way to joy, healing, and hope. I have found a home, yes, but I have also found myself.

This journey, on which I never intended to embark but to which I am irrevocably committed, has led me to cross borders both literal and figurative, to challenge myself to see the world differently, to find strength and courage I never knew I had. For this richness in my life, for a faith that shows me how love can triumph over fear, I am eternally grateful.

NANCY PALMER JONES: I grow up white European American in the 1950s and '60s, first in the multicultural city of San Antonio, Texas, and then in the segregated suburbs of Dallas. My early awakenings to the impact of race and racism are unforgettable and painful. When I am eight years old, for example, my mother, also white, tells me that I can't develop a friendship with the only African-American boy in my class because, she says, "we just can't let this get started."

That day in 1960, my mother speaks out of her own embeddedness in white supremacy culture. She wouldn't have used that name for it, and its demands don't chime with her heart, but they are all she knows. I already sense that there's something terribly wrong about her perspective, but in third grade, I feel powerless to change it.

My first understanding of my whiteness, then, is one of loss: I'm not supposed to build relationships across the barriers of race, ethnicity, and class; my beloved mom holds a view that I'm not sure I can trust; and I have hurt my longed-for friend. A journey of broken-openheartedness begins.

It makes some sense, then, that my first vocations as a professional actress and freelance book editor focus on telling and embodying complex human stories. These vocations expand my circles of friendship and connection, bridging differences not just in race, class, and ethnicity but also in sexual orientation and gender identity. They show me how to make art as part of a team. I experience the abundance of life that comes from creating multicultural community. And I still have almost everything to learn about my own identities. I am only just beginning to awaken from the trance of whiteness, though I wouldn't have dared to call it that at the time.

In 1997, I am living in New York City. The flame of my acting career has gone out, and I am heartbroken again. Distanced from organized religion since high school—the theater has been my church and source of spiritual growth—I am hungry for new kinds of meaning making, spiritual depth, and ways to give back. A friend suggests that I visit the Unitarian Universalist congregation just blocks away from my apartment.

From my first Sunday in that sanctuary, the core messages of Unitarian Universalism give me a sense of homecoming, direction, and hope. I start volunteering at the after-school program run by our partner church in East Harlem. There I am trained and supervised by adults of color; I become part of a team with African-American and white volunteers, and I bond with children from the neighborhood who give me glimpses into their varied lives. At the Booker T. Washington Learning Center, I get a sense of what embodying my new faith means.

The next year, I find myself sitting in another sanctuary crowded with hundreds of people, all of us there to celebrate Rev. Marjorie Bowens-Wheatley's installation as associate minister at the Community Church of New York City. I have been taking adult religious education classes with Marjorie; in conversations after class about our lives and my emerging call to ministry, our friendship is born.

At Rev. Marjorie's installation, Rev. Bill Sinkford calls for "more white people in our antiracism movement." His words ring a loud, resounding gong that echoes through my head and heart. That's the moment when my real re-education as a white person begins.

My teachers on this journey—both white and of color, teachers in the flesh and on the page—help guide me. Rev. Josh Pawelek, a white ally and accomplice, suggests that every paper I write in divinity school can explore its subject through an antioppressive lens, and I strive to meet this challenge. I work for a year as a field-education student in the Unitarian Universalist Association's Faith in Action Department, where I read and summarize the literature on whiteness. I'm astonished by how explicit and longstanding this body of work is, going back decades. It is little known among Unitarian Universalists at the time. It transforms me.

In 2001, Rev. Marjorie asks me to co-edit what will become *Soul Work: Anti-Racist Theologies in Dialogue* (published in 2003). Witnessing, recording, and working with the essays and conversations that grow out of the Soul Work consultation mark a significant stage on my journey. During my internship in Massachusetts, I lead an adult religious education class in studying *Soul Work*. I get a sense of what it's like to try to meet everyone just where they are on this journey.

In 2005, I am called as senior minister to the First Unitarian Church of San José (FUCSJ). The city of San José's extraordinary diversity reminds me of my early years in San Antonio. FUCSJ's clear commitment to multiculturalism chimes with the longings of my heart. In many ways, this is my real homecoming; it's when my real work begins.

In the years since, my understanding of my own identities continues to shift, expand, and grow clearer. After the end of my second marriage, for instance, having experienced heteronormative privilege all my life, I finally begin to claim my true sexual orientation, first as bisexual, then in less binary language. When Karin and I model naming our identities for our conversation partners in this book, my list grows into something like this: I am a white, cisgender woman in her sixties, temporarily able-bodied, middle class with an upper-middle-class background, an artist, a Unitarian Universalist minister, and queer, all-gender loving. This exploration of my own identity and of all the ways in which centering and marginalizing have affected and do affect my sense of wholeness forms a crucial part of my journey.

With each stage of awakening and of developing my antiracist and multicultural skills, I have experienced the full range of feelings: fear, inadequacy, heartbreak, anger, and impatience with myself and others, as well as joy, compassion, curiosity, delight, and love. My world is infinitely more complex, more beautiful, more real, and more satisfying than when I began.

IN SUM: Our complementary identities—lay leader and settled minister, Asian American and white European American, younger and older, scientist-engineer and artist-writer—encourage us to name our different perspectives and notice how they affect every aspect of writing this book together. As we will share in the concluding chapter, we too are on a journey of deepening love and trust as we build our cross-cultural friendship.

OUR HOPES FOR THIS BOOK

This book invites you into the stories of people and congregations that are on the road to creating multicultural, antiracist Beloved Community. We have included mistakes and failures as well as breakthroughs and successes because these stories, to be useful, must be *real*. At the end of every chapter, you will find a section titled "Questions for You and Your Congregation" to help you apply these stories to your own journey and discern your own next moves.

Although the solo reader will find here food for thought and ideas for individual action and change, we recommend reading this book in community. Whether you choose just one other person or you form a circle of companions within your congregation, ministerial chapter, or interfaith community, reading and discussing this book with others models a fundamental truth about multicultural work: At its heart, it is always about the relationships we create and the care that we bring to these relationships. Taking the time to build these relationships is part of the work we're describing.

Storytelling, too, takes time, and in that sense, it is an act of resistance in a culture like ours, which values the quick and efficient. Stories take longer to unfold and ask more of the reader or listener than does a list of to-dos. The interweaving strands of the stories we tell—their loop-de-loops and muddy patches, their forests of details and their bright shining moments—all help to paint a fully human picture of what's at work in each congregation.

In *The Power of Stories: A Guide for Leading Multiracial and Multicultural Congregations,* Rev. Dr. Jacqui Lewis uses "story" as a verb. She urges congregational leaders to "story" a new vision of spiritual community that embraces differences across race, ethnicity, culture, sexual orientation, gender identity and expression, physical and mental abilities, and more.

Such stories transform us—readers, hearers, and tellers alike—into participants in the act of creating something new. We experience joys, sorrows, anticipation, disappointment, hope, frustration, and wonder together. We come away from these stories with lessons learned to guide our actions and with a new vocabulary to name the meanings we discover along the way.

The complex stories we share here show that it takes intentional work and persistent commitment to build multicultural, antiracist Beloved Community. Mistakes and misgivings abound and are inevitable. But unexpected miracles of joy and transformation are abundant too. The journey itself; the companions who join in; the sometimes fleeting, often sacred sense of completeness that emerges in the midst of the journey; the satisfaction that we are living our faith—these elements make all the hard work meaningful and worthwhile.

We co-authors, too, have a sense of mission and vision. We want this book to make some small contribution to the process of re-storying Unitarian Universalism. We want to help move this faith that we love farther along on its path toward a multicultural reality. We want these stories of transformation—both individual and institutional—to inspire our readers to take the risks, make the mistakes, discover the creativity, and be enriched by the joys of multicultural work. Because the need for multicultural Beloved Communities in these United States is so urgent, we want to light a fire under us all.

OUR THANKS

Readers will find a long list of our acknowledgments at the end of this book. Here we want simply to thank *you*. Whoever you are, wherever you are, by reading this book you become partners with us on this journey. By entering into these stories together, we draw the circle of connections wider still, and we take another step closer to multicultural Beloved Community. Thank you!

Nancy Palmer Jones
San José, California

Karin Lin
Cambridge, Massachusetts

March 2019

Some Words about Language

THE WORDS WE USE MATTER. They have an impact on readers' and listeners' minds, hearts, spirits, and actions. When we write and talk about issues of race and ethnicity, striving to illuminate the truths of people's experience, the words we choose become even more tender and impactful.

At the same time, language evolves. Over the course of our own involvement in Unitarian Universalism, we have witnessed shifts and expansions in the language that describes both the roots of the problems that we are writing about and the goals toward which our religious movement is striving. After years of describing "racism" and "racial prejudice" as the problem and "racial justice" as the goal, many Unitarian Universalists in the 1990s and early 2000s become clearer about the centrality of "white privilege" and the need to awaken to the sometimes subtle, often overt systems of hierarchy and oppression that offer white people privileges and access to power while denying them to, or limiting them for, others.

During the writing of this book, we witness another important shift. Led and taught by leaders of color, more and more Unitarian Universalists are beginning to name the system of racialized oppression in the United States as *white supremacy culture*. With this system identified as the problem, the goal becomes to "dismantle white supremacy culture" and to "build the Beloved Community where all souls are welcomed as blessings and the human family lives whole and reconciled," as the UUA's Leadership Council puts it in 2008.

Each shift in language gets at a deeper analysis of what keeps this country and its people stuck in life-destroying divisions. Each shift helps people name the difference between personal prejudice and systemic oppression. Each shift awakens more folks with power and privilege to the unfairness and destructive impact of these hierarchies. Nothing can change at its root until people with power join with marginalized people to choose a new way of being and living.

Our readers and listeners won't agree on the meanings of certain words we use. They won't agree on which words they prefer. The impact of the words we choose may be harmful despite our good intentions, and for this we apologize in advance. We welcome the chance to acknowledge our mistakes and to continue to learn and grow.

Still, we must capture this moment in time with the language that we have found most helpful. So we offer here a brief description of what we mean as we use certain words throughout this book.

ALLIES AND ACCOMPLICES: The terms *allies* and *accomplices* refer to different types and gradations of support and solidarity that people from dominant groups can offer to those in targeted or oppressed groups. *White allies*, for example, educate themselves and others about the history and ongoing impact of white supremacy culture. They attend to the voices of people of color and show up with empathy and compassion when these friends and colleagues are hurting. They interrupt instances of racism in interactions they witness. They work for systemic changes that reverse institutionalized oppression.

But as more and more white people have claimed the term *ally* without necessarily demonstrating these actions, the word has lost some of its power and significance. In a keynote address to Loyola Marymount University's 2019 Advocacy Teach-in, Dr. Stefan Bradley, associate professor and chair of African-American studies, states, "I need an accomplice, not an ally." Loyola Marymount social justice intern Raven Yamamoto elaborates in her response to Dr. Bradley's address: "You risk nothing by calling yourself an ally, but you risk everything by embodying the role of an accomplice in the fight for freedom by sacrificing your own."

Accomplices, then, take the attitudes and actions of allies further. White accomplices seek and respect the authority of people of color; they ask, rather than assume that they know how to help. Following the lead of organizations led by people of color, accomplices take part in civil disobedience and other actions to overturn unjust laws. They focus on dismantling white supremacy culture, element by element.

In a 2017 blog post written in the wake of white nationalist riots in Charlottesville, Virginia, queer advocate of color Dr. Jon Paul writes an article with the same title as Dr. Bradley's address: "I need an accomplice, not an ally." Dr. Paul explains the distinction between ally and accomplice as a matter of *feeling* versus *doing*. Being an accomplice, he says, "is about being complicit in the struggle towards liberation and being okay to take a step back to move marginalized people forward. . . . Telling someone that you are an ally at this moment in history only reassures us that you see the problems that we face. We just want to know are you ready and able to do something about them."

BELOVED COMMUNITY: The phrase *Beloved Community* was first used by philosopher and theologian Josiah Royce in the early twentieth century. In the 1950s and '60s, Dr. Martin Luther King Jr.'s writings and speeches created vivid expressions of the Beloved Community.

In chapter 1, we quote the UUA Leadership Council's powerful description of Beloved Community as a place "where all souls are welcomed as blessings and the human family lives whole and reconciled." We also draw on other experiences and definitions of Beloved Community throughout this book. In our Introduction, for example, we have quoted UUA president Susan Frederick-Gray's description of Beloved Community as "a community that practices a radically inclusive and compassionate, antiracist, anti-oppressive, multicultural, multigenerational faith within, and acts powerfully in partnership and solidarity for justice and liberation beyond."

In her essay in *Unitarian Universalists of Color: Stories of Struggle, Courage, Love, and Faith*, Yuri Yamamoto—musician, diversity activist, and hospital chaplain resident—offers this description:

> To me a beloved community means a sanctuary where all of us can express ourselves authentically and celebrate who we are without the fear of rejection. It is not a place where only like-minded people gather or where everyone is simply nice to each other by withholding their feelings and opinions. In a beloved community, we are committed to candid conversation and love because of our many—and sometimes painful—differences. The road to build such a community is extremely long and rocky. It may be a never-ending process rather than an attainable goal.

ETHNICITY: *Ethnicity* refers to a group's shared national or cultural origin, tradition, or heritage. In a racialized society, people are privileged or discriminated against on the basis of their ethnicity, as well as their assigned race. In this book, we tend to use *race* and *ethnicity* together to capture the ways that white supremacy culture uses these differing identities to create and discriminate against an "other."

FAITH: Because Unitarian Universalism welcomes a wide range of belief systems and theologies, not all Unitarian Universalists are comfortable with the term *faith*. We use *faith* to mean trust and commitment, especially the trust and commitment given to one's deepest values. In the phrase "Unitarian Universalist faith," *faith* means "a religious movement united around these deepest values." Chapter 1, for example, "The Call of Our Faith," describes our search for a compelling expression of the values that call all Unitarian Universalists to the work of building multicultural, antiracist Beloved Community.

IDENTITIES OF OUR CONVERSATION PARTNERS: We have begun almost all our interviews with our conversation partners by saying, "We know identity is a complex thing. We humans all have multiple identities, and different aspects of our identities will be more or less important to us at different times in our lives. We'd like to know how you want to be identified." Then we would offer our own identities, which we describe in the Introduction. Throughout this book, we name the racial and ethnic identities that our conversation partners claim. We recognize that identity is not static, nor are the names used to describe different groups. May these identities add to the richness of the stories we tell here.

INTERSECTIONALITY: People and groups may be targeted by more than one system of oppression, on the basis of many aspects of their identity. Ableism, classism, heterosexism, cisheteropatriarchy, transphobia, and other hierarchical systems amplify the impact of racism and white supremacy culture for those whose identities and life experiences place them in more than one targeted group. We are deeply aware of the importance of intersectionality, though we have focused on issues of race and ethnicity in this book.

MINISTERS AND THEIR TITLES: How people are referred to—full name, first name, or surname; with or without titles and honorifics—is a significant issue, especially in light of longstanding patterns of disrespect and disprivilege. Matching the style of our conversation partners' names and titles to their personal preference is a sign of respect, gratitude, and care.

For this reason, the styling of ministers' names and titles does not remain consistent throughout the book. In general, we introduce ministers with their title (or titles) and full name and then refer to them as "Rev." with just their first name. In references that follow quickly on each other, we often alternate using the title and first name with using just the first name.

When a minister's preference varies from these general rules, or when a congregation uses a different pattern, we follow the guidance of our conversation partners about their congregation's culture. At All Souls Unitarian Church in Tulsa, Oklahoma, for example, the congregation uses a minister's title and last name or just their first name. At First Parish, Cambridge, the custom is to use first names only, after the initial introduction.

Our conversation partners have had a chance to review their sections and let us know how they would like to be named. We hope that we have followed their guidance to the letter! Where we have made mistakes, we heartily apologize.

Names are important. Using the correct name and title is one way in which we co-authors strive to honor our conversation partners.

MULTICULTURAL: *Multicultural* can refer to communities that gather together across many kinds of difference. In this book, we focus the word *multicultural* on issues of race and ethnicity. At least one of the congregations we study—All Souls Unitarian Church in Tulsa, Oklahoma—has chosen the term *intercultural* over *multicultural* to describe their work on building Beloved Community. The Spring Institute for Intercultural Learning on its website describes the difference it sees between the two terms:

> **Multicultural** refers to a society that contains several cultural or ethnic groups. People live alongside one another, but each cultural group does not necessarily have engaging interactions with each other. . . .
>
> **Intercultural** describes communities in which there are deep understanding and respect for all cultures. Intercultural communication focuses on the mutual exchange of ideas and cultural norms and the development of deep relationships. In an intercultural society, no one is left unchanged because everyone learns from one another and grows together.

In our usage, *multicultural* and *multiculturally competent* communities demonstrate the kind of transformation that the Spring Institute reserves for *intercultural* ones.

MULTICULTURAL, ANTIRACIST BELOVED COMMUNITY: Over and over in this book, we use this phrase to describe the way of being and living toward which the congregations we study are moving. Any Beloved Community worth the name will be *multicultural*—that is, welcoming to and inclusive of a variety of cultural identities and expressions and in relationship with groups and communities from a range of cultures and ethnicities. And any Beloved Community by definition will be *antiracist*—that is, actively and intentionally working to dismantle systems of racism and white supremacy culture in its midst and beyond its walls. Still, we feel it is important to make these aspects of Beloved

Community visible in this book by explicitly naming these attributes.

MULTICULTURALISM: Our usage of *multiculturalism* matches the definition given by the online *Collins English Dictionary*:

> **Multiculturalism** is a situation in which all the different cultural or racial groups in a society have equal rights and opportunities, and none is ignored or regarded as unimportant.

An American source, *Webster's New World College Dictionary*, gives an equally useful definition:

> **Multiculturalism:** the policy or practice of giving overt recognition to the cultural needs and contributions of all the groups in a society, esp. of those minority groups regarded as having been neglected in the past.

MULTIRACIAL, INTERRACIAL, AND CROSS-RACIAL: These terms are particularly difficult to distinguish. Here's how we've tried to be consistent: We use *multiracial* and *interracial* to describe joint communication and work by people of more than one race—for example, a *multiracial team*, an *interracial marriage*. We use *cross-racial* to describe engagement that specifically crosses and addresses a racial divide, as in *cross-racial conversations*. Please see the description later in this section that covers our usage of the term *race*.

PEOPLE OF COLOR: In a well-researched Wikipedia entry, we find a definition for *people of color* that matches our intent:

> The term encompasses all non-white people, emphasizing common experiences of systemic racism. . . . Because the term "people of color" includes vastly different people with only the common distinction of not being white, it draws attention to

the fundamental role of racialization in the United States. Joseph Tuman argues that the term "people of color" is attractive because it unites disparate racial and ethnic groups into a larger collective in solidarity with one another.

We recognize that this term, like others related to race and ethnicity, is painful for some readers, and it represents one of many heartbreaking choices we have made. Some colleagues use "members of the global majority" as an affirmative and more accurate description. But for us right now, "people of color" continues to underscore that in the United States, many people from many different parts of the world and different locations in this country, people with many different group histories and many different presentations in terms of skin color and appearance, share "common experiences of systemic racism."

RACE: Race is a social construct. Biologically, there is only one race, the human race. Many people object to the use of the word *race* as a descriptor because racial categories have no scientific basis. The term is particularly problematic when applied to Latinx or indigenous people. As Rev. Lilia Cuervo says, being Latinx is a matter of culture, not of race.

On the other hand, in a racialized society like that of the United States, everyone is assigned a race, or a "racialized identity," and that identity has real effects, for good or ill, on individuals' and groups' life experiences, opportunities, access to power, and more. We use the word *race* in this book to draw attention to the way white supremacy culture is structured around hierarchies based on skin color, country of origin, culture, and many other attributes.

RACISM: *Racism* is the combination of prejudice (based on race or ethnicity) and the power to make decisions and access resources.

"WE": Unless otherwise noted, "we" stands for us co-authors, Karin and Nancy. When we use the personal pronoun for more people than just ourselves, we strive to be diligent about identifying who is included in the "we."

WHITE SUPREMACY CULTURE: The term *white supremacy culture* is a catchall phrase to describe the "set of institutional assumptions and practices, often operating unconsciously, that tend to benefit white people and exclude people of color," as religious educators Aisha Hauser, Christina Rivera, and Kenny Wiley write in the resources created for the "UU White Supremacy Teach-ins" in the spring of 2017. They continue,

> Why "white supremacy" as the term here? It conjures up images of hoods and mobs. . . . In 2017, actual "white supremacists" are not required in order to uphold white supremacist culture. Building a faith full of people who understand that key distinction is essential as we work toward a more just society in difficult political times.

Aisha, Christina, and Kenny point congregations toward the article "White Supremacy Culture" by Kenneth Jones and Tema Okun, who identifies as a white social justice activist and antiracism trainer. In it she lists fifteen characteristics of white supremacy culture, including perfectionism, individualism, power hoarding, fear of open conflict, and the belief that "progress is bigger, more." The antidotes she offers include creating a culture of appreciation, emphasizing teamwork, making power sharing an explicit value, being courageous about raising hard issues (rather than overvaluing politeness), and attending as much to the relationships and the process by which work gets done as to the outcomes.

Many institutions use the assumptions and practices of white supremacy culture as standards against which to measure success, without recognizing the harm these standards do both to people of color and to white people. Such assumptions and practices act as barriers to other cultural ways of being.

We highly recommend Jones and Okun's full article, which is listed in the Resources section, especially as we refer to white supremacy culture throughout the book.

CHAPTER ONE

The Call of Our Faith

BE IT FURTHER RESOLVED that the General Assembly urges the Unitarian Universalist Association, its congregations, and community organizations to develop an ongoing process for the comprehensive institutionalization of antiracism and multiculturalism, understanding that whether or not a group becomes multiracial, there is always the opportunity to become antiracist.

—"Toward an Antiracist Unitarian Universalist Association," Business Resolution passed at General Assembly 1997, Phoenix, Arizona

With humility and courage born of our history, we are called as Unitarian Universalists to build the Beloved Community where all souls are welcomed as blessings and the human family lives whole and reconciled.

—"A Vision for Unitarian Universalism in a Multicultural World," Unitarian Universalist Association Leadership Council, October 1, 2008

WHAT IS IT in Unitarian Universalism's core message that demands that its people work toward building multicultural, antiracist Beloved Community? What in Unitarian Universalism's central theology *requires* us to do this work if we want to call ourselves Unitarian Universalists? How can we articulate this call of our faith in compelling ways?

These questions have troubled and consumed us since long before we began the writing of this book. Unitarian Universalism is famously noncreedal, which means there is no "belief test" for claiming a Unitarian Universalist identity. The religion's Fourth Principle expresses Unitarian Universalist communities' commitment to affirming and promoting a "free and responsible search for truth and meaning." In fact, most Unitarian Universalists agree on the value of the search more than we do on any particular outcome. The degree of freedom of conscience and belief promised to individual Unitarian Universalists remains a distinguishing characteristic of the faith; for some, it is the main draw.

Is it even possible, then, to claim that Unitarian Universalist theology *requires* us to build multicultural, antiracist Beloved Community? And if so, where and how is this core requirement expressed?

Neither of us claims to be a theologian. And yet we sense that our faith's very celebration of the "free and responsible search for truth and meaning" calls *all* Unitarian Universalists to be just that: practical theologians who express, in words and deeds, the ultimate meaning of our faith. Our process in this chapter, then, is to create a conversation on the page among voices from a variety of locations, all of whom are striving to do just that.

As we wrestle in this chapter with the question of why we must do the work of multiculturalism and antiracism, we invite our readers to wrestle with us. The words and ideas that we offer here inspire and fuel our own commitment to the work. May they encourage the search in our readers as well.

THE BACKGROUND FOR
OUR SEARCH

On our bookshelves sits a row of books from the late 1990s and early 2000s that focus primarily on Christian congregations striving to build multiracial, multiethnic communities. Some of these books come out of the National Congregations Study—research conducted in the late '90s that produces such titles as *United by Faith: The Multiracial Congregation as an Answer to the Problem of Race*; *People of the Dream: Multiracial Congregations in the United States*; and *One Body, One Spirit: Principles of Successful Multiracial Churches*. The Resources section at the back of this book lists these and other titles. Although some of Christianity's claims differ from those of our faith, the authors' insights offer background and help us prepare for our own research with Unitarian Universalist congregations.

We are particularly struck by the authors' claim that multiracial congregations have an overarching goal that surpasses racial and ethnic diversity. Something bigger than the richness of diversity itself demands that these congregations persevere in the countercultural project of bringing diverse folks into community together. That "something more," the authors suggest, springs from the call of their faith.

In the Introduction to *United by Faith*, for example, the authors—Curtiss Paul DeYoung, Michael O. Emerson, George Yancey, and Karen Chai Kim—wonder whether the core message of Christianity demands that, "as much as possible," its believers *ought to* create multiracial congregations. But these authors—like most Unitarian Universalists—wonder whether members of their faith can come to consensus about anything they "ought to" do. Their uncertainty reminds us that every single religion encompasses many different expressions. Claiming one unifying identity statement is tough for all of us, whether we are Christian, Jewish, Muslim, Hindu, Buddhist, Unitarian Universalist, or something else.

The authors of *United by Faith* then zero in on how Jesus' vision of a "house of prayer for all nations" (Isaiah 56:7; Mark 11:17) urges the move to multiculturalism. Guided by this vision, Jesus' earliest followers set themselves free from their monoracial worldview and begin creating multiracial, multicultural communities. Under the leadership of the apostle Paul, this "theology of oneness"—the understanding that, through Jesus, there is just one human family, one human race—eventually becomes an established part of the Christian message. To follow Jesus' Way, the authors conclude, Christians are called to do this work.

Still, the lived experience of Christianity in the late twentieth and early twenty-first centuries remains as diverse as that of any religion. DeYoung, Emerson, Yancey, and Kim suggest that the theology of oneness must first deepen into a "core belief" in order for it to have its full impact on the lives of its followers. A *core belief*, they say, is a "nonnegotiable commitment and mindset . . . [residing] in the depth of our souls." In other words, Jesus' life and teachings represent a change in mindset, a revolution in worldview that demands a life built on the recognition of oneness. But that demand can only be accepted and embraced when taken into the depths of Christians' souls. Then and only then do multiracial, multicultural congregations become necessary expressions of this theology.

Most religions' ideals remain aspirational; they are hoped for rather than attained. The National Congregations Study defines a multiracial congregation as one where 20 percent of the members come from racial groups different from the majority. According to that measure, only about 7.5 percent of all Christian congregations are multiracial in the late 1990s. In a 2010 Faith Communities Today study, the figure rises to 13.7 percent. That's still small. In contrast, we co-authors note, the proportion of multiracial congregations in non-Christian faiths surpasses one-third.

Still, the authors of *United by Faith* find in the foundational stories and scripture of Christianity a distinct and compelling call to the work of building multicultural, antiracist Beloved Community, whether or not this aspiration is achieved.

IN THE FOREGROUND

As we write our own book about congregations striving to build this kind of community, we wonder where Unitarian Universalists can find a similar compelling call. In a noncreedal faith, where do we turn for such clarity?

We could rely on the faith's theological underpinnings, including those verses from the prophet Isaiah and Jesus that *United by Faith* draws on. After all, our religion grows out of Jewish and Christian roots.

We could look to the core beliefs that led some Unitarians and Universalists to participate in the nineteenth-century abolitionist and twentieth-century civil rights movements. For many individual followers, their faith demanded their participation in those contemporary struggles for justice, equity, and compassion. On the other hand, most local and national Unitarian and Universalist institutions didn't follow suit.

Or we could depend on Unitarian Universalism's Seven Principles, adopted by congregational delegates in 1985. The Principles, many Unitarian Universalists feel, create a roadmap for what it means to live a faithful life in our religious communities. The First and Seventh Principles—affirming and promoting the inherent worth and dignity of all and the interconnected web of all existence—lay the groundwork for a religion of radical inclusion and empowerment, while the Second through Sixth offer pointers for how to live these aspirations into being.

Any of these sources might suffice, although our religion's history shows that they haven't yet created a unifying call that convinces enough Unitarian Universalists to create lasting institutional change. What's more, the urgency of the times in which we live invites us to listen instead for more contemporary voices, and especially for those that have been silenced in the past. Unitarian Universalism's conviction that "revelation is not sealed"— that new truths are constantly emerging—teaches us to look and listen now for fresh expressions of this religion, in the words of those who have been marginalized for too long.

In the foreground of our hearts and minds, then, rise the voices of Unitarian Universalists of color preaching and teaching in the second decade of the twenty-first century. Also in the foreground shine our own lived experiences of recent prophetic calls to multiracial, antiracist Beloved Community within our congregations and in our national movement. Justice General Assembly 2017, reshaped at the last moment in response to the disruptions in Unitarian Universalism that spring, blazes as one such lived experience for both of us.

A word of reassurance: Although we are inspired by events that happen close to the time of our writing, the words and images we offer here transcend the specific moments when they occur. The reader doesn't have to have been present at any of these experiences to feel the resonance of what is said and modeled there. Beyond the timeliness of our own context, we are looking for those theological expressions and wrestlings that might represent fresh "revelations" and that might inspire Unitarian Universalists, too, to be "united by faith."

A TALE OF TWO GENERAL ASSEMBLIES

For a moment on June 22, 2017, when Lena K. Gardner, executive director of Black Lives of Unitarian Universalism (BLUU), introduces elder and mentor Dr. Mtangulizi Sanyika at the Unitarian Universalist Association's Justice General Assembly (GA) in New Orleans, we sense time folding back on itself.

Almost fifty years earlier, at the 1969 GA, a third of the attendees are people of color. White Unitarian Universalists' active engagement in the Civil Rights movement of the 1960s has thrown open the doors of the predominantly white religion, and people of color have resonated with its commitment to progressive action. Together, these congregants have helped to reshape Unitarian Universalism into a much more diverse association.

But at that 1969 GA, the UUA Board announces that it must de-fund a $1-million grant promised to the Black Affairs Council (BAC) just the year before. Anger, grief, and fear break the delegates into factions with different ideas about how to proceed. Dr. Sanyika, then named Hayward Henry and chair of the Black Affairs Council, leads a walkout. Hundreds of African American delegates, other people of color, and many white allies leave the building. For some, that departure lasts only a little while. For many, like Dr. Sanyika, now a Presbyterian elder, it lasts a lifetime. The possibility of multiracial, multicultural Beloved Community on a large scale within Unitarian Universalism recedes.

The wounds and rifts of the late 1960s, a turning point now called the Empowerment Controversy in the Unitarian Universalist Association, form part of Unitarian Universalism's present DNA. They still impact even those Unitarian Universalists who have never heard the story. They echo in the responses roused by the UUA staffing disruptions in spring 2017 and by the Board's subsequent decision to fund Black Lives of Unitarian Universalism for $5.3 million over the following three years. They strengthen the longing for reconciliation and redemption that this new moment offers.

So on this June day in 2017 when Dr. Sanyika, a vital presence in his seventies, stands on the General Assembly stage beside

Lena Gardner, a young leader in her twenties, the four thousand Unitarian Universalists in the convention center can feel two powerful movements coming together across time and generations—the Black Empowerment Movement, as manifested within Unitarian Universalism in the 1960s, alongside Black Lives of Unitarian Universalism, a movement of the 2010s.

Dr. Sanyika describes how Unitarian Universalism "used to be my spiritual home, but white supremacy swept me away." Yet he remains committed to the struggle—"not to the *structure*," he clarifies, "but to the struggle and the justice that need to be done" within this religion. Something has called him back to help lead in this new moment of crisis and opportunity.

Dr. Sanyika then offers these reflections on the faith's compelling call:

> Unitarian Universalism at its finest and at its best is an instrument to transform humanity so that it can evolve to its highest level of consciousness and potential. At its best! And it must constantly be vigilant to denounce all forms of human oppression, exploitation, degradation, domination, and control in any form that it comes.
>
> Unitarian Universalism at its best is a transformative agent for justice and liberation and peace in the world. At its best! But it can't do that if it marginalizes humanity. If it leaves anybody out at the table, you cannot fulfill that mission. You cannot fulfill that mission by being partial to some and not fair with all. Justice and equity must define who you are and what you do with who you claim to be. Because it's not just *saying* what you believe that matters, it's what you *do* with it.

Unitarian Universalism as a "transformative agent for justice and liberation and peace in the world"—this is our *identity*, as Dr. Sanyika names it. But he warns us listeners that we can't begin to fulfill the promise of this identity until we believe in our souls that the "virus of racism and white supremacy is still around us." This virus metastasizes and sneaks up on us whenever we stop paying attention, whenever we fall asleep. We need to remain mindful that "Unitarian Universalism is still under construction." Finally, he sums up: "You still have a long ways to go. So don't be infatuated with yourself, please."

The audience erupts in laughter and applause. The call for Unitarian Universalists to dismantle the culture of white supremacy rings clear, set in the overarching context of the faith's potential—"at its best!"—to be an agent of transformation for individuals and society. At the same time, Dr. Sanyika's image of Unitarian Universalism as a faith "still under construction" invites an attitude of humility, curiosity, and responsiveness, without losing any of the urgency of the renewed movement for change.

"It's not just *saying* what you believe that matters, it's what you *do* with it," Dr. Sanyika emphasizes. He draws a direct line from the core messages of the religion to how it calls for us to live. With Unitarian Universalism's plurality of theologies and multiple sources of wisdom and spiritual practice, Unitarian Universalists tend to be more interested in how beliefs make us act than in what the beliefs are. Ours is a practical theology. If we take this faith seriously, it must have a real and discernible impact on how we live. Any compelling expression of the theology that calls us to multiculturalism and antiracism must have this practical thrust.

A PROPHETIC AND UNFULFILLED RESOLUTION

The day after Dr. Sanyika stirs the convention delegates with his presence and his words, the cochairs of the Journey Toward Wholeness (JTW) Transformation Committee, Rev. Theresa Inés Soto and Rev. Wendy von Courter, move to the same podium to give their report. Justice General Assembly 2017 marks the twentieth anniversary of the Business Resolution titled "Toward an Antiracist Unitarian Universalist Association," passed in Phoenix, Arizona, at GA 1997, which sparked the creation of the JTW Transformation Committee.

Rev. Theresa and Rev. Wendy point out the bright promises of the resolution and lift up the pain made so evident in the spring of 2017 from the failure of Unitarian Universalism to fulfill it. We have failed "to move far enough, fast enough, and true enough to that resolution—or truly, to the call of our faith," they lament.

They distinguish between anti-oppressive *programs* and an anti-oppressive *ethos*. The programs that some congregations have used in the past twenty years have offered education about systems of oppression, institutional racism, and personal prejudice. Such classes, conversations, and inventories can help unmask the systems of racism and white supremacy embedded in Unitarian Universalist communities. They have led to some progress— but not nearly enough. Unitarian Universalists, Rev. Wendy and Rev. Theresa urge, need to move deeper into the implementation of a "worthy, yet amorphous ethos."

They then invite thousands of Unitarian Universalists to affirm the 1997 resolution by reading it aloud. As the words scroll across the huge screens and the dull roar of raised voices and united breath fills the hall, the resolution takes on some of its original power. It hints at this "worthy, yet amorphous ethos." Although we co-authors hear in its words a subtext aimed primarily at white members of the religion, still the resolution serves as another expression of *why* Unitarian Universalism calls all its participants to this work. Here is our summary of its text:

- The resolution's "Whereas" clauses cite the Second and Sixth Unitarian Universalist Principles, which affirm and promote "justice, equity, and compassion in human relations" and "the goal of world community." These two Principles, the resolution suggests, require us to do the work of multiculturalism and antiracism.

- The resolution then lifts up the faith's successes and failures in the "struggle for racial justice." It refers to the lessons of history and calls for an understanding of intersectionality and interconnectedness before the religion can cast a larger vision. This web of connections—to the past and to other oppressions—gives the work a strong and nuanced context.

- It acknowledges that "racism and all its effects" cannot be dismantled "without deliberate engagement in analysis and action" and intentional institutional commitment. Explicit intention, analysis, and action are key elements for change.

- It points to the dangers for everyone, and for the planet itself, of the "deepening divisions in our world caused by inequitable and unjust distribution of power and resources." Already in 1997, the resolution makes clear the relationship of antiracism to environmental justice.

- It then underscores Unitarian Universalism's commitment to "faith in action . . . in the spirit of justice, compassion, and community." Again, ours is a *practical* theology.

- The resolution recognizes that this work involves not only individual self-examination and change but also institutional education and transformation. One without the other will not create lasting transformation.

- Finally, the resolution calls for particular actions. It recommends offering specific trainings and workshops, forming committees to monitor progress, deepening "relationships with all people of color" to establish accountability and to honor cultural authenticity, and organizing with other international and interfaith groups that are doing this work.

In short, the resolution asserts that, to be true to the call of Unitarian Universalism, we Unitarian Universalists must dismantle systems of hatred, discrimination, and supremacy rather than perpetuate them. We must work collaboratively rather than in isolation. We must intentionally educate and act for justice and equity rather than imagine that change will happen without an explicit commitment (through generational change, for example). And we must establish accountable relationships rather than sidestep mutual responsibility and impact. These elements will show up in the Common Threads that we list in chapter 2.

As the congregational stories in chapters 3 through 7 show, the resolution's specific recommendations still provide direction for communities on the road to multicultural, antiracist Beloved Community. The names and content of the specific programs continue to change, but these recommendations remain valuable. For all its wordy formality, the resolution offers another way to express the call of Unitarian Universalism to the work of dismantling oppression and building Beloved Community.

And yet . . . twenty years after its passage, as Rev. Wendy and Rev. Theresa point out at Justice GA 2017, the resolution, on its own, has not led to an antioppressive *ethos*—a way of being that embodies Unitarian Universalism "at its best." For such an ethos to capture and transform hearts, minds, bodies, and spirits, faithful people need a compelling lure—a statement of theology, of core beliefs and shared ethics, of lived experience, that makes it clear that we simply cannot call ourselves Unitarian Universalists if we are not engaged, individually and corporately, in the work of antiracism and multiculturalism.

In the next sections, we offer examples of pithier statements. We tease out how these statements might offer such a lure. The search for the heart of this call continues.

WHOLE AND RECONCILED

In October 2008, the lead staff of the Unitarian Universalist Association, a group known as the UUA Leadership Council, compose this "vision for Unitarian Universalism in a multicultural world":

> With humility and courage born of our history, we are called as Unitarian Universalists to build the Beloved Community where all souls are welcomed as blessings and the human family lives whole and reconciled.[2]

"The Beloved Community where all souls are welcomed as blessings and the human family lives whole and reconciled"—this vision gleams with promise. For us co-authors, the statement encompasses the key elements of a compelling call to multicultural, antiracist Beloved Community:

- It asks for an attitude of humility and courage and for an awareness of both the gifts and the crises in our religious history, whether from long ago or just last week.
- It points to the goal of building Beloved *Community*, since Unitarian Universalism, as a covenantal faith, simply cannot be lived in isolation.
- It affirms the faith's welcome across many diversities.
- It lifts up the possibility for reconciliation, with a clearsighted recognition of the harm done and an invitation to repair the brokenness of life and spirit that white supremacy culture inflicts.

[2] The UUA's Leadership Council in 2008 consists of Bill Sinkford, Helene Atwan, Taquiena Boston, Tim Brennan, Judith Frediani, John Hurley, Harlan Limpert, Beth Miller, Kay Montgomery, Meg Riley, Tracey Robinson-Harris, and Mark Steinwinter.

- It expresses the intention to grow together into a fullness of life that allows a new and more expansive wholeness to be created out of the brokenness of our hearts.

Like the 1997 resolution and the rousing 2017 speech by Dr. Sanyika, the Leadership Council's words are powerful and inspiring.

The problem is that we Unitarian Universalists—like the members of every religion—often don't live up to these ideals. Pointing out where and when we go astray is another way of zeroing in, by contrast, on the core message of our faith. This truth telling adds to our self-understanding, and self-understanding is essential for doing the work of building multicultural, antiracist Beloved Community. The next sections lift up a few voices that show Unitarian Universalists how we fall short and where we may still find hope.

BOTH BROKENNESS AND BEAUTY

In Unitarian Universalism, Rev. Abhi Janamanchi, senior minister of Cedar Lane Unitarian Universalist Church in Bethesda, Maryland, explains, "There is a level of brokenness that I really don't see us getting out of any time soon. . . . But I have found from experience that when we get to that really low place, where we think we couldn't go any farther, we suddenly find that there is yet another basement level that we find ourselves crashing into." Disappointment on disappointment—this is the story that many Unitarian Universalists of color tell about the institutions and communities where they have fallen in love with the faith and then felt left out by it.

Still, Rev. Abhi goes on, "Hope is what happens next: how we do find it within us to get up and begin that long arduous trek"— the trek back into right relationship, into a deeper awareness of the impact of ongoing oppressions on all of us, and toward the fulfillment of the promises of this inclusive faith. Although Unitarian Universalist communities may make mistakes over and over, they also can face their failures and try again, with broken-open hearts, to build the kind of multicultural, antiracist Beloved Community that is truly countercultural.

Abhi's own experiences in Unitarian Universalism fuel his understanding of the faith's possibilities as well as of its short-comings. As an immigrant, arriving in the United States with his family from India, he has received a warm welcome and extraordinary generosity from the Unitarian Universalist congregations that have called him as their minister. Yet at times, he and his family have also been made to feel like "the other" in deeply hurtful ways. For people of color, "the *struggle* to belong," Abhi reflects,

is part of the journey to belonging. And that struggle is going to be a constant companion in the journey. This is not something where I will one day feel I have arrived. And that's partly because those of us who are people of color in this movement pin our hopes more on the *aspiration* that this faith represents than on the *reality* of this faith. And that's a very different mode than many of our members and colleagues who are fed by the reality of our movement! There's nothing wrong with that—I choose not to make that somehow a deficiency. It is the reality, and in order to feel a sense of belonging, I feel I need to embrace that reality while working to embody a different reality. But there's a cost attached.

For many Unitarian Universalists of color, "there's a cost attached" to staying and struggling in partnership to bring to life this imagined but as-yet-unfulfilled reality. That cost drives some people away, as it did Dr. Sanyika in the late 1960s. Rev. Abhi makes the choice, again and again, to stay.

A large part of his choice lies in a central theme for his theology. Abhi identifies as a Unitarian Universalist Hindu—"in that order," he gently insists, because "Unitarian Universalism helps me to be a better Hindu." One doesn't cancel the other, Abhi says. Rather, "it's both/and."

Throughout Rev. Abhi's expression of Unitarian Universalism runs this strong "both/and" thread, which draws on many sources. Hinduism, for example, encourages being comfortable with multiplicities of all sorts, rather than forcing a sense of uniformity. Such a uniformity, Abhi explains, can create a false dichotomy, an "either/or way of looking at things: you're a sinner or you're blessed, you're good or bad." White supremacy culture encourages an either/or way of thinking; this leads to "us/them" polarizations, the potential for a damaging level of self-righteousness, and a sense of scarcity that pits one group against another.

In both/and theology, all humans have this streaky nature, a mix of beauty and brokenness. Hinduism's sacred stories, which include multiple expressions and embodiments of the holy, capture these complexities in ways that allow everyone to find themselves reflected. If taken into Unitarian Universalists' souls as core beliefs, these ideas—that the holy appears in many forms, and that all of us humans are embodiments of beauty and brokenness—would indeed compel our Unitarian Universalist communities toward radical inclusion.

Rev. Abhi acknowledges how far this religion has to go to reach its aspirations, and he works to "embody a different reality"—a both/and reality—for this faith. In the midst of this work, how does he retain his hope that Unitarian Universalism as an institution and Unitarian Universalists as a group can change? What is so strong about the call of this faith that he feels we Unitarian Universalists can move from the aspirations that draw many people into this faith, to a lived reality?

Rev. Abhi calls himself a "hopeful pessimist." He turns to Vaclav Havel's understanding of hope to explain. In *The Power of the Powerless* (1978), Havel writes, "Hope is not a prognostication—it's an orientation of the spirit. . . . Hope in this deep and powerful sense is not the same as joy when things are going well or the willingness to invest in enterprises that are obviously headed for early success, but rather an ability to work for something to succeed." Havel's words echo Abhi's commitment to staying with the uncomfortable present reality even as he works toward its transformation.

Rev. Abhi also finds strength in the Unitarian Universalist belief that "revelation is continuous, it's never sealed." Our calling, then, is to "remain awake." He goes on:

> That's a deeply powerful and disturbing call. Because in order to be truly awake, we need to be truly aware of what we are confronted with, to look through the masks and the fog that cloud our ability to see the world as it is, in order to be more present and to serve the world. And to me when I look at our broken and muddled attempts at times to do this work [of multiculturalism and antiracism], it is that larger call that seems to kind of keep us going, even when we stumble and fall.
>
> But we need to make a sustained commitment. I feel we have tended to make a seasonal commitment. . . . What would it be like if we make a commitment to remain awake going forward? . . . That would call for a fundamental change in how we are as a religious community, [and for] some very deep paradigm shifts in how we function as a religious community, both at the congregational level and at the institutional level— and that's one heck of a scary proposition.

The co-existing truths of belonging and exclusion, the inherent brokenness and beauty of human beings, the call to remain awake when the urge to return to sleep is strong—for Rev. Abhi, the reality of these elements living side by side in our faith forms the core both/and message that compels us to do the work of building multicultural Beloved Community. To take any of these elements seriously requires huge paradigm shifts, as anyone who has tried to maintain a both/and, brokenness-and-beauty perspective in the midst of a heated controversy can attest. Staying awake and staying in the struggle become practical expressions of this challenging theology.

THE "CALL OF SOMETHING MORE"

In her poem "Call of Something More," Rev. Marta I. Valentín names the core of our faith and, like Rev. Abhi, unearths a fierce hope out of the failures of its lived reality. Rev. Marta identifies as *puertorriqueña* and is minister in a shared ministry with the Unitarian Universalist Church of Medford, Massachusetts. She offers this poem at the 2017 Berry Street Conference. The half-day conference is a longstanding annual gathering of ministers, open to clergy and laypeople alike, that precedes GA.

In June 2017, the Berry Street Conference takes a nontraditional form. Instead of a single speaker, it features multiple voices, all speaking to the disruptions of the past spring and to the institutional flaws that have made those disruptions inevitable. By reshaping its format, the conference models the collaborative, multivocal Common Thread that runs through multicultural, antiracist work.

Rev. Marta's poem lays bare the spiritual journey of many Unitarian Universalists of color—a journey that mirrors co-author Karin's experience and that of many of her friends of color. Karin describes how the journey of "come-inners" discovering the faith often begins with an almost instant infatuation with Unitarian Universalism's core message of welcome. In her poem, Rev. Marta paints a picture of jumping for joy, grinning hugely, and dancing in the aisles when she first experiences that welcome "*tal como soy*" (just as I am). She hears with delight the words that claim she is a valued human being who is wanted and needed and "might eventually be loved."

But all too soon, Rev. Marta comes to see that even "*this* sacred theology" can be twisted into "painful, spirit-crushing lies" in the ways that Unitarian Universalists live out the faith. Speaking in the voice of people of color new to the faith, Rev. Marta laments, "We learned that not all of us were accepted, / some were 'too much,' and others 'not enough,' / even as we were offered marginal platforms, / to teach the pale center."

At this moment of disillusionment, many Unitarian Universalists of color must make a choice: to leave, despairing that Unitarian Universalism will ever live up to the promise of its theology, or to stay, reclaiming the faith and fighting to build it anew from within. Those who choose to stay bring great gifts because, as Rev. Marta's poem proclaims,

> We humans of color have always reached for something more,
> exercising and building up quite a resilient muscle
> that is necessary against the many gatekeepers
> still trying to deter us.
> Being resilient in the face of dissenting voices is a gift we bring.

But staying is not easy, Rev. Marta goes on, "especially when our Latinx history is ignored" and microaggressions compound the pain of tokenization.

Despite what it costs to stay, Rev. Marta offers a vision of fierce hope for the faith:

> *If* the pale center responds to the call for something more
> they will turn and face the edges where we are,
> a rainbow of faces and cultures
> engaging in a Unitarian Universalism

that breathes love into its very core
from our well-worn hearts;
they will find us no longer waiting
but creating a Unitarian Universalism of our own
for everyone.

Like others in the conversation whom we have assembled here, Rev. Marta's expression of Unitarian Universalism emphasizes its practical, lived theology. It matters less which words capture the core of this theology and more what actions express it out loud. At the margins, Rev. Marta urges, a "rainbow of faces and cultures" already embodies a Unitarian Universalism with love at its core—"a Unitarian Universalism of our own / for everyone." The "call for something more" demands that those who have traditionally held the center—the dominant white culture—turn and rediscover the faith at its edges. There, through the recognition of pain and disillusionment, of voices too long silenced, and of the fierce hope these people embody, all Unitarian Universalists just might find, once again, reason to dance, in body or in spirit.

A NEW PRINCIPLE

At Justice General Assembly 2017, Paula Cole Jones says to the gathered crowd, "For some of us, Beloved Community is a core theological principle—it's a core spiritual principle. And some of us are working toward that becoming perhaps another one of our Principles, so it's explicit, so we don't miss it." A practical spirituality speaks through the actions of its followers. Still, the words that sum up that theology have power too. Words and actions—a crucial both/and.

Paula Cole Jones, who is African American, is the founder of ADORE (A Dialogue on Race and Ethnicity), a former president of DRUUMM (Diverse and Revolutionary Unitarian Universalist Multicultural Ministries), and an independent consultant specializing in multicultural competencies and institutional change. She reflects on how "our Principles were passed twelve years before we stepped into the antiracist commitment of our Association, and we haven't gone back and really integrated that into our Principles. What does it mean for us to live as an antiracist faith community? We need something explicit around the Beloved Community and our work around dismantling racism and oppression."

She and Bruce Pollack-Johnson, who is white and part of the Unitarian Universalist Church of the Restoration in Philadelphia, have proposed an Eighth Principle to join Unitarian Universalism's existing seven. The Eighth Principle currently reads,

> We, the member congregations of the Unitarian Universalist Association, covenant to affirm and promote: journeying toward spiritual wholeness by working to build a diverse multicultural Beloved Community by our actions that accountably dismantle racism and other oppressions in ourselves and our institutions.

Just like the concepts of love and justice, equity and compassion, the concept of the Beloved Community has history and meanings beyond any specific religious affiliation. Taking the phrase from the early-twentieth-century philosopher and theologian Josiah Royce, Dr. Martin Luther King Jr. in the 1950s and '60s fills out the vision of people all over the world sharing the earth's riches; eliminating poverty, hunger, and homelessness; eradicating racism, discrimination, and all forms of oppression; and solving disputes through peaceful reconciliation and nonviolent conflict resolution. In the Beloved Community, an all-inclusive spirit of kinship will prevail, the King Center website summarizes. In the Beloved Community, "love and trust will triumph over fear and hatred. Peace with justice will prevail over war and military conflict."

For more and more Unitarian Universalists, the creation of Beloved Community represents an overarching, unifying goal. The call to create such communities demands Unitarian Universalists' participation in the work of undoing oppressive systems and building accountable, loving relationships.

The Black Lives of Unitarian Universalism Organizing Collective heartily endorses the incorporation of the Eighth Principle. "While Unitarian Universalists have no creeds to which one must attest, our living tradition is a faith guided by principled action," BLUU's web page on the Eighth Principle states. "As such, we wonder why the dismantling of white supremacy, as implicated in the 8th principle, has not been formally included in our covenant as Unitarian Universalists. . . . We will not be satisfied by practices that call for community without full and explicit recognition of the need for equity and justice."

The long process of seeking to integrate the Eighth Principle into the bylaws of the Unitarian Universalist Association begins in 2018. But even before this Principle is adopted—if and when it is—some Unitarian Universalist congregations have already incorporated it into their covenants and strategic planning. The Eighth Principle combines aspects of many of the faith statements we have included here. It explicitly states that spiritual wholeness requires creating diverse and multicultural communities. And it points to the actions—dismantling white supremacy culture and other oppressions, with accountability—that will embody this theological call.

CENTERING HOPE

When we invite the various expressions of faith in this chapter into conversation with each other, several themes emerge. The

Unitarian Universalist promise of an all-embracing love and an all-inclusive honoring of each person's worth and dignity draws people of all colors to this faith, but the religion's institutions— its congregations, its regional and national structures—have yet to fully embody this promise. The conversation partners in this chapter suggest that the way forward lies in Unitarian Universalists

- awakening to the world as it is . . .
- centering the voices that have been marginalized or outright silenced for centuries . . .
- understanding and resisting the systems that keep oppressive practices in place . . .
- acknowledging the pain and harm that result from remaining embedded in white supremacy culture . . .
- and steadily—with a renewed, resilient commitment, a dedication that does not wane or falter over the long haul—replacing the ways of white supremacy culture with the ways of love, in its most effective, tangible forms.

In the Unitarian Universalist faith, "revelation is never sealed," as Rev. Abhi reminds us. Ours is a religion designed to evolve. These moves are possible and are already in motion in the congregations we study.

Rev. Bill Sinkford provides a hopeful closing word for this chapter on the call of our faith. At the end of the interim co-presidents' report to Justice General Assembly 2017, Rev. Bill says,

> The final message we would pass on is a message of hope. There is a reason that people of color have become Unitarian Universalists . . . from the very beginnings of this faith and still today. There is a fundamental hope in our values and our aspirations that speaks to persons across the boundaries of race and culture and language and economic circumstance and

ability. It is the empowerment in our Unitarian legacy and the love of our Universalist promise that draw people to us and that keep us here.

It is our culture and not our theology that has been our biggest obstacle. And because that is true, our final message is a message of hope. We can change our culture if we have the will to do it.

In this book, we look at congregations that are striving to change their culture. The next chapter describes some Common Threads that we have found running through the stories of these congregations. These practices can help us Unitarian Universalists to change our culture and build multicultural, antiracist Beloved Community.

QUESTIONS FOR YOU AND
YOUR CONGREGATION

1. Which expressions of faith described here are most compelling for you, especially as they call for the work of building multicultural, antiracist Beloved Community? How would you express this call?

2. If you are reading this book in a group, what consensus can your group create about expressing the "call of our faith"? How can this expression be shared with your community or congregation and used to offer an overarching standard for your work on multiculturalism and antiracism?

CHAPTER TWO

Common Threads

- intentionality
- relationships, relationships, relationships
- leadership that's diverse, committed, and collaborative
- education for multicultural competencies and antiracism
- institutionalized structures that support the multicultural, antiracist mission
- multicultural is multigenerational
- worship that speaks to the heart and that centers diverse voices, styles, and cultures
- social justice and community engagement
- adaptability and entrepreneurship
- a willingness to take risks and to feel uncomfortable
- patience, perseverance, courage, and humility
- a palpable aliveness and love

IN THE 1990s, the Unitarian Universalist Association creates a hopeful logo for the original Journey Toward Wholeness campaign. The logo shows a gently winding two-lane roadway, leading up and over a hill. The destination, it suggests, can't quite be described, but it's just over the horizon. All we need to do is set out on the journey.

But now we co-authors understand that the "road" to such Beloved Community is not a single highway. Rather, we think of it as many intersecting paths. Each path includes loop-de-loops and detours; crossroads at which crucial decisions must be made and a "wrong" turn may lengthen or thwart the journey; roundabouts where, when folks can't figure out the "right" exit, they end up circling and circling. "Right" and "wrong" are in quotation marks here because there just aren't many absolutes on this journey.

Some paths feel like highways, where dangerous merges bring high-speed roads together from myriad directions. Some paths feel grueling, where the way forward must be hacked through dense underbrush in uncharted territory.

The work of building Beloved Community doesn't have a single roadmap. There is no digital mapping system that will take us directly to our destination.

Instead, this work is complex and messy. Congregations on the journey to multicultural, antiracist Beloved Community make halting, uncertain progress at times, and at other times feel a rush of emerging life, partnership, and joy. The work is hard, and it's worth it.

Here's the good news: We don't have to start from scratch, and Unitarian Universalists are not alone in doing this work.

EARLIER LISTS OF CORE PRINCIPLES

In chapter 1, we refer to the National Congregations Study, the late-1990s research that focuses primarily on Christian congregations striving to build multiracial, multiethnic communities. The books that result from this research offer us early inspiration. So do Mark DeYmaz's *Building a Healthy Multi-ethnic Church*; Gordon Dragt's "16 Tips for Turning Your Church Around"; Jacqueline J. Lewis's "Ten Essential Strategies to Grow a Multiracial, Multicultural Congregation" (a workbook that forms the seed of her and John Janka's *The Pentecost Paradigm: Ten Strategies for Becoming a Multiracial Congregation*); Manuel Ortiz's *One New People*; and Howard Thurman's *Footprints of a Dream*. Almost all of our early resources suggest "core principles" for congregations hoping to bring people from different races, ethnicities, and cultural backgrounds together into one anti-oppressive institution of faith. Across this literature, these lists of core principles share many similarities. In each case, the authors' actual experiences turn their list into a living document.

When we first dive into this project, these lists echo in our mind. They offer on-ramps for congregations as they begin the work. They can serve as fresh guides when congregations get stuck. They remind us of the essential qualities that we all need, and they hint at ways to measure our progress through the developmental stages of creating Beloved Community.

So we too want to give our readers a list. But as we get to know the congregations in our study, as we encounter their lay and ordained people, and as we ponder our own experiences, we grow increasingly uncomfortable with calling our list "core principles" or "essential strategies." These phrases imply an "expert's" voice; they hint at valuing efficiency and quickness over depth and the long haul. "Core principles" and "essential strategies" would sound like we are offering you a how-to guide, after all. These terms just don't work for us.

Instead, building multicultural, antiracist Beloved Community is "heart work," as Rev. Melissa Carvill-Ziemer says at Ministry Days before the start of Justice General Assembly 2017. It's a complex, interwoven process of building relationships while also creating the space to analyze how power works in any given system. To do this work, congregations must ask: Who has power in the here and now, and who doesn't? Who benefits and who doesn't from hierarchical systems created long before we current strugglers were born?

This heart work asks participants to hold each other's differing experiences and needs in a loving, sustainable container, while also urging growth and change. But participants must also address all the aspects of parish ministry that go on whether a congregation is monocultural or multicultural: worship, pastoral care, religious education, social justice work, administration, and more. Congregations on the way to multicultural Beloved Community look at these common congregational elements through a multicultural, antiracist lens.

Participants in building Beloved Community weave all of these elements—the heart work, the power analysis, the ongoing congregational work—into a complex tapestry. So in this book, the phrase "core principles" has evolved into *Common Threads*.

OUR COMMON THREADS

Our Common Threads include most of the shared elements from the lists in earlier resources, along with some of our own. No one congregation embodies all of these Common Threads, and congregations almost never implement them fully. The Common Threads do not constitute a step-by-step to-do list. Congregations can enter into this work at multiple points; they can pick up one or more of these elements at any stage in their development. We witness most of these Common Threads running through the life of each of the congregations we study.

Here, then, are our Common Threads. In the sections that follow, we look more closely at each one.

- **Intentionality:** Congregations ground their journey in an overarching goal or sense of call, made explicit in their mission and vision.

- **Relationships, Relationships, Relationships:** Building and tending to healthy relationships within the congregation and beyond are central to the work.
- **Leadership That's Diverse, Committed, and Collaborative:** Ministers, staff, and lay leaders are passionate champions for the multicultural, antiracist mission. Whenever possible, they represent a wide range of identities.
- **Education for Multicultural Competencies and Antiracism:** Through classes and trainings that speak to different generations, congregants can name the impact of white supremacy culture and other oppressive systems of power and privilege. They explore the congregation's history and the wider community in which they dwell in order to draw on strengths and reconcile mistakes from the past.
- **Institutionalized Structures That Support the Multicultural, Antiracist Mission:** Congregations adapt their governance and committee structures to make them more inclusive. They work to eliminate barriers to participation in leadership.
- **Multicultural Is Multigenerational:** Children, youth, young adults, and adults worship, learn, and grow together, honoring their different styles and needs. They stay in touch with changing expressions and expectations of family life across racial, ethnic, and generational differences.
- **Worship That Speaks to the Heart and That Centers Diverse Voices, Styles, and Cultures:** Worship in these congregations touches congregants' hearts, bodies, and spirits as well as their minds. It includes music, language, and art from many cultural sources. Such inclusion is authentic and accountable because the congregation has relationships with people whose cultures are represented.
- **Social Justice and Community Engagement:** The congregation works in partnership and solidarity with traditionally marginalized groups at the local, state, and national levels for

justice and equity for all. Congregants—especially those from the dominant culture—know how to follow leaders of color as well as how to use their own power appropriately for change that benefits those at the margins.

- **Adaptability and Entrepreneurship:** The work of creating multicultural, antiracist Beloved Community keeps evolving. These congregations adapt their initial plans to meet changing times and contexts. They develop a gift for improvisation and joy. They are on the journey for the long haul.

- **A Willingness to Take Risks and to Feel Uncomfortable:** Taking risks—especially, risking "failure"—creates discomfort in most congregational systems. Yet in the work of building multicultural, antiracist Beloved Community, if some folks are not uncomfortable, then the congregation or community may not be moving into the areas that need the deepest change.

- **Patience, Perseverance, Courage, and Humility:** This work is messy, and it never ends. Well-trained and well-intentioned people will keep making mistakes. Conflict is inevitable. Patience, perseverance, courage, and humility are prime habits of the heart in building multicultural, antiracist Beloved Community.

- **A Palpable Aliveness and Love:** Congregations on this journey have a sense of aliveness and enthusiasm for the work. Everyone has the chance to feel more whole and "seen" in such communities. The spirit of love is palpable in the congregations that commit to this soul work.

All of these Common Threads are easier to grasp through story, example, and experimentation than through lecture and description. The following sections draw on wisdom and examples from a wide range of sources as well as on the lived experiences of the congregations we study.

INTENTIONALITY

In 1996 in *One New People*, Rev. Manuel Ortiz offers various "models for developing a multiethnic church" and acknowledges that "racial reconciliation will not happen on its own." Intentionality, our first Common Thread, shows up at the top of the list of core principles in almost all the earlier literature about multicultural, multiracial, multiethnic congregations.

Congregations need a "common purpose that *supersedes* racial equity," writes Michael Emerson in *People of the Dream*. At the same time, these communities "need to become convinced that they cannot be fully mature in their faith and reach their goals *apart* from racial equity" (our emphasis added).

For just this reason, we spend chapter 1 wrestling with Unitarian Universalist theology. The overarching goal—the sense of call that is bigger than, but also makes necessary, the hard work of building multicultural, antiracist congregations—provides the compelling motivation for congregations to get started and to keep going. The *why* precedes the *how*.

In *Footprints of a Dream*, Rev. Dr. Howard Thurman describes how creating an explicit statement of intent is a crucial step in the creation of the Church of the Fellowship of All Peoples in San Francisco—the first intentionally interracial church in the United States, founded in the 1950s. The Fellowship's explicit statement, called "The Commitment," initially causes dissent among the members, and it drives some people away. But that's a necessary risk. As Dr. Thurman affirms, "if we did not have some kind of verbal platform on which to stand, all authentic growth would be cut off."

The thread of intentionality runs through all the congregations we study. At All Souls Unitarian Church in Tulsa, for example, longtime congregants and new members sign a huge poster that displays the congregation's Centennial Vision 2021 statement.

They commit to helping create a community "bursting with people from a diversity of theologies, philosophies, ethnicities, cultures, colors, classes, abilities, generations, sexual orientations, and political persuasions, all dwelling together in peace, seeking the truth in love, and helping one another." Congregational leaders use this statement of the overarching goal to assess every decision they make about resources and programs.

In sum, then, to be effective about building multicultural, antiracist Beloved Community, congregations have to be intentional. The congregation can express that intentionality by:

- making a fierce commitment to an overarching goal grounded in a sense of call
- creating a mission or vision statement that makes multiculturalism, antiracism, and antioppression an explicit part of the congregation's identity
- allowing these expressions of intent to determine where the congregation puts its resources (money, time, programs, staff) and how members and friends relate to each other, as well as how they act in their wider communities

RELATIONSHIPS, RELATIONSHIPS, RELATIONSHIPS

"All of life is based on relationships," Manuel Ortiz writes. The second Common Thread for congregations creating multiracial, antiracist Beloved Community underscores the centrality of relationship building. This includes relationships both within and beyond the congregation.

Healthy congregations and communities always depend on the quality of their relationship building. But once a congregation commits to building multicultural, antiracist Beloved Community, its participants' capacity to build authentic, accountable relationships across all kinds of differences becomes crucial. Devoting time and resources to learning how to be in right and loving relationship across differences is central to the work. It is both the condition and the means for living into every other Common Thread on our list.

The vision crafted by the Unitarian Universalist Association's Leadership Council, quoted in chapter 1, offers a rich call to relationship. In this vision, Beloved Community is a place "where all souls are welcomed as blessings and the human family lives whole and reconciled." To welcome all souls as blessings, to reconcile and make whole the human family, people must be able to perceive and embrace the full humanity of everyone they meet, whether that person is a newcomer to the congregation, a stranger on the street, or a community member with whom they are engaged in a joint project. To witness to each person's brokenness and beauty, to their unique personality and their complex identities, requires congregants' ongoing commitment to their own self-knowledge and to their capacity to grow.

In a racialized society, members of the dominant group (and sometimes members of targeted groups as well) often assume that all, or even most, members of a targeted group will feel or act the same way and want the same things. In worst-case scenarios, these assumptions become stereotypes and prejudices that diminish or exclude those who don't fit the dominant group's norms. A focus on relationship helps people understand the personal within the systemic. It debunks any generalizations about a group of people and allows the range of opinions, experiences, histories, personalities, and perspectives among people in any group to become visible.

Rev. Dr. Kristen Harper, in her essay in Rev. Mitra Rahnema's *Centering: Navigating Race, Authenticity, and Power in Ministry*, offers an example of how relationship building over time can transform a congregation's capacity both to hear the real trauma that ministers of color experience and to honor these ministers' power and authority. Rev. Harper's experiences demonstrate the complexity of issues such as inclusion and exclusion, superiority and inferiority, and power and authority that often operate in multicultural relationships. Writing about these experiences again in 2019, Kristen describes them this way:

> When I first arrived at the congregation I now serve, I preached a sermon during Black History Month on "Driving While Black." I shared my experiences of being pulled over half a dozen times by white police officers in white neighborhoods when I was trying to make pastoral visits and officiate at beachside weddings. Although I did not feel angry when I was relaying these stories, some of the congregants commented on how "angry" I seemed. The unconscious projections and assumptions brought by white congregants into our relationship led them to see only an "Angry Black Woman" and not their minister attempting to invite them into a different view of the world in which we were all living.
>
> These projections and assumptions about me as a person of color continued until I felt I could no longer share my experiences and those of other people of color with the congregation and still maintain my position. For years I remained silent about the personal and systemic racism occurring to and around me. At the same time, I continued to show them compassion and care, knitting myself into the church and community. As our relationship grew, their trust in me grew and their ability and willingness to hear the pain of people of color—my own and others'—grew too. Many of the projections and assumptions were brought to the surface, named, and dispelled.
>
> In 2016, after the deaths of a number of Black and Latinx people at the hands of white police officers and vigilantes, I preached a sermon in which I passionately expressed my anger, sadness, and frustration over the continued marginalization

and dehumanization of people of color. When I completed my sermon, the congregation stood and applauded. Afterward, many of the longtime white members expressed their gratitude for my courage and leadership as well as their empathy that I and other people of color continue to suffer from the racism embedded in our culture.

Sixteen years later, I am probably more angry, more passionate, and more committed than ever, yet my feelings and experiences no longer threaten or cause paralyzing guilt for members. Undaunted we stumble forward and backward together, transformed by the power of our openness and brokenness.

Rev. Harper's story reveals the meaningful ministry that can take place when people are willing to do the excruciatingly slow and painful work of reflection on both an individual and communal level. It speaks to the transformations that are possible when relationships become a community's top priority. At the same time, it touches on the additional cost that many ministers of color must bear in this dance of relationship building.

In the congregations we study, the Common Thread of "relationships, relationships, relationships" shows up again and again. At the First Unitarian Church of San José (FUCSJ), for example, engagement in faith-based community organizing has changed the congregation's culture. One-to-one conversations with community members from a variety of faiths and ethnicities have given FUCSJ members—both white and of color—fresh insight into the fear and pain that immigrant families experience. The sense of family kinship becomes real and specific for congregants and community members. They develop a commitment to showing up for each other.

Within each congregation we study, the practices that support healthy relationships become increasingly important. Direct and regular communication, in person whenever possible; using "I" statements; deep listening; sharing air space and avoiding cross-talk; understanding cultural differences; trying on ideas that differ from one's own; practicing confession and acknowledging hurt ("oops" and "ouch," as youth groups put it)—these practices honor the inherent worth and dignity of every participant, while making room for voices that have been historically marginalized. Many congregations use the Visions, Inc., Covenant for Dialogue, as adapted by Rev. Leslie Takahashi, Rev. Nancy Palmer Jones, and Dr. Mark A. Hicks. It is available as part of "Beloved Conversations," a curriculum for exploring the role of race and ethnicity in individual and congregational lives offered by Meadville Lombard Theological School. When such relational covenants are woven into a congregation's culture, everyone is better prepared to deal with the conflicts that inevitably arise in the work of building multicultural, antiracist Beloved Community.

In sum, then, to be effective about building Beloved Community, congregations:

- place the slow, steady process of relationship building at the heart of their life together
- support healthy relationships in every aspect of congregational life, spanning all kinds of differences and especially understanding and embracing differences in race, culture, and ethnicity

LEADERSHIP THAT'S DIVERSE, COMMITTED, AND COLLABORATIVE

Diversity among ministers and lay leaders is a key principle in creating and maintaining multicultural churches, as George Yancey points out in *One Body, One Spirit*. Members and newcomers need to see people who share their identities in visible positions of leadership, both lay and ordained. Diverse leadership communicates the congregation's commitment to welcoming all and to including many voices in worship and decision making.

In *Unitarian Universalists of Color: Stories of Struggle, Courage, Love, and Faith* (edited by Yuri Yamamoto, Chandra Snell, and Tim Hanami), Latoya Brooks describes what she feels when she walks into her first Unitarian Universalist church. She notices right away that a Black gay man serves as the minister. "I loved seeing someone who looked like me," she says. "I didn't feel 'othered' or an outsider. I felt empowered seeing him in a position of power and spiritual leadership in a faith tradition that has few ministers of color." Rev. Dr. Jacqui Lewis and John Janka echo this experience in *The Pentecost Paradigm*. "When people come to worship, whether for the first time or the hundredth time," they write, "the unspoken sermon is whom they observe in leadership."

Congregations on the road to multicultural, antiracist Beloved Community strive for diversity among their lay leaders too. Leaders of color take their place on the Board; they lead and participate in key committees; they show up as greeters and worship associates during worship and other major congregational events. Such lay leadership expands the range of voices and experiences engaged in the major decisions about how the congregation will move toward its goals. And in the process of governing and managing the congregation, leaders of color and white leaders build relationships across difference that can model joy and aliveness for the whole community.

In congregations whose leaders are all white, the minister's passionate commitment to the call to multicultural, antiracist Beloved Community makes a big difference in the congregation's journey. These white ministers intentionally model approaching their own mistakes with a spirit of humility, openness, and curiosity. They engage in their own ongoing education around issues of multicultural competencies and systems of power and privilege.

When the Unitarian Universalist Church of Annapolis (UUCA) calls Rev. Fred Muir as senior minister in 1984, the lead staff is all white, as is he. But Rev. Fred is already committed to changing himself, the community he serves, and the wider faith through understanding and dismantling racism, white privilege, and white supremacy culture. Over the thirty-two years of his ministry at UUCA, he remains a steady advocate for the hard work and the heart work, the experimentation and the relationship building that the journey requires. He shares stories with the congregation about his own growth and transformation. He inspires lay leaders to take risks and dedicate their time and resources to this work. When congregants ask him to be actively involved in an antiracism program, he shows up. As Marlene Browne, an African-American member, says, "Without the minister's support, I mean, who's going to follow?"

Justice General Assembly 2017 lifts up another important dimension for leadership in building multicultural, antiracist Beloved Community. Through efforts that include the interim co-presidents' opening armchair conversation (described in our Introduction), the use of "tri-moderators" (three moderators lead the business of the assembly, instead of one), and core presentations that also use the big black armchairs so that multiple leaders can speak, Justice GA demonstrates that multicultural leadership is multivocal and collaborative. When the Unitarian Universalist Association's Board members take their seats in the armchairs, each member's thoughts, feelings, and responses to the changes afoot in the religion have space for expression. The thousands of Unitarian Universalists in the convention hall get a personal feel for each of these decision makers. They witness how this collection of individuals comes together to form a leadership group not afraid of difference and conflict but, rather, willing to learn and collaborate with and across those differences.

The practice of *shared ministry* can mirror this multivocal, collaborative leadership style on the congregational level. Aisha Hauser reports that at East Shore Unitarian Church in Bellevue, Washington, where she serves as director of lifelong learning, collaboration is encouraged and welcomed. When ministers and congregants practice this collaborative leadership model, they build skills that transfer to the work of justice in the wider community.

Still, we need to offer several major caveats when we talk about "diversity in leadership" in predominantly white congregations. Congregations longing for more racial and ethnic diversity in their pews may call a minister of color—and then think that their work is done. Asking ministers and members of color to do the "spiritual domestic labor" of diversifying the congregation racially and ethnically reinscribes white supremacy culture instead of dismantling it. Too often, congregations simply hope or assume that the minister or lay leader of color will teach about white supremacy, racism, and other oppressions; will take the lead in changing institutional structures; will welcome and integrate newcomers of color into congregational life; and more. These expectations tend to burn out or drive out Unitarian Universalists of color, both lay and ordained.

Congregations that have done considerable work around awakening to the impact of white supremacy culture on their lives communally and individually—even congregations that have shifted their institutional structures and common practices to reflect their multicultural competencies—can make some of the same mistakes. Their capacity to embrace different degrees or combinations of culturally defined "difference" (including class, skin color, sexual orientation, physical abilities, and gender identity) may limit their ability to see their new minister or lay leader as a whole person rather than as a representative of an entire group.

Congregations that are ready for such diversity in leadership own the need for ongoing education, awakening, and monitoring of their journey toward multicultural, antiracist Beloved Community. Some of the congregations we study demonstrate the mix of blessings and difficulties that calling a minister of color brings.

To ensure the flourishing of leaders of color, congregations must invest in antiracism training and remain awake to the dangers of tokenism. With these foundations in place, it also matters that the congregation's key leaders (ordained, lay, and professional staff):

• represent a wide range of identities
• champion the multicultural, antiracist mission
• demonstrate that multiculturalism is multivocal and collaborative

EDUCATION FOR MULTICULTURAL COMPETENCIES AND ANTIRACISM

The work of building multicultural, antiracist Beloved Community cannot happen without ongoing training, religious education, and faith formation in antiracism and multicultural competencies. These programs help congregants of all ages wrestle with the ways that systemic racism, ethnocentrism, and white supremacy culture impact their own lives and the life of the congregation. They give participants practice in shifting away from the norms of white supremacy culture and engaging in new ways of being.

When we first start this project in 2014, we enter into it with at least one assumption about what congregations need to learn in order to make any progress at all toward their multicultural, antiracist mission. We put it this way: "Until a congregation reaches a tipping point in the number of white folks in the congregation who understand the concept of white privilege, a congregation can't really make any progress."

"Understanding white privilege" is shorthand for awakening to this country's system of racial hierarchy. Now we use the term "white supremacy culture" to describe this system. Regardless of the language used, what matters is that congregations come to understand the histories and the present-day manifestations of racialized systems.

Congregations get started on this process in many ways. They may watch a movie together and hold discussions afterward. Paying attention to the themes, actors, and filmmakers of recent releases can point congregational leaders toward films that serve as important cultural markers.

Congregations may read or listen to a book together and use a study guide to take the conversation deeper. Like the list of possible movies, this list grows every month. The UUA's annual Common Read offers good suggestions. Other books offer valuable starting points too. We list many of them in our Resources section, along with some films.

Congregations may bring in trainers who specialize in the work of antiracism and multiculturalism. In the congregations we study, some leaders and members take the Intercultural Development Inventory, which is based on the idea that people in dominant as well as targeted groups—white people and people of color—all grow through certain developmental stages in their capacity to understand, respond, and relate to cultural differences. Congregations can use this tool and then create a plan to help people grow in intercultural competencies.

Many follow the curricula developed by Dr. Mark A. Hicks, Angus MacLean Professor of Religious Education at Meadville

Lombard Theological School. "Building the World We Dream About" and "Beloved Conversations" develop congregants' capacity to have "holy conversations" about power and difference in a racialized society.

Congregations also subscribe to resources created by Unitarian Universalists of color. These resources, developed with congregants of color in mind, enrich the spiritual lives of members and friends across differences in race, culture, and ethnicity. The monthly Black Lives of Unitarian Universalism (BLUU) Spiritual Subscription Box (#BLUUBox), for example, offers prayers, reflections on contemporary issues, suggestions for social justice actions, historical profiles of Black Unitarian Universalists, ways to connect, audio links to meditations, and more. "Culturally relevant. Spiritually grounded. Family friendly. Action oriented," BLUU's description of this resource reads, and it goes on, "With content grounded in the lived experiences and diverse perspectives of Black Unitarian Universalists, this subscription box is a wholly unique opportunity to connect one's belief to faith-led action while building community with others who are dedicated to justice-making and liberation through our shared faith." Black and non-Black congregants benefit from this resource that centers the voices and experiences of Black UUs.

Similarly, congregations intent on the journey to true Beloved Community apply a multicultural, antiracist, antioppressive lens to all their educational and spiritual resources. Every experience becomes an opportunity for ongoing training and reflection.

For example, Gail Forsyth-Vail, interim faith development director for the Unitarian Universalist Association, adds questions with an antioppressive focus to the themes offered by the Soul Matters Sharing Circle. Soul Matters is one of many theme-based resource groups used by Unitarian Universalists. Here's a sampling of how these questions deepen the themes:

- **sanctuary**—"For whom has [our congregation] been a sanctuary up to now, and in what way? Who is missing from that picture?"
- **possibility**—"What would it mean to decenter white culture, history, and perspectives in our congregation and community to make room for those whose culture, history, and perspectives are often on the margins?"

Most of the congregations we study offer some form of training and engagement every year, intentionally expanding the number of people who share a common understanding as well as offering increasing levels of complexity and integration for those who have already begun. Chapters 3 through 7 bring many of these training opportunities to life.

All this training and education, though, must take into account each congregation's specific context. Understanding the surrounding community helps a congregation hear its specific call to the work of antiracism and multiculturalism. Exploring a congregation's history gives leaders and congregants a sense of the strengths and the brokenness in the inheritance it carries. We dive into the history and context of each of the congregations we study in order to lift up what's in their DNA. Our conversation partners have found inspiration in stories from their congregation's past, as well as reminders of mistakes that still echo in the present.

In sum, to be effective about building multicultural, antiracist Beloved Community, congregations:

- build their multicultural competencies and awareness of white supremacy culture through ongoing trainings and learning opportunities
- use every aspect of congregational life as part of the curriculum for multiculturalism and antiracism

- explore the congregation's history and its wider context to see what strengths and what mistakes form part of its inheritance for this work

INSTITUTIONALIZED STRUCTURES THAT SUPPORT THE MULTICULTURAL, ANTIRACIST MISSION

Congregations intent on building multicultural, antiracist Beloved Community examine and shift their organizational structures to support the work. What institutional structures and practices need changing in order to break free of the systems founded on white supremacy culture? How can congregations embody a more flexible, less oppressive way of working together? What institutional structures and practices need to be put into place to help keep the congregation accountable and on track?

Most of the congregations we study develop new institutional structures that provide accountability, assessment, and lived experiences of multicultural ways of being. These congregations often set up a special team or structure for monitoring their faithfulness to their overarching goal and for measuring their growth. Whether a team is called the Racial Justice Team, the Transformation Team, or something else, it takes on the difficult task of examining all aspects of congregational life for their adherence to or variance from the mission. It makes them accountable to the mission and to the groups most impacted by white supremacy systems. The evolution of structures at All Souls Unitarian Church in Tulsa, Oklahoma, offers a great example, as we describe in chapter 5.

Some congregations launch this process by noticing and naming how congregants currently work together. The First Unitarian Church of San José uses process observation at each meeting of its Board and of its Program and Operations Council. A leader volunteers to serve as process observer for a particular meeting and then watches how the group fulfills its work and how the members relate to each other. The questions the observer strives to answer are listed on a printed form for easy reference. They include:

- Are we fulfilling the work of the congregation in a way that supports our mission, vision, and ends?
- Do the agenda and discussion demonstrate FUCSJ's commitment to antiracism, antioppression, and multiculturalism (AR/AO/MC)? Do leaders share responsibility for raising AR/AO/MC concerns?
- Does the leadership demonstrate accountability to marginalized groups and/or to people not represented at the table? Are marginalized communities invited to be a part of the discussion?
- Do leaders share air space and listen deeply; work with each other with respect, compassion, and humor; and generally embody our Unitarian Universalist Principles?

At the end of the meeting, the process observer shares what they have noticed, offering affirmations and specific examples as well as suggestions about how the group can improve. Asking the questions over and over, naming how folks attend to this over-arching sense of call, even passing out the process observation form to all members at the beginning of the meeting so that the questions are present in everyone's minds and hearts—these practices shift cultural habits toward a new way of being together.

The Board of Trustees at the First Unitarian Church of Portland has made the practice of process observation even more focused on dismantling white supremacy culture. For their fall 2018–19 retreat, Board members read "White Supremacy Culture" by Kenneth Jones and Tema Okun. They choose to focus for that congregational year on shifting their behavior around four habits of white supremacy culture: fear of open conflict, a belief in a right to comfort, a sense of urgency, and valuing of objectivity. The process observation form names some of the antidotes for each of these behaviors, and the process observer for each meeting notes the strengths, questions, and issues that arise around these behaviors.

For example, to counteract the habit of urgency, Board members strive to set realistic timelines, to consider the time needed to complete tasks, and to put off decisions if additional information or work is needed. They also have a shared understanding of the process that they have put in place for making decisions in urgent situations. Tracking these behaviors in every meeting over the course of the year reminds Board members that they can choose behaviors that include and honor many voices and many styles of processing information and making decisions.

First Parish in Cambridge, Massachusetts, and the First Unitarian Church of San José, California, also use the spiritual practice of Mutual Invitation in their leadership gatherings, small groups, and some worship settings. In *The Wolf Shall Dwell with the Lamb*, Rev. Dr. Eric Law describes this practice, which ensures that everyone in the room shares power and airtime. He developed it when he noticed that people from some cultures often need to be invited to speak, while others—especially those from dominant cultures—take for granted their right to contribute and may dominate conversations, usually without noticing they are doing so. In Mutual Invitation, the conversation's facilitator invites a member of the group to speak first about the question at hand. That person may speak, pass, or "pass for now," but whatever their choice, they get to invite the next person to share. Everyone gets the opportunity to invite; everyone receives an invitation. Everyone has the chance to speak and be heard, uninterrupted. This practice shifts the pace of conversations. It demonstrates a both/and approach to a theme rather than an either/or assumption of "one right way." With Mutual Invitation, each conversation becomes intentionally multivocal and collaborative. Relationships grow sweeter and deeper as everyone gets to be known and heard.

In sum, then, this Common Thread calls on congregations to:

- adapt their governance and committee structures and institute practices that ensure more inclusivity and accountability
- share the responsibility for the congregation's multicultural development
- demonstrate that multiculturalism is multivocal and collaborative

MULTICULTURAL IS MULTIGENERATIONAL

"Multicultural is multigenerational!" reads a sign posted in Aisha Hauser's office at East Shore Unitarian Church (ESUC) in Bellevue, Washington. From her vantage point as a religious educator of color, Aisha looks out on the all-too-often closed spaces of Unitarian Universalism and longs for more openness and flow among generations, cultures, and ways of worshiping and learning.

She points to the practice of many congregations on a Sunday morning of having children and youth leave the sanctuary after the opening of worship to go to a separate space for their age-segregated classes. During a Beloved Conversations session at ESUC, a Bolivian congregant reports how he feels when he and his family, including young children, first arrive at the church. "You tried to take my children away!" he says. "You wanted to send them to another place!" On the East Shore campus, the religious education building is the farthest from the sanctuary.

"Everything in my whole life before I became a Unitarian Universalist was multigenerational," Aisha says. Aisha, born in Egypt and raised Muslim, immigrated to the United States with her family when she was a child. In her culture of origin, children and adults are comfortable sharing the same space, and children hear adult conversations all the time. There is no separating children into another room—"there isn't another room!" Aisha exclaims.

The conversation about all-ages worship services is very much alive in Unitarian Universalist congregations, partly as a move toward multicultural Beloved Community, partly in response to radical changes in family life over recent decades. Some congregants object to the noise and disruption they may experience when worshiping with young children in the room. They are accustomed to a style of worship that favors quiet, contemplative practices, with sermons that resemble lectures aimed at a highly educated crowd. We look more closely at worship style in the next section, but here, it's good to point out that such expectations mirror the characteristics of white supremacy culture, with value placed on perfectionism rather than on the lively, unpredictable semi-chaos of multigenerational space.

Kim Sweeney, the author of a discussion guide titled "The Death of Sunday School and the Future of Faith Formation" and facilitator of workshops on the topic, emphasizes that prioritizing multigenerational experiences in congregations does not mean making either/or choices. Congregations can offer all-ages worship, family worship, and age-segregated religious education in varying combinations. What's important for this Common Thread is that children and youth are included in the congregation's vision for its multicultural growth.

In chapter 3 we describe an engaging all-ages Flower Communion service at the Unitarian Universalist Church of Annapolis,

Maryland, created by Rev. Christina Leone Tracy. The service demonstrates how a multicultural, multigenerational lens can transform and enliven a familiar story from Unitarian history.

Congregations on the road to multicultural, antiracist Beloved Community also look at the religious education curricula they offer children and youth through an antioppressive lens. Religious educators and lay leaders use their own multicultural competencies to enrich existing curricula with questions that deepen and widen the focus, such as: Who is included in this story? Whose cultural values does this curriculum represent? How is our congregation in relationship with the cultures represented here? Inviting children and youth to engage with age-appropriate questions about inclusivity, relationship, and representation models an awareness that they can use throughout their lives.

We can't leave this Common Thread without mentioning one misconception about the inevitability of certain kinds of generational change. Some older white Unitarian Universalists express the belief that issues of racism and white supremacy culture will no longer be relevant as today's younger generations grow into adulthood. The older adults point to the shifting demographics of the United States and the move toward a "majority minority" country. They watch their children and grandchildren living and learning in multicultural and mixed-race settings and assume that the relationships the younger generations form now will eliminate systems of racial and cultural hierarchy in the future.

Sadly, this hope, and even these childhood experiences, will not on their own overcome the power and inertia of social systems set in place centuries ago. That's why multicultural competency trainings are so necessary for all ages. Change won't come without intentionality. Change only happens when community members of all ages practice new ways of being together over and over and over.

In sum, congregations on the road to multicultural, antiracist Beloved Community:

- demonstrate that multiculturalism is multigenerational
- experiment with all-ages worship styles that embody the messages of love and inclusivity at the heart of the Unitarian Universalist faith
- adapt religious education curricula in age-appropriate ways to include a multicultural, antiracist lens

WORSHIP THAT SPEAKS TO THE HEART AND CENTERS DIVERSE VOICES, STYLES, AND CULTURES

In *Footprints of a Dream*, Rev. Dr. Howard Thurman writes that multiracial, multicultural churches must create religious experiences "by which the sense of separateness will be transcended and unity expressed, experiences that are deeper than all diversity but at the same time are enriched by diversity." In the early twenty-first century, worship services remain a vital expression of what a congregation values and an important opportunity for participants to practice living their faith out loud.

In the United States, Unitarian Universalist worship has its roots in the Puritan tradition of the eighteenth century. A stripped-bare sanctuary and music that consisted of chanted, unaccompanied text helped to focus congregants' attention on the words. Those words were almost always drawn from a single source—the Christian Bible—and worship featured the faith leaders' lengthy interpretations of it.

Although worship styles and sources have evolved and expanded over the succeeding centuries, many Unitarian Universalist congregations at the beginning of the twenty-first century still favor a quiet, word-driven worship experience. This preference discourages folks for whom vibrant, embodied worship is a part of their cultural upbringing. It also leaves out those who long for more spiritual freedom of expression, and it usually fails to keep younger congregants engaged.

Unitarian Universalist congregations on the journey to multicultural, antiracist Beloved Community know that worship needs to embody the multivocal, collaborative, heart-centered values that allow a wide range of people to feel spiritually at home.

In her essay in *Centering: Navigating Race, Authenticity, and Power in Ministry*, Rev. Dr. Kristen Harper describes some of the barriers she encountered when trying to introduce multicultural elements to worship. "Music," she writes, "is one of the few ways I feel connected to spirit, to the divine, to others [in worship]." Early in her ministry, Rev. Harper tried integrating chanting, stomping, and clapping into her services. "I wanted to help evoke in members feelings of connection and transcendence that I had experienced through movement and song in the Black churches I had visited." While still singing the Unitarian Universalist hymns she loves, Rev. Harper tried to add diverse cultural expressions and the chance to "clap and shout and vibrate with rhythm." Many in the congregation responded with "not-so-quiet resistance and resentment."

How do worship leaders in congregations striving to build multicultural, antiracist Beloved Community introduce change, handle resistance, and manage congregants' conflicting worship preferences? We co-authors can see classic elements of white supremacy culture at work in keeping Unitarian Universalist worship constricted. Perfectionism may demand a certain musical sound and a rigid order of service. The right to comfort makes it hard for longtime members to give up the familiar word- and idea-driven worship that they were grateful to discover years before. Individualism—especially Unitarian Universalism's historical emphasis on individual freedom—combines with consumerism to create an approach to worship that is more about getting one's own needs met than about experiencing a transcendent unity with others whose worship preferences may differ. Worship leaders in the congregations we study encourage a spirit of generosity among congregants during worship. They invite participants to notice when they are *not* responding to some aspect of worship and to remember that this very element or style might be just what their neighbor in the sanctuary needs. Can they generously rejoice that their neighbor is getting the experience they need and hang on, knowing that what they need is around the corner too?

A growing number of Unitarian Universalists have experienced worship "conversion experiences" by attending the Leading Edge Conference—now called the Revolutionary Love Conference—held each spring at Middle Collegiate Church in downtown Manhattan. Worship at Middle Church offers vibrant and diverse music, dance, moments of intense quiet, rousing preaching, and direct connection to experiences in the wider world to bring its multiracial, multicultural, multigenerational, LGBTQIA-friendly congregation into joyous expressions of unity-with-diversity. As Rev. Dr. Jacqui Lewis describes in *The Pentecost Paradigm*, every choice of word, music, movement, and leadership in worship furthers the congregation's multicultural, antiracist mission. One Easter, a visual artist paints the worship elements as they unfold in real time, filling her canvas with color. At the 2016 Leading Edge Conference, Middle Church's multiracial, multigenerational Jerriese Johnson Gospel Choir offers a version of "Glory," by John Legend, Common, and Che "Rhymefest" Smith, that has the packed congregation shouting, crying, clapping, and breathless with wonder.

Not all congregations have the wealth of artistic resources that Middle Church enjoys. But worship leaders can leap over such limits with a little creativity and relationship building.

Nearby high schools and music and arts programs, for example, may serve as sources for varied worship elements and diverse participants.

At the same time, heart- and soul-stirring worship that creates unity-with-diversity is not either/or—either lively and loud or quiet and restrained. Howard Thurman describes how, at the Church of the Fellowship of All Peoples in the mid-twentieth century, music is only one connecting element. Meditation and prayer invite congregants to turn inward to encounter their truest self, their own sense of the holy. When a worshiping group creates the shared quiet together, Dr. Thurman points out, even this most private of experiences can lead to a sense of unity.

A congregation's authentic context may inspire multicultural worship that draws on rituals and practices from contemplative traditions. Rev. Abhi Janamanchi, for instance, has noticed increasing numbers of Asian Americans visiting Cedar Lane Unitarian Universalist Church in Bethesda, Maryland. Unitarian Universalism, through its Transcendentalist ancestors, he points out, already has a "deep connection to Eastern spiritual traditions." To meet the needs of these new potential Unitarian Universalists, Rev. Abhi wants to create what he calls the new "Spirit Experience." He envisions

> multicultural, multifaith worship experiences, particularly honoring and celebrating Eastern religious or cultural observances . . . that might actually provide a space that is outside the Protestant box. . . . We try to fit everyone into [that box] on Sunday mornings, which is a huge turnoff for people who are non-Christian and also have been impacted by colonial Christianity. . . .
>
> Unitarian Universalism, at least on the conceptual level, is an expansive vessel, and I feel we can do that work in partnership with integrity. To me that is part of being awake. But I'm doing it sideways because I know the congregational system is

not equipped to handle that kind of a fundamental change to its DNA yet.

Rev. Abhi acknowledges that transforming worship style is a slow, developmental process that requires risk taking, patience, perseverance, and an entrepreneurial spirit. The "expansive vessel" of Unitarian Universalism can help create multicultural, interfaith worship spaces when congregations work with integrity and in partnership with those for whom other traditions are home base.

In the chapters to come, we describe in detail some great examples of the multicultural, multigenerational, transformative worship that we encounter on our site visits. Some of these models are adaptable for other congregations, especially if worship leaders ask permission from the originators of these services, the conversation partners we mention here. We have already experienced this cross-fertilization in our own congregations. This is another kind of collaboration that a multicultural, antiracist mission and vision can spark.

Congregations also benefit from a wealth of resources that can open up worship styles and sources. The Unitarian Universalist Association offers a webinar and follow-up conversation titled "Decentering Whiteness in Worship" on its website. As mentioned earlier, Black Lives of Unitarian Universalism (BLUU) offers a monthly Spiritual Subscription Box (#BLUUBox) that includes reflections, prayers, history, suggested social justice activities, and more. The resource has been created specifically for Black Unitarian Universalists, but its creators say, "The BLUUBox is for all people." It also offers opportunities and information for white people and non-Black people of color and for people who are not Unitarian Universalists.

One other crucial element characterizes the worship experience at each of the congregations we study. These congregations demonstrate a palpable warmth and inclusive welcome for all who enter. We feel this warmth from the moment we approach the sanctuary. We see and hear it intentionally woven into the words, images, and gestures used during the service. And we watch the welcome extended through conversations after worship is over. This characteristic of congregations on the road to multicultural, antiracist Beloved Community weaves itself throughout many of our other Common Threads. It underlies "relationships, relationships, relationships," of course, as well as all the habits of the heart we list below. There are important nuances to consider about how a congregation communicates its warmth; chapter 4 suggests some of these. But when this warm welcome is informed by congregants' training in multicultural competencies and antiracism, it shines as a natural expression of the congregation's joy in being together.

In sum, the worship experience continues to be a primary portal for entry into congregational life and thus is crucial for embodying multicultural, antiracist Beloved Community. Congregations on this journey experiment with worship services that

- explore a range of styles, media, locations, and times
- honor and include diverse voices and cultures, without misappropriating cultural resources from traditionally marginalized groups
- demonstrate a warm, multiculturally inclusive welcome to all visitors, newcomers, members, and friends

SOCIAL JUSTICE AND COMMUNITY ENGAGEMENT

High on the list of Rev. Gordon Dragt's "16 Tips for Turning Your Church Around" sits this reminder: "Keep opening more doors into the church from the community and into the community from the church." A congregation's community engagement and social justice work open another portal for the journey toward multicultural, antiracist Beloved Community.

In *People of the Dream*, Michael Emerson and Rodney Woo describe the journey of the Wilcrest Baptist Church in Houston, Texas. When Pastor James Darby joins the ministerial staff of this mostly white congregation, he clarifies that he alone, as an African-American minister, can't "diversify" the church. Instead, he leads the congregation out into the surrounding African-American community, and the relationships that form start to change the composition of the church itself. He begins by inviting the congregation to join him in an act of witness and solidarity. On an evening shortly after the shooting death of a young Black neighbor, the minister leads some 125 congregants on a march from the church to the place where the shooting occurred. The neighbors peer out their windows and step out of their houses to watch; a few even join the march and participate in the prayers that the pastor offers. Dr. Woo, then lead minister of Wilcrest Baptist, remembers it this way: "For a few moments, we all saw the power of transcending the limitations of racial division and inequity." After that night, the congregation has a new sense of calling: "to walk by faith across racial and cultural lines, to live a common humanity."

As these walks through the neighborhood continue, the neighbors begin to visit the church. They bring their children to congregational activities and religious education classes. Some of the adults become members themselves. The work for justice in the wider community, the engagement with neighbors—these become important strands in the congregation's movement toward multiracial community.

In one way or another, all the congregations we study follow this model of building multicultural community: engaging with neighboring communities in a variety of ways and working for justice in partnership with their neighbors. They have all learned that if "diversifying" the congregation itself is the real underlying goal of such engagement, neither the neighborhood projects nor the diversification will succeed. When marginalized communities sense that the relationships others are attempting to form with them are mostly about helping white folks to feel good about themselves, they will find even genuine demonstrations of solidarity and partnership difficult to trust.

But when such engagement arises out of a congregation's real sense of call—a desire "to live a common humanity"—and when it is accompanied by trainings and reflections that support the congregation's growing multicultural competencies, then the multiracial relationships that bloom become as important for the congregation's journey as its own demographics. As we describe in chapter 4, the Immigration Small Group Justice Ministry at the Unitarian Universalist Congregation of Phoenix (UUCP) follows the lead of their partners in Puente Arizona, a migrant justice organization. The UUCP team offers what the community asks for rather than imposing their own ideas about what's needed. In between moments of direct engagement, the white members of the small group spend time reflecting among themselves about how their antiracism and multicultural competencies are serving or impeding these relationships. As a result, both UUCP and Puente partners express joy and appreciation for what they are creating together.

To be effective, this Common Thread, in particular, must be finely interwoven with the Common Threads of "relationships, relationships, relationships" and "education for multicultural competencies and antiracism." But we also can't imagine a congregation getting very far on its journey toward multicultural, antiracist Beloved Community without a powerful commitment to the work of social justice and community engagement. For all the heartbreak and frustrations that accompany such work, the resulting relationships bring a broken-openhearted joy to the lives of all involved. And action for justice is the best antidote that we know for the fears of collapse that weigh down so many people of faith as we write.

In sum, congregations on the journey:

- build working relationships with community members, characterized by partnership, solidarity, and a commitment to justice and equity for all
- follow the lead of members of traditionally marginalized communities and—especially when congregants are members of dominant groups—remain steadfast about building their multicultural competencies

HABITS OF THE HEART

The last four Common Threads are not so much actions to take as habits of the heart that are nurtured and cultivated by congregations striving to build multicultural, antiracist Beloved Community. These ways of being are closely intertwined; in fact, our brief descriptions earlier in this chapter mix and match elements that we mention in the slightly longer sections below.

The stories we share in the next five chapters offer rich examples of these qualities at work in congregational life. Here we offer brief summaries that hint at those deeper learnings.

Adaptability and Entrepreneurship

"This is an age that calls us to *experilearn*," says Karen Bellavance-Grace in *Full-Week Faith*, a report she wrote as a 2013 Fellow of the Fahs Collective. *Experilearning*—a word she first encountered in an online conversation with religious professionals in 2011—means opening minds and hearts to new possibilities and then trying new ways of doing things and learning from the results. Congregations on the journey to Beloved Community make a habit of experilearning. Because they are committed for the long haul, they recognize how the work keeps evolving as the times and the context change.

The Unitarian Universalist Church of Annapolis, Maryland (UUCA), for example, launches its entrepreneurial AWAKE Ministries with a particular vision for the time of its services and the participants it will draw. At first, AWAKE avoids Sundays so that congregants from many different faith communities can gather without losing their worshiping time in their home congregation. As the AWAKE team reflects on its experiments, the team keeps trying out new combinations of times and locations. They keep asking such questions as: What is UUCA's overarching goal in offering these new ministries, with their alternative worship style? How do changing demands on people's time, and the challenges of commuting influence when and how worship is offered? Eventually, UUCA comes to focus its adaptations on its own Sunday morning worship styles, allowing AWAKE's style to transform most Sundays with its lively, engaged spirit.

In *People of the Dream*, Michael Emerson emphasizes that "what works today cannot be assumed to work tomorrow." Congregations can expect to make adjustments and to make them often, in light of their larger purpose.

In sum, congregations on the journey to multicultural, antiracist Beloved Community:

- continually try out new ways of being and doing
- demonstrate their willingness to experilearn

A Willingness to Take Risks and to Feel Uncomfortable

Developing an entrepreneurial spirit and increasing the capacity to experilearn imply that a congregation has strengthened its willingness to take risks. But this willingness deserves its own

Common Thread. After all, risk taking is often uncomfortable, even triggering, for people, especially if they are already living in uncertain times. Risking "failure" threatens some people's sense of security and pricks at others' pride. The vision of Beloved Community may serve as a bright guiding beacon, but the journey is never simple and straightforward.

Elements of white supremacy culture, so deeply woven into white-dominant congregational life, complicate the journey regardless of congregants' best intentions. For example, the drive for perfectionism, as Kenneth Jones and Tema Okun describe it, shows up as a "tendency to identify what's wrong" rather than an "ability to identify, name, and appreciate what's right." When congregations are in the midst of change, it's all too easy to fret over what appears to be going wrong (lower attendance rates, for example), rather than celebrating the changes that are creating deeper, warmer relationships across difference within and beyond the congregation. When "perfection" is the goal, people view mistakes only as a problem, rather than as a resource from which to learn and grow.

In white supremacy culture, either/or thinking—which holds that a change or a suggestion is either good or bad, right or wrong—takes precedence over both/and, the recognition that most of life is complex and nuanced, and that there are multiple ways to move toward a goal. Either/or thinking acts like a constraint, narrowing congregants' field of vision, restricting their options, almost always inviting fear and defensiveness.

When the habits of white supremacy culture remain at work in congregational life, risk and discomfort are inevitable as the congregation strives to become multicultural and antiracist. For white folks, challenging long-held assumptions, changing habits that may be unconscious, and encountering differences in experiences and perspectives can trigger fears, frustrations, and uncertainties.

For people of color, the work may disrupt whatever comfort and security they have already found in their community of faith. It may make others' hurtful words and experiences even more obvious and retraumatizing. And it may simply become too wearying and uncertain to be tolerable.

With such difficult feelings aroused in most participants, conflict is inevitable. As a community sets out to build multicultural, antiracist Beloved Community, it must develop healthy ways of dealing with disagreements. In "Ten Essential Strategies to Grow a Multiracial, Multicultural Congregation," Jacqui Lewis urges congregations to create a "theology of conflict in your context that sustains you on the ride. Preaching and teaching about conflict normalize it. It is part of life. It is deeply spiritual, and is the space in which we grow."

Each of the congregations we study experiences conflict and discomfort on their journey. The choirs at All Souls Unitarian Church in Tulsa, Oklahoma, for example, drop into a painful passage of mutual hurt and misunderstanding over differences in style, expectations, and communication. Their journey to a deeper empathy and a sense of reconciliation speaks to the possibilities for growth and change. These possibilities depend on people staying with the conflict and discomfort until these experiences yield what they have to teach.

Many passionate champions for the work of building multicultural, antiracist Beloved Community have said that people doing the work must "get comfortable with being uncomfortable." Author and activist Luvvie Ajayie speaks to this way of being in her TED Talk of that name, urging people to have the courage to do what's difficult and scary, like speaking hard truths about unjust systems, in spite of fear.

In some contexts, this encouragement to "get comfortable with being uncomfortable" applies most to people in traditionally dominant groups. Those in targeted groups often experience discomfort as part of their daily lives. Kenneth Jones and Tema Okun lift to the surface the expectation in white supremacy culture of the "right to comfort" for white people, especially those who are middle or upper class. She offers compassionate antidotes for this habit: "Understand that discomfort is at the root of all growth and learning; welcome it as much as you can; deepen your political analysis of racism and oppression so you have a strong understanding of how your personal experience and feelings fit into a larger picture; don't take everything personally."

In sum, congregations on the road to multicultural, antiracist Beloved Community:

- recognize that discomfort and conflict are inevitable
- allow leaders to bring these conflicts out into the open in order for a healing path to appear
- keep strengthening their willingness to take risks and to learn from whatever happens

Patience, Perseverance, Courage, and Humility

Progress in building multicultural Beloved Community moves s-l-o-w-l-y and unevenly. At different times, congregants will find themselves at different locations on the journey: sometimes deeply engaged, at others mildly interested; sometimes doubting the whole process, exhausted by the ongoing difficulties, or resisting change; and sometimes finding again the joy of renewed life, deepened relationships, and the power of living in equitable and loving community. Congregations must commit to staying on the journey for the long haul, across changes in ministries, shifting conditions in the wider world, and many generations. Approaching the work with patience, courage, curiosity, and humility becomes a way of being that can lift the sense of burden or weariness and allow congregants to appreciate every phase of the journey.

Some of the congregations we study have been on this journey for decades; others have begun it more recently. All can find in their histories both cautionary tales and great strengths. The congregations that build into their process ample time for self-reflection—for an honest assessment of those moments when they have lived up to their vision of multicultural, antiracist community and those when they have fallen short—demonstrate the most consistent growth.

Gordon Dragt's "16 Tips for Turning Your Church Around" includes this good advice: "Be prepared for hard work, perseverance, and an adventurous journey. Transformational leadership is not for the faint-of-heart."

In sum, congregations on the road to multicultural, antiracist Beloved Community:

- know that this work is both/and, accept that it is never done, and commit to the long haul
- recognize that conflict is inevitable and approach it with a spirit of courage, curiosity, and humility
- demonstrate patience and a readiness to confess mistakes and begin again in love
- meet congregants where they are and help them to heal and grow from there

A Palpable Aliveness and Love

If these Common Threads seem daunting, that's no accident. Building multicultural, antiracist Beloved Community is a countercultural move; it requires leaders and congregants to work together to dismantle centuries of systemic oppression and to change unconscious or semiconscious ways of being that keep the human family divided.

But our list of Common Threads would not be complete without this final note: Congregations on this journey feel a sense of aliveness and enthusiasm for the work. They experience the joys of working toward and living in diverse Beloved Community. In these communities, everyone has the chance to feel more whole and alive.

The aliveness and joy are palpable as soon as we enter these communities. We sense them in our own congregations, and we feel them in the other three congregations we study. Our conversation partners share their stories with us with a generosity, vulnerability, and authenticity that are awe-inspiring. Even in the painful stories about conflict, disappointment, or harm done, the leaders and congregants express love for and commitment to the people with whom they are building community. Their impatience—"we're so close; can't we just get there?"—arises out of their faith that what has seemed impossible really is attainable. Already in love with our own congregations, we fall in love with these companions on the journey too, and we find ourselves strengthened and encouraged by their work.

In sum, this work is messy, and it's "partial"; it is never truly complete. *It is also worth it.* It is soul work to which our faith calls all of us, and thus it truly is a "journey toward wholeness." The congregations on the journey to multicultural, antiracist Beloved Community, then:

- experience a sense of aliveness and enthusiasm for the work
- are places where joy is evident, even in hard times

FROM COMMON THREADS TO PARTICULAR STORIES

These Common Threads offer a glimpse of the big picture. They point to some of the major ingredients of the work of building multicultural, antiracist Beloved Community.

But the real work of building such Beloved Community lives in the particulars—the day-to-day choices; the large and small leaps of faith; the synchronicities and moments of grace; the mistakes and misgivings; the seeming miracles of healing and reconciliation; the conflict, the pain, and the joy of relationships made and broken and made again; and the sheer steady attentiveness of the human beings involved. These truths only grow clear when we dive into the stories of the congregations we visit. Chapters 3 through 7 invite our readers to visit these congregations with us.

QUESTIONS FOR YOU AND
YOUR CONGREGATION

1. Which Common Threads surprise or intrigue you in the list we have offered here?

2. Which Common Threads are already weaving through the work of your congregation or community? Which ones could use your attention, research, and intentionality? Make a note of these strengths and growing edges. Then, as you read the congregational stories in the chapters to come, notice how this list may change.

CHAPTER THREE

"Stumbling in the Right Direction"

UNITARIAN UNIVERSALIST CHURCH
ANNAPOLIS, MARYLAND

Excitement and passion and frustration and anger and confusion and understanding—it's all happening at the same time. . . . It's messy. And we're not done. We have a lot of work to do.

—Betsy Kraning, UUCA Music Director

This congregation is stumbling . . . but it's stumbling in the right direction.

—Andrew Bain, UUCA congregant

"DELIBERATE, INTENTIONAL, and often slow change"—that's how Rev. Dr. Fred Muir describes the path to multiculturalism that the Unitarian Universalist Church of Annapolis (UUCA) has followed. The stories we share about UUCA show how actions fueled by a persistent dedication to building multicultural, anti-racist Beloved Community can change a congregation's culture in large and small ways.

We experience a palpable warmth and joy at UUCA. The congregation offers many opportunities for personal and communal spiritual growth, as well as many chances to make changes for the good, both within the congregation and in the wider world. Its embrace of a multicultural way of being suffuses the congregation with a sense of aliveness and hope.

Still, antiracism work "is messy," UUCA music director Betsy Kraning says. Even congregations that are well on the road to multiculturalism can often only claim, as congregant Andrew Bain does, that they are "stumbling," but they are "stumbling in the right direction."

In this chapter, we offer some of the details that mark UUCA's progress, and we explore a few examples of the inevitable conflicts. This work is not either/or; it is not either a "success" or a "failure." It's both/and—both life-giving relationships and destructive harm, both entrepreneurial leaps and defensive setbacks. At UUCA, we see how a fierce commitment to the vision keeps the balance tipping toward learning, healing, growth, and hope.

COMMON THREADS

By the time we visit UUCA in 2015–16, Rev. Fred has served as senior minister for more than thirty years. During that time, he has dreamed of and promoted, launched and supported, encouraged and applauded every step the congregation has taken on the journey. He has mourned and bemoaned the missteps and setbacks too.

What motivates his dedication to the journey? "It's soul work," Rev. Fred says. The minister's passionate championship of the multicultural mission and vision is a strong Common Thread at UUCA.

Here are some of the other Common Threads we'll see running through this chapter:

- **a clear sense of an overarching goal**—Rev. Fred describes UUCA's goal as "to find, create, embrace, and be the deep and abiding *completeness* that comes with multiculturalism."
- **knowledge of the community's context**—UUCA's passionate champions for multiculturalism have studied the church's history and the demographics of their location. They know what they are up against in Annapolis.
- **ongoing training**—Every year, trainings of various lengths and from different sources widen the circle of participants in the multicultural mission and vision. The result is that many in the congregation now share a common language around this work.
- **institutional structures**—Ministerial and lay leaders develop different committees, councils, working groups, and small group ministries to keep them accountable to their multicultural vision. They institutionalize this commitment by recording it explicitly in their bylaws.
- **diversity in leadership**—UUCA's ministers represent a range of races, ages, and theologies.
- **worship that speaks to the heart and centers diverse voices**— Leaders experiment with different worship styles and a wide range of worship resources.
- **multicultural is multigenerational**—Centering children and youth lies at the heart of UUCA's journey toward multiculturalism and antiracism.
- **adaptability and flexibility**—Congregational leaders experiment with different worship styles, institutional structures, and more. They adapt and change in light of what they learn.
- **social justice and community engagement**—UUCA members practice and build their multicultural competencies by collaborating with their neighbors. They learn how to follow as well as how to lead.

- patience, perseverance, courage, and humility—UUCA's story, like that of all the congregations we study, demonstrates that conflict is inevitable, the work is messy, and it never ends. Congregations on this journey must learn to expect and accept these aspects of the work. There are power struggles, disagreements, misunderstandings, micro- and macroaggressions, and more at UUCA. These cause distress and division. Equally important, the congregation works through them to build a stronger community.

WHAT'S IN THE WATER?

Annapolis, Maryland's capital, has a vivid history when it comes to racism, segregation, and white supremacy culture. In the late eighteenth and early nineteenth centuries, the bustling port city was a landing place for enslaved Africans. Kunta Kinte, the central character in Alex Haley's novel *Roots: The Saga of an American Family*, first arrived in America at the Annapolis dock.

Today a cluster of statues stands on the dock: the Kunta Kinte–Alex Haley Memorial. It depicts Haley reading his novel to a circle of children. Tourists walk past them or among them. "Never forget," the memorial seems to say, "this place grew out of a fierce injustice."

Maryland can claim a more progressive heritage too. Sitting just below the Mason-Dixon Line, the state remained in the Union during the Civil War. Harriet Tubman, Frederick Douglass, and Thurgood Marshall all began their lives in Maryland—a fact of which Marylanders are rightly proud.

Nevertheless, Annapolis and Anne Arundel County remain deeply segregated by race and class. The Annapolis area has the largest number of subsidized public-housing communities for low-income residents in the county, while other residents have great wealth.

The Unitarian Universalist Church of Annapolis sits on several sloping acres above a neighborhood of winding streets, compact brick and wood-frame houses, and large, well-kept yards. This area appears to be primarily white middle class but not completely segregated.

For example, just up the street from UUCA, at the top of a rise, sits St. Philip's Episcopal Church, a largely African-American congregation. St. Philip's history reveals the fault lines that undergird Annapolis. Back in 1870, the white women of St. Anne's Episcopal Church, which was founded in colonial days, establish St. Philip's Colored Mission as a Sunday school for African-American children. The intent seems to be not just Christian outreach but also segregation. Sure enough, within a few years, St. Philip's becomes the Episcopal congregation for African-American families. Today, St. Anne's and St. Philip's are still largely segregated.

UUCA and St. Philip's are a short walk away from each other. The relationships they build are part of UUCA's journey. And that journey really begins with the calling of Rev. Fred Muir as senior minister in 1984.

CALLING REV. FRED

Rev. Fred arrives at UUCA with a vision for a socially engaged Unitarian Universalism. His commitment to the work of dismantling racism has roots in his teenage years in Oak Park, Illinois, when his Disciples of Christ minister helps him to see the racial injustice all around him. By the time Rev. Fred arrives at UUCA in the mid-1980s, he has begun to analyze racism within Unitarian Universalism itself.

In a chapter on UUCA intended for the 2012 *Mosaic* book project (which was never completed), Fred, who is white, writes that in the wake of the Empowerment Controversy of 1967–72, the Unitarian Universalist Association and most of its congregations "never fully addressed the racism of its members and the systemic racism that shaped (and is shaping) its theological, spiritual, and institutional culture and story." Our own chapter 1 briefly describes the Empowerment Controversy, when the UUA made a promise to its African-American members and then reneged on it. Whites and African Americans formed a variety of multiracial groups, often with conflicting ideas about how to move forward. In the years that followed, "there was little to no UUA or UUCA interest or effort in renewing the promise which had been imagined for decades," Fred recalls.

In Rev. Fred, UUCA has called a champion for building multicultural, antiracist Beloved Community. His arrival launches the congregation's long, slow progress toward change.

INSTITUTIONALIZING THE FOCUS

As soon as the Unitarian Universalist Association's Journey Toward Wholeness (JTW) and Jubilee antiracism trainings become available in the late 1990s, Rev. Fred brings them to the congregation. More than seventy people participate in the first weekend-long training. The numbers of participants reveal UUCA congregants' hunger for the journey. Afterward, twenty-five of them sign up to form a JTW Committee. Fred calls the committee the "first intentional, ongoing commitment ever made by the congregation toward antiracism and multiculturalism." That first step is crucial.

Darrel Nash, an older white UUCA member, knows he wants to be part of the Journey Toward Wholeness Committee as soon as he finishes the weekend training. This first committee, though, focuses outward, following a familiar pattern for Unitarian Universalist congregations. The committee offers workshops and service opportunities in the wider community. It participates in interfaith rallies for racial understanding. It joins the local NAACP chapter. These are worthy efforts, but they don't get at the core issues within the congregation itself. "Instead of a 'journey,'" Darrel tells us, "it was . . . ," and he draws a circle on the table. His eyes tear up as he remembers the frustration.

Marlene Browne, an older African-American member, recalls a similar frustration. "I wasn't impressed with the work the committee was trying to do. I thought they were missing the mark and *missing* the mark. But I kept going because they were trying. And it became clear to me that Fred, the minister, wanted something to happen." The sense of intention, and the minister's commitment, keep Marlene engaged.

Still, a congregation's first steps on the journey may not take them where they want to go. The first course correction occurs when Rev. Fred and some of the committee members, like Marlene and Darrel, realize that the congregation must look at the impact of racism within its own walls. Rev. Fred, with Rev. John Crestwell and Rev. Christina Leone Tracy, describes this crucial move "from outreach to inreach" in "Turning Toward Wholeness," an essay in *Turning Point: Essays on a New Unitarian Universalism*, a collection Fred edits almost twenty years later. If the dream of building multicultural Beloved Community at UUCA is to come about, then the people already in that community will need to transform themselves.

Evelyn Spurgin, a white woman who at one point serves as president of the congregation, describes the impact of this shift on her: "When the focus was on antiracism, that clicked for me. At the beginning, it was on 'How can we get more African Americans?' But with antiracism, that wasn't the goal." As Karin likes to say, "Diversity in the pews is not the goal. Rather, it is evidence that you have reached—or, better, that you are *approaching* the goal."

The new Antiracism Transformation Team (ARTT), created in 2000, consists of an intentionally multiracial group of congregants who meet once or twice a month. Darrel and Marlene are both members. The team attends antiracism trainings in Chicago and Kansas City. But Marlene still feels that "we don't seem to be getting anywhere," and she finally realizes that Rev. Fred needs to be actively involved with this work, on the committee level as well as from the pulpit. "Without the minister's support," Marlene says, "I mean, who's going to follow?"

So now the congregational leaders recognize that they have crucial work to do at UUCA itself, and the senior minister visibly endorses and participates in their work. They launch a series of annual trainings and educational opportunities, which have become the norm for this congregation. In addition to the Journey Toward Wholeness materials, UUCA uses structured gatherings like ADORE ("A Dialogue on Race and Ethnicity") and curricula like "Building the World We Dream About." It brings in well-known trainers like Paula Cole Jones, Phyllis Braxton, and Robin Di-Angelo. It works with the Intercultural Development Inventory.

The language and the focus of these trainings range from talk of racism and antiracism, to explorations of white privilege and white supremacy culture, to understanding models of racial identity development and the development of intercultural competencies. As always, the models overlap and amplify each other. As always, some models appeal to some congregants and turn others off. Different methods reach different people. Early participants find that the newer models deepen their understanding. The learning process, like the rest of the work, never ends. But the culture of the congregation begins to change.

The ARTT experiences its own journey of transformation, becoming a tight-knit group over time. In this "bold space" (not a "safe space," for no space is fully "safe" if *safety* means "without conflict"), the team members share truths about their racial experiences in ways that the general culture usually doesn't allow. Members of color share stories of their encounters with racism within the congregation and beyond. White members slowly come to grips with their own privilege. The intimacy that develops is rewarding and palpable.

Some congregants who aren't part of the team feel jealous, even resentful: What are those folks doing in ARTT that makes them feel so special? "A lot of people viewed us as a special exclusive committee," Marlene remembers. These congregants wonder why they are excluded.

We see this pattern in almost all the congregations we study. To develop authentic relationships across differences like race and ethnicity, congregants need to gather in small, mixed groups. These relationships create lasting, rewarding bonds—and can cause resentment among those not part of the group. Some of this is natural: Most of us humans hate to miss out on healthy opportunities for belonging, especially when the belonging promises such life-affirming friendships. We don't want to be the ones not invited to the party.

But it's also true that many white congregants are used to having easy access to all the spaces and gatherings in their communities. Limiting white access in order to make room at the table for others feels uncomfortable for many white people. It even feels threatening to some, who worry that the multiracial groups are becoming "too powerful" and have too much sway with congregational decision makers. Deep down, we believe, such fears are rooted in the very structures of white supremacy, which create norms for who is in power. These fears illustrate how wily and surreptitious implicit bias can be.

Congregations can respond to these tensions by creating more and more opportunities for congregants of all identities to participate in the work. UUCA leaders discover that they have to be intentional about how they invite folks to attend trainings and workshops. ARTT not only announces the ADORE curriculum in the Sunday bulletin but also sends out individual invitations to members of key committees. Every singer in the choir, for example, receives an invitation, and everyone shows up for at least one session. UUCA leaders experiment and learn—experilearn—about which methods best communicate how important multicultural antiracism work is to the whole congregation.

UUCA experilearns with the committee structures that support the work too. Just as the Journey Toward Wholeness Committee gives way to the Antiracism Transformation Team, so too, over the course of ten to fifteen years, ARTT evolves into the Antiracism Council and eventually into the Building Beloved Community team. The most effective approach changes as the trainings deepen congregants' understanding of white supremacy culture and their multicultural competencies. The desire to balance and coordinate UUCA's inward-turning and outward-focused social justice work drives the evolution of these committees. UUCA's story demonstrates how natural it is for committees to come and go as new ways to serve the overarching goal grow clearer.

MAKING THE COMMITMENT EXPLICIT

During its tenure, the Antiracism Council takes up the next big task in institutionalizing UUCA's antiracist, multicultural mission. They work with the Board to propose an addition to the congregation's bylaws and hold six months of conversations with congregants about the change. Taking time to get widespread congregational buy-in pays off. At the congregational meeting, the new wording passes with 92 percent of the vote. Now the bylaws include this strong statement:

> UUCA is committed to becoming and sustaining an antiracist, antioppressive, and multicultural religious community where people of all races, ethnicities, and colors see their identities reflected and affirmed in all aspects of congregational life.

Once this change is in place, the Board begins to include a new sentence in its annual list of goals for the senior minister and staff: "A commitment to antiracism, antioppression, and multiculturalism will shape all participation in the Unitarian Universalist community." The minister and staff must then come up with ways to measure their progress toward these goals. They feel empowered to make decisions and suggest changes that fulfill this commitment. These explicit statements are strong pillars that can support further institutional change.

By about 2009, then, the Unitarian Universalist Church of Annapolis has woven many of our Common Threads into the fabric of congregational life: It has a minister and a growing number of key lay leaders who passionately support and champion the work of building multicultural, antiracist Beloved Community. It has made multiculturalism, antiracism, and antioppression explicit parts of its identity through the bylaws change and the leaders' goals. It has plunged into a series of trainings. These trainings transform individual lives and influence the language used in many parts of congregational life. Some of those transformations—and the relationships that make them possible—lead to the next big leap on UUCA's journey.

RELATIONSHIPS, TRANSFORMATIONS, AND THE NEXT BIG LEAP

When UUCA participates as a pilot congregation in the year-long "Building the World We Dream About" curriculum in 2007, member Rusty Vaughan's wife urges him to take part. Rusty is a rangy white man in his late sixties. His first thoughts about the class include "I'm not a racist. Dunno anybody who's a racist. Used to know a lot of them. It's probably not going to be much, but what the heck, let's go, we can always leave." He feels curious, wondering, "What are 'these people' going to talk about?"

Looking back, he can see that in his mind "it was still 'we' and 'they.'"

"Building the World We Dream About"—a curriculum written by Dr. Mark Hicks and available free from the Unitarian Universalist Association—uses a range of techniques: art, movies, quotations, and stories from Unitarian Universalists of color, caucusing by racial or ethnic identity, skits and exercises that demonstrate concepts of privilege and microaggressions, and more. Its length—twenty-four two-hour sessions, often offered over the course of a year—discourages some congregations from using it. But its length can also make possible deeper, more trusting relationships among congregants, especially across differences in race and ethnicity. It can prompt white participants to recognize their own racialization and begin to understand its implications. Many come to see how white privilege intersects with other aspects of their identities. Rusty describes his own aha moment:

> We're about six months into the program. On a Sunday afternoon, we're about halfway into the two hours. All of a sudden, something snaps. I have a come-to-Jesus moment. Everyone stops talking; everyone is looking at me. Diane Goforth [a longtime UUCA member who is facilitating] looks concerned and says, "What's wrong? Do you want to talk about it?"
>
> I say, "I can't explain it, but I just got it." I had listened to just enough stories and heard a number of perspectives, not just from African Americans but also from Puerto Ricans and Asian Americans. I'm thinking, "No shit? You had a problem? People treated you differently?!" Finally I got it.
>
> I have to say, that was the beginning of the rest of my life.

Over the next decade and more, Rusty devotes much of his energy to his ongoing journey. He joins Coming to the Table, a national organization that brings the descendants of enslaved people together with descendants of enslavers to build relationships, to work for racial healing, and to help create a "thriving, inclusive, and compassionate democracy for the future of this country," as its president, Fabrice Guerrier, describes it. Eventually, Rusty hosts an interfaith chapter of Coming to the Table at UUCA, and he plays a crucial role in the movement to hang Black Lives Matter banners at local churches.

But the long slow arc of this learning process for white people can be frustrating for people of color. Marlene Browne describes the journey of a white man on the ARTT: "It took him two years to understand that he's been privileged his whole life! How do you break through to a congregation and get them to understand they've been privileged all their life? They think 'privilege' is something very special, but it's really the difference between going into a department store and being followed, versus being able to browse and try on things."

Sadly, this is the way the system of white supremacy works. Something that seems so obvious to those targeted—such as being followed in a store because of the storekeeper's implicit bias—remains invisible to white people. Whites benefit from the system in simple ways, like being able to shop without being harassed, as well as in large ones, like facing less risk of incarceration and of violence on the street. These benefits form an invisible "norm" for many white people, especially when their whiteness intersects with other dominant-culture identities—being middle or upper class, cisgender, straight, middle-aged, able-bodied, and more. No wonder the language of "waking up" and "staying woke" is so prevalent among the white people and people of color who are determined to dismantle unjust systems like white supremacy.

At least one African-American member of ARTT quits, "fed up with how little we know about white power and privilege," Diane Goforth, who is white, remembers. "It takes us almost three years to learn to be a community just among ourselves," she says. The ARTT has a mandate to help the congregation "wake up" to its issues with racism and white privilege, but its members realize that they need to learn how to do this work themselves first.

The team uses the method of caucusing to help take their conversations deeper, with white members gathering in one area to take up the question of how to move forward, while people of color gather in another to reflect on the same question. Both Marlene and Diane remember what usually happens when the two groups come back together.

"We white folks," Diane remembers, "would always come back with charts and blueprints and ideas from our heads, and the people of color caucus would come back with their hearts." As Kenneth Jones and Tema Okun write, white supremacy culture encourages most white people to focus on efficiency and outcome, while nondominant cultures place a higher value on relationships and process. ARTT offers a space where members can see these differences clearly.

Finally, though, the day comes when the two caucuses come back together and something new happens. The people of color return with a longing for a minister of color. Marlene remembers the message as a nudge—the group says, "You know, a minister of color would be good"—while Darrel Nash hears their words as a clarion call: "We're not going anywhere unless we have a minister of color here at UUCA!" Whether the request is gentle or forceful, Diane Goforth names this as the breakthrough moment. The white folks set aside their plans and say to their kin of color, "How can we help?"

These stories of relationship building and transformation illustrate one of the reasons why building multicultural, antiracist Beloved Community is such long-haul work. Is there a shortcut for waking up to the truths of how white supremacy culture keeps many people trapped in unjust and inequitable lives? Is there a speedier way to create authentic relationships of depth across race and culture? These questions themselves spring from the urgency in our country and in Unitarian Universalism as we near the end of the second decade of the twenty-first century. In many ways—both physical and spiritual—they are questions of life and death. We hope that in learning these stories of slow transformation, our readers will find ever stronger motivations and means for moving the work forward.

CALLING REV. JOHN

When Darrel thinks about his work on the search committee that brings Rev. John Crestwell to UUCA in 2009, he can't help crying. The sense that the committee was doing something crucial and historic in the life of the congregation remains great, even years later. In many ways, the calling of Rev. John, who is African American, marks the moment when the real work of building Beloved Community begins. John's very presence brings all the issues—the struggles and the joys—of creating multicultural community to the forefront of UUCA life.

For the search, UUCA turns again to resources from the UUA, drawing on the Diversity of Ministry Initiative (DOMI). The Initiative's website explains that it "seeks to foster, create, and sustain healthy, engaged, long-term ministries for ministers and religious professionals who identify as people of color, Latina/o, Hispanic, and/or multiracial/multiethnic." DOMI is created in 2006 because UUA staff recognize that ministers and other religious professionals of color face extraordinary difficulties in getting and retaining jobs and ministerial settlements in Unitarian Universalist congregations. To reverse this pattern, the UUA's Diversity of Ministry Team establishes a program that offers preparation and ongoing support to both congregations and religious professionals seeking a long-term match. This need for additional support signals how white supremacy culture still

impacts relationships of power—such as those with ministers—
in Unitarian Universalist congregations.

The Diversity of Ministry Team helps bring Rev. John and
UUCA's Search Committee together, but many Unitarian Universalists already know of him. John comes into Unitarian Universalism from the Methodist church and then serves at Davies
Memorial Unitarian Universalist Church in Clinton, Maryland,
before coming to UUCA. His book, *The Charge of the Chalice*,
tells Davies Memorial's story of intentional multicultural and
multiracial growth over a few years' time. Rev. John and Rev.
Fred have established a supportive collegial relationship, and
Unitarian Universalists who have read Rev. John's book find
inspiration in his work. All these experiences create a good starting point for this match.

Still, some UUCA members are skeptical about calling an
associate minister. The congregation has recently experienced a
failed call for an assistant minister (a younger white woman) who
some wanted to be their new associate minister. But Rev. John
himself doesn't feel this skepticism when he arrives in September 2009. In the chapter on UUCA intended for the unfinished
Mosaic book, he writes, "I did not share the congregation's grief
or concern. I only knew what I felt and saw—love, acceptance,
and eagerness to begin a relationship. Still, as a Black man, I was
slightly apprehensive with this group of mostly white folk who
were being overly nice." John's words—"mostly white folk who
were being overly nice"—convey the characteristic twinkle in
his eye, as well as acknowledging a lifetime of experiences with
racism.

In general, the congregation feels a tremendous sense of
energy and great enthusiasm for Rev. John's new role with UUCA
as associate minister of outreach, leadership, and evangelism.
"I'm the MOLE!" Rev. John chuckles, creating an acronym out of
his title. For those who have actively participated on the journey

toward multiculturalism and antiracism for the previous ten years, this call sums up all the work that they have done.

When the congregation officially installs Rev. John in April 2010, Rev. Fred offers the Charge to the Minister. Rev. Fred begins with W. E. B. Dubois's words:

> Now is the accepted time, not tomorrow, not some more convenient season. It is today that our best work can be done and not some future day or future year. It is today that we fit ourselves for the greater usefulness of tomorrow. Today is the seed time, now are the hours of work, and tomorrow comes the harvest and the playtime.

Then Rev. Fred goes on, addressing Rev. John directly:

> You and I and this congregation share a vision of Beloved Community, and we are excited about this moment. . . . John, don't waste your time here. It's your time. Do what you have to do. Do it now. . . . Plant the seeds and eventually will come the harvest. . . . Everything you do won't work but don't give up. . . .
>
> John and I, we share a destination. We don't know exactly how we are going to get there. The map has not been written . . . but we share a common destination. . . . My charge to you, John, is to keep your eyes on the prize and hold on. . . . You are ready to fly because of your spirit, and I want you to take me, I want you to take *us* with you on that flight. . . . But keep your eyes on the prize and hold on to your soul!

Fred then quotes another white minister, Gordon Dragt, who in the 1990s helps lead Middle Collegiate Church in Manhattan toward its multicultural, antiracist mission: "Keep one foot in the center and one foot dangling over the edge!" And he concludes with an enthusiastic exhortation: "John Crestwell, we want you to be just who you are. We did not call you in order to be somebody else. . . . We are going to be uncomfortable and that's okay. Share your spirit, your passion with us."

Rev. Fred's words lay down a strong foundation for the new ministry. There will be discomfort, he predicts, and it's okay to be uncomfortable. This idea can be tough to accept for folks in the dominant culture, who are used to one particular way of "doing church" and accustomed to having their tastes and choices catered to.

Fred asks Rev. John to let his entrepreneurial spirit soar, to take risks, to make mistakes and not give up. There's no map, he reminds everyone, and that's an invitation for the whole congregation to grow a spirit of trial-and-error experimentation, to be willing to fail and to learn from mistakes, and to keep on moving forward. It's a countercultural—and truly multicultural—message.

Most of all, Rev. Fred asks Rev. John to be "just who you are." As Rev. John's supervisor in the years to come, Rev. Fred stays true to that message. His long ministry has taught him that authenticity is essential, not only for a healthy relationship between minister and congregation but also for the minister's own physical, mental, emotional, and spiritual survival. Throughout his time with UUCA, Rev. John gets to be exactly who he is.

As Rev. John listens to Rev. Fred's charge at the launch of his UUCA ministry, he feels "a kind of affirmation I've rarely known in my life. I feel home as a Unitarian Universalist minister. The phrase *settled ministry* means something that day."

In the *Mosaic* chapter, Rev. Fred underscores the significance of calling Rev. John. He describes three young African-American children bobbing up and down in their chairs in the sanctuary on a Sunday morning, trying to get a better view of Rev. John up on the chancel. "Here's what I know," Fred writes,

John's ministry is a significant reason—maybe *the* reason—for the broadening and deepening of this congregation's membership. What he is and symbolizes, those three children and their parents, and those who, like them, walk into our building every Sunday searching for a faith community that reflects back to them a future they search for and of which they are a part—these are tipping points that form the saving promise of and for Unitarian Universalism. These are some of the necessary and special ingredients that will help us create and sustain a Unitarian Universalism that mirrors the promise of an increasingly pluralistic and multicultural country.

Calling Rev. John infuses UUCA's many champions of multiculturalism and antiracism with a joyous sense of hope and possibility. The strengths they have already built—a willingness to be flexible and adapt existing structures to make them more effective, an emerging understanding of white power and privilege, and the capacity to build deep, authentic cross-racial relationships—are great resources as Rev. John begins his ministry among them.

In June 2012 Rev. Peter Morales, then UUA president, invites Rev. John to lead the Sunday morning worship service at Justice General Assembly in Phoenix, Arizona, an honor that marks national recognition of his ministry. Open to the public, this service sums up the heartbreaking, hopeful, dramatic experiences that Unitarian Universalists have shared throughout the week, witnessing for the inherent worth and dignity of immigrants and learning about the state's discriminatory practices.

Rev. John invites the UUCA ministerial team to lead worship with him. They offer a music- and story-filled service that culminates in Rev. John's rousing sermon, "Justice Is Love in Action." The service packs a powerful message and lifts UUCA's multicultural, antiracist journey onto the national stage.

Back at home in Annapolis, Rev. John's focus in his ministry includes a passion for the kind of personal growth that can transform lives that have felt stuck or limited. He wants his ministry to help community members develop emotional literacy (the capacity to name and work with our own and others' feelings), build life skills (from the simplest to the most complex), and deepen intercultural competencies. To answer these needs, he conceives of AWAKE Ministries, and Rev. Fred offers his enthusiastic support.

AWAKE stands for "Actualize your Wisdom, Awaken to your Karma, and Engage the process." The full name speaks to Rev. John's eagerness to break out of the intellectual box of "heady" Unitarian Universalism. UUCA ministers and congregants call the ministry simply "AWAKE." The acronym captures the ministry's energy and overall intention, to help folks *wake up* to their life potential.

AWAKE launches in 2013. In April 2015, when we settle into the sanctuary for our first experiences of worship at UUCA, we can feel and see the impact of the congregation's work over the previous years. In this chapter, we offer in-depth descriptions of these services because they demonstrate how, with intentional planning, every word and gesture can support the multicultural message.

"DIFFERENCES MAKE US STRONGER"

When we arrive for the first of two Sunday morning worship services on April 19, 2015, we find Rev. Christina Leone Tracy darting among the clusters of congregants who linger on the patio in front of the main church door. Serving as UUCA's faith development minister, Rev. Christina, a white young adult, is in charge of today's Flower Communion services. She nabs volunteers for the play that will form the heart of each service. Still, in the midst of urgently pulling together this improvisational bit of fun, she pauses to greet us newcomers warmly. One eye focused on the congregation, another looking out for newcomers, Rev. Christina models the multitasking that Sundays demand.

Just inside the door, Rev. John leans on a small portable podium where newcomers fill out nametags and everyone can catch a glimpse of the schedule for the day. He offers hugs, handshakes, and hellos to people entering for worship. The relaxed warmth of his greeting, calling folks by name, says, "We're *all* at home here."

The buzz in the sanctuary finally settles at the ringing of a bell. Every week, UUCA plays a recording of the bell that calls Unitarians to worship in its partner church in Transylvania. This service will appeal to each of our senses with its message about connections that span time, space, and differences. In fact, next up, an older white man reads the chalice lighting words as a young child lights the chalice. "Multicultural is multigenerational"—this Common Thread runs throughout the all-ages services this morning.

Then the large screen on the wall behind the chancel lights up with the Call to Worship. The screen is a result of AWAKE's efforts to make services more contemporary in style. Rev. Christina and Rev. John stand close to each other to lead the responsive reading, their light and dark skin side by side—another Common Thread, diversity in leadership, made visible. People of color can see themselves reflected in congregational leadership, and so can young adults and white people.

The Call to Worship, written by Rev. Christina, reminds us congregants that we are welcome just as we are, *and* we are committed to change. It reads,

REV. CHRISTINA: We come to worship in a community filled with love, surrounded in our challenges, comforted in our sorrows, embraced in our joys . . .

CONGREGATION: We come to be transformed.

REV. JOHN: We come to worship to fill up our hearts, to sit in silence, to move, to sing, to renew our spirits in this sacred time, set aside from all the busyness of the day-to-day . . .

CONGREGATION: We come to be transformed.

REV. JOHN: We come to worship so that we can go back out again, eyes wide open to the injustices and oppressions of the world, but not overwhelmed. Open, ready, and strong . . .

CONGREGATION: We come to be transformed.

REV. CHRISTINA: We come as we are—young, old, able-bodied or differently abled, a rainbow of skin colors and hair colors and eye colors, a bouquet of experiences and gifts and talents. We come as we are, knowing that we will never leave this place the same as when we entered . . .

CONGREGATION: We come to be transformed.

Which minister reads which lines feels significant. Rev. Christina offers the opening invitation to create a pastoral space large enough to hold all our joys, sorrows, and challenges. Rev. John lifts up singing and moving our bodies as forms of renewal of the spirit—styles that his AWAKE Ministries have brought to this congregation. Then he reminds us that the experience of worship offers not just a sanctuary but also a doorway that leads us "back out again, eyes wide open to the injustices and oppressions of the world, but not overwhelmed. Open, ready, and strong." In these few lines, the two have captured both the inward- and the outward-turning work of the congregation.

With the last line, Rev. Christina brings it all home. The fact that the white minister names the embracing of diversity makes it clear that this work belongs to all of us. "We come as we are—young, old, able-bodied or differently abled, a rainbow of skin colors and hair colors and eye colors, a bouquet of experiences and gifts and talents." All of these diversities, including people of color of all ages, are visibly present in the congregation this morning.

It is also visible that the congregation remains predominantly white and older. Rev. Christina's words, then, reflect both an emerging reality at UUCA and an aspiration. She and Rev. John name this aspiration up front—literally at the top of the service, from the front of the sanctuary—calling the congregation to grow into its multicultural, multigenerational, antiracist mission. "We come to be transformed," voices of all ages respond.

The play that Rev. Christina has created features four flowers with different personalities: Sunny, the happy sunflower; Violet, shy and quiet; the loving Rosey; and a bold dandelion named Dandy. Rev. Christina invites congregants to write their names on flipchart sheets under the name of the flower they feel most like today. Soon the sheets are almost full. The exercise taps into how well congregants can sense and name how they feel; it gives them a chance to practice emotional literacy.

The script tells the story of Rev. Norbert Čapek, a Czechoslo-vakian Unitarian minister in the 1920s and '30s. Rev. Christina doesn't mince words about Čapek's era. Next door in Germany, the story script says, the National Socialists—the Nazis—are work-ing to build a "'master race' where just one skin color" is valued. The words have potency in UUCA's multiracial congregation of 2015; they ring ominously as this book is being written a few years later, as white nationalists in the United States become emboldened to express their hateful beliefs in violent words and acts.

Čapek, deeply disturbed by the Nazis' racism, encounters Violet, Sunny, Rosey, and Dandy on one of his long walks and has an idea: "I can bring you to my church!" he cries. "I can invite all the people of my church to bring a flower, and our church will be made beautiful by all your different gifts, and that will help us realize how beautiful we all are, and how full and diverse our own church is, and that each of our gifts is necessary!"

A few moments later, when the volunteer flower arrangers bring forward the Flower Communion bouquets, the diversity gleams. Some of the arrangements are tall and spiky, others low and soft. Yellows, reds, blues, and the dark green of leafy branches light up the front of the sanctuary. With Nazi oppression freshly brought to our minds, the bouquets' colors stand out all the more. "Differences make us stronger and more beautiful together," Rev. Christina says.

Then she invites congregants to come forward to choose a flower, not to keep for themselves but to give to the person behind them in line. She invites us not to focus on our own needs and wants but to enter into generosity and other-centeredness. Again, the congregation weaves an interconnected web of "young, old, able-bodied or differently abled, a rainbow of skin colors and hair colors and eye colors, a bouquet of experiences and gifts and talents." By the end of the service, every person in that sanctuary has connected with at least two other people—one from whom they received a flower and another to whom they gave one—across differences in roles, ages, abilities, races, and cultures.

People with a wide variety of emotional and intellectual styles can find themselves in these Sunday morning services. Congregants develop their emotional literacy in choosing which of the play's four flowers best represents them this morning, yet the service also speaks to the intellect. History comes alive when it is told so boldly, proving that multigenerational services don't have to be "dumbed down," as some Unitarian Universalist congregations fear.

Each element of the service supports the theme and taps into one or more of our senses. Congregants get to use their bodies in ways that feel comfortable, or just the right amount of uncomfortable. Folks of all ages and abilities scrunch down in their seats like a seed in the warm dark earth and then grow into a tall, waving, sunlit flower. Some roll or walk over to a softly running fountain where they can light a candle of joy or sorrow in silence. There's time for sharing life passages aloud too. Although each of these services is attended by nearly two hundred people, the warmth of care in them feels intimate. Rev. Christina seems to know the names of all the children, and Rev. John takes part in the flower skit alongside congregants of a variety of ages. The congregation feels no gulf between young and old, minister and laity.

Over and over, the Unitarian Universalist theology of respect, love, and value for all beings, and of inclusion and interconnectedness among us all—the very theology that demands our move toward building multicultural, antiracist communities—is named explicitly and experienced in our bodies. "We are here to be transformed," and on this day, the transformation that all of us in that room want is the certainty that "differences make us stronger and more beautiful together." These embodied, multicultural, multigenerational services create a palpable joy and connection among congregants across many kinds of differences. UUCA's "soul work" on its journey toward multiculturalism and antiracism shines throughout this Flower Communion Sunday.

A HOLY CONVERSATION

These worship experiences leave us co-authors feeling enlivened and a little in awe. After worship that morning, we host a small group conversation about UUCA's multicultural mission and vision. The group's reflections make the morning's harmonious picture more complex.

About fifteen congregants with diverse experiences and opinions gather to share how they feel about the work of multiculturalism and antiracism at UUCA. Andrew Bain, a Black UUCA member originally from Trinidad, is among the first to speak. He lays bare his experiences of microaggressions in the congregation, such as being asked to join committees not because of his talents and experience but because of the "amount of melanin in my skin." He admits that he has almost left the congregation because of these stings.

Diane Goforth exclaims, "It hurts my heart that Andrew could come here and run into a community that thinks it's welcoming and doesn't know it's not!" In her eighties and going strong, she reiterates her determination to help the congregation grow into a multicultural, antiracist Beloved Community.

Guinn Sherlock, a white congregant in her forties, speaks hesitantly. "I thought I heard an underlying message in some sermons that white people are bad because they are white," she says. But then she hesitates. Was that really what was said? "Maybe I'm not hearing with the right ears," she adds.

We recognize something of our own congregations in most of these stories of mistakes and misgivings. Yet we also witness how this diverse group listens, almost without cross-talk, as each person speaks for a couple of minutes. They are all honest, interested, self-reflective. Some stories hurt; some seem borrowed from an earlier era. But the circle holds; everyone stays in the conversation. That the diverse experiences and opinions are expressed so openly and held so respectfully demonstrates a level of trust and multicultural competency that feels hopeful. This is what we call a holy conversation.

Robin Gilmore—young, white, and transgender—sums up the conversation when they compare their experiences at UUCA to their visits to other Unitarian Universalist congregations. At least "UUCA is facing the problem" of racism and white supremacy, Robin says. "And there's tension, but a lot of other congregations aren't even having the conversation." (Our conversation takes place two years before more than seven hundred UUA congregations hold "White Supremacy Teach-ins" in the spring and fall of 2017.)

Andrew, despite his painful stories, agrees. "Yeah," he says, "this congregation is stumbling, but it's stumbling in the right direction."

The conversation makes us all the more eager to experience AWAKE worship later that afternoon.

"AUTHORS OF OUR OWN STORY"

When Rev. John and the UUCA leadership first launch AWAKE Ministries in 2013, AWAKE's services are held on a weekday evening once a month, so as not to conflict with Sunday morning services at UUCA and other congregations. The leaders hope that people of color from a wide range of religions and denominations will participate in AWAKE's energized, theologically inclusive style. "The service will be contextually cultural and will use an emergent church model," reads an early description.

"This is both Fred's and my idea," Rev. John remembers. "We feel that while we are doing most of the right things to grow a racially diverse church on Sunday, it will take some time to get there. Fred and I want to speed the process up by offering a different kind of worship service during the week. The worship will be high-energy and high-spirit. We will have life coaches, healing rituals, and of course a band."

As it turns out, though, only a handful of non–Unitarian Universalists show up for these services. Perhaps "coming up the hill" to an unfamiliar church in a largely white neighborhood feels daunting for people of color in segregated Annapolis. And showing up on a weekday evening doesn't appeal to either UUCA members or newcomers. So, with a characteristic willingness to try another tack, Rev. John and Rev. Fred move AWAKE to Sunday afternoons, with a twice-monthly potluck and worship service. The overall mission is the guide; the specific strategies can change.

When we visit in April 2015, casseroles, salads, and pies crowd two long tables snugged up against the wall of the foyer. Rev. John's eyes grow big at the size and the quality of the spread. "This is *amazing!*" he raves again and again.

About two dozen people pile their paper plates high and sit at a set of long bare tables. Because the numbers are small, the racial mix is even more visible than it is at the morning services. Teenagers and young adults of color show up, along with some of the people of color and older white folks who have attended morning worship. People greet each other warmly, asking specific questions about one another's lives. They know each other's stories well.

Another dozen people have arrived by the time we move into the sanctuary for a worship service titled "Authors of Our Own Story." The congregation of thirty-five or so sits scattered among the forward-facing seats in the large room. Rev. John perches on a stool on the chancel platform. The band raises the energy with an opening praise song, the lyrics scrolling across the screen. Those who can rise are on their feet; those who are seated have their arms in the air.

Music floods the service. A guest musician offers a song that issues from her gut and soars to the skies. Joshua Long, an African-American young adult who serves as UUCA's director of contemporary music, sings a brand-new song he has written for AWAKE and then teaches it to the congregation.

Josh's enthusiasm is palpable. Joining the UUCA staff is a "great blessing," he says. He has played "in almost every Christian denomination through my life," but when he discovers UUCA by attending AWAKE's 2014 gospel concert, he finds his faith and theology reflected in the worship services. He loves that AWAKE speaks to both heart and mind. The music that he has already created fits right in, and he feels inspired to write more.

This AWAKE service uses the popular television show *Game of Thrones* to continue the congregation's emotional literacy training. Using brief video clips, we congregants ponder how much each of the troubled characters in that drama creates their own life story and how much they allow others to determine their fate. Rev. John shares leadership of this section with Dayna Edwards, a white woman in her thirties who is one of AWAKE's designated life coaches. Dayna's own interracial marriage has spurred her to develop strong multicultural competencies. Again a white woman and a Black man, this time a layperson and an ordained minister, lead together from the chancel. Rev. John's original vision of life-coach ministries in AWAKE hasn't caught on, but his dedication to shared ministry continues in worship.

"Who has written your story up until now?" Rev. John asks. "Whom have you been trying to please? Turn the page in your book. Become the author of your own story. We are works in process, constantly evolving. Don't let anyone else define who you are."

Folks in the room share aloud some of their struggles: worries about family members wrestling with addiction, uncertainty about work, a hunger for a deeper spirituality. The honesty with which this small diverse community holds the pain of its members and their willingness to be vulnerable in public feel striking in a Unitarian Universalist setting. The dominant white middle-class culture encourages most Unitarian Universalist congregants to present as at least "okay," and perhaps better. The informality of the potluck and the intimacy of the sharing in worship create an atmosphere that invites people to come as they are. The emphasis on empowerment, actualization, and self-determination feels relevant and practical for everyone in the room. The use of a pop-culture source, the shared ministry, the depth of sharing, the life skills the service builds—all these elements contribute to the multiculturalism this worship represents. These approaches aren't the only way to get there, but they point to the freedom that exists in worship design when it decenters the white-dominant culture.

One more element caps our experience with AWAKE on this Sunday. Toward the end of the service, Rev. John encourages people to come forward for a private prayer or blessing. He always invites other ministers in the room to participate in the healing ritual; today we are here, so he asks Rev. Nancy to join him. Music plays softly in the background as a half dozen folks bring their whispered longings, sometimes with tears, to the ministers.

This practice first begins during a Sunday morning worship service a few years before, when the theme of the month is Healing. UUCA's ministers take a risk, not sure whether anyone will come forward or what they will bring. After an initial trickle, long lines form in front of each minister. Even the people who remain seated report how powerful the ritual is to witness. By April 2015, this "altar call" forms a part of every AWAKE service. The ministers' risk taking opens a new way for the community to offer a healing presence.

Rev. John's ministry and the evolution of AWAKE have opened other doors too. At the potluck, Heather Millar, a white woman who has co-facilitated "Building the World We Dream About," says, "I couldn't say that I was a Christian in this church for a long time." But, she says, a constructive dialogue opens up when a UUCA humanist complains online that "we are too God-centered." In response, congregants form an email group where they can talk openly about the range of their theologies. "It gets us talking about what we really believe, where we really are," Heather remembers. Instead of feeling pressured to remain silent about their differences, they become curious about each other's experiences, and they value the conversation. When Rev. John launches the AWAKE services and a contemporary choir called Spirit Singers, the theological languages used in worship expand.

Darrel Nash recalls his longing for more spiritual depth—a longing that lives quietly within him for decades after he joins

UUCA. But "when Rev. John tells me what AWAKE is going to be like," Darrel tells us, "I get excited. And when it is implemented, it just more than meets my expectations: the music, the talk, the interactions, the people going deeper one-on-one. . . ." His voice drifts away into simple emotion. Darrel attends both the morning and the afternoon worship services faithfully.

Multicultural, multifaith worship services in Unitarian Universalist congregations often welcome a wider than usual range of theologies and an experience of deeper spirituality. This wider, deeper spirituality runs through all the congregations we study.

Still, Darrel, like Rev. John, worries about the small attendance. "The big disappointment with almost everyone who has wanted AWAKE is that the attendance is way, way smaller than what we wanted. We were hoping that people from other congregations would come because it doesn't interfere with anyone's Sunday morning worship service. And some of this happened, but we just haven't had the attendance that we had hoped for."

AWAKE's worship services represent a culture change at UUCA, and participants relish this accomplishment. Still, AWAKE's current manifestation doesn't match the original vision, and that, of course, raises questions.

QUESTIONS STIRRING

Despite the intimate atmosphere in the Sunday afternoon AWAKE service, then, the services raise questions, with accompanying tensions. We list some of these questions here, elaborating on some of them and leaving the rest for the reader to ponder.

We start with something seemingly insignificant. During the service, we wonder why some people sit so far apart from others. This separation doesn't break down by race or ethnicity; it's not that the white congregants are sitting with whites, while people of color sit with other folks of color. Perhaps these separations boil down to personality differences or emerge simply because some folks arrive after the service begins. But the impact is notable. The scattering of folks around the large room diffuses the energy of the service. Is the sanctuary the wrong room for this service? Matching the space to the size of the gathering, whenever possible, can shift the feel of a service from isolated to united. With so many empty seats, the small congregation has a beleaguered, almost defiant feel to it. The intimacy feels a little fragile. Choosing and setting up the space well are important considerations for entrepreneurial multicultural ministries.

Next, would other kinds of outreach efforts have brought in more people from the wider community? Or was that dream unrealistic from the get-go, given Annapolis's segregated context? Setting the goal as "bringing people in" is rarely the most effective way to build multicultural, antiracist Beloved Community. That goal can lead to discouragement, and such discouragement can keep congregants from appreciating the real transformations already afoot. Comparing AWAKE's current accomplishments to the original expansive vision emphasizes one particular outcome—and perhaps reinforces perfectionism—rather than celebrating the ongoing process of culture change.

Perhaps most important for us, we wonder why more UUCA congregants don't make the effort to show up for a program that furthers their stated mission. Did the original understanding of AWAKE as a separate set of ministries make it seem extraneous, perhaps not even intended for UUCA members themselves? In the Sunday morning services, congregants raise their voices to say, "We are willing to be transformed." AWAKE offers just such an opportunity—why don't more people dive into it?

Most humans are uncomfortable, at least at first, with what feels new or different. And folks from dominant cultures don't often have to stretch out of their comfort zones. Many need encouragement to learn how to feel comfortable with discomfort. Is discomfort the main issue?

Some UUCA members, including some of AWAKE's supporters, admit that it's too hard to fit both the morning and afternoon services into their schedules. Others say that AWAKE is just not their thing; they don't like the style of the music or the preaching. Still others bring up their distaste for the "God language." Robin Gilmore, whom we met earlier and who sings with the chancel choir, sees the phrase "God language" here as "code for Black culture." When the mostly white chancel choir sings of God, Robin says, congregants don't seem to notice. But when the Spirit Singers use similar language, some congregants protest that it doesn't fit their understanding of Unitarian Universalist theology.

What is the deep-down source of this discomfort? Is it the theology or the style or—as hard as it is for many white folks to admit—is it implicit bias and the norms of white supremacy culture that make some people find AWAKE uncomfortable or even distasteful? No doubt the answers vary from person to person, but they all need to be explored.

By the time we make our second visit to UUCA, in May 2016, the ministers have moved the AWAKE services into the Sunday morning rotation. Once a month, the Sunday morning services follow AWAKE's liturgy and use its lively worship style. In this new arrangement, UUCA congregants who feel uncomfortable with AWAKE simply stay home on those Sundays.

Shauntee Daniels, an African-American member, says that moving AWAKE to Sunday mornings is fine, but "I'm not fine with the fact that I can see how it's not supported. I'm not fine with the fact that you can obviously see there are people who don't come to church that day. They'll come the other three Sundays. To me, that's an outward defiance that—well, I'm not going to accept it." To integrate AWAKE into UUCA's Sunday morning repertoire is "fair," she says, "it gives a little change to the service. We have services for everybody."

Shauntee brings up the example of her own experience with UUCA's Darwin Day:

> Fred has Darwin Day for Darwin's birthday. First time I went there I was like, "What the heck?" But it was okay. I'm no atheist or agnostic by any means, but I'm not going to say, "Today's Darwin Day, I'm not gonna go." You can almost take any sermon by any minister and apply it to your life, if you're willing to stretch yourself. This is *healthy!*
>
> So God-talk doesn't work for some. But I know there are people who are part of the Mindfulness Practice group, the Buddhists, who come to AWAKE to be supportive.

Shauntee wants to ask those congregants who stay away on the AWAKE Sundays, "Why are you so resistant to having something different?"

Rev. Fred, too, feels frustrated with the lower attendance on those Sundays. Personally, he would relish the high-energy worship style *"every"* Sunday, he says. "You saw it all," he says to us co-authors about the Sunday morning AWAKE service we experience in May 2016, "the loud singing, people clapping their hands, hands up in the air, tears!" He characterizes traditional Unitarian Universalist worship as still stuck in an old white Protestant model: "an intellectual sermon, European white-dead-man music, and the choir singing. And," he insists, "we can do all that—within a month we do it all! But there's some folks, that's all they want. They don't ever want to hear God, they never want to hear Jesus, they never want to hear scripture, they never want to hear anything else. They come up from that UU humanistic point of view, and that's all they want to hear."

For white Unitarian Universalists who have fled the more dogmatic or oppressive religious institutions of their upbringing, the evangelical language and style of AWAKE's services trigger old traumas, despite the radically inclusive message. How do Unitarian Universalists hungry for change bridge such gaps?

Let's face it: These questions are hard to answer and will no doubt draw protests from some of the good folks themselves at UUCA. Like many UUCA leaders, we feel both compassion and frustration: compassion for the reasons that folks share for not attending and supporting AWAKE and frustration because the power and beauty of the services that we attend in 2015 and 2016 make us wish that more people would benefit from them. The questions we have raised represent a good sample of the struggles that congregations on the road to multiculturalism face.

We close out this exploration of questions by circling back to the original issue—attendance. Attendance numbers are often used as a measure of the success or viability of a multicultural program, including worship services. This brings up some key issues, which show up in several of the congregations we study:

- Is attendance a reasonable measure of the value of a program? Are congregants "voting with their feet"—that is, with their presence or lack of presence—on the value of a particular program? If so, why are they voting as they are? How much influence do the norms of white supremacy culture have on how members respond to change?

- What are the best measures of success and growth in our congregations and their programs, especially as cultural and generational norms about churchgoing continue to shift? We know that attendance at services in brick-and-mortar sanctuaries is declining in most Unitarian Universalist congregations, as it is across religions. How do the numbers and the mission intersect? What weight is given to each?

- Should a sparsely attended service or program continue to receive congregational resources? How does a congregation manage its financial and human resources in order to support and fulfill its multicultural, antiracist mission and vision?

At UUCA during the time of our study, the money questions grow more and more pressing. At first, grants from the Unitarian Universalist Funding Program underwrite the majority of AWAKE Ministries' expenses, but as those grants run out, AWAKE depends more and more on a special fund managed through UUCA itself. In 2015 and surrounding years, some congregants make annual pledges both to UUCA and to AWAKE. By the time we visit, AWAKE's budget has been cut almost in half. Still, the rumblings about money grow louder.

THE GRUMBLINGS OF CRITIQUE

By 2016, UUCA has made great leaps on its journey toward multicultural Beloved Community. But the murmurs of dissatisfaction and the grumblings of critique from a small cadre of congregants are growing increasingly audible. As often happens when a predominantly white congregation calls a minister of color, much of this critique targets Rev. John specifically.

When UUCA first calls John, many congregants understand outreach to the wider community to be the main mandate of his ministry. Rev. Fred supports the evolution of Rev. John's ministerial focus from outreach to program development. But some congregants feel disappointed, confused, or angered by the changes. They may not understand how and why the vision has shifted; they may not agree that it needed to shift.

At the same time, a small group of congregants express discomfort with Rev. John's preaching style and the "God language" that he brings into worship. Robin points out that if the worries about "God language" in the Spirit Singers' music are actually a cover for discomfort with cultural differences, then the complaints about John's preaching style feel coded too. Worship in the African-American tradition is often stereotyped as involving "God language" and gospel music (in fact, AWAKE offers spirited music in a wide range of genres, of which gospel is just one). Black ministers and musicians in Unitarian Universalist congregations hear these stereotypes often. In truth, Rev. John explains, "I don't use 'God language' any more than Fred or Christina."

The dissent of the longtime members who avoid John's Sunday morning worship services puts a damper on others—the vast majority of members—who either appreciate the changes or simply want to support their ministers and the congregation as a whole. A sense of tension between some factions in the congregation begins to replace the enthusiasm and unity that greeted Rev. John when he first arrived. These shifts represent a familiar story, and they lead us to our next set of tough dilemmas.

WHEN THE MINISTER OF COLOR GETS CRITICIZED

Often, when a minister of color arrives in a predominantly white congregation, the congregation rejoices. It celebrates the change and relishes high hopes for the transformation that most congregants long for. Underneath the celebrations there usually lies an implicit—and sometimes explicit—desire for a "savior" in the hard work of building multicultural, antiracist Beloved Community. Congregations often hope that the minister of color will step right into that savior role.

As time goes by, the congregation's original high hopes for the new ministry usually aren't quite realized. This is life, after all, and dreams often don't come true in the ways we first imagine. Dreams of building multicultural congregations may be based on unrealistic assumptions, especially on the part of the white-dominant culture. The expectation that Rev. John will go out and "bring in" people of color from the wider Annapolis community is one of those unrealistic assumptions.

At the same time, as lay members and ministers get to know each other better, both the ministers' and the congregants' all-too-human limitations and failings become evident. The minister of color usually receives most of the criticism and blame for whatever is not going according to plan. It's hard to sort out whether that particular congregation's needs are simply not a match for that particular minister's gifts or whether the unacknowledged white supremacy culture is doing its work to try to maintain the white-dominant status quo.

So, for example, in 2016 Rev. John reports that, where his detractors are concerned, "no matter what I do to prove to them that I'm good enough, I have to keep proving myself. I could give them evidence after evidence, and it's just like, 'We don't want you to have that much power. You don't deserve it. You're not smart enough. You're not refined enough.' But I don't want to be! I want to be who I am."

These words pierce our hearts. They lift up the desire for authenticity in any ministry. They remind us of the wry axiom among people of color that they have to be twice as good in order to make their way in this culture. And the reference to "refinement" points to the intersection of race and class in the work of multiculturalism.

L. E. Gomez is a UUCA member of African descent, born and raised in New Jersey. He spells out some of the complexity around race and class. "That's part of the dilemma we face here," he says. "There are extremely well-educated people of African descent [whose] vernacular is informed by that education and that culture," but when someone arrives who doesn't share that kind of education and culture, "the pushback is huge. It's almost like an anaphylactic reaction. It's like, 'What?! No! That's not what we meant'" when congregants sought a leader of color.

For Shauntee Daniels, this explains some of the "defiance" she witnesses in the congregants who don't support AWAKE. "They don't like John," she admits bluntly. "One African-American group leader says that the reason some people don't give John a lot of respect, it's not because he's Black, it's because he didn't come from one of the Ivy League schools—that it's more about his background from Southeast D.C. than about him being an African-American minister."

Rev. John was born and raised in Washington D.C. From 1995 to 2011, he lives in Prince George's County, Maryland, a predominantly African-American area near D.C. In the minds of many older white Marylanders, "PG County" still stands for "ghetto," and for some UUCA members, Rev. John "comes from" there. So the stereotypes of "lower class" and "uneducated" get projected onto him, despite all his achievements. His presence at UUCA draws these implicit biases into the open. This process is uncomfortable yet necessary; the congregation must make visible the invisible racism and classism that have many folks in their grip.

Exploring and accepting a different ministerial "vernacular"—one that is informed by the minister's unique life experiences and perceptions—is part of broadening and deepening multicultural competencies. The pushback to Rev. John's style illustrates how tough the combined race-class divide is to bridge.

In "Trust Thyself," his essay in *Centering: Navigating Race, Authenticity, and Power in Ministry*, Rev. Walter LeFlore asks, "What happens when a congregation calls a minister of color?"

An important factor is the degree to which a minister of color is perceived to be "different." The greater the perceived difference—in color (degree of darkness), style (often noted as degree of stereotypical behavior traits), class identification (or perception thereof), or use of "proper" language—the more that difference will affect how that minister is received.

Rev. Walter then asks a series of questions crucial for predominantly white congregations when they call a minister of color:

> Are the potential ramifications of a minister of color the elephant in the room, or is the manifestation of differences anticipated so that the community can openly and honestly address any issues that may surface or lurk in the background? Who is responsible for raising the issue of difference when it is perceived as a possible dynamic in the congregation's everyday life? Do both the minister and the congregation understand that issues of authority, perceptions of competence or performance, and expectations of the minister may well be affected by dynamics of difference? Does at least one party to this dance of relationship recognize and understand these dynamics, and are they competent at navigating the turbulent and muddy waters of difference, especially differences based on race?

Walter's questions point to the possibility of open, honest, self-aware dialogue about difference—dialogue that takes place both among congregants and between congregants and their ministers. Congregations need to put in place structures and agreements about where and how these dialogues will occur as soon as they embark on this journey toward multiculturalism. More often, though—in an all-too-human pattern—it takes a crisis to bring these dialogues to the fore. Such a crisis forms part of UUCA's story.

EVERY MINISTER NEEDS THE CHANCE TO GROW

But before we get there, we need to take up another angle on this issue of critiquing the minister of color. How do congregations and ministers of color best promote the minister's growth? After all, every minister, no matter what their identities, has both strengths and areas that need improvement. In a good match between a congregational minister and a congregation, the minister's strengths fit the vision that the congregation has for itself during that chapter of its life. In a healthy congregation, this vision will include the congregation's understanding of how it needs to change and grow rather than a wish to simply maintain the status quo.

A good match decidedly does not mean that the minister is "all things to all people." That's an all-too-common misunderstanding of the minister's role, exacerbated by this country's consumer culture.

In fact, a congregation's hunger for a "perfect" match—and then the judgment that often arises when a minister's limitations become visible—reflects the value that white supremacy culture places on perfection. Choosing multicultural standards instead would mean placing a higher value on a minister's vulnerability, humility, imperfection, capacity to build relationships, and willingness to grow, while still honoring and nurturing that minister's current strengths. It would also mean that ministers themselves could name their strengths and limitations. They would show up "just as they are," as well as ready to learn.

These are tall orders for any minister and congregation. Gauging whether their relationship and covenant continue to grow in healthy ways and figuring out what to do if they don't lie at the heart of a wise and well-crafted evaluation process, no matter what the minister's identities. When a minister of color serves a predominantly white congregation, the process requires extra doses of awareness and multicultural competencies.

First of all, let's face it: Racial stereotypes and white supremacy norms will almost inevitably factor into some congregants' critiques of their minister of color. As Robin DiAngelo explains in

What Does It Mean to Be White?, such implicit biases don't mean that the people holding them are "bad." Rather, these assumptions, discomforts, and judgments simply underscore how powerful this system is and how long it has held this country in its sway. Trainings, readings, and holy conversations that bring these "invisible" (to most white folks) assumptions into conscious view will help ensure that these assumptions don't influence the evaluation process unjustly. A growing capacity to "call each other in"—that is, to remind each other of these influences and the ways in which institutionalized racism affects all our perceptions—serves congregations well as they strive to deepen their relationships with each other and with their ministers of color. Humility on the part of congregants and staff is key, along with the willingness to recognize that good intentions do not guarantee good impacts. For instance, congregants may intend to conduct a fair and thorough evaluation process or to offer an occasional helpful comment as feedback to the minister, but when implicit bias drives the critique, it can have painful and unfair results. White congregants and staff members must acknowledge and respect the deep hurt of repeated micro- and macroaggressions borne by their ministers and colleagues of color.

At the same time, ministers of color, like all ministers, make mistakes in their ministries. Like all ministers, they have crucial areas where they need to figure out how they will grow and change professionally. Like all ministers, they have limitations that even the most self-aware cannot see.

How do ministers of color and their congregations establish practices for giving and receiving healthy constructive criticism? Congregants may worry that *any* criticism of the minister of color will automatically be labeled racist. Unsure of whether their own implicit biases are at work in their critique or, worse, whether they are stuck in a presumption of "white innocence," as DiAngelo calls it—"*I'm* not racist!"—they may stifle their feedback. Unexpressed dissatisfaction can quickly fester and turn poisonous if it spreads through a gossip grapevine in the congregation.

How, then, do ministers of color get the chance to grow within their ministries—a chance that all ministers need? Building trust lies at the heart of dismantling such barriers to relationship and growth for both the congregation and the minister. To build trust, everyone must make an unwavering commitment to deepening their self-awareness. Congregants must become more aware of the influence of white supremacy and racism on their expectations. Ministers must become more aware of their own strengths and limitations. All must deepen their understanding of what such holy conversations sound like.

Often, these holy conversations grow out of the inevitable conflict that arises when congregations embark on the journey toward multicultural, antiracist Beloved Community. UUCA experiences some classic cases of conflict, and it creates opportunities for redemptive holy conversations. We turn now to this part of the story.

THE URGE TO ENGAGE AND THE BLACK LIVES MATTER BANNERS

"White people will talk you to *death!*" African-American theologian James H. Cone exclaims at the Unitarian Universalist Association's Soul Work Consultation in early 2001. He expresses a classic impatience with the ways that white people can get stuck in discussions *about* undoing racism without taking any actions to actually undo it.

Some white allies get tired of all this talking too. Two such folks at UUCA are Linda Mundy and Rusty Vaughan.

Linda Mundy comes to UUCA in 2012, just as Rev. John is launching AWAKE. She participates in "Building the World We Dream About," and it deepens her understanding of her own white privilege. She begins working for a nonprofit started by an African-American colleague. Their purpose is to grant scholarships and offer mentoring to students of color entering college. Linda wants to put her privilege to work "in a way that could be supportive to people that need it. And when I say 'need it,' I don't mean need *me*, I just mean need a scholarship, need mentoring, need my access."

As her community connections continue to grow, she becomes more impatient with both the inward focus of the antiracism work at UUCA and its sometimes scattered energies. Linda notices that longtime participants in antiracism work, like Diane Goforth and Darrel Nash, are "meeting and meeting and writing and writing," trying to form a more cohesive social justice profile for the church, but she doesn't see it coming together. "Trust me," she says. "I definitely think there's internal work always to be done—but to really experience growth, you just gotta go out there and take a chance."

In 2014, searching for people in the congregation who share her enthusiasm for accountable multicultural work that reaches into the community, she meets Rusty Vaughan. Rusty, responding to the killing that summer of Michael Brown in Ferguson, Missouri, is determined to hang a Black Lives Matter banner at UUCA, and his passion is convincing. Linda and Rusty submit a proposal to UUCA's Executive Team, which consists of the ministers and a few key staff members. Empowered by the bylaw that states, "UUCA is committed to becoming and sustaining an antiracist, antioppressive, and multicultural religious community," the Executive Team accepts the proposal and sends it to the Board. The Board approves, and Rusty and Linda schedule the hanging of the banner for just after worship on a Sunday in August 2015. Congregants of all ages troop out to the edge of UUCA's property, near the neighborhood entrance, to watch the banner rise.

Rusty wants to ask other churches to display the banners too, so he and Linda create a packet of information and make appointments with the ministers or lay leaders of neighboring churches. Pretty soon, the Quakers, the United Church of Christ, and St. Philip's Episcopal Church have banners up as well.

Most members of UUCA feel proud of these efforts. But Linda and Rusty are not closely woven into the congregation's organizational structures. "We're a little show on the side, doing our thing," Linda says. She and Rusty keep the ministers and the Embracing Racial and Cultural Diversity (ERCD) group informed. ERCD is one of the many groups gathered under the Antiracism Council umbrella. But mostly Rusty and Linda are busy building accountable relationships with their interfaith partners.

And then the vandalism begins. Over and over, under cover of night, someone defaces the banners with white paint or cuts the word *Black* out of them. Rusty keeps supplying new ones. When St. Philip's Episcopal Church has its banner cut down and stolen, UUCA members, led by Unitarian Universalist youth, march a new banner over to their neighbor. UUCA gets good press about this partnership and its efforts to replace the damaged banners.

But eventually, Rev. Fred says, UUCA has to realize that the vandalism is stressful, especially for the historically African-American congregation of St. Philip's, who are the people most at risk. After their ninth banner is vandalized, St. Philip's congregants replace it with a "Dismantling Racism" banner. That banner remains untouched.

UUCA experiences its own rumblings about the Black Lives Matter banners. Some congregants confess that they don't really know what it means to hang one. What is the congregation endorsing? And why wasn't there a congregational meeting before the banner went up? What was the process for deciding whether to put it up anyway?

WHO HAS THE AUTHORITY TO DECIDE?

These growing murmurs pluck at another common experience for congregations building multicultural, antiracist Beloved Community. What governance structures allow a congregation to be quick and flexible in showing up for its own members and for the wider community as allies and partners in justice struggles? Who has a voice in those structures? The old model of one-voice, one-vote democracy, in which every issue must come before all the members, no longer serves most congregations, especially those with more than about two hundred members.

UUCA, like many such Unitarian Universalist congregations, moves to a form of policy governance around 2007. In policy governance, a small executive team, usually consisting of the minister (or ministers) and staff, sometimes with a lay member as liaison, makes operational decisions for the congregation. The Board partners with the members and ministers to set larger policy and create a vision for where the congregation is going.

Policy governance is a more nimble way of operating. The Executive Team has the power to respond quickly to major issues, whether that's replacing a broken boiler or making a statement in response to a hate crime committed in the neighborhood. At the same time, the lay members serving on the Board are freed up from the day-to-day tasks of running an institution and can stay focused on the congregation's vision of what it wants to be and do for the people and the communities it serves.

But this form of governance gets mixed reviews in Unitarian Universalist circles. Some congregants are confused or irritated by it. They feel left out of decision making and may see the process as contradicting the Fifth Principle, in which congregations covenant to affirm and promote "the right of conscience and the use of the democratic process within our congregations and in society at large." Longtime members and those who have belonged to small fellowships may be used to having a say on almost every issue that the congregation faces. In addition, many white congregants are used to being in control, or at least having a crucial say, in almost all the spaces they occupy. Most congregations that implement policy governance adjust the model to match their particular culture.

Rev. Fred describes policy governance from a minister's perspective:

> In a position as the senior minister or CEO, with all of the authority and power that comes with that, it is so much easier to—or let me put it this way, it's much *harder* to remember how important it is to make sure the congregation is aware and on board with what is going on. Because I have the authority and the power to make decisions, and because under policy governance I am in constant conversation with the staff, I can very easily isolate myself and isolate the team from the rest of the congregation. And so we can talk about things and talk about things for months and almost flip into the illusion that everybody knows about what we're talking about when they don't at all. And why would we think they do, because we haven't been talking to the congregation? And so that's one of the downsides. There are lots of upsides, and I'm really really glad we're in policy governance, but there are some things we have to be very mindful about, and sometimes it's easy not to be very mindful.

The issues of who is making the decisions and how people respond to them grow more complicated when the decisions relate to race. A group of UUCA congregants say that they object not to the Black Lives Matter banner itself but to being left out of the decision-making process. "I don't have a problem with the message, just how we did it," these congregants report. The Black Lives Matter banner becomes a point of focus for issues that almost always come up in the work of multiculturalism and antiracism.

First, when change is afoot in the congregation and in the wider culture, how do congregational leaders get buy-in from congregants for the new vision, the new way of being? How much communication is enough? How much buy-in is necessary?

In the case of the banner, the UUCA ministers and Board reason that they have a mandate for supporting Black Lives Matter. After all, the congregation has voted to change the bylaws to explicitly name their multicultural, antiracist vision. Then they vote to call Rev. John in 2009. Aren't these actions enough of an endorsement?

Linda Mundy sees problems with relying on the long-ago vote. "We should be evolving and changing with that original decision," she says. Taking a shortcut can look to the dissenters, or at least to those not in the inner circle, like defiance or simply like a lack of caring about those who are not in the know.

Second, when does pushback on a decision represent a fear of loss of control? As Shauntee Daniels suggests, "the outside world is changing. In Annapolis especially, the majority has always been very well educated, white—that's probably [who's] been at church since its inception. Now [some members of that group] have no control. Things are just moving and changing, and they're like, 'This is the only place I can control. I give large contributions.'" Rev. Fred mentions the cultural changes on the local and national level too, and he empathizes with congregants who "feel as though they are losing control over something [the church] that's really really important to them."

When the decision that is being challenged reflects systemic inequity and refers to identity, as the Black Lives Matter campaign does, then the conversation must include a recognition of the racial power structures at play. The conversation is no longer just about a process moving too quickly or not including enough voices. It's about being accountable to members of the affected groups—that is, to Black people when it concerns Black Lives Matter.

L. E. Gomez says, "There's no way that I would not stand with Black Lives Matter or any sort of pushback against institutionalized racism. But what I think is, we keep missing the point because we keep fighting the wrong fight. . . . It never gets deep, it never gets more sophisticated. We never talk about truly deep change and understanding of the level to which racism is inculcated in our society. . . . It's not the primary conversation—we tend to start to have arguments at the level of 'Put a sign out there.' 'Nah, I'm not so sure.' 'Put a sign out there.' 'Ahhh, I'm not so sure.' That's not the point. The point is the *reason why the sign needs to be there*."

Board president Ken Apfel, a white UUCA member, says that policy governance is only a piece of the problem. Yes, a good deal of administrative and executive authority has now moved to the ministerial team, and some congregants want to be more involved in "thinking about day-to-day directions and activities." But the more important question, Ken says, is, "Where does the leadership come from on underlying directions? Clearly the ministers have been supportive of moving strongly in the direction of multiculturalism, and many members have too, but there are lots of others who are saying, 'This train is going on, and I'm not part of it. What's going on here? I've lost my voice.'"

After the Black Lives Matter banner goes up, the people who feel they have lost their voice begin to gather. Long-held resentments, confusions, and disgruntlements start to bubble to the surface.

CONFLICT IS INEVITABLE, AND IT'S MESSY

Knowing that conflict must and will happen on the road to multiculturalism doesn't make it any easier once it comes. The mishmash of strong feelings and opposing ideas is messy, to say the least. It's also almost always painful for everyone involved.

The stakes are high when conflict erupts. Some members of targeted groups, together with their allies, fear that the congregation will step back from its commitment to radical inclusion and reinscribe or deepen the hurts and injustices that they experience every day. The whole project could be halted or dismantled, which would mean the end of a dream and the loss of a community that they love.

Some who come from dominant groups fear that the congregation is changing its character beyond recognition. New forms of worship may not be as comforting or stimulating to them as earlier, more familiar ones. New ways of making decisions may shift the congregation's understanding of the democratic process or may lift up priorities that these folks don't share. They too fear the end of a dream and the loss of a community they love.

With the stakes so high, all kinds of difficult things can happen. People may present their arguments in such a way that they put others down, or worse. Others may explode and use words that sting and wound. Poorly managed conflict can get into the DNA of a congregation and cause lasting damage. The congregation may split; members or ministers may leave.

But the kind of conflict that arises from doing multicultural and antiracism work brings benefits too. First and foremost, an explicit conflict gets people's thoughts and feelings out in the open, rather than shared behind closed doors or in private virtual spaces. If leaders can manage the conflict in such a way that everyone grows their capacity to speak, hear, and witness, then people with vastly different views and experiences will get to see and hear the cost of each other's hurts and fears, including both the cost of oppression and the cost of change. Such spiritual growth can increase the congregation's capacity for compassion and ultimately lead to deepening its multicultural competencies.

Many of these elements are present when conflict erupts at UUCA in the spring of 2016. A small group of unhappy congregants asks for time on the agenda at the April Board meeting, and Board president Ken Apfel gladly agrees.

Among his identities, Ken lists "white old guy." He headed the Social Security Administration during the Clinton administration, and he brings a love of building community across diversities to his engagement at UUCA. "The interconnection, the social action, the striving for something bigger and deeper and more connected all have been profoundly rewarding for us at UUCA," he says. He has participated in "Building the World We Dream About" and other antiracism activities, and they have made him long to "find ways for people to talk to one another and listen better" as the congregation makes its decisions. Facilitating a Board meeting where congregants can present their dissatisfactions seems like a good step in that direction.

We talk with congregant Michael Willis about how this meeting with the Board comes to be. Michael describes himself as an "older white male of European descent," the partner of Betsy Kraning, UUCA's music director, who is also white.

Michael and a group of six long-term congregants, some of whom have served on the Board and been instrumental in bringing policy governance to UUCA, meet ad hoc every couple of weeks for three or four months, refining their sense of what needs fixing, integrating what they hear from other congregants. The group, all of whom are white, is "pretty close to closed," Michael says.

Still, news of their work leaks out to other congregants, partly because one member of the group—apparently without the knowledge or consent of the others—places a series of phone calls to certain UUCA members, asking if they approve of the "direction of the church" and urging those who are unhappy to reduce or eliminate their annual pledges. These phone calls, in turn, grant some people permission to voice their unhappiness in public. Rev. Fred describes one such outburst, by an antagonist who has spent a couple of hours in pastoral conversation with Fred earlier that week: "On Easter Sunday, he gets up during the sharing and basically just blasts me." Fred begins to cry as he tells us this story. "I was stunned, stunned to the point where I didn't know what to do, didn't know what to say." The outburst—during the Easter service, no less—leaves Fred feeling vulnerable and the congregation unsettled.

Responding to the disruption on Easter, Rev. Fred sends out a congregational letter later that week, urging people to engage in direct and compassionate communication. But even this letter feels overly critical to some in the unhappy group. Is the minister trying to shut down their freedom of speech?

At the same time, the semi-surreptitious phone calls anger those who do believe in the church's direction. The calls feel like a kind of blackmail aimed at the congregation's leadership. Some supporters of the church's vision actually raise their pledges.

By the time the April Board meeting comes around, then, conflict and polarization have already rippled through the congregation. The Board is meeting in the congregation's library, and the room is packed to overflowing. Some people have shown up to support the group presenting their concerns, others because they worry how these concerns might diminish or derail the congregation's multicultural mission.

The critics present a four-page spreadsheet listing their concerns. Michael Willis sees his role as helping to modulate the tone of the presentation, from angry and complaining to reasoned and nonjudgmental. Still, the spreadsheet inevitably triggers emotional responses. The critics' complaints cover areas of management, ministry, budget, Board, and membership. They cite data showing how membership numbers and total pledges have fallen over the past five years and how the number of staff members has increased over the past two decades. These congregants worry about a lack of short- and long-term planning for the congregation's future and about how much input the membership has in decisions regarding UUCA's overall direction. They question the number of ministers (three full-time ministers and an intern for a congregation of just under four hundred members), and they point out a lack of structures to hold the senior minister accountable. They ask the Board to increase its transparency and improve its communication with the congregation, to develop performance metrics for the senior minister, and to develop a strategic plan and annual review that will include membership input.

The group feels that Board president Ken Apfel is responsive to their concerns. "Not 'yes, yes, yes,'" Michael Willis admits, but clearly Ken "thinks we raised some valid concerns, and the Board seems to be saying this is a great opportunity to reevaluate our vision, our governance."

But other congregants in the room are deeply uncomfortable with the group's presentation. Conversations in the weeks before the Board meeting influence what they hear as the complaints' subtext.

For instance, Andrew Bain remembers a conversation after worship a few weeks earlier in which a congregant complains about the direction of the church. "What do you mean by that?" Andrew asks. Like many champions of UUCA's mission, Andrew sees complaints about the congregation's governance structure as a cover for resistance to its multicultural, antiracist vision. "What is the greatest failure of policy governance?"

The congregant cites the Black Lives Matter banner as a prime example. This congregant says that "he is all for Black Lives Matter, but we should have followed a different process.

That knocked the wind out of me," Andrew reports. "Maybe to another person that would not be such a big thing, but to a Black person . . . There was no way I could walk away from that."

Andrew and others at the Board meeting hear the presenting group's desire for more congregational input in decision making as revealing their disapproval of the congregation's taking a stand on antiracism issues like Black Lives Matter. They hear the group's worries about the number of ministers on staff—while understandable from a budgeting point of view—as code for their dissatisfaction with Rev. John's ministry. They hear the presenting group's concerns about the senior minister's lack of accountability as critiques of the changes that Rev. Fred has supported to create a multicultural, antiracist community. And they hear the concerns about the ineffectiveness of the diversity efforts as rendering invisible the people of color who are already congregation members, both those who have been members for a long time and those who are new.

The fallout from this Board meeting is difficult, to say the least. Tempers rise. Hallway conversations and Facebook posts name the presenting group's concerns as racist. The term *racist* causes more anger and polarization. Although the presenting group comes away encouraged that the Board has heard their concerns, many people of color and their allies feel hurt and frustrated that some people can't see how these concerns relate to race.

PATTERNS OF CONFLICT IN MULTICULTURAL COMMUNITY

Some of our conversation partners at UUCA say that this Board meeting is "not the subject of your book." As Ken Apfel sees it, the presenting group's concerns are not explicitly about race but are explicitly about church direction, governance, and budget priorities. "But race is in the room," we reply. Once the work of building multicultural, antiracist Beloved Community gets under way, participants need to be courageous about asking how issues of racism influence their interactions, especially when conflict arises.

The Board meeting and the responses to it feel like a classic case of "intent versus impact"—a distinction that must be understood in antioppression work. The stated *intent* of the presenting group is to get the congregation "back on track" and to preserve its future. For the most part, their concerns focus on governance and budgeting issues. These are legitimate areas for debate in a faith tradition where members "co-own" the congregation.

Nestled among these concerns, though, are critiques of the senior minister's decision making and of the effectiveness of AWAKE Ministries. Since both Rev. Fred and AWAKE are so identified with the work of creating multicultural, antiracist Beloved Community, then the *impact* of the group's concerns and the manner of their presentation necessarily feel, to those who support that work, like an attack. And it feels like an attack not just on the ministers but on all those who have the most to lose if this work diminishes or ceases—namely, people of color and their allies and accomplices. In the racialized culture of this country, issues of who has the power and authority to make decisions are directly related to whether centuries of privilege for some and oppression for others are corrected or the status quo is maintained.

The conflict at UUCA mirrors patterns that we and other researchers see across faith movements and in the wider world. Often—especially in Unitarian Universalist contexts—the white folks offering the critiques build their case on logic and statistics. They can come across as the "reasonable" and "rational" parties. The people of color, reacting to the subtextual attacks, are sometimes labeled "hot-headed," "emotional," or "oversensitive." Our conversation partners at UUCA report just such generalizations at work in this conflict.

If we look at this pattern with a mind and heart focused on compassion, what do we see really happening? We offer here our own partial, empathetic imaginings, along with the voices of our conversation partners, as we take a closer look.

THE CHALLENGES OF CHANGE FOR WHITE PEOPLE

Change always involves loss, and this is especially true for those who have benefited from the old way of doing things. Even when everyone agrees that the old way needs to go, there's still the loss of the familiar and an awkward period of adjustment to the new way of being or doing.

For many Unitarian Universalists whose identities place them in the dominant culture—white European Americans, when we're talking about race and ethnicity—the changes that multicultural, antiracist community requires are particularly difficult to manage because they are changes to what has seemed "normal" and natural to them. Folks not awake to their own socially constructed power and privilege—as well as some who are working hard to wake up—often aren't aware of how much they are accustomed to having the decision-making power. The congregants at UUCA who feel that they are "losing their church" believe that they don't have power because the Executive Team, or the Antiracism Team, or the Board seems not to represent them on particular issues. Yet these congregants still stand within the dominant culture, where their voices and power are privileged daily.

Some congregants say that they don't object to the Black Lives Matter banner itself, just to the fact that they didn't have a voice in the decision to hang it or didn't understand the issue well enough. Is their objection racially motivated? Not necessarily in the sense of racial *prejudice*, per se. Still, race is in the room. Their emphasis on having a voice comes across to others as valuing their own agency over the reasons "why the sign needs to be there in the first place," as L. E. Gomez says. This is systemic racism at work.

For white folks, then, sharing power means diminishing the power of one's own dominant voice. This can feel painful and even unfair. Learning to step back when one's own ideas are bubbling up, as bright and worthy as always, takes a lot of practice and self-discipline. More important, some white people whose intersecting identities put them in a different targeted group (transgender folks, queer folks, disabled folks, women, to name a few) are still striving to make their voices truly heard. Figuring out how to be in solidarity, how to see intersecting oppressions, and how to be a follower rather than a leader on issues of racial and ethnic oppression requires mindfulness and ongoing training for all white people.

Finally, many Unitarian Universalists come into Unitarian Universalism because of the sense of choice it gives them. Worshiping and working with "likeminded" people, not having to hear traditional creeds or dogmas from religions that may have wounded them in the past, and feeling a sense of agency and ownership in their faith communities are among the benefits cited by longtime Unitarian Universalists. Any changes to their original understanding of this faith may feel like a loss.

RESPONSES FROM PEOPLE OF COLOR

People of color can be hurt by conflicts like the one that surfaces at UUCA because they feel betrayed by friends or coreligionists in their spiritual home and because these betrayals build on a lifetime of enduring both microaggressions and blatantly racist words and deeds.

People of color at UUCA have participated in the hard work that the congregation is doing to raise awareness of the cost of white supremacy culture to this society, to our congregations, and in congregants' personal lives. These folks of color experience the progress and the shining moments. They feel the deepening sense of community and real welcome in the congregation. They begin to be able to see themselves in the pews, on the chancel, and in the forms that worship takes.

How much more hurtful, disappointing, and infuriating it is, then, when—even after all this work—some white congregants can't see the impact of their statements or can't name what underlies their opinions about Rev. John, AWAKE, and Black Lives Matter. Sure, this work hasn't reached everyone, but when so many opportunities have been offered for people to participate, it grows harder to understand how and why some people aren't on board.

After a series of conversations that hurt him deeply—like the one about the Black Lives Matter banner—Andrew Bain decides he can no longer hold back. "So I, at that point, get fed up and decide I'm not going to remain quiet, and I start to let other people know: 'These are things that people are telling me. . . . This is being said to my face. This doesn't feel good, this sounds like an attack.'"

When Andrew hears the presentation at the Board meeting, some of the group's statements sound racist to him, and he confronts one of the group members in the hallway after the meeting. Even when Rev. John, in the coming weeks, asks Andrew to tone down the rhetoric, Andrew says, "I won't. I realize that what I'm saying can make people uncomfortable, but that was kind of the point. Basically what we had reached was, I thought, a point of impasse. Either you will grow, or we will lose the friendship. It's either I take that, internalize, and die an early death, or they take it and realize they have some growing to do."

Andrew's anguish and fury make even some allies at UUCA uncomfortable. Often in Unitarian Universalism's predominantly white congregations, one person of color (or one individual in any targeted group) becomes the "identified problem"—seen by others as the perpetually angry, emotional, "oversensitive" one. But such a characterization distracts from the larger systemic issue.

Andrew's distress reminds us of Dr. Martin Luther King Jr.'s 1963 *Why We Can't Wait*. "Perhaps it is easy for those who have never felt the stinging darts of segregation to say, 'Wait,'" Dr. King writes. "But . . . there comes a time when the cup of endurance runs over, and [people] are no longer willing to be plunged into the abyss of despair."

In the same season when Andrew is being pushed to his limit by these conversations at UUCA, the 2016 U.S. presidential campaign has unleashed a flood of racist, misogynistic, ableist rhetoric. That rhetoric emboldens some citizens to use hate speech or physical violence more loudly and more often—a situation that only grows worse as the following years unfold. The fact that Andrew gets "fed up" at UUCA is a symptom of a larger unrest and a sense of life-or-death urgency among many targeted groups across the country.

L. E. Gomez sees that connection. "I think the pushback [against UUCA's multicultural antiracism work] is more like our national dialogue," he says, where "the terminology is 'take back our country.'" So when the "people who are the squeaky wheel with regard to the pushback" at UUCA use language like "take back our church," L. E. goes on, it sounds like "kind of a coded message which is bigoted. For the informed, it's not so coded, but it becomes hurtful, and I don't think it's intended as hurtful, but it's so defensive that it can't help but be that way."

THE STRUGGLE FOR A COMMON UNDERSTANDING OF RACISM AND WHITE SUPREMACY

Trying to unpack the different hurts on all sides reveals just how hard it is to get at a common understanding of the impact of racism and white supremacy culture on all of us in this country. When Andrew and a white ally use the word *racist* to describe the critiques that the white folks present at the Board meeting, the critiquers are offended. They believe that they have eliminated any hint of personal prejudice or discrimination from their concerns.

In *What Does It Mean to Be White?*, Robin DiAngelo describes how the dominant culture still presents racism as consisting of individual acts of meanness and prejudice rather than focusing on larger systemic issues related to the unequal distribution of power, resources, and access. The narrower definition understands racism as an individual binary—an either/or that categorizes individuals as either racist, and therefore bad, or not racist, and therefore good. But DiAngelo points out that "these categories are false, for all people hold prejudices, especially across racial lines in a society deeply divided by race." Even when individual acts embody racism, she goes on, "*these acts are part of a larger system of interacting and interlocking dynamics.* The focus on individual incidences prevents the personal, interpersonal, cultural, historical, and structural analysis that is necessary in order to challenge this larger system."

These two different understandings of racism are at play in almost every congregation. Surely they influence the conflict at UUCA too. In the concerned group's critiques, for example, congregants of color and their allies hear echoes of systemic issues. When budget woes are to be solved by cutting a major focus of the multicultural mission and/or the staff that supports it, this looks like assigning resources inequitably. On the other hand, if the white congregants understand racism as an individual binary, then using the word *racist* attacks their personal integrity.

Even after all the antiracism work that UUCA has done, these different understandings of how to define the core issues are bound to create even more conflict and mutual distrust. And given the hurts on all sides, it's easy to see how the conversation at UUCA becomes polarized.

L. E. Gomez suggests that at UUCA, "we keep fighting the wrong fight. So merely to blame is useless. . . . We never talk about truly deep change and understanding of the level to which racism is inculcated in our society. It's a sophisticated matter to look and see how our systems of function fundamentally discriminate against other people."

Betsy Kraning also insists that UUCA needs more training, more conversation in order to get more people to understand multiculturalism and antiracism. Betsy sees other white congregants pushed to accept a decision that they don't really understand, like the one to hang the Black Lives Matter banner, and, she says, "it almost feels like UUs are already supposed to know it all. We're supposed to already get it and understand it. And we're all so smart that we're supposed to understand we need to do it this way or that way. That's why I'm saying, I dunno, I think slower is better. More education, more talking, more conversation. Build those bridges. . . . Have conversations."

Both these suggestions can be discouraging to those who have worked so hard for decades now, offering so many trainings and programs, building a large core of congregants who share a complex analysis of these issues. But these comments illustrate a couple of Common Threads:

- Understanding systemic racism theoretically is very different from understanding it in one's own behaviors and in a congregation's institutional structures.

- And even when a congregation pours time and resources into developing these understandings, this work is never done. We can always go deeper.

THE HEALING CIRCLE

Rev. Christina sees the angry and hurtful exchanges that precede and follow the April Board meeting as the inevitable eruption of the discomfort and dissension that have been percolating just below the surface of congregational life for quite a few years. She chooses a vivid metaphor: "It's a boil. We have to lance it. It's nasty, gross, painful, but it has to happen."

The image of lancing a boil captures just how uncomfortable the conflict can feel once it comes to a head. And it suggests a way forward: Leaders have to get these conflicts out in the open for a healing path to appear.

As one response to the conflict in the spring of 2016, the ministers invite a regional UUA staff person to lead a "listening circle" on a Sunday evening at UUCA, a few weeks after the Board meeting. "We anticipate thirty to forty people," Rev. Christina says, because of the short notice, but "we get seventy-five." The desire for healing and progress is strong, and UUCA members keep showing up.

At this gathering, everyone has time to share in pairs and then to speak to the whole circle for a minute and a half uninterrupted. The crowd does not represent a full cross-section of the congregants with different opinions and perspectives; it leans more toward those who already support the multicultural mission and vision. These supporters are, after all, in the majority in the congregation as a whole.

Still, many participants find the conversation powerful. Ken Apfel remembers, "People speak their minds and hearts. Several people have concerns they raise that are about race and about the hurtfulness that can be said. Others talk about how concerned they are that they aren't able to speak their minds for fear that they will be viewed as racist. There is some good stuff that comes out of that session."

Diane Goforth experiences a personal transformation during the one-on-one sharing. Though she is a passionate champion of UUCA's multicultural and antiracist vision, she has criticisms of Rev. John's worship services. She tells her conversation partner, "I don't get much new out of what he says, to the point that I don't go much of the time when he's preaching. . . . He's really good one-on-one and for people who are hurting, but that's not where I am."

Her sharing partner, in contrast, says "she absolutely loves John and AWAKE, that for her that's exactly what she needs and she loves to come to church for that." And Diane thinks, "'Man, what a snob I've been.' It's just like I don't get gospel music, I love classical, but I don't want to have *just* classical, because then I'd lose my gospel friends. So now I'm going to support John more than I used to because she said what she said. She needs him."

When it comes time for the ninety-second individual sharing around the circle, Rev. John speaks bluntly about some of his experiences at UUCA. "There are racists in the church," he says to the group. "You won't believe some of the things that have been said to me. People have asked me if I write my sermons, if I get help writing my sermons." One person, who hasn't attended any of UUCA's trainings on antiracism and multicultural competencies, has said that John's writing sounds "like a fifth-grader's."

People in the circle gasp. Although some congregants have heard murmured critiques of Rev. John's ministry over the years, the echoes of racial stereotypes in these statements shock the listeners.

Such individual acts of racial prejudice targeting Rev. John are profoundly hurtful not just to him but also to the community.

To understand these acts, congregants need to see how infected everyone in a white-supremacist system is by the images and messages in the culture all around them. Hearing that such stereotypes still have a grip on members of their own congregation wakes some in the circle up to the larger system. Rev. John's honesty motivates more congregants to call out coded racist statements when they hear them. The movement toward building multicultural, antiracist Beloved Community grows stronger as a result.

The healing circle has its limitations. Some of the critics of the congregation's direction opt out of participating. The brief time available limits how deep the conversations can go. Still, the gathering models the kind of holy conversation that can help move a congregation forward together. Thoughts and experiences that need to be aired, yet never have been, are heard and absorbed. Empathy grows, and a sense of interconnectedness deepens. In the aftermath of conflict, it is a step in the right direction.

SPARKLING MOMENTS AND ALMOST-MIRACLES

These stories unpack some of the difficulties and downsides of multicultural antiracism work. Yet in the midst of these struggles, UUCA experiences moments when all the hard work comes together. Such moments can feel almost like a miracle of harmony and completeness.

The practice of Appreciative Inquiry invites congregational leaders to find the sparkling moments when their community embodies the hoped-for change, even if only for a few hours. Next, the leaders analyze and intuit what makes these moments possible: What leads up to them? What conditions make them likely to happen? Then they, working alongside community members, set about creating the conditions for more and more of these sparkling moments to occur. Eventually, this way of being becomes the new normal in the community's life.

In the midst of the discontent among some members of UUCA, just such a shining moment occurs on a Saturday afternoon and evening in April 2016. The afternoon begins with about eighty people watching and discussing Shakti Butler's film *Cracking the Codes: The System of Racial Inequity*. It concludes with a full house for UUCA's second annual gospel concert, this year called the Black Lives Matter Concert. Both events reveal a community well on the road to transformation.

MAKING MISTAKES AND MODELING TRANSFORMATION IN PUBLIC

The afternoon workshop grows out of the relationship that Rusty Vaughan and Linda Mundy have built with Father Randy Callender, the priest at St. Philip's Episcopal Church, during their Black Lives Matter campaign. Linda and Fr. Randy co-facilitate the conversation of Butler's film. Butler has designed *Cracking the Codes* to be shown in three parts, so that participants can share their responses after each part, and Linda and Fr. Randy meet a day early to plan how they will work together and who will lead discussion of each part.

The real moment of transformation comes in the midst of the workshop. About halfway through the movie, Fr. Randy shares a story about his experience as an African-American minister in a predominantly white religion. He describes offering a sermon early on in his ministry and having an older white person say to him afterward, "That was nice, dear. You're pretty smart for a Black person." This kind of microaggression, he tells the workshop participants, is an example of how he gets second-guessed as a Black man.

Randy and Linda have decided on a discussion question to follow this story, and so Randy asks it now. But Linda, looking out at the participants, feels that the question is much too complicated for the time that they have. So she suggests, "I think what he meant was, you can do part A or part B. Let's just simplify it." Here's how she describes what happens next:

He looks at me and I look at him, and I realize, *What does this look like? It looks like I totally second-guessed him.* So I said, "Fr. Callender, did I just do what you were talking about?"

And he says, "Why, yes, you did, Linda."

And of course my very first reaction was I need to explain to everybody it really wasn't that, that he and I had written the question yesterday and I realized it was a dumb question, but I just went *No.* I went with it somehow. So I said, "I am *so sorry!*" I blushed. Everybody just started laughing and so I started laughing too, and then he came over and he just hugged me and he wouldn't stop. It was so awesome.

I just knew, *Shut up, Linda. Don't start with your stupid explanation.* Because I am one of those people who will run my mouth and hurt people's feelings and make excuses and tell you why you shouldn't feel that way about something I said, and that's really who I am. So it has been such a great learning experience.

Well-intentioned and well-trained white antiracist allies are going to make mistakes and commit microaggressions in relationships with people of color. "There's no way you cannot, unless you just sit in your house," Linda says. "That's the only way you can *not* make mistakes on this stuff." And even if they stay at home, well-meaning and well-trained people can make plenty of mistakes online.

At the *Cracking the Codes* workshop, Linda makes a public mistake. She has the awareness to catch it, take responsibility for it, and apologize without defensiveness. The result is a deepening of relationship and a learning opportunity for everyone in the room.

Often, people in the midst of awakening to systems of racism and white supremacy become paralyzed by their fear of making such mistakes. They grow scared of speaking up or reaching out. As Linda says, "You know enough, yes, about your own racism and prejudices. You don't necessarily know what to do with it. You're working on it, you're trying to improve. You're just scared to go out in the real world to do anything because what if I step on somebody's toes, what if I hurt somebody, what if I make an idiot of myself, what if I really mess something up, right?"

As always, we Unitarian Universalists need both/and—both the internal work and the application of that work in our wider communities. Linda and Rusty's impatience with the inward focus of UUCA's groups and trainings leads them to build real relationships in the interfaith community. Now they can make mistakes and be forgiven because they and their relationship partners have gotten to know each other. They have built enough trust to be real.

"I love what the UUCA ministers have talked to us a lot about," Linda says. "You still have that sacred conversation where we're all there, we all have that common goal—that we want to grow, we want to learn, we want to learn how to be better people, we want to learn to understand the person next to us. That's a really important lesson for us."

EMBODYING THE VISION OF THE WORLD WE DREAM ABOUT

That very evening, Betsy Kraning leads UUCA's second annual gospel concert. As soon as UUCA hangs their first Black Lives Matter banner, Betsy knew she wanted to create a Black Lives

Matter Concert. She has spent a year building and deepening relationships with participants from around the area.

She has partnered with Rusty Vaughan to coordinate the afternoon's and evening's activities. After the *Cracking the Codes* workshop, folks grab a bite to eat and stroll through a marketplace featuring local vendors, many from Annapolis's African-American community. UUCA groups involved in undoing racism and building multicultural community sit at tables where people can learn more about their work. The president of Maryland's NAACP brings volunteers to register voters.

Betsy, who taught music in the Annapolis area for forty years before retiring, brings to her work with UUCA a vision for how music can support and advance the congregation's multicultural mission and vision. This evening, the concert features some of her former students, now young adults who leap at the chance to help when she tells them it's a "dismantling-racism concert." During the year of preparation, Betsy has also built a relationship with Rhonda Winfrey, the director of Expressions Dance Company, a group of African-American young women who concentrate on doing service in the community. Their performance brings movement into the sanctuary. Poets, soloists, a jazz band, and an a cappella group of older African-American men called the Gospel Travelers join the lineup.

Attendees describe the evening as "magical."

Betsy also invites Diane Goforth to offer a brief testimony. Diane prefers to stay as far away as she can from a gospel concert. "Gospel (and most pop music) sounds like ear-splitting noise to me, and it's very hard to hear the words. Give me my Mozart and my tenor section in the choir!" she exclaims.

Diane opens her testimony by describing her early cultural elitism. She is a third-generation Unitarian and fourth-generation Universalist who grew up in Concord, Massachusetts, home to

Ralph Waldo Emerson and Henry David Thoreau. In her childhood, she says, "I thought I was at the pinnacle of civilization, to which I felt the rest of the world should aspire." But when she moved to Annapolis in the 1960s, her world opened up. Hoping to follow her upbringing by "doing justice and loving mercy," she volunteered in jail, advocated for prison reform, and ran an HIV program. She describes her first revelation: "I realize that my culture was so narrow and I am not special any more than all people are special," she says. "I am now a recovering racist, learning how to walk humbly."

She has used this term "recovering racist" to describe herself before, but this evening she adds that she is now also a "recovering elitist." She describes a brand-new realization:

This morning I was listening to Beethoven's Ninth on TV. Tears were streaming down my face, I was so powerfully moved by this deepest expression of my culture. And as I experience today's events I know that most of you are as moved by gospel music as I was by my Eurocentric symphony.

Neither culture is better than the other. They are just different, and we have so much to learn from each other. There is not only room but a need for both in this sacred space, and at almost eighty-four, I want to spend my remaining days making sure that no one who shares my religious values ever walks through these doors and feels unwelcome. If we can't build Beloved Community here, how can we hope for it in the larger world?

When she's done, Gerald Stansbury, Maryland's NAACP president, tells the crowd how much it means to him to hear Diane admit to being a recovering racist. He marvels at the crowd too. Usually when he sees Black and white people in the same room, they are sitting on different sides, he says. "But here you are all mixed up *together*!"

The Black Lives Matter Concert, Betsy Kraning reflects later, is much more than just a "fun night. It is doing the work." Then she lays out the conditions that make its success possible:

> All year I have taken people along with me as we have been coming together, talking, planning, discussing feelings about antiracism, going out into the community, getting people involved, making connections, telling them about UUCA and our antiracism work and efforts and intentions and putting together this magical evening as we recruited performers in the church and in the community. . . . When we join together to make music, we are a beloved community made up of beautiful differences and coming together for a common goal.

Rev. Fred describes UUCA's multicultural, antiracist mission as the commitment "to find, create, embrace, and be the deep and abiding *completeness* that comes with multiculturalism." For a few hours, during the Black Lives Matter concert and the workshop that precedes it, UUCA congregants and their neighbors embody that completeness.

Jane Carrigan, who identifies as Cape Verdean American, sums up the wonder—we might call it the miracle, or almost-miracle—of all those elements of hard work, relationship building, art, and grace coming together into one sparkling moment: "It was wonderful. . . . The entire sanctuary was full of two hundred or more people of every color and every hue to celebrate Black Lives Matter. That's what we need to see!"

FINDING A WAY FORWARD

When we visit Annapolis for the second time, on Memorial Day weekend of 2016, we find congregants' and ministers' feelings about the conflict and its aftermath still fresh and raw. The level of distress among ministers and congregants six weeks after that April Board meeting is discouraging.

On the other hand, the fact that the Black Lives Matter workshop and gospel concert have taken place in the midst of all this turmoil feels hopeful. That Saturday event also highlights how hard it is to ensure that everyone in a congregation will experience the joy and completeness that multicultural, antiracism work can bring.

Betsy sums up the mood for us: "Excitement and passion and frustration and anger and confusion and understanding—it's all happening at the same time. . . . It's messy. And we're not done. We have a lot of work to do." We can sense the mixity of it all. Frankly, after the high of our first visit to UUCA the year before, the congregation's difficulties in recent months make us feel more than a little concerned.

So when we attend worship on that Sunday morning of Memorial Day weekend, and it is an AWAKE service led by Rev. John, and the sanctuary is packed, we are surprised and heartened. Yes, it's the first service in the summer schedule, when the congregation goes from two morning services a week to one, and yes, the dedication of Rev. Christina's and her spouse Brian's beautiful baby Nevan is a huge draw. Still, the warmth and connectedness among the diverse folks gathered in the sanctuary are palpable, and the service's title—"Covenant, Communication, Collaboration"—feels tailor-made for the hopes and struggles UUCA faces in that moment.

At one point in the service, Rev. John asks, "What would happen if I really *saw you*—saw the God within you?" He asks us congregants to turn to each other and look for the God in each other. We stare into each other's eyes. It's a little awkward. One of us—Nancy—finds herself thinking, "I know I'm supposed to feel something, but can I really?" It's *practice*, she reminds herself, and she repeats internally, "Breathing in, breathing out, I am a step closer to seeing the God in you and to letting you see the God in me."

When we confer later about the experience, we agree: Rev. John has offered everyone there—the supporters, the dissenters, the curious, and the wary—a way forward. There is in each of us God, the Spirit of Life, the holy, the beautiful and unique and worthy—a broken-openheartedness that can turn into a raw talent for connection. What happens if we build a congregation on *that*?

After the service, we hear people who have been doubtful about AWAKE and Rev. John's ministry go up to John and say, "I liked it. That was a great service."

The congregation is stumbling, but stumbling in the right direction.

"Given how hard this work [of creating multicultural, antiracist Beloved Community] is," Rev. John reflects, "what gets us up to do it every day?" Then he answers his own question: "We ministers are doing this not just because we're getting paid but because in our heart we know this is the right thing to do. This is a call, and we're willing to sacrifice our time, our peace, and our sleep to do it."

"THE CHURCH IS GOING TO BE JUST FINE"

Lay members, too, offer glimpses of a way forward. Linda Mundy, for example, ponders the ongoing worries about the budget and comes back to some core truths about building multicultural, antiracist community. Even though cuts may be necessary to arrive at a fiscally sound operation, "we have to make that investment in our dream, what it is that we want our community to be in the future. And it may not turn out how we think it's going to. When we get there, it'll probably be something different than we originally envisioned, but it'll probably be better." Investing resources in the dream, letting go of specific outcomes, participating in the journey, in the experilearning, and in growth of many kinds—these too are necessary steps.

Shortly after our visits to Annapolis, Rev. Fred announces his retirement, effective January 1, 2018. And Rev. Christina is called to serve as senior minister at the Fox Valley Unitarian Universalist Fellowship in Appleton, Wisconsin, where she begins in the fall of 2017. The congregation is in a time of great transition. Such transitions cause stress in an institution yet also fling open the doors for fresh visioning and commitment. Ken Apfel, who continues as Board president through this transition time, lifts up one more sparkling moment from the spring of 2016, as a lure toward UUCA's future.

That spring the congregation celebrates its sixtieth anniversary with a morning-long party and presentations. Toward the end of the morning, the leaders show a video of Rev. Fred offering the Charge to the Minister at Rev. John's installation in 2010. We quoted his charge earlier in this chapter.

It's an "unbelievably powerful moment," Ken says, both at the time of John's installation and during the anniversary party in 2016. At the time of the installation, Rev. Fred's words are "all part of the celebration of new choices, new beginnings, real commitments, and a unified vote." But in the mix of emotions in the spring of 2016, they are equally powerful.

"It's a statement of where we have come as a congregation," Ken reflects, "and of what Fred's charge, which was really *our* charge to John at that time, was. It's a right-between-the-eyes 'Look it, this is your opportunity. Take it, go for it, make it happen! Lead us!' It was very powerful."

Josh Long uses the same word—*powerful*—for his experience of the video during the anniversary party. His response sums up this part of UUCA's journey and what it can hope for, if it stays true to its vision. We let Josh, then, have the last word:

The charge that Fred gave was saying we are intentionally getting an African-American minister, and it's going to be uncomfortable, we're not going to like it, they're going to do things that are unfamiliar to us, and that is all good. . . . And hearing that, when we are in the middle of that right now . . . [We get that] this is all a part of it. You don't get a Black pastor and all of a sudden everything's good—African Americans, people of color start flowing in. That's not how it works.

Josh laughs at that thought, and we join him. Then he goes on, more quietly, "That's the *beginning*, actually. So it's, um, it's— yeah. So watching that video was just like, man, the church is going to be okay. The church is going to be just fine."

QUESTIONS FOR YOU AND YOUR CONGREGATION

1. Which of the Common Threads that run through the Unitarian Universalist Church of Annapolis's story are strongest in your faith community or congregation? Which ones need more attention?

2. What do you know about the context of your wider community? What is its history with racism or ethnocentricity? In your congregation's context, is antiracism work countercultural, or are there movements and events on which you can build?

3. In your faith community or congregation, what sparkling moments on the road to multicultural, antiracist Beloved Community provide a foundation for the work to come? What can you build on?

4. What is the balance between the outward-turning justice, advocacy, and service work that your congregation does and the inward-turning education and institutional change needed to become a Beloved Community?

5. What kinds of conflict have arisen in your community or congregation as you take steps on the journey toward multicultural, antiracist Beloved Community? What approaches to working with conflict have helped your community to heal and keep moving forward on the journey?

CHAPTER FOUR

"The Exploration of Difference"

UNITARIAN UNIVERSALIST CONGREGATION
PHOENIX, ARIZONA

It's one thing to want diversity how you imagine it. It's
another thing to accept diversity in style of conflict. You
say you want to be "radically inclusive," but you might
not be comfortable with how diverse it becomes! But
that's not your problem. You're here to be part of a multicultural congregation.

—Sam Kirkland, UUCP member

As Unitarian Universalists, we try to be a big-tent faith.
One of the challenges of being a big tent is that we try to
find the commonality [among all of us], and we avoid
talking about difference. . . . Real multiculturalism happens in the exploration of difference.

—Rev. Susan Frederick-Gray,
then UUCP's lead minister

THE UNITARIAN UNIVERSALIST CONGREGATION of Phoe-
nix (UUCP) gains national attention in 2010 when it calls Unitarian Universalists to show up for protests against Arizona's infamous
anti-immigrant legislation, SB 1070. In late May and again in late
July of that year, hundreds of Unitarian Universalists pour in

from all over the country. Local congregants offer homestays and prepare meals for their visitors. Together, they march, chant, and engage in civil disobedience; some get arrested alongside leaders from the immigrant community.

Two years later, thousands of Unitarian Universalists arrive in Phoenix for Justice General Assembly (GA) 2012. At the conference, regular business takes a back seat to education around immigration reform, social justice workshops, and a candlelight vigil outside then-sheriff Joe Arpaio's Tent City jail.

These public moments lift UUCP's profile as a justice-oriented congregation. Still, building multicultural, antiracist Beloved Community is always a forward-and-back journey, and a congregation's inner work is always more complex and nuanced than public sound bites can capture. In this chapter, we share some of the personal stories that illustrate how UUCP's journey feels for those who are in it for the long haul.

COMMON THREADS

Here are some of the Common Threads that weave through UUCP's story:

- **multicultural is multigenerational**—Centering children and youth is in the congregation's DNA. The importance of their religious education program keeps the congregation focused on growing engaged citizens and creating a more just world for the generations to come.
- **flexibility and persistence**—UUCP's early members demonstrate a willingness to be flexible and creative over the long haul and in the face of daunting obstacles in the surrounding environment. These character traits become powerful resources for the congregation.

- **social justice and community engagement**—UUCP's passion for social justice is also in its DNA. But only when this work evolves into real partnerships with local community organizations can the congregation's internal work on multiculturalism and antiracism really begin.

- **the minister's passionate engagement, the offering of trainings, and the creation of various structures and strategies**— All these help to move the work of multiculturalism and antiracism forward.

- **humility and warmth**—UUCP leaders are honest about how much the congregation has to learn on its journey toward multiculturalism and antiracism. At the same time, congregants' warmth toward members and newcomers alike, across all kinds of diverse identities, offers a strong foundation on which to build Beloved Community.

- and of course: **Conflict is inevitable, the work is messy, and it never ends.**

LOCATION, LOCATION, LOCATION

The Unitarian Universalist Congregation of Phoenix sits on ten acres of stark desert beauty, its buildings flanked by large cacti and low brush. When UUCP first purchases this land in the late 1950s, it lies in unincorporated Maricopa County. Congregants are urged to go take a look at it and offered these directions: "Drive to the end of the paved road. Then walk four telephone poles to the edge of the parcel."

Today, the dirt road has been replaced by Lincoln Drive, and a variety of faith traditions now have nearby campuses. This whole area belongs to the township of Paradise Valley, the wealthiest of the Phoenix suburbs. The township's developed land consists mainly of multimillion-dollar homes on large lots.

The Phoenix metropolitan area, like Annapolis, is deeply segregated. No public transportation runs past UUCP's campus. Paradise Valley residents have voted to keep the closest bus stop a mile away to the east. How can UUCP resist the appearance of being set apart and well-to-do? How can UUCP leaders make the congregation accessible to Phoenix's financially and ethnically segregated residents?

These are just some of the challenges the congregation faces. In fact, finding the right location has been a recurring theme in UUCP's story from the start.

WHAT'S IN THE DNA?

In January 1947, the Unitarian Universalist Congregation of Phoenix, then brand new and known as the First Unitarian Church of Phoenix, moves its worship services from a member's home to a school auditorium in downtown Phoenix. The school won't let the fledgling congregation rent the classrooms, so the volunteer religious education teachers offer classes outdoors. The kindergartners meet at the sandbox. The first and second graders gather on the steps of the fire escape. The third and fourth graders camp out on the baseball bleachers. When older children show up, their classroom is the back of a volunteer teacher's station wagon.

These scrappy solutions to the problem of limited space show how central children are for this congregation. They also underscore UUCP's inventive, determined spirit. Such characteristics still serve the congregation well.

The urge to work for justice shows up right away too. In 1947 the congregation's first settled minister, Rev. Laurence Plank, pulls together a cross-racial, nondenominational group at the YWCA for a series of conversations about race. These conversations precede by many years the national dialogue on civil rights. In 1952, they influence the passage of a state amendment that desegregates Arizona's schools—two years ahead of the *Brown v. Board of Education* Supreme Court decision that makes desegregation the law of the land.

At least a few members of color are part of this predominantly white congregation from the beginning. Dr. J. Eugene Grigsby Jr. and Thomasena Grigsby are prominent members of Phoenix's African-American community. Eugene, an artist and educator, founds the Consortium of Black Artists and launches an annual art show at UUCP that continues to this day.

Lincoln Ragsdale, a former Tuskegee airman, also joins the congregation early on. A successful businessperson, Ragsdale lives in an exclusive area of Phoenix. The local police often stop him. "I look suspicious," Lincoln used to say. "And all you have to do to look suspicious is to be driving a Cadillac and be Black." Through Lincoln Ragsdale's experiences, UUCP members learn about racial profiling well before the term becomes commonplace.

Meanwhile, during the McCarthy era, UUCP gains the reputation of being a "Communist-front group," thanks in part to rumors spread by dissatisfied conservative members when they leave the congregation. At least one continuing church member loses his job simply for belonging to UUCP. The congregation gets booted out of one rental arrangement after another, as city organizations—from the local school to the YWCA—grow leery of associating with such a liberal group. The stresses of planting a Unitarian "outpost" in a conservative Western city take their toll.

At last, with the congregation on the verge of disbanding, a congregant loans UUCP a parcel of land. For the next few months, congregants of all ages spend their Sundays erecting their own small building. Determination, stubbornness, and a willingness to tackle the work on their own keep the congregation afloat.

Rev. Arthur Olsen arrives as UUCP's minister in 1957, and his fierce denouncement of fascism from the pulpit draws new members from throughout the area. UUCP explodes in numbers and quickly outgrows its worship space. The congregation purchases land "way out in the desert" and builds anew.

Today, when Jim Sorgatz, a UUCP member who is white, thinks about the congregation's history of being attacked and turned out of its sanctuaries for its liberal and progressive views, he sees a kind of posttraumatic stress in the very shape of the present building. A massive windowless wall faces the street. The main doors open off the large parking lot and are set back from the road. For a long time, the congregation had no sign to proclaim its Unitarian Universalist identity. "It's like a fortress," Jim says, "kind of in hiding." Perhaps the building symbolizes a hunkering down, reflecting a fear that more conflict might tear the congregation apart.

Indeed, along with its stubborn persistence, the congregation in those early decades also has a tendency to fight over its theologies and its recurring financial woes. Individual members say they'll leave if the congregation does not follow their direction. In a covenantal institution, a focus on individual needs and opinions can quickly devolve into an "ideology of individualism," as Rev. Fred Muir puts it in *Turning Point: Essays on a New Unitarian Universalism*. This kind of individualism, he writes, stands in stark contrast to the "joy and celebration of *individuality*," where people's unique personalities and contributions add richness to the group, even as the group's needs rank higher than any one person's.

The paradigm of "rugged individualism," which is characteristic of white supremacy culture, can keep people isolated from each other. It can hamper congregations' ability to unite around a mission and move forward together. UUCP will have to find ways to break away from this paradigm—to move from "I" to "we"—if it hopes to lean intentionally toward multiculturalism.

RESONANCES FROM THE CIVIL RIGHTS ERA

In 1963, as UUCP's new minister, Rev. Ray Manker, steps into the pulpit on his second Sunday, the Sixteenth Street Baptist Church is bombed in Birmingham, Alabama. Four children die in the attack, and many others are wounded. The news shakes the Phoenix congregation. Two years later, UUCP sends Ray to Alabama to accompany Rev. Dr. Martin Luther King Jr. on the last leg of the Selma-to-Montgomery march. Congregants feel a sense of pride and participation because their minister is there.

Around the same time, UUCP member Robert Finley heads up Phoenix's LEAP Commission (Leadership through Education and Action for Phoenix). The Commission seeks to reverse the causes of racial inequity through cross-racial partnerships between churches and community centers. When UUCP partners with the Booker T. Washington Community Council, it gains its first experience of accountable relationship. Church historian Frances Bishop writes, "When the plan [for the partnership] is presented to the congregation for adoption, it is made very clear that we are not going in to *help* people but rather to *work with* people." The Booker T. Washington Council outlines the community's needs, and the Unitarian Universalists accept them, "rather than making any suggestions from our church." The experience of the predominantly white congregation honoring the needs of the African-American community, instead of imposing its own vision, gets rooted in the congregation's DNA. It reemerges decades later in UUCP's work with immigrants' rights groups.

The late 1960s also see the installation of a statuary group, "That Which Might Have Been, Birmingham, 1963," in UUCP's memorial garden. The life-sized sculpture, by UUCP member and artist John H. Waddell, imagines the four girls killed in the Birmingham church bombing as the young women they might have become. His good friend, the African-American artist Eugene Grigsby, helps ensure that the sculpture group gets installed on the UUCP campus. Grigsby's approval gives the congregation a sense that it is appropriately accountable to the African-American community and that it is personally connected to the bombing and to the Civil Rights Movement. The statues are a source of pride and inspiration.

Yet decades after its installation, the sculpture causes alarm in visiting Unitarian Universalist leaders of color and provokes complex thoughts and feelings about the relationship of race, art, interpretation, and ownership. Has the white artist reinscribed white ownership of Black bodies by presenting them as nude? Hope, pride, anger, and confusion—the conflicting feelings that the sculpture evokes remind us of the feelings that often arise in conversations about race and white supremacy culture.

One more important piece of history forms part of the mosaic of UUCP's background: In its first fifty-five years, the congregation is twice led by ministers of color. Rev. Wilbur Johnson, an African-American Methodist interim minister, takes charge during Rev. Manker's sabbatical in 1971. In 2000, the congregation calls Unitarian Universalist minister Rev. John Burciaga, its first Latinx minister, who serves for five years. These ministers of color and the sustained membership of congregants of color do not change the overall demographics or culture of this predominantly white congregation. But they do lay a foundation for deeper relationships across race and ethnicity, which the congregation can draw on when the real work of building multicultural, antiracist Beloved Community begins.

THE REWARDS AND THE LIMITS OF OUTWARD-FOCUSED SOCIAL JUSTICE WORK

The outward focus of UUCP's early social justice work bears fruit. Not only do UUCP leaders help establish statewide desegregation but they also launch the Arizona chapter of the ACLU. The congregation votes to participate in the Sanctuary Movement of the 1980s. And it continues its relationship with the Booker T. Washington Child Development Center in downtown Phoenix, which now serves a largely Latinx population.

This work in the community draws people to the congregation. Katie Resendiz, who serves UUCP as director of children's ministries and identifies as a Latina lesbian, observes, "Doing the work out there in the world has gotten the congregation more of [the public's] attention and made it a welcoming place. More people are coming for that reason. More people put their shoulder to the wheel." A vital social justice program is one of our Common Threads in creating multicultural, antiracist Beloved Community.

But in between these sporadic successes in the community, the congregation tends to settle back into the comfort of its routines and the immediacy of its own members' life passages. The social justice work continues but is driven by the interests of individual energetic congregants rather than by a shared explicit mission or overarching goal. This pattern continues until 2007.

On its own, an outward-focused social justice program will not translate into building multicultural, antiracist Beloved Community within the congregation itself. That vision requires a willingness to engage in inward transformation. UUCP's sometimes-subtle, sometimes-not-so-subtle aversion to internal conflict—a legacy of its early history—can hamper this internal work. But all this begins to change when, through two tragic events, the external work becomes deeply personal.

THE PUBLIC BECOMES PERSONAL

In the early 2000s, Julie Erfle, a white woman hungry for a progressive faith community, falls in love with UUCP and its cooperative preschool. She dives into active engagement with the congregation, teaching the "Our Whole Lives" sexuality education curriculum, participating in numerous committees, and attending every Sunday with her growing family. Her spouse Nick, a Phoenix police officer working nights and weekends, isn't able to join her there often, but the congregation holds an important place in their lives.

Then, in September 2007, during a routine traffic stop, Nick, just thirty-three, is shot and killed by an undocumented Latino immigrant. The young assailant has a criminal history (including domestic abuse) and had previously been deported. Nick's death could not be more devastating. Given the rhetoric around immigration at that time, it also could not be more ripe for political exploitation.

In the immediate aftermath of this tragedy, UUCP congregants show up for Nick's family with an outpouring of support. Rev. Roberta Haskin, the interim minister, works with Julie to plan the wake at UUCP and the funeral, which is held at a larger evangelical church in order to accommodate all the mourners, who come from across the city. Julie remembers feeling "proud to be a Unitarian Universalist," as her minister and UUCP's choir lead the service that celebrates Nick's life.

In the months that follow, Julie steps back from UUCP; as she puts it, "everything changes" when just getting through each day is a challenge. But as she witnesses politicians and nativist groups using Nick's death as a battle cry to target and disparage all immigrants, she feels called to step forward publicly. She begins to work with various politicians, faith groups, immigration attorneys, and law enforcement to support comprehensive immigration reform. She speaks up for policy changes that would "put public safety and humanity on an equal footing."

Before Nick's death, immigration reform had not been "at the top of my to-do list," Julie says. Called by love and a passion for justice, she lives her Unitarian Universalist values out loud by taking up this issue.

Meanwhile, those congregants at UUCP already engaged in the struggle for immigrants' rights feel even more deeply motivated in the aftermath of Nick's killing. Others who had not been as aware of the fraught issue begin to get involved too. Some congregants are inspired by Julie's courageous positions in the face of harsh conservative criticism. Although her work and theirs operate on parallel tracks rather than in conjunction, UUCP's commitment becomes more personal—and more powerful—because of the relationships that congregants have built with the family before this tragedy. Relationships, as our Common Thread says, can turn abstract, philosophical affiliations into real, nuanced, grounded calls to action.

Then, in 2009, a second event catapults UUCP into a still deeper engagement with immigration issues. That year, without warning, Immigration and Customs Enforcement (ICE) deports the mother of two beloved UUCP congregants. ICE sends her back to Mexico after she has worked for twenty years in the United States and raised her children, Daniel and Geraldine, here.

Jimmy Leung—a Chinese-American radiologist and then a lay member of UUCP—and Rev. Susan Frederick-Gray take up this story in their chapter for the unfinished *Mosaic* book:

> The deportation denies this working family its wholeness during some of the most important moments in their lives, including Geraldine's high school graduation and the birth of the first grandchild, Daniel's daughter Isabella. Geraldine is a citizen, but her older brother Daniel has no status, despite

having lived here since he was seven years old and being married to a U.S. citizen and now a father. Both are young teachers in our religious education program and much beloved by our children and parents. Every Sunday that they cheerfully help take care of our children reminds the congregation of how injustice and pain borne by some members make us all unwhole.

As a result of these two horrible events, one of the most contentious issues in local and national life becomes a matter of personal concern for UUCP congregants. The congregation wakes up to the varied stories of undocumented immigrants. "Our collective mindfulness about immigration and local people of color begins to transform from a third-person point of view to a first-person point of view," Jimmy and Rev. Susan write. Similarly, UUCP's social justice work begins to move from the "I" of individual interests to the "we" of common cause.

IMMIGRATION REFORM AS A MINISTRY

UUCP's Social Action Committee, supported by Rev. Susan, decides that immigration reform ranks as a full call to ministry for the congregation, rather than just one of its many social justice concerns. Individual congregants, including Jane and George Pauk, have already planted the seeds of relationship with local groups working for the rights of migrant workers. Now the whole congregation embarks on a process of education, engagement, and reflection. Workshops, movie nights, and worship services focus on the plight of immigrants, especially those from the south. Members show up to protest police collaboration with ICE and the workplace raids of Sheriff Joe Arpaio, whose goal is to deport undocumented workers and break up Latinx families. In June 2009, the Unitarian Universalist Association honors UUCP for its engagement with the immigrants' rights groups Tonatierra and Puente by giving it the Bennett Award for Congregational Action on Human Justice and Social Action.

The next year brings the major protests against the anti-immigrant state bill known as SB 1070. UUCP, taking direction from its local immigrant partners, becomes a hub for organizing Unitarian Universalist and interfaith resistance. On May 29, 2010, some five hundred Unitarian Universalists from around the country join 50 thousand protesters marching to the Arizona state capitol, led by groups such as the National Day Laborer Organizing Network (NDLON) and Puente Arizona. Because of their bright yellow "Standing on the Side of Love" t-shirts, the Unitarian Universalists become known as "the Love People." Jimmy and Rev. Susan describe the impact of the experience on UUCP members:

> For many UUCP members it is the first time we have such a personal shared experience with our migrant and immigrant neighbors. For the congregation as a whole, it is the first opportunity in many years for us, as a group, to practice social justice outside of a Unitarian Universalist milieu, in a cultural context distinct from our own.
>
> In contrast to the Unitarian Universalist experience, for the vast majority of the marchers, the May 29 protest is merely one of many events in a long, long struggle for freedom and human rights. They have no expectation of help from allies outside of their own community, and most have no idea who we are or why we are marching. We march side by side with the migrant and immigrant families and leaders chanting, "¡Sí, se puede!" We sing songs, we share water, but it is clear to everyone that we do not come as, nor are we expected to be, saviors, or sponsors, or observers.

This experience marks a turning point in UUCP's social justice activism. It creates a new "subconscious paradigm for the congregation," as Jimmy and Rev. Susan put it. For decades, much of UUCP's social justice work has followed the sponsorship model, where individual congregants or small groups of them would lead or put money into a movement for change. But now, Jimmy and Rev. Susan say, "those who march, including many congregants of color, clergy, and lay leaders, see firsthand the power and spiritual reward of a multicultural witness experience. Although no laws are changed that day, a greater benefit occurs: Hearts are changed, and relationships begin to form." The move from *sponsorship* to true *partnership* has begun.

CIVIL DISOBEDIENCE AND CHANGES WITHIN

Puente Arizona and the National Day Laborers Organizing Network call for an even more intense and engaged protest just two months later, on July 29, 2010, when SB 1070 is supposed to go into effect. Sheriff Joe Arpaio has planned massive raids on immigrant communities for that day. Again, hundreds of Unitarian Universalists fly in from all around the country, including us co-authors. We join the Arizona congregations in solidarity with the immigrant communities.

This multiracial, multiethnic, multigenerational outpouring makes national news as thousands of protesters take to the streets and some engage in civil disobedience. In the middle of a busy downtown intersection, Latinx, indigenous, and Unitarian Universalist protestors sit down in a circle, arms linked, singing and chanting under the hot midday sun. Battalions of police in riot gear wait for the command to arrest them.

A few blocks away, leaders from Puente and NDLON, along with Rev. Susan, the UUA's then-president Rev. Peter Morales, and other Unitarian Universalists, chain themselves together to block an entrance to Sheriff Arpaio's county jail. They, too, are arrested. Nearly thirty Unitarian Universalists and many more Latinx and indigenous protestors go to jail that day.

Inside the jail, the Unitarian Universalists experience the humiliating, intimidating treatment already familiar to immigrants. Some with white skin or clergy status sustain injuries, but these are minor compared to the harsh physical and emotional abuse inflicted on protestors of color. These differences in treatment, based on skin color and apparent economic or educational status, bring home to the Unitarian Universalists the concept of unearned privilege. Across religious, racial, ethnic, language, and class boundaries, the protestors feel a sense of kinship. The physical harm done to some protestors has a deep emotional and spiritual impact on everyone.

For UUCP, their lead minister's arrest and night in jail become a defining moment. Daniel Mendez, whose mom was deported the year before, says that friends of his who don't attend UUCP "notice when Rev. Susan gets arrested. She is actually going to go out and do something about [justice] to show her support, whether it's immigration or equal marriage." He adds his own feeling: "It's really great to see her do that stuff." His spouse Tiffany Mendez, who is white, confirms, "Yeah, she's not all talk." As we have seen in our Common Threads, the minister's passionate engagement in the work of building accountable relationships and showing up for multiculturalism, antiracism, and other justice issues makes a difference in the congregation's visibility and credibility in the wider community.

These events create deep relationships that change how some UUCP congregants—and other Unitarian Universalists—view their partners in the work. Again, Jimmy and Rev. Susan capture this transformation:

What many Unitarian Universalists find in our Latino and indigenous allies are not people who define their identity by the tremendous oppression and marginalization to which they have been subjected. It was only our unfamiliarity and our own lens of privilege that allowed Unitarian Universalists to see our allies in this way. Instead what we find in our allies are some of the strongest, most dignified, empowered people we have ever met. We find a people with a sense of community so deep that it can hold its families together and raise their children under a tyranny that most Unitarian Universalists would never know. They teach us the source of their strength—personal and communal spirituality, grounded in Mother Earth and in universalism. Our allies become religious teachers and social justice teachers who resonate deeply with our Unitarian Universalist faith.

When we read this account, we notice the humility in these leaders' self-reflection, as they acknowledge the Unitarian Universalists' earlier mistakes and assumptions. Clearly, taking part in a bold public action has a profound internal effect on the congregation.

Similarly, Justice General Assembly, held in Phoenix in 2012—although it is controversial and fraught for many Unitarian Universalists, including some of color—promotes a further sense of engagement. Many UUCP members are proud of their congregation's growing accountability. They feel inspired by their spiritual learning and appreciative of the focused energy.

As Jimmy Leung sees it, the immigration ministries help the congregation move out of its fellowship model, a culture that is common among Unitarian congregations started in the late 1940s and 1950s. In many of these fellowships, individuals' needs and initiatives keep folks separate, and the congregations' energies remain diffuse and sporadic. With its immigration work, UUCP experiences the power of partnership and humility. Many congregants discover how to be led rather than lead. They experience how much they can learn from other cultures. The movement from "I" to "we" gains momentum.

Through conversations in planning meetings and during the shared time in jail, some members of the immigrant community become curious about these "Love People." The theologies and spirituality of their new Unitarian Universalist friends resonate with their own. In the immediate aftermath of the activism in 2010–12, more Latinx visitors show up for UUCP's Sunday morning worship services. Several become active members of the congregation. The "we" at UUCP grows larger. Building multicultural Beloved Community within the congregation gets real.

The newcomers of color help bring into focus the racial and ethnic diversity already present in the congregation. How are all these members being served? How can the congregation provide translation into Spanish for those who need it? What other barriers to full participation and inclusion exist within a culture that is still predominantly white and upper middle class? The congregation will have to take up all these questions in the months and years to come.

On the other hand, not all long-term UUCP congregants support the anti-SB 1070 actions and the events around Justice GA. What happens in the months following Justice GA qualifies as the most persistent Common Thread for congregations building multicultural, antiracist Beloved Community: conflict is inevitable.

INTENTIONALITY, BACKLASH, AND DELAYS

After Justice General Assembly 2012, Rev. Susan and the UUCP Board turn their attention to institutionalizing the congregation's multicultural mission and vision. Crafting an intentional statement of commitment to the goal of building multicultural,

antiracist Beloved Community is one sign that a congregation—
or at least its leadership—is serious about making the internal
changes that this goal requires.

UUCP's newly adopted policy-based governance structure
requires that the Board establish "ends statements." The ends
statements are an excellent way to express the congregation's commitment; they name the goals toward which UUCP is working.

The Board divides its ends statements into three sections:
"Within," describing the goals for congregants' personal growth;
"Among," describing how the congregation hopes to be in community together; and "Beyond," describing the congregation's
way of being in the world beyond its walls. In January 2013, when
the Board presents the ends statements to the congregation, the
second section reads,

> **Among:** UUCP is a healthy, vibrant, multigenerational, and
> multicultural religious community filled with committed
> evangelical Unitarian Universalists.

One word in this draft sets off a firestorm of responses. Interestingly, it's not the word *multicultural*. It's *evangelical*. For some
Unitarian Universalists, this word triggers visceral memories of
their earlier, deeply wounding religious experiences, especially
when those churches tried to exclude people on the basis of their
sexual orientation, gender identity, or theological beliefs or
doubts.

The word hints at historical abuses too, such as the forced conversion of indigenous peoples by our Unitarian and Universalist
ancestors. Other congregants object to the word on intellectual
grounds, insisting that we Unitarian Universalists "don't evange-
lize"—meaning that we don't reach out to try to bring people into
our congregations. There's confusion here with the word *prosely-
tize*, but either way the feeling is strong: Only religiously conser-

vative churches do that. Besides, in white middle-class culture, one rarely speaks of religion outside one's own faith community.

Champions of the word *evangelical* feel that Unitarian Universalists' shyness about sharing their faith has kept the movement small both in numbers and in spirit. The Board wants to reclaim this language from our Universalist heritage. Some congregants remember what it feels like to share a jail cell or a community-organizing event with Latinx community members when the conversation comes around to each person's religion. The Unitarian Universalists can still see the curiosity and light in their new friends' eyes as the UUs spell out their religion's particular message of all-inclusive love and respect, made visible in Unitarian Universalists' everyday relationships and through their work for justice, accompanied by a generous freedom to seek and choose one's specific spiritual path. If those conversations count as evangelism, then these Unitarian Universalists are eager to make them part of UUCP's culture.

As the conflict heats up, the Board tries to say, "Look, we can be together and not agree." But others fear that when conflict arises, it will never subside or be tolerable. UUCP's ways of dealing with conflict are embedded in its DNA. In its early years, disagreements about theism and humanism, as well as politics, would send some congregants packing. This leaves remaining congregants eager to avoid direct conflict with each other.

But avoiding conflict can lead to harbored resentments suddenly blowing up like a "time bomb," as Jimmy Leung describes it. Jimmy, who is serving as congregational president when the ends statements are presented, reflects on the congregation's patterns:

> The congregation has this dichotomy: They want to get along, yet they also want their own way. So historically what has happened, when they run across something they don't like, they'll pack it away and make a booby trap out of it. They'll tuck it

away, and then somebody comes along, not knowing the booby
trap has gotten set off. That's what happens to Rev. Susan,
that's what happens to me, with the whole *evangelical* problem. . . . [At that time,] we haven't gotten to the point where
we can have tough conversations with each other, and do the
healing. Tough conversations are not really part of the DNA
here, because they've had tough conversations before, and
they've gone really badly.

As emotions rise in this particular conflict, some congregants
use harsh and hurtful language in angry emails directed at Rev.
Susan and Board leaders. The congregational leaders, no doubt
weary from years of preparing for that June's Justice General
Assembly, are vulnerable. Their own enthusiasm for the new
vision of multiculturalism and their readiness to move ahead
with the congregation's internal transformation make the conflict
equally emotional on their side. In her annual report at the end of
this church year, Rev. Susan says that this issue makes "for a very
difficult spring," taking an "emotional toll on leadership that we
are still healing from" months later.

Might this conflict have been one of those "time bombs" actually related to something else, such as resistance to the focus on
immigration reform and to the dream of building multicultural
Beloved Community? We don't want to minimize the genuine
feelings that people on each side of the conflict express. But we
notice that such distracting arguments tend to rise up just when
the journey toward multiculturalism goes deeper.

The conflict culminates in a no-holds-barred congregational
meeting in which each side gets to express its response to the
word *evangelical*. Those who object to it speak of the pain they
still carry from experiences in the conservative Christian world.
Among those who support it, Jan Kaplan, a white member, says,
"I don't just want to be an evangelical for Unitarian Universalism.

I want to be a *jihadist* for Unitarian Universalism!" The whole room laughs; the word's supporters cheer. Everyone seems to understand the reference to the personal spiritual struggle that is the true definition of *jihad*.

At the end of this meeting, those on both sides of the argument feel relieved because they have had the chance to vent openly and be heard. The participants have managed to stay in the room with each other. That counts as a change and a success for UUCP. They reach across to their friends on the other side of the conflict. They shake hands, hug, and congratulate each other on their capacity to be so honest.

Jimmy, though, finds such apparently easy reconciliation frustrating. It feels like another way of avoiding actual engagement with differences. Sure, the differences were expressed, but where is the willingness to find a compromise, the ability to relinquish one's own desires for the good of the whole? His frustration drives him to leave the congregation for a while.

Wrestling with differences and finding a way to an authentic resolution are necessary skills for congregations that want to embrace multiculturalism. In her annual report, Rev. Susan gently calls for further sessions where the congregation "might improve our capacity for dealing in productive ways with differences, disagreements, and change."

Looking back on the conflict a few years later, Susan tries to sum up why such disagreements occur: "As Unitarian Universalists, we try to be a big-tent faith. One of the challenges of being a big tent is that we try to find the commonality [among all of us], and we avoid talking about difference." Those commonalities, she suggests, may actually just be a projection, based on the dominant norm. The emphasis on commonalities becomes a kind of wishful thinking, a glossing over of core differences, an inability to see beyond one's own experiences. "People want comfort," she exclaims, echoing Kenneth Jones and Tema Okun's characterization of the "right to comfort" as an element of white supremacy culture. A desire for comfort often takes precedence over a real engagement with difference.

Then Rev. Susan adds, "And Unitarian Universalists want to vote on *everything*." The insistence on voting can be a dodge—a dodge for some who don't want to give up accustomed power in the face of culture change, and a dodge for others who don't want to do the hard work of mutual understanding and consensus building when conflict is in the room. "Real multiculturalism," Rev. Susan sums up, "happens in the exploration of difference."

UUCP's Board finally solves the problem of the troublesome word by substituting the new word *uuvangelical*. But we can't help noting the loss of clarity that comes with this compromise. What does *uuvangelical* actually mean? Is it supposed to indicate a uniquely Unitarian Universalist way of spreading the good news of our faith? How does that way differ from other evangelisms? Is it just another word for what we have already been doing—or not doing—all along? Or does the creation of this new "UU" word embody a sense of fun and compromise? Clarifying the word's intention might support UUCP's multicultural mission.

In the end, the Board moves forward with the ends statements, including this revision. Rev. Susan, following policy-based governance procedure, adds an executive interpretation to each one. The second statement then looks like this:

Among: UUCP is a healthy, vibrant, multigenerational, and multicultural religious community filled with committed uuvangelical Unitarian Universalists.

Executive Interpretation: UUCP has adequate resources to fund a growing, thriving ministry. UUCP has an adaptive culture that does not reflect just one dominant culture. UUCP provides activities and worship that engage people and families across the generations. Members are passionate about UUCP and quick to share about its ministry and invite their friends and neighbors.

With the acceptance of the ends statements, UUCP now has an explicit statement of its mission and vision. The executive interpretations list some of the steps necessary to get there. Still, the conflict over the word *evangelical* has left a renewed tenderness about the congregation's decision-making process and how to bring people along when they differ. Rev. Susan's interpretation offers ambitious words: "UUCP has an adaptive culture that does not reflect just one dominant culture." But she and the congregational leadership know that they first need to lay down the fundamental building blocks for a more cohesive, warm, engaged congregation—one that doesn't get bogged down in conflict—before more radical change can occur.

WELCOME IN WORDS AND SYMBOLS

To create a cohesive, warm, and engaged congregation, UUCP leaders pour their energies into transforming their culture of welcome. In chapter 2, we name the importance of a "warm, multiculturally inclusive welcome." In fact, in every one of the congregations we study, members of color always mention the quality of the welcome they experience when they walk in the door.

At UUCP, Jeff Newman, a longtime member who resists identifying by race, says that UUCP's welcome is its "biggest story." Jeff presents as Asian American, his daughter as white. At another Unitarian Universalist congregation they visit, they receive lots of smiles from the congregants, but no one speaks with them. They have the opposite experience at UUCP: "Whatever race, skinny or fat, you're going to get swarmed," he promises. "The congregation wraps you in its love and warmth. It's palpable. You can feel it."

Longtime UUCP members have been working on demonstrating their warmth for each other and for newcomers ever since the 1970s, when their African-American interim minister, Rev. Wilbur Johnson, chides them for being distant and restrained—a common characteristic of white upper-middle-class culture. In a highly individualistic culture, people don't want to intrude on others' space. In more communal cultures, warm embraces and expressions of affection help bind people together in kinship.

Balancing extroverted expression and introverted restraint is always tricky, for these traits show up in different measures in people from all races and cultures. UUCP manages this balancing act by providing a welcome table by the main entrance to the sanctuary, staffed by its membership coordinator and another volunteer. They offer nametags to all newcomers and can also have a quieter conversation with seekers who want it.

Another land mine in the welcome field is the tendency in Unitarian Universalist congregations to "swarm" folks with an identity considered "other" and therefore much desired to add diversity in the pews. Same-sex couples, trans people, people of color, and young adults may be targeted in this way. Elena Perez and Katie Resendiz describe the contrast between the welcome they receive at other congregations when they are first looking for a faith community and the one they experience at UUCP. Elena, who identifies as a "Native American gay woman, sound engineer, and foster parent, who has evolved into a parent," says that at other congregations, "we hadn't cared for the nametags and the overly friendly thing. We went to churches where they clearly said, 'Oh, look, two lesbians and a Black kid!' "—implying that they would be a "catch" for that congregation. Elena would think, "No, I'll be stepping out now."

"A lot of the progressive churches around here are older and dying out," Katie explains. "So as a younger family, they want us."

At UUCP, in contrast, they experience a more relaxed and natural welcome. Elena finds a volunteer job right away as a sound operator. Getting involved right away—"that's the hook," she says. Katie dives into religious education work. Finding a role to play in the community opens a path to engagement for each of them and keeps them coming back.

Newcomers from traditionally marginalized communities can sense whether a congregation is welcoming them as people or desiring the identities they represent. Yet each person's experience can be different. Sylvia Sharma's first impressions, for instance, differ from Elena's and Katie's. Sylvia identifies as a "heterosexual female, raised in California, Chicana, aged sixty-nine, grandmother, mother, daughter, and Mexica." When she first arrives at UUCP, it's "a little bit gushy-gushy, a little overkill," she says, "like, 'we're so glad you're a minority coming here.'" But she becomes a member of the congregation because of "its position on the immigration marches. These people are not just do-gooders but will take action." At justice actions in Arizona, she says, white people are often missing. "But here is this congregation showing up." From Sylvia's account, it's clear that a congregation's gestures of welcome extend well beyond its own doors.

Visible symbols of inclusion help make many newcomers feel at home. At UUCP, visitors and longtime members notice the rainbow flag, the artwork on the sanctuary walls—often the children's own drawings—and the banners outside the front door that reflect the congregation's vision. One of them offers an image of two hands, one brown, one white, clasping each other in friendship and solidarity.

Jim Sorgatz, who identifies as "a Unitarian Universalist gay white male," says that for him, displaying the rainbow flag is "pretty much all it takes" to communicate that a congregation is gay-friendly. Before coming to UUCP in 2010, he and his partner try out another congregation in town because it advertises that it welcomes the LGBTQ community. But once they show up, "there is nothing at all that indicates it, nothing that says, 'We're a Welcoming Congregation.'"

The next week when he and his partner visit UUCP, "it is the opposite," he says. What's more, the Unitarian Universalists "welcome us just like every other couple." And he adds, "The posters out front have made the church look so much more welcoming, by showing diversity in the panels." UUCP's signage continues to evolve to match its vision.

Elena Perez describes taking newcomers on a tour of UUCP's campus. When they walk into the memorial garden and see the sculpture of the four girls killed in the 1963 Birmingham church bombing, "I think it makes [visitors] feel like this is a good place to be," she says. "When you see the sculpture, and you think, the injustice, the significance of the sculpture itself—it riles something in you and you feel like you're in the right place. Then I read the history and thought, Oh, my goodness, the artist was in this congregation fifty years ago. The congregation has been dealing with racial justice issues for a long time, when those girls were alive."

For Elena, the controversial sculpture group shows up as a significant marker of the congregation's commitment to racial justice. It, too, becomes a symbol of welcome.

In the early fall of 2015, some congregants start pushing the Executive Team to purchase or create a Black Lives Matter (BLM) sign and hang it outside the church. One white couple with African-American children feels a particular urgency about UUCP making this public statement.

Mindful of the earlier conflict over *evangelical*, Rev. Susan wants to start the process by holding congregational conversations about the Movement for Black Lives, which the sign represents.

She envisions nuanced sharing about the conflicts between law enforcement and communities of color, especially the African-American community. Congregants need an opportunity to air their differences of opinion and experience in a healthy, productive way.

But before these conversations can happen, one congregant produces the banner and brings it to church. The Executive Team compromises by placing it inside the sanctuary that Sunday. Some UUCP members respond right away. Celso Salinas-Mireles says, "When I saw the BLM banner—wow. I felt like crying. I just love that about UUCP; they really walk the talk. It's great to talk about it, but to spend time to design something that people can see—I definitely appreciate that. To make a statement—everybody who comes in, they see it."

It takes a while for the banner to be moved outside. Heidi Singer, who is white and who facilitates UUCP's 2013 offering of "Building the World We Dream About," grows impatient. "I don't know why it has to take this long. I'm kind of unclear on what exactly [the congregation needs] to do or say or be to be ready to put it out. Because the fact is, we'll never be ready. It's like having kids. If you wait until you're ready, you're never going to do it. Like, love is not a feeling, it's something you *do*. Being multicultural is something you *do*."

Today the Black Lives Matter banner hangs alongside the others that greet people as they move from UUCP's parking lot to its front door. Adding this sign makes the congregation's commitment to its multicultural, antiracist vision even more visible.

STRETCHING THE HEART AND SHIFTING THE EGO

In Rev. Susan's sermons at UUCP, she often talks about "stretching the heart and shifting the ego." To make these changes, congregants who long to create multicultural, antiracist Beloved Community need to make time for a spacious spiritual practice of self-reflection as they engage in multicultural, multiethnic partnerships and social justice actions.

UUCP leaders know they need to create a better balance between the congregation's longstanding outward focus on service and action in the community and its emerging inward focus on personal and congregational transformation related to multiculturalism and antiracism. In 2014, they discover a great model in "Small Group Ministry for Social Change," a program developed by the Boulder-Denver cluster of Unitarian Universalist congregations. The model definitely invites participants to "stretch the heart and shift the ego."

In "Implementing Small Group Social Change Ministry," Boulder-Denver cluster members Kelly Dignan and Kierstin Homblette Allen describe the goals of this program (our emphasis added):

As Unitarian Universalists, our faith calls us to be agents for social change. However, sometimes this work can feel draining, daunting, or disconnected from our spirituality. Engaging social change efforts through the format of small group ministry addresses both *the yearning to grow spiritually in community* and *the call to transform ourselves and the world. . . .* Using this format encourages us to focus more on spiritual and social transformation and less on tasks, campaigns, and the roller coaster of political wins and losses. *Our Small Group Ministries are places where we can take risks, make mistakes, learn together, and deepen our engagement of social change, spiritual growth, and the connections between the two.* Small Group Social Change Ministry asks us to take the time to reflect on how we are connected to that which is larger than ourselves and how that connection transforms us and calls us to walk beside our partners as we endeavor to create the Beloved Community.

To launch what UUCP decides to call its Small Group Justice Ministry, a group of congregants gather to choose a focus among the many issues that are alive in the congregation and the wider community. Participants propose a range of ideas. Some leave when their issue isn't chosen. But the majority decide to continue UUCP's immigration work using this new model.

The group forms a covenant and a charter, and the members make a commitment to stick together for the long haul. Then they choose a community partner to approach. Puente Arizona, which organizes for migrant justice, is a natural choice, because its relationship with UUCP is already longstanding.

Even so, this new UUCP group takes nothing for granted. They follow best practices for accountable relationships with traditionally marginalized groups and start by saying, as Rev. Susan reports it, "We are starting this group, and we would like to partner with you. Would *you* like us to partner with you? And if you do, what would you like us to do?" Much as UUCP congregants, decades earlier, turned to the Booker T. Washington Community Council to ask what it wanted them to offer, so too the Immigration Small Group Justice Ministry recognizes Puente's self-determination and its knowledge of what it truly needs.

Sandy Weir is a founding member of the group. Sandy identifies as white and is already a passionate proponent of UUCP's immigration justice ministries. She serves as the Arizona immigration ministry organizer from 2011 to 2013. Sandy imagines that the new small group will be racially and ethnically diverse; she hopes that the congregation's undocumented immigrants will feel welcome and empowered in this group.

But the group remains all white, and Sandy has to adapt her vision. Instead of a multicultural group, it becomes more like a caucus, and this becomes an advantage for the culture change at UUCP. Such whites-only caucuses allow white allies and accomplices to "talk, educate, respond, and inform each other better,"

Rev. Susan reflects. "If hurtful things are said there, they don't have to be absorbed by people of color."

The group asks Sandy to reach out to Puente, with whom she has already established a relationship. When she asks Puente if they want the UUCP group's partnership, the Puente leaders say—as Sandy puts it—"Duh, don't you already do that?" Yes, she explains, but "some people unfamiliar with your organization will be coming." The Immigration Small Group Justice Ministry welcomes congregants who have not been involved in the previous years' activism.

Puente asks the group for help working their community garden and providing childcare for their monthly Monday night organizing meetings. The latter would allow all Puente members caring for children to attend the meetings. Puente leaders also require that UUCP participants receive an orientation from Puente itself.

These are not the exciting jobs some UUCP members may have envisioned, in which they and their immigrant partners would make change together. But the white Unitarian Universalists stay humble and true to their promise to show up in the ways that Puente needs. Over time, the UUCP team members discover that in interacting with the Puente children and parents— sometimes stumbling, sometimes communicating deeply—they stretch their hearts and shift their egos. This, it turns out, is exactly the change they need.

The small group also agrees to let the whole congregation know about any actions or marches for which Puente wants support. They promise to *accompany* their community partner— an evocative word that describes the social change work they are doing. For example, in 2015, with short notice and little advertising, the Immigration Small Group Justice Ministry manages to rally about forty Unitarian Universalist laypeople to march with Puente and its allies on a Thursday afternoon, and Rev. Susan brings a dozen Unitarian Universalist clergy from the annual ministerial chapter gathering. As this spontaneous response shows, UUCP's sense of accountability to Puente has grown stronger as the relationships have deepened.

What distinguishes the small group justice ministry model from most other opportunities to do community organizing and direct service is the time the group spends on its own mutual support and internal reflection. The first hour of their monthly gathering includes a chalice lighting, then a spiritual practice designed to deepen participants' sense of presence and attentiveness. Next, one participant reflects on a recent experience, responding to this prompt: "Share an experience related to the issue of focus for your small group social change ministry that created an emotional shift in you and made you feel connected to something larger than yourself."

Often, as Sandy puts it, the experience is of a moment when "oops, my privilege showed," or it's an "example of reconciliation" in their interactions with their Puente partners. To offer these reflections, small group members draw on the multicultural competencies and antiracism trainings they have received from consultants like Beth Zemsky and in programs like "Building the World We Dream About." Telling the small group about a new insight or connection reinforces all that learning. It allows the "emotional shift" to travel deeper into the members' bones.

After the small group members listen without judgment to their colleague's reflection, they have time to offer responses: How do they feel about the experience shared? What have they learned from it about the practice of accompanying? How does hearing about it connect them to a sense of something larger than themselves, and how does that connection sustain them? In the process, the listeners, too, experience shifts in their perspectives, and their insights further the growth of the participant who shared.

In the second hour, the group manages its work: What have they accomplished? What's coming up? Who will do which tasks and when? What plans do they need to put in place? What do they need to share with the wider congregation? The meeting's agenda thus reflects the balance of inner work and outward focus.

During one of these reflection times, Sandy shares a realization that has caused her some embarrassment. In the telling, though, it becomes a deep learning experience for her and the whole team. The incident occurs during the two-week *huelga de hambre* (hunger strike) that Puente family members hold in the winter of 2014 to demand that Immigration and Customs Enforcement release detainees and halt their unnecessary deportation and to expose the human cost of tearing away members of the community. The strikers camp in front of the ICE offices in downtown Phoenix, eating nothing but keeping up their spirits by chanting, singing, and welcoming supporters who visit.

Sandy lives close by, and she visits often. She has been accompanying Puente for three years by this time and has already learned a good deal about how she can show her respect for the group's leadership: "listening and asking rather than dominating," she reminds herself. Eventually, she begins to bring her violin, playing soothing tunes from some distance away. Then the strikers ask her to play more, and she draws closer and takes requests. She brings the Unitarian Universalist Spanish hymnal, *Las voces del camino*, and accompanies a Puente leader on "Sólo le pido a Dios." The bond among them grows stronger.

But progress for the strikers' cause is slow. One detainee who joined the hunger strike from inside the detention center has already been deported. One day, as Sandy sits with the strikers, she looks up at the imposing ICE building and blurts out in frustration, "If we had any *power*, this would be over by now!"

A Puente leader whom she knows well looks at her with fury. Sandy immediately understands what she has done. He must be thinking, "This white lady with all kinds of privilege and power has the audacity to say that!" She silently chastises herself: "Shame on you, Sandy! Aren't you seeing power *personified* here?"

Sharing the story with the small group allows all of them to reflect on their unconscious assumptions. What is power, really? One definition says that it is the capacity to make change. What does power look like then? It doesn't always look like the dominant culture, the group of white congregants agrees. Who has real power? An organized grassroots group of people can have an impact on a huge institution. At least one detainee is released before the hunger strike ends—that's power.

Power has not always been a central concept in UUCP's work on multiculturalism. In fact, Sandy suggests, the difference between the work required to build a multicultural community and the work needed to ensure that such a community is also antiracist and antioppressive lies in the degree to which the community understands and works with concepts of power. Sandy's mistake with the hunger strikers takes her on a journey through "regret at having said that, to feeling thankful for the forgiveness that followed, which leads to a deeper realization of the power present in the hunger strike and the strike's importance in empowering more people."

Using the social justice small group ministry format, Sandy models how making a mistake can actually lead to deeper connections. Being willing to step out of one's comfort zone and risk making mistakes—this is a Common Thread among congregations striving to build multicultural, antiracist Beloved Community. It's also an explicit expectation in "Small Group Ministry for Social Change."

The transformation runs deep on both personal and communal levels. Through the generosity of spirit and time offered by Puente, and through the white congregants' consistent engagement, showing up month after month as they are asked, gradually the Puente members and the UUCP group come to see "each other in our wholeness," Sandy feels—"all of us needing family ties, work, the arts, physical comfort," all of them both broken and beautiful. The Immigration Small Group Justice Ministry provides a pathway to building relationships—and to stretching hearts and shifting egos.

THE EXPLORATION OF DIFFERENCE

"Real multiculturalism happens in the exploration of difference," Rev. Susan says. Exploring cultural and individual differences adds complexity and texture to our understanding of what it means to be human and alive. And such exploration—as the Immigration Small Group Justice Ministry finds—is the only way to create authentic cross-cultural relationships.

Still, we overstressed human beings have inherited a tendency to clump people into groups and generalize about their characteristics. Earlier in our evolution, this tendency may have helped some groups to survive. Now some of us may fear that we don't have the mental and emotional energy to observe and appreciate every individual's unique qualities and to understand what those differences could mean for creating relationship.

But such generalizing tendencies can lead to all kinds of stereotypes, held consciously or unconsciously by congregants, and these can cause enormous harm. One of those generalizations, for example, takes the form of an assumption that all people of color share the same experience of Unitarian Universalism.

In fact, in all our time with UUCP, what is most moving for us co-authors is the diversity of perspectives, experiences, voices, and identities of the people of color who become our conversation partners. They share with us different interpretations of UUCP's style of welcome. They have different responses to the microaggressions they encounter. They openly acknowledge that they are at different stages of their own racial identity development. There is nothing surprising about these differences, of course. In fact, assuming that people who share just one aspect of their many identities must be somehow "the same" diminishes the full complexity of human life. And that's the opposite of what our Unitarian Universalist faith calls us to do. Yet this diversity of experience remains invisible to the dominant cultural group until authentic, respectful, open-ended cross-cultural relationships grow deep and personal.

So this dive into relationship with a small sample of folks reminds us that no group is a monolith. Listening to the varied experiences of individuals from nondominant groups and integrating them into the work of multiculturalism, antiracism, and antioppression flies in the face of the value that the dominant culture places on efficiency and swift results. It adds to the messiness and never-endingness of this work—and it also adds immeasurably to the joy.

SOMETIMES ASKED TO BE A TOKEN, ALWAYS ACTING AS A BRIDGE

When we meet Celso and Ileana Salinas-Mireles at a coffee shop in the fall of 2015, Celso wears his signature black motorcycle jacket. On the back, a wreath of colorful embroidered flowers surrounds the words "Black Lives Matter." The jacket symbolizes the intersectionality and partnerships that Ileana's and Celso's lives embody.[3]

---

[3] Two years after our visit to UUCP, Celso dies tragically in a motorcycle accident. We leave this section in the present tense to match the style of the rest of this book, but we also feel that in this case, the present tense honors the lasting legacy that Celso's life leaves to all of us who have known and loved him.

Both identify as DREAMers—that is, undocumented immigrants who have come to the United States as children. Ileana, who arrived in the United States at age fifteen, adds "100% Mexican" to this identity, though in truth, she identifies with her new home too. After all, it's in the United States that she goes through "my identity crisis, getting to decide who I want to be and going to college." Identity is "complicated," she laughs. Maybe we need percentages that go higher than a hundred.

Celso, who arrived in the United States at age three, describes himself as a "Mexican transplant and technological entrepreneur." He meets Ileana in 2008 while they are both students at Arizona State University. When a new state law eliminates the merit-based scholarships that they and some other undocumented students have received, the group forms the Arizona DREAM Act Coalition and begins to organize.

Ileana discovers UUCP when she finds a job teaching Spanish for Social Justice at the Arizona Workers Rights Center. The center is partly funded by a grant from the UUCP Foundation, and UUCP members are among her students. They invite her to visit the church. She finds the congregation really welcoming, and she recognizes faces she has seen at the immigration marches. "They were trying to get themselves out there, and that made me feel like I could trust them," she remembers. Social justice work, as an expression of the congregation's deepest values, creates a foundation for trust.

Celso, who once considered becoming a Catholic priest, grows disenchanted with his original faith as his organizing work teaches him more about the church's role in systems of power and oppression. When he finally joins Ileana for Sunday mornings at UUCP, he appreciates the congregation's openness and lack of dogma. "Everything is just love—I can get behind this," he thinks.

In 2015, they live in a home between two Phoenix neighborhoods—one upper middle class and white and the other poorer and full of immigrants of color. Once again they find themselves "at the border," as Celso puts it. "We're always a bridge, I guess." They sense they play that role in the congregation too.

Ileana sings with the choir, for example. She has been asked to teach Spanish pronunciation for some of the choir's songs. Celso, in turn, gets asked to play the guitar and sing in Spanish in worship. Do they feel tokenized—asked to do these things because they are Latinx, rather than simply in appreciation of their particular gifts?

At first, Ileana says, teaching pronunciation to the choir feels intimidating. But as time goes on, she interprets it to mean "I have value here, I have a role, I can help the music to sound better. And that's nice."

"Even at UUCP," Celso adds, multiculturalism "needs to start somewhere. There need to be *some* Latinos." They move into these roles with a youthful, openhearted energy.

That year, some of UUCP's worship associates who are white pause in their planning of the Día de los Muertos service, worried about cultural misappropriation. They turn to Celso and Ileana for advice. Celso surprises them with the news that, growing up in northern Mexico, he didn't celebrate this famous holiday as a child.

"They might have been worried about cultural appropriation," Ileana explains, "but we're like, 'Woohoo!'" Celso remembers encouraging them: "Yeah, we're *glad* you're doing this!"

"I feel safe in this group of people," Celso tells us, partly because many of UUCP's white congregants are trying so hard to be accountable. He goes on, "Multiculturalism is inefficient at its core—that's not my quote, but it's invaluable. And one of the byproducts is tokenization."

Multiculturalism is inefficient at its core—this could be one of our Common Threads.

Partly because of his personality style and perhaps largely because of the strength of his own identity, Celso takes a larger view of his role in the congregation. "If you want to be on the frontier," he says, "if you're one of the few Latinos in the community, there's work involved. Don't just dismiss that as tokenization. You can see it from another perspective—see it as an opportunity to have a voice and to signal to people like you, 'You belong here,' and to people not like you, 'You belong here too.' I get why there's that concept of tokenization and the pushback to it, but I also think that that sometimes gets in the way."

Celso feels that being on the frontier is part of who he is; it's a way of life. "You have to get out of your comfort zone," he says. "I've never really felt that I belonged anywhere." But at UUCP, that's starting to change.

"We just feel very connected to the congregation," Ileana sums up. "One friend asked me, 'Oh, really? You feel comfortable in that community?' Like, 'you're not with your people.' I never even thought about that. We can relate to what is being said, the covenant, the music. Everything I hear challenges me to think about different perspectives. Many times, as we get out of service, we look at each other in awe of what we experienced, and we comment on how amazing it is to have heard that message and how it relates to what we are going through in our lives. That's what keeps us here—and the fact that we are open."

AMBIVALENCE AND BELONGING

Michele Morgan and Sam Kirkland sit in the front row of the sanctuary every Sunday morning. They make sure to greet African-American newcomers. Like Ileana and Celso, they understand the power that their welcome can have for newcomers of color, and they want to support the congregation's inclusive mission and life-saving message in every way they can.

But the stories we hear from Sam and Michele also include important areas of ambivalence. They know themselves well and are clear-eyed about the influence of white supremacy culture on Unitarian Universalist congregations.

"I identify very strongly as Black," Michele says, adding that she is fifty-five years old, a physician, and has been married to Sam for thirty years. They have two adult children, and she has been a Unitarian Universalist for almost twenty years.

Michele and Sam find Unitarian Universalism in a small town in Michigan. When they move to Phoenix in 2007, they seek out UUCP right away. By the time we speak with them, Michele has already served on the Board. "I find the Unitarian Universalist worldview to be parallel to my own," Michele says. "They want to do the right thing. They want to be fair."

Sam describes himself as "fifty-nine years old, an African-American male, pretty much heterosexual. I'm a retired auto worker, into labor education, and a life coach. I'm very active in the church. I would say I am a *strong* member of UUCP, but a *devout* member of the Unitarian Universalist Association." Sam's values align with Unitarian Universalism's Seven Principles so deeply that he feels "driven" to take part in the faith. At UUCP, he teaches "Our Whole Lives" and serves on the Vision Task Force.

"Unitarian Universalists have been on the right side of every social justice issue," Sam says. "And they've stepped across a couple of lines to do it." The thought brings tears to Sam's eyes.

But we notice that Michele and Sam both use "they" when each of them talks about Unitarian Universalists, even though Sam and Michele have identified as Unitarian Universalist for two decades. We ask them about that.

Michele thinks about it for a moment, then offers, "It might be that 'one degree of separation' thing—that I'm not feeling so deeply integrated where I am such a minority." Then she elaborates:

It's challenging being in a denomination with so few African Americans. It's hard to feel completely at home. I consider church to be part of people's personal lives. Being African American, I'm used to being in a work situation where I'm the only one. I'm from Detroit, so in my personal life, I'm used to it being *all* Black. In Detroit, the [UU] congregation was predominantly white. That put me very much in contact with white people who want to do the right thing. The whole denomination is very challenged to attract Black people to Unitarian Universalism because people do consider [church to be] their personal lives. Black people think, "I work forty hours a week; I don't want to be with white people at church."

How, then, does she see UUCP's call to create a multicultural Beloved Community?

"They would like that to happen," Michele says. "But always when people want that, there's a certain amount of ambivalence. They want it on paper, then there's what it would feel like if it happened."

Naming and addressing this ambivalence in the congregation are crucial steps on the journey to becoming a multicultural, antiracist community.

"That's part of what I brought to the Vision Task Force," Sam offers. "It's one thing to want diversity how you imagine it. It's another thing to accept diversity in style of conflict. You say you want to be 'radically inclusive,' but you might not be comfortable with how diverse it becomes!" He chuckles a little. Then he goes on, "But that's not your problem. You're here to be part of a multicultural congregation."

"Or to *work* with it," Michele adds.

For all the challenges, Sam and Michele feel a profound commitment to UUCP. In Phoenix, Michele says, the congregation offers "one of our major contacts with people." And Sam tagteams, "Most of our good friends are from the church."

"It's nice to come somewhere and you know there's not going to be a lot of nonsense," Michele says. "I'm always working with myself to feel more comfortable and to feel more included because there aren't really any other Black people. But this is true in Phoenix at large. I'm used to more Black people. But I am thrilled to have found Unitarian Universalism as a church because it provides what I need from a religious home. I think it's a good fit. I'm glad I'm here. I'm glad I found this church."

Sam offers one more story to sum up how he feels. When Michele has "some significant health challenges"—as he says this, his eyes well up again—"we weren't certain how she was going to be. I brought that anxiety to the church, and they've been phenomenal. So, I tell you, I'll be an 'African-American Unitarian Universalist,' but I'll be a *Unitarian Universalist* because this is a dang awesome thing for any race!"

CEYSHÉ NAPA'S STORY also embodies the interweaving of ambivalence and belonging. Ceyshé's primary identity is Navajo. She grows up on the reservation until she is eight, when her father moves the family to Phoenix so that he can go to school. Her father, a "very conservative Christian," and her mother, a Baháʼí, do not ask their children to follow either faith, so Ceyshé grows up skeptical and unchurched. She and her spouse Terry used to drive past the UUCP campus on the way to a movie theater, and she would say out loud, "Unitarian Universalist—what are those? Sounds like some sort of alien worshiping. Who *are* these people?"

Then she and Terry bring her niece and nephew into their family. Like many people raising children, Ceyshé longs for a supportive community where these children can learn ethics and morals without narrow dogma. Deep down, Ceyshé yearns for such a community for herself too. "I would see my cousins, who were Christian," Ceyshé recalls, "and it felt like they belonged. They had this passion in them. It wasn't a passion I identified with, but I was like, wow, they really feel this, and they live for it, and it gives them something special. I never really had that in my life."

She knows what she wants: "a faith community of equity that respects all people." At the time of her search, Arizona had recently amended its constitution to define marriage as between one man and one woman. She wants a faith community that supports equal-marriage rights and that honors the inherent worth and dignity of LGBTQ people.

What's more, Ceyshé wants a religious community "that also allows you to be Native, to be Navajo." Some of her Native friends have been excommunicated by their religion for attending Native ceremonies. She doubts that religion and Native spirituality can go together. But Navajo spirituality and traditional ceremonies are central to who she is.

Can she find a faith community that meets all these criteria?

At a loss for where to look, she takes a "Belief-O-Matic" quiz on Beliefnet.com and scores 100 percent Unitarian Universalist. "So I was like, this looks really interesting, and I kind of Wikipedia'd it to see if there was anything around here, and it was that church, the one I was making fun of and categorized as weird!" Ceyshé loves the irony—both that she would find Unitarian Universalism through a quiz and that she would end up going to the church she has laughed about.

As she experiences Unitarian Universalism through UUCP, she comes to see that the dichotomy between religion and her spirituality doesn't exist here. In American Indian traditionalism, she explains, religion and spirituality aren't separate. They are a "way of life. This is what you do, this is how you live, and it's not because someone told you to, it's not because you go to church every Sunday." She experiences the same quality in Unitarian Universalism. "It doesn't feel like religion. It feels like a way of life," she affirms with relief. Following the practices of Navajo spirituality and becoming a Unitarian Universalist—both "shift how you live your life." At UUCP, she finds a community of belonging, much like the one she envies in her Christian friends. "It fills that space," she says. Early on, Rev. Susan asks Ceyshé to join the Multicultural Task Force. In some ways, it's a natural fit. Her parents "always talked about how everybody is equal, and about multiculturalism, even though they didn't use that word. We would talk about different cultures and countries and the people that lived there. And so I think that's something that Navajos also crave, is learning about different cultures but also being able to share."

Ceyshé joins the Multicultural Task Force in 2009, as it is just beginning. "They are trying to hammer out a vision—just in general, how do you want to go about this?" she remembers. "Because I had never done that type of work before, I felt very lost. My mentality at that time is, you set out to do this work, and the work just happens." She laughs and shakes her head. "I didn't have a realistic expectation about how long the process was going to be and how important that front work is, about defining your mission, your values, your scope. I'm very impatient, trying to do the front work: When are we going to start *doing stuff*? Yet you have to do the planning." Ceyshé isn't an "expert" on the committee; she discovers how much she too has to learn.

Ceyshé's mother tells her Bahá'í friends that her daughter is now attending a Unitarian Universalist congregation. The friends say, "Aren't they just so smart and so rich?" Ceyshé brings that overall impression back to the Multicultural Task Force. "Our congregation at that time is fairly advanced in age, predominantly white, very well educated, and I might be the only Native person there," she remembers. "The whole congregation needs to do this work, to diversify. And I think the congregation as a whole, they're very aware of it. I know that they want to bring in more cultures, more diversity, but it's hard work."

When asked if she sees barriers to Native participation in Unitarian Universalism and at UUCP, Ceyshé answers right away, "Trust is an issue." Most of her Native friends have no idea what Unitarian Universalism is. She doesn't know many Native liberal Christians who might have crossed paths with Unitarian Universalists. The religion "sounds so foreign—and you can't just go down the street to get to this church. We need a satellite location in downtown Phoenix. We need something that is on public transportation, that is fairly easy to get to." The question of access should be a high priority.

But she senses ambivalence about this idea among some congregants. She suspects that some folks like being in Paradise Valley "because it separates us from 'those people.' Nobody has said those words, but I feel I can pick up a general attitude, a general feeling from people, that they don't want to move. Because this is a plush community. There's status, prestige. There's no public transportation, and that's a strategic policy by the city, by the town of Paradise Valley. But downtown Phoenix is centrally located, and there are a lot of different ethnicities and cultures there."

A congregation's location conveys a message about its identity and culture. Many congregations won't have the flexibility or resources to start a second campus, let alone to move. But recognizing the barriers that a church's location presents can help a congregation strategize how to communicate its message and imagine new ways to take that message beyond its walls.

Like Sam and Michele, Ceyshé sees how UUCP has plenty of room to grow toward its multicultural mission and vision. And to her, as to them, it already feels like home.

MICROAGGRESSIONS AND REPAIR

Sylvia Sharma—Californian, Chicana, Mexica—remembers a time when another Native member of the congregation wears his beaded necklace to Sunday worship. She watches as a white congregant picks up the necklace with their left hand, asking, "Did you make this?" For Native peoples, such a necklace is a sacred object, not to be touched and certainly not to be touched with the left hand. This is a microaggression—one of those unintentionally hurtful moments that have a cumulative effect.

The person who does this "doesn't know they are hurting people when they touch someone's necklace," Sylvia says. She has theories about why such microaggressions happen: sometimes it's a simple lack of "manners" and of "relationship skills classes." But sometimes it's a product of Unitarian Universalists' individualism. "Unitarian Universalism has had a history of being a bright light" for social justice, Sylvia says, citing the faith's work with Planned Parenthood, the League of Women Voters, and more. "We relish highly educated, well-grounded personalities. We've evolved: We have sacred truths, and they're individual."

Perhaps this emphasis on individual self-determination gets in the way of people learning the customs of an unfamiliar tradition in which communal respect is key.

Sylvia witnesses even more troubling microaggressions at UUCP. She watches as a white member assumes that if UUCP were to attract more African Americans, the congregation would need to offer "drug education classes." Ouch! The association between Blacks and drug addicts is a direct product of white supremacy culture. But what's particularly troubling for Sylvia is that the white ally who also witnesses this microaggression fails to intervene. Sylvia doesn't want to "have to be the policewoman in the room."

One Sunday in worship, Rev. Susan uses a story that she borrows from the British philosopher Bertrand Russell. It concerns two Catholic priests who argue about whether it is appropriate to smoke while they pray. Each writes a letter to the pope, and the pope answers yes to each one—it's okay to smoke and it's not okay—because the priests have framed their questions in different ways. Susan's intention, she remembers, is to "illustrate that how we frame our questions actually shapes the answers we get."

But to Sylvia, who has just returned that Sunday from four days and nights of Native sun dance, the story seems to be making fun of the conjunction of smoking and spirituality. In some Native ceremonies, tobacco and pipe smoking play a central role. And Catholicism's history of colonialism and genocide in indigenous communities makes the story even more painful. Rev. Susan hadn't looked at the story through an indigenous lens.

"I gave her corn, I gave her tears," Sylvia says, to represent how hurtful Rev. Susan's lack of multicultural sensitivity was. They reconcile as Susan recognizes the pain she has caused. Nevertheless, "we are frustrated," Sylvia says, speaking for many people of color she knows. "You climb the mountain, you think you have a chance, and it just doesn't happen."

Sylvia first hears about Diverse and Revolutionary Unitarian Universalist Multicultural Ministries (DRUUMM) during her conversation with us. She picks up on this resource with pleasure. "Maybe that's the hope," she says: "an institutional structure so that minority people like me can meet each other on common ground." She hopes DRUUMM offers a virtual journal or network; she wants her own children to find a way to a Unitarian Universalist congregation.

Despite her discouragement, Sylvia remains passionate about her UUCP membership. She lifts UUCP up as "a good place to raise children," not least because "we embrace biracial children." Her own daughter is biracial and now in a biracial marriage. "And white congregants know that Christianity is not the beginning of the world," Sylvia goes on—a particularly important point for all those aware of the genocide of Native peoples by the early Christian immigrants to this country. She sums up how she feels about UUCP:

I'm never going to give up. I go there for the joy of going there. It's the best we have. You can't lose hope in humanity. We have a long way to go to be a loving humanity. I think the congregation tries. And it's refreshing. Over the years I've made a lot of good friends there. But because I'm a minority, I don't trust a lot of white people. Still, I'm hopeful, and I won't give up. I see there's strong leadership. I don't see it falling apart; I see the place thriving.

Sylvia's story echoes Ceyshé's words: "Trust is an issue." It also shows how trust can be built over time. The *impact* of all those microaggressions, the hurt they cause, is important, along with the lack of awareness and education that makes it easier for them to occur. But the congregation's *intention*—and the evidence of its actions, as it tries to grow more multiculturally competent— matter too, when it comes to building trust.

JUST AS IT IS FOR SYLVIA, the congregation's embrace of multiracial families is a big draw for Katie Resendiz and Elena Perez. In contrast to other churches they tried out, at UUCP "it's very specifically Unitarian Universalist and welcoming and safe for interracial and biracial families," Katie says.

They are also impressed with the accountability and awareness that they see growing among white staff and congregants at UUCP. Elena, who is Native American, remembers witnessing a specific microaggression: "A few months ago, we're at community night. Kristina [who was then the membership and volunteer coordinator] and Rev. Susan are talking to Katie about something, and they use the term 'the natives are getting restless.' Oh, man. I hear stuff like this all the time, and it's a question of, do I interrupt or just let it slide? Is it worth the effort for me at this time?"

Elena finds the stereotyping comment disappointing, but she lets it go. Then, the very next day at church, Kristina finds her and says, "I realized what I said, and I don't ever want to use that language again. I'm really sorry, and I hope you can forgive me." "I've never had anyone do that before," Elena marvels. "She went home and had a realization and came and made good on it. The fact that she even noticed was amazing; that was really encouraging. People have no idea the culture that they're pulling from" with certain expressions. "I don't speak up very often in situations like that. When—it's never an *if*—people say things like 'we're going to get together and pow-wow,' I can say, 'No, we're not. Could we have a *meeting* instead?' Some people will get defensive, but someone in this place will realize the harm done. I think Rev. Susan in particular is very open to those discussions."

Katie takes up the thought. "One of the ways women and minorities get shut down is when we're told we're being too sensitive. I don't have to worry about that here."

"Yeah, you might get annoyance," Elena adds, "like, 'I don't get why you feel that way, but I hear you.' Even acknowledging the feelings is a start."

Elena and Katie have ideas about how UUCP might live out its multicultural mission even more richly. "There are times when I feel like the older population is overlooked," Elena says. "There are key members over sixty-five, grandmas and grandpas, who are very active and respected, but there are other times when I would like to see more respect paid to the older population of the church."

"Part of being multicultural is recognizing the diversity we already have," Katie reflects. "So much oppression happens because people have to sublimate their identities. In our eagerness to go around and 'get' people of all different colors and orientations, we also have to look at the resources we have and celebrate those." She imagines multicultural conversations that could include something like: "You're eighty—that's amazing! I'm thirty-six!" "You grew up in Ohio—that's amazing!" Every aspect of diversity in identities and backgrounds adds a richness to congregational life. Katie and Elena would like to see them all celebrated.

These stories from Sylvia, Elena, and Katie lift up a small sample of the kinds of microaggressions that occur in congregations all the time. Yet they also demonstrate how accountability, awareness, and a commitment to growth can build a strong enough foundation of trust that relationships can be repaired when such mistakes happen. Our next two stories make our exploration of microaggressions even more complex.

HUMOR, COMPASSION, AND THE INEVITABLE MISTAKES

Jeff Newman sees humor, curiosity, and good intention as the best approach to dealing with a highly racialized society. "There are so many ways you're going to step in it," he acknowledges. "If you learn to let it be funny, it's funny. But if you're not willing to let it be funny, it's just ridiculous."

He remembers how a white congregant at UUCP, struggling to remember the name of another member of color, dances around describing that person, not wanting to mention their racial identity. "Dancing around it can be as insulting as saying the wrong thing," Jeff points out. "You gotta dive in and have some humor about it."

Asked how he identifies, Jeff pushes back at first: "I'm wary of giving a list. With people who don't know me, I can get miscategorized." But then he launches into a list rich in details: he is fifty-eight, a "computer guy" who is fluent in English, Spanish, Portuguese, and, at one time, Mandarin, with a "WASP dad from New Jersey," a diplomat, married to a "Chinese mom from Beijing." Jeff grows up in Paraguay but also lives in Uganda, Chile,

Taiwan, and other countries, as well as many parts of the United States. Like Sam Kirkland, he teaches "Our Whole Lives" to middle school youth at UUCP. He is cisgender, straight, and "very comfortable with all sorts of variations and ideas."

"I don't approach people with a consciousness of race," Jeff says. "I identify mostly as white, but I don't know what that means. Culturally I'm more Latino because I lived in South America and am married to a Mexican woman."

When people first meet Jeff, they see him as Asian American. But, Jeff says, "I don't remain part of 'the other' for very long after I open my mouth. If I talk to white people, I'm white. Around Chinese New Year, I want in on the feasts. Around Latinos, I'm Latino. But when I lived in Taiwan, *I* was 'the other.' Because of where I grew up, immersed in many cultures, I'm very talented at being a chameleon."

Jeff brings an international perspective to issues of race and ethnicity in the United States. Like many immigrants, he doesn't automatically think in terms of hierarchies of power and the social structures that give advantages to some and disadvantages to others. His approach focuses on the relationships.

For instance, when Jeff experiences a common microaggression—being mistaken for another Asian-American congregant—he focuses on the relationship with the person who makes the mistake:

> I don't look that much like Jimmy Leung. We're the same height, we both wear glasses. But I have long hair in a ponytail [Jimmy has short hair]. Twice at least, I've had someone come up to me and start talking to me, and I realize they're continuing a conversation with Jimmy. It's horrifying. Not because I'm insulted, but because I realize that this earnest white person standing in front of me will realize in the next few seconds that "I've made this mistake of 'all Asians look alike.' " I haven't figured a way to let them down gently.

I guess what I'd like to say in your book is, hey, it's not that big a deal. I was not insulted. People are *so* politically correct that it can hinder [relationship building]. I suspect that these two people [who mistook me for Jimmy] had a hard time approaching any Asian after that.

During Jeff's tenure on the Multicultural Task Force, he notices how hard it is for the group to decide what *multiculturalism* even means. "And once you define multiculturalism, are we as a congregation willing to change to *become* that?" he wonders. But counting up the percentages of people of color in the pews feels like "a really dumb way to measure multiculturalism," he says. Rather, "it should be measured by whether people who are aligned with our values want to be here."

The focus needs to be on retaining those people who give UUCP a try. "Personally, if I see someone who's not white, I make a point to go and talk to them." By welcoming the visitor, he's saying, "Help me paint this church in color."

"It's not because I resent the color of the church, or the whiteness of it," he adds quickly. "I don't want to insult anybody. But I think we put a little too much into trying to get people *in*. I think we'd be doing better trying to *retain* people. And I think we do that just by being friendly."

Most of us humans tend to interpret new evidence as confirmation of the beliefs and theories we already hold. This tendency is called *confirmation bias*. "If I'd come in here with the idea that people were discriminating against me, I'd have had ample evidence to support me," Jeff acknowledges. His hearty welcome to people of color, and his very presence at UUCP, can contradict a visitor's expectation of feeling alienated, hurt, or simply of not belonging.

But of course this work of welcoming must not fall to people of color alone, let alone to all people of color—and not just because not all people of color want the job. It's even more important that white congregants become aware of their own microaggressions and other forms of discrimination, and work to stop making these mistakes, which confirm the expectations of many people of color.

Yet Jeff feels empathy for folks trying to get the work of undoing racism right. He longs for everyone to feel more compassion and find more humor in the inevitable mistakes people—especially white people—make. His own humor is sometimes sardonic and biting, sometimes silly and refreshing. It almost always cuts through the tension and creates new common ground.

Jeff sums up how he feels about UUCP with unbridled enthusiasm:

> I love the place, right? I've been here through thick and thin. I love the people here, I love the programs, I'm deeply involved in the youth program.
>
> I'm gonna tell you one of the reasons I love my congregation. And this is gonna sound unbelievably racist at the same time. One year, a long time ago, we celebrated Kwanzaa. I don't know if we had any Blacks attending on a regular basis then. As part of it, we sang Negro spirituals. I saw these old white ladies earnestly singing Negro spirituals. I loved them because they were earnestly singing Negro spirituals with all their heart. They were failing miserably at it. It's like white Protestants doing samba. But it's all earnest. They're willing to step up and look foolish in order to build a bridge, to make the world right for someone else. They're willing to put it all on the line.

Sometimes, Jeff implies, the work of multiculturalism and antiracism is not about getting every gesture "right." Yes, there is a difference between intent and impact, as one of the Golden Rules of antioppression work puts it. It matters what impact our actions have. They may cause hurt or harm despite our best intentions. At the same time, there is not a binary either/or here. Intent also matters, and it can influence the impact of one's actions. As Jeff's story shows, sometimes when the spirit shines forth and people are willing to take risks "to make the world right for someone else," that intention, however clumsily executed, has a positive impact and helps to build the bridges needed for Beloved Community.

RACIAL IDENTITY DEVELOPMENT AND THE BURDENS OF LEADERSHIP

"We Asian Americans are chameleons"—Jimmy Leung uses the same metaphor that we hear from Jeff Newman. Jimmy goes on, "We're natural assimilators—we're *supposed* to assimilate. So I have spent most of my life assimilating. But I'm not a very good assimilator!" he laughs.

This expectation of assimilation creates particular pressures for Asian-American Unitarian Universalists, Jimmy and co-author Karin agree. In 2015, we begin by asking Jimmy about the central elements in the work of multiculturalism, but the conversation quickly evolves into a deep sharing about identity development.

What's central to multiculturalism, Jimmy feels, is the understanding that the dominant white culture is only one of many cultures rather than a "default set of values that everybody should buy into." In white supremacy culture, a white perspective is accepted as the norm and the particular characteristics of this culture become invisible to those who don't question it.

At UUCP, "you talk to people who are very in favor of multiculturalism," Jimmy explains. "They'll say, 'Yes, we should do that,' but when you push it a little bit past the skin, they reflect their own personal experience onto everybody else. When you confront them with 'How do you become a multicultural congregation?'

they say stuff like, 'Well, people just need to know about us [Unitarian Universalists] more. We just need to be louder about what we do.'" Jimmy laughs. "No," he says, and shakes his head to indicate that's not enough.

Outreach, social justice, and advocacy work in the community are crucial aspects of a congregation's welcome and visibility. But on their own, they won't dismantle a congregation's dominant cultural style, which may feel unwelcoming or exclusive to some people from marginalized groups. Many Unitarian Universalists share the misunderstanding that building multicultural, antiracist Beloved Community is simply about creating better outreach to a broader section of the city. The conversation that Karin and Jimmy share on this subject is rich and includes their reflections about their own racial identity development:

KARIN: You said this thing about people saying you just need more outreach in order to be multicultural. When I started trying to have this conversation at my old congregation, that's where I was actually. Because I had so assimilated myself into the dominant culture that the concept that it could be anything different, I didn't even imagine that. I thought, this is just the way it is. I've noticed this particularly among first-generation Asian Americans—we don't know how to be Asian Americans. Nobody taught me how to be Asian in a white society—

JIMMY (*breaking in*): You're talking to my soul, sister! You're bringing up deep stuff inside of me right now.

KARIN: Back then I had never heard of white privilege. So I'm wondering, where did you develop that consciousness?

JIMMY: That's one thing that I will always be grateful to Unitarian Universalism about—it really taught me that.

KARIN: The shorthand I use to talk about it is: My whole life I thought I was a flawed white person.

JIMMY: I do too!

KARIN: With Sam and Michele—just the way they articulate who they are: "We are Black, and we are in a white denomination, and we have chosen to accept this role." Whereas with me and a little bit with you, Jimmy—there is no place where I know who I am. And because people always say, "Oh, you're home, you're UU, you can be anybody you want," we think, "OK, maybe this is the place. Maybe *this* is the place where I can be, and not be sure who I am" . . . and it's not.

JIMMY: Maybe we're hydroponic plants. Our roots always have to be in some liquid form. That's a really good contrast—between Sam and people like me and you. If [the congregation] did no further multicultural work, Sam would stay; I would not. One of the mistakes that we make in Unitarian Universalism is that we don't understand that spectrum.

Unlike Jeff Newman, Jimmy doesn't want to be responsible for greeting every Asian or Asian-American visitor to UUCP. His first thought is that he "doesn't want to form an Asian clique. I don't want my colorness to define who I am." Gradually, he realizes that this reluctance comes from a deeper place:

It's my own anti-Asian racism. That's one of the things I learned about in Unitarian Universalism, too, is how we can internalize the racism directed at us. So, yeah, Rev. Susan said to me one time, "Well, I'm glad we have people of color so that when somebody who's a newcomer of color walks in, there's somebody to talk to them." And I said, "You know what, I feel anxious when you say that, because when somebody Asian walks through the door, I so don't want to talk to them. And it's not because I don't think Asians should be coming to the UUCP." I don't even know why it is. Part of it is the reaction to that whole internalization. I don't want just me and the new Asian to sit in the corner talking to each other. Now, Jeff Newman can do that. He's a different kind of guy. He doesn't have the internalized, subconscious anti-Asian feeling that I have. And that's the other thing I'm grateful for: that [being UU] has allowed me to really confront this in myself. I realize that all these times in my life when I was just ashamed of who I am were really not my fault. I mean, maybe it *is* my fault, but there were external reasons for it as well. It's not the white people telling you that you got to be like white people. It's the other Asian people telling you that you got to be like white people. It's my own mother!

Through all of these revelations, Jimmy has come to see how much Unitarian Universalists of color need pastoral care and spiritual direction designed specifically for them. Dr. Mark Hicks, the Angus MacLean professor of religious education at Meadville Lombard Theological School, has focused on developing just such resources, shifting the perspective in religious education from assuming that white participants will form the majority in any given program to centering the experiences of people of color. Although the need remains great, recent years have brought the development of more resources specifically designed for congregants and religious professionals of color. DRUUMM, LUUNA (the Latina/o Unitarian Universalist Networking Association), Black Lives of UU, and the annual Finding Our Way Home conferences provide community and opportunities for spiritual growth. Two books published in 2017—*Centering: Navigating Race, Authenticity, and Power in Ministry*, edited by Mitra Rahnema, and *Unitarian Universalists of Color: Stories of Struggle, Courage, Love, and Faith*, edited by Yuri Yamamoto, Chandra Snell, and Tim Hanami—offer stories written by Unitarian Universalists of color for colleagues and congregants of color. White readers can build their cross-racial understanding by reading these books too.

As Board president and as an active member during his years in Phoenix, Jimmy helps lead UUCP's antiracism and multicultural work. The slow progress of the congregation's multi-cultural work sometimes feels to him like confronting a wall, as we have seen in the conflict over the term *evangelical*. "The worst part of it is losing the hope. I don't know if this is ever going to happen," he laments. He doesn't realize how much he needs a place to lay down the burdens that he carries. "I didn't even know I was carrying those burdens around. I didn't know enough to be able to say to the people around me, 'We need to talk about this so we can unpack this, so we can unburden each other.'" Again, the congregation's capacity to engage in the tough conversations can determine whether leaders of color can stay with the congregation or will need to step away.

But Jimmy's gratitude for all that he has learned and experienced through Unitarian Universalism brings him back after he takes a restorative break. As an example of what the faith has offered him, he holds up a pivotal moment on his own journey toward understanding multicultural identity and accountability. At the 2012 General Assembly in Phoenix, he attends a workshop on multiculturalism. The room is packed. At one point, a participant at the open microphone uses the expression "Chinese water torture." Jimmy can't remember the context, but he can still see what happens next. Rev. Fred Small, then senior minister at First Parish in Cambridge, Massachusetts, goes up to the microphone and gently describes how and why that phrase is hurtful by perpetuating a stereotype of evil Asian characters.

"I was sitting in the back," Jimmy says, and when he sees Rev. Fred's actions, "something inside of me just clicks. I'm like, 'Oh, my God, I've never had this kind of experience.'" To see someone with authority, who doesn't look like Jimmy, standing up for him is revelatory. "I realize . . . that I couldn't have done that. I knew it bothered me, but I didn't have the skills to do that. I just ate it. And here's somebody saying, 'You don't have to eat that.' That was amazing."

In that moment, Jimmy feels his own consciousness raised about the impact of microaggressions. He experiences how an ally's or accomplice's response can help change the world.

SUMMING UP WITH A SUNLIT SOCIAL HOUR AT UUCP

UUCP, like all of our congregations on the journey toward multiculturalism and antiracism, is a work in progress. In fact, we know that this journey never ends. When we visit UUCP in 2015, we see that congregants may not share a common language around systems of power and privilege and the work of dismantling white supremacy culture. But a growing group of passionate champions, both white and of color, are leading the way, and the minister's enthusiastic support is a crucial element of the work. UUCP's history of long-term accountable relationships and its sheer capacity for warmth are huge gifts for its journey. Our brief visit gives us a taste of all these elements.

We attend Community Night on our very first evening in Phoenix—and our first encounter is with an older white man who assumes that Karin is Chinese. He begins to offer his own experiences with China as a way to connect with her. This is a microaggression—assuming and labeling someone rather than asking—with which Karin is so familiar that she barely even registers it. But it's an uncomfortable start. Later, as we ask a small group of white congregants about UUCP's multicultural mission and vision, those present don't feel a deep connection with it. Some seem uncomfortable with conversations about difference and power.

Yet in the days that follow, our conversations with staff members, congregants of color, and white allies and accomplices bring us the vivid stories we have shared in this chapter. The long arc of UUCP's journey toward multicultural Beloved Community rolls out before us. Our visit culminates with experiences in worship and the social hour that follows.

As the service ends on that bright November Sunday, the greeters fling open the glass doors from the sanctuary to the courtyard, and congregants stream out into the sunshine. Worship has featured a Bread Communion, an annual intergenerational harvest festival. Families and individuals have brought bread that represents their heritage: a grandmother's recipe or a traditional loaf from their family's country of origin, no matter how recently or how long ago the family emigrated. This multicultural celebration does not address the nuances of colonialism and postcolonialism, of privilege and disadvantage in different cultures. That's not its purpose. Instead, it honors the truth that all of us humans have our complex stories.

When the doors open, children race to the playground at the far end of the courtyard, still clutching slices of homemade banana bread, challah, or pan dulce. Jimmy Leung, now returned to worship after his time away, plays a pickup game of soccer with the youth, relishing the high energy of the moment.

Adults pause at the large standing panels in the middle of the patio, looking at the photos and text describing UUCP's engagement with Puente Arizona. Members of UUCP's Immigration Small Group Justice Ministry introduce congregants to Puente organizers who are here for the day. With newcomers, they share stories about the 2010 marches protesting SB 1070. More recent pictures show UUCP members offering childcare during Puente meetings downtown, as their partners have requested.

Inside the social hall UUCP spotlights the work of a different congregational team or committee each week. On this Sunday, two groups share the spotlight for the day. UUCP's Nominating Committee and the Immigration Small Group Justice Ministry have tables in adjacent corners. Congregational leaders purposefully set the two groups next to each other to show that inward-turning work like governance and outward-turning work like community building and social justice are both essential for keeping the congregation healthy and engaged.

Amid the usual chaos and noise of social hour, many congregants reach out to newcomers, including us, asking us about our project and our home congregations. Karin and Jimmy have a long conversation with a first-time Asian-American visitor. Nancy talks with Jeff Newman.

Later, on a bench shaded from the hot sun, Nancy interviews two UUCP children. Nancy Schwartz is the eleven-year-old daughter of Melissa Schwartz and Desira Amiday. Henry Frederick-Gray is the nine-year-old son of Rev. Susan and her minister-spouse Brian, who then serves a Christian Church—Disciples of Christ congregation in nearby Scottsdale. If being multicultural means being multigenerational, as one of our Common Threads holds, then what will these children say about the congregation's mission?

REV. NANCY: What does *multiculturalism* mean to you guys?

NANCY S.: Multiculturalism means having all races kind of fit into one place.

HENRY: Everybody being able to live together in peace.

REV. NANCY: How's the congregation doing along those lines?

NANCY S.: I've seen people from England, Ariza who's Native American, I don't remember his name but there's a tall African-American guy . . .

REV. NANCY: Sam Kirkland?

NANCY S.: Yes!

REV. NANCY: What do you think makes it possible for people to feel comfortable here, to be all in one place?

NANCY S.: I actually don't really know. Friendship? Treating well of others?

HENRY: I think it feels pretty nice to have a bunch of people around who are all, "I'm okay with you being different."

Though these two white children can't name exactly how the congregation teaches its ethic of radical inclusivity, they can feel its impact. Eventually we co-authors find an open space at one of the long tables in the social hall and sit down with Puente organizer María Cruz Ramirez for a conversation in Spanish about UUCP's partnership with Puente. María gets tears in her eyes when she remembers the demonstration at Sheriff Joe Arpaio's Tent City at the 2012 Justice General Assembly. To see "buses, buses, buses coming" from the convention center to the dark street just beyond the razor-wired fences of Tent City—"to see all these people, not necessarily undocumented, but documented people who want to help" arriving for that protest—is moving and powerful for her. "I want to say thank you because our problems are your problems, because even though you are from here, or you have documents, also our problems affect you, and all of us have to fight so they don't affect *anyone*" any more. There are many organizations that help Puente Arizona, she tells us, but the Unitarian Universalist Congregation of Phoenix is the only congregation that has become such an active partner.

Not everyone we speak with that Sunday can name ways that the congregation strives to fulfill its multicultural mission and vision, even with the Puente partnership so visible on this day. But the community's warmth, the congregants' eagerness to connect, and the presence of children threading their way through the clumps of adults create a lively, swirling energy for this social hour. Harnessing this energy, harvesting the gifts of its creative, determined past, and building on the foundations for multicultural, antiracist Beloved Community that it has already put in place—these steps will surely carry UUCP forward on its journey.

QUESTIONS FOR YOU AND
YOUR CONGREGATION

1. At UUCP, when the struggle for immigrants' rights becomes personal, the real work of building multicultural, antiracist Beloved Community can begin. What stories and experiences have made this work personal for your congregation or faith community?

2. Do members of your congregation work primarily in silos or in partnerships? What are the advantages and disadvantages of each of these approaches to doing social justice work and to building multicultural, antiracist Beloved Community?

3. Who in your congregation has a story to tell about a learning journey, much as Sandy Weir shares her story here? How can this kind of sharing become a spiritual practice for learning and change in your community?

4. Does your congregation have a tendency to see any one group as a monolith? How can you create possibilities for listening and sharing that will celebrate the exploration of difference?

CHAPTER FIVE

"A Fierce Conversation with Life"

ALL SOULS UNITARIAN CHURCH
TULSA, OKLAHOMA

Our church is an embodiment and celebration of the world as we hope it will one day become. A climate of profound hospitality, love, and acceptance radiates from our campus and our members. Our sanctuary is bursting with people from a diversity of theologies, philosophies, ethnicities, cultures, colors, classes, abilities, generations, sexual orientations, and political persuasions, all dwelling together in peace, seeking the truth in love, and helping one another.

—All Souls Unitarian Church, Centennial Vision 2021

[Now] we're all in this together, in this fierce conversation with life . . . And if these are the terms, then I want to be real, because I *have* to be real, and we *need* church.

—Pat Newman, All Souls congregant

IN THE UNITARIAN UNIVERSALIST WORLD, All Souls Unitarian Church in Tulsa, Oklahoma, is among our most famous congregations. In 2008, a Pentecostal congregation, largely Black, merges with the mostly white Unitarian Universalist congregation.

207

The story is recounted in newspaper and magazine articles, in radio broadcasts, and in the Netflix movie *Come Sunday*: Bishop Carlton Pearson's rise within evangelical Christianity, his leadership of a Pentecostal megachurch, then his conversion to a universalism that he calls the Gospel of Inclusion and the resulting departure of the majority of his congregation; his growing friendship with All Souls' senior minister, Rev. Marlin Lavanhar, as they explore and celebrate their common beliefs; the decision of All Souls' leadership to offer the remaining Pentecostal congregation worship space for free during the summer of 2008; and then the decision to merge the two congregations. The merger represents a kind of miracle in Unitarian Universalist and Pentecostal circles.

But it's not just All Souls' fame that sparks our desire to include a chapter about the congregation in this book. It is also our own curiosity. What happens after the merger, when all the press coverage dies down? What does the congregation look and feel like almost ten years later? What paths do these diverse congregants and leaders discover and create as they strive to build multicultural, antiracist Beloved Community? In this large congregation—the largest brick-and-mortar Unitarian Universalist congregation in the world—resources for staff and programming are not as tight as they are in smaller churches. Do we find our Common Threads weaving through the story even here, or does this story look different from all the others?

This chapter describes our exploration of these questions with All Souls and its people. Of our five chapters on congregations, this one, we confess, is most likely to show the ragged seams in our process. After all, All Souls' context and its trajectory do feel larger than life. Making choices about what to include and what to leave out is particularly hard here. We speak with a good-sized sampling of congregants and staff in person and over the phone. During our site visit, we connect with even more people through a wide variety of gatherings. Yet we can only include a fraction of these voices in the pages that follow.

Similarly, our reflections capture just a moment or two in time. Yet All Souls' congregational life—like that of all our congregations—moves and changes quickly, as the church community responds to events in both national and local arenas, deals with the deaths of beloved leaders and congregants, and adjusts its focus, methods, and messages to match the current moment. These changes are perhaps even more swift in this large congregation, which has enough resources to make a degree of nimbleness possible.

In light of these concerns, we find it particularly telling that our Common Threads shine through All Souls' story, as they do through our other congregations'. The stories we share here lift up a few of these threads that may inspire, provoke, or puzzle our readers, no matter what the size and location of their communities.

More than anything, we are struck by the tenderness of the work of building multicultural, antiracist Beloved Community in this large congregation. Most visitors to All Souls sense the congregation's liveliness and joy, and we do too, when we show up for worship there. But All Souls' leaders, including the ministers, have a much more nuanced experience. They feel in their bones the mistakes, misgivings, and miracles of this work. The vision of what the congregation might become feels personal to them; it demands all they have to give. A misrepresentation of congregational life can set the work back, as can their own stumbles in speech or action. Holding the needs, fears, hurts, and longings of such diverse congregants in their minds and hearts while still striving to move ever closer to the overarching institutional goal—it's an enormous task, often conducted in full view of a critical audience.

For all these reasons, we approach telling our own partial version of the story with an extra dose of humility. Yet we can't resist sharing the energy and enthusiasm we feel for what All Souls' journey can teach us all.

COMMON THREADS

Almost all the Common Threads that we have listed in chapter 2 show up in All Souls' story. Here are some of the most significant:

- **the power of intentionality**—Although the merger of Bishop Carlton Pearson's New Dimensions congregation with All Souls Unitarian Church occurs without much advance planning, the congregational leadership quickly recognizes the need for an overarching vision. The congregation's Centennial Vision 2021 explicitly names its goal of a sanctuary "bursting with people from a diversity of theologies, philosophies, ethnicities, cultures, colors, classes, abilities, generations, sexual orientations, and political persuasions, all dwelling together in peace, seeking the truth in love, and helping one another," and the invitation to the congregation to sign on to the vision statement—literally to sign the poster—helps root the early changes in a long-term process of transformation.
- **diverse and engaged leadership and diverse worship styles**—The diverse worship styles at All Souls deserve particular attention, since the congregation now includes a wide range of theologies. One of the worship services intentionally conveys a Pentecostal feel with a Universalist message, a style that Bishop Pearson calls "Unicostal." Diverse leadership and worship styles are visible and audible expressions of All Souls' vision for a multicultural, antiracist Beloved Community, and they may seem inevitable in light of the merger. But in truth, they take ever-renewed commitment, attention, and flexibility. All Souls' leadership continues to attend to these elements.

- **education for multicultural competencies and structures that institutionalize the multicultural commitment**—The details of All Souls' thoughtful programming and infrastructure, often revised to better build what leadership calls *intercultural* competencies, can provide valuable models for other congregations.

- **adaptability, patience, perseverance, courage, humility**— When such a large group of people strives to do something as countercultural as building antiracist community in Tulsa, they need every ounce that they can muster of these finer human virtues.

- **relationships, discomfort, conflict, and transformation**— Personal relationships drive every stage of the merger's story, from its first radical moves, through the inevitable discomfort and conflict, to the powerful transformations that many members and staff experience in this community.

- **work that is messy and never-ending, yet loving and life-giving**—All Souls' story shows how these Common Threads do not show up in a particular order—that's why we call them *threads* rather than *steps*. They interweave and sometimes tangle, get sorted out and grow stronger, then get tangled again. Leaders focus on one of these threads, then another, or they pick up several at a time. But the aliveness and love at All Souls sing out through the relationships we witness there and through its diverse worship services. We begin our story, then, with worship.

TRUTHS TOO BIG FOR ONE EXPRESSION

When we visit All Souls in January 2016, we make a point of attending all three Sunday morning worship services. Each has a distinct character and sound; each has its own religious language. All Souls' leaders offer these different forms of worship intentionally, knowing that in a large multicultural, antiracist Beloved Community such as theirs, congregants need many forms of religious expression. Yet all three services express the same core truths of this religion. And the different forms appeal to folks across differences in race, ethnicity, and culture, as the congregants present at each service that day show.

The Traditional Service at 10:00 A.M.

On Sunday, January 10, 2016, snow dusts the ground on the large campus of All Souls Unitarian Church and mounds on the beak of the penguin sculpture outside the religious education wing. Early arrivals for the first of the three worship services cross the parking lot gingerly, tightening scarves and buttoning coats as they try to avoid dark splotches of ice. It feels good to step inside the main door of the building that houses the sanctuary. The steam heat and the first set of greeters are equally warm.

At the welcome table, which stretches across the large central foyer directly in the path of the newcomer, a multiracial team of members offers nametags, pamphlets, and event flyers. The foyer bustles with families, couples, and singles making their way to worship.

Inside the sanctuary, the white walls, the high peaked ceiling, and the tall windows on each side and at the back of the chancel create a sense of spaciousness and quiet. People settle in the pews and listen to the prelude played on the organ from the choir loft at the back, then rise to sing the opening hymn. The ministers—senior minister Rev. Marlin Lavanhar, executive director Rev. Barbara Prose, assistant minister Rev. David Ruffin, and affiliate minister Rev. Gerald Davis—process in. The first three wear clergy robes and stoles, while Gerald wears his stole with a dark suit.

All Souls' website describes the Traditional Service as offering a "forward-looking, honest approach to faith in a world with diverse religious expressions and traditions. Our ministers draw from the wisdom of the world's great religions to make their messages relevant to our times, always leaving room for personal experience and particular understandings of God." The service mirrors the worship format handed down to Unitarian Universalists from our Protestant ancestors. The hymns come from *Singing the Living Tradition*, the gray 1993 hymnal that features many familiar Protestant tunes, though some of them have been given more inclusive Unitarian Universalist words. The choir, under the leadership of longtime director of music Rick Fortner, sings an anthem about ringing out the old and ringing in a happy new year, the arrangement rich with classical harmonies. There's a formal flow to the congregants' rising and sitting down, the reception of the offering and the invitation to prayer. Congregants—the majority are white, with biracial couples and other people of color scattered among them—can follow along in their printed order of service.

The announcements, though, reflect the liveliness of this large congregation: "Come help reassemble the float for the Martin Luther King Day Parade this afternoon! This year the theme is 'One Race: The Human Race,' and we are invited to wear something that represents our culture. Bring your Black Lives Matter and Get Out the Vote signs and join us on Monday, January 18." Tulsa's Martin Luther King Jr. Day Parade is the second largest in the nation, and All Souls has won the prize for best float several times in recent years.

Then, when Barbara takes the pulpit to preach, something in the atmosphere shifts ever so slightly.[4] Barbara, a white woman in her fifties, preaches with her whole body. Her arms spread wide to encompass the room or sweep to the side to mime setting aside

---

[4] At All Souls, the custom is to call ministers by their first name or by their title and last name.

214 MISTAKES AND MIRACLES

an idea to which she will return later. She uses ideas from Brené Brown's *Rising Strong* to talk about truth—this month's theme—and the hero's journey. She lays out the steps on this journey: "Be me; be all in; fall, get up, do it over again." "Say it with me," she calls out, and counts off the steps again. She scrunches down toward the pulpit to indicate a fall, then squints up with one eye to encourage everyone to see the world from a new angle when these inevitable falls happen.

When she cites a passage from Christian scripture—John 14:6, where Jesus says, "I am the way, the truth, and the life; no one comes to the Father except through me"—she gives it a progressive interpretation. In many conservative Christian readings, this passage is used to argue that Christianity is the only, or at least the best, way to salvation and a connection with the holy. But in Barbara's reading, Jesus is really calling for authenticity.

"If you're not you, how will you come to know your own capacity to love?" she asks. "If you're not you, how will you come to know your own God, the God that lives in you, the God that *is* you?" Rather than being a message of exclusivity, Jesus' words point to faith, courage, and a universal love. "If this way works for you, don't deny it," Barbara translates. "You are known and loved no matter what, but you'll only know that that love is true and real in your own life when you dare to be who you really are."

She cites Mahatma Gandhi saying the same thing: "Truth is God." Then she asks the congregation, "How will you express the truth that is you?" Mindful of the mix of theologies now present in All Souls' congregation, Barbara uses Christian scripture, but she feels free to expand and play with it to pull out a Universalist message.

She has a written text for her sermon, but her tone is conversational, and clearly she improvises some of the time. She calls to people in the pews by name and laughs with Rick Fortner, who sits up in the choir loft, about a question he asked that prompted a major turn in her message. When she encourages people to talk about the forbidden topic of shame, she invites them to shout "Shame!" Then she adds, "We better say this together too: Shame is a big fat liar!" The people in the pews, for the most part staring straight ahead and listening with solemn faces, robustly repeat the words with her.

All Souls' core message, summarized in its tag line "Love Beyond Belief," holds that people with a wide range of beliefs, drawing on all the world's religions along with the wisdom of science and of direct experience, can be united by love. The Traditional Service, as we discover on that January Sunday, offers a powerful, energized expression of this core message, set within a meditative container. The use of elegant music and the formal flow of worship elements create that container. Amid the formality, the worship leaders' more relaxed play brings a contemporary freshness to the whole experience.

The Point at 11:30 A.M.

At 11:30 on Sunday mornings, All Souls' members, friends, and visitors have a choice: they can go into the large social hall for the Humanist Hour, also called "The Point" (but never "worship" or even a "service"), or they can go to the sanctuary for the Contemporary Service. "We need not worship alike to love alike," All Souls' website proclaims. When we visit, we choose the gathering that speaks most directly to each of us: Karin goes to The Point, and Nancy goes to the Contemporary Service.

The Humanist Hour develops after the New Dimensions congregation has joined All Souls. In the early years after the 2008 merger, the Contemporary Service strives to speak to a wide variety of theologies: the Universalist Christianity of New Dimensions members, the atheism and agnosticism of many longtime members of All Souls, and many others. All Souls' leaders recognize that trying to be everything to everyone limits the full expression both of humanism and of the spirited "Unicostalism," or Neo-Pentecostalism, that New Dimensions adds.

In response, the leaders create the Humanist Hour and schedule it for the awkward time of 8:30 in the morning. For a couple of years, All Souls offers a full menu of three services every Sunday. But the Humanist Hour grows smaller and smaller, while the Contemporary Service continues to try to speak both to those who want spirited, embodied worship and to those who long for a more intellectual, quieter time but can't make it to church by 8:30 or 10:00 A.M.

In 2014, the ministers move the Humanist Hour to 11:30 A.M., allowing each of the later services to bloom into full expression. Now All Souls' website explains, "Our 'Humanist Hour' offers a variety of speakers, poets, and professors sharing reasoned commentary relevant to life in the here and now for those who want to be part of a community that welcomes questions, enjoys conversation, and cares deeply about ethics."

When Karin visits on that early January morning in 2016, one white male attendee sums up The Point like this: "No hymns, no prayers, no up-and-down stuff."

At one end of Emerson Hall, a stage rises a few feet from the floor. There is no pulpit in sight. Though spacious, the room is more intimate and less formal than the sanctuary. Stackable chairs set up in rows face the stage and soon fill with 150 people or more. Racial and ethnic diversity is less obvious at this service than at the others; most attendees on this Sunday are white. Onstage, Rick Fortner plays jazz piano at intervals throughout the forty-five-minute gathering.

Rev. David Ruffin offers the central talk. Wearing a suit but no stole, he perches on a tall chair onstage and refers to notes on his cell phone. At one point, David invites Rick to share the reading of a passage with him, but the text on the cell phone screen is too small for Rick to read. This dilemma gets a chuckle of recognition from the group gathered in the hall.

David tackles the theme of the month—truth—using popular and contemporary references. He draws on *The Big Short*, a 2015 film offering an acerbic look at the lies promulgated by Wall Street bankers and brokers that created the subprime mortgage crisis and led to the 2008 economic crash. He quotes the classic 1992 courtroom drama *A Few Good Men* in which Marine Colonel Jessup (played by Jack Nicholson) shouts at a young defense attorney, "You can't *handle* the truth!" David puts a fresh spin on the famous line, suggesting that we humans often don't want to handle the existential truth that we are not in control of how our lives unfold. How can we become comfortable with uncertainty? he asks.

Using completely different sources from those that Barbara references in the Traditional Service, David mines some of the same themes: life brings unexpected twists; we will fall, make mistakes, and have to recover; we have to work to remain true to ourselves; there are no easy answers. In this congregation, as in Unitarian Universalism as a faith, the very action of seeking the truth—wrestling with questions, thinking critically, using one's own experience and wisdom to discern personal and communal truths—is not only permitted but expected and encouraged.

The Contemporary Service at 11:30 A.M.

The band is already playing as people gather for the Contemporary Service in the sanctuary. Pastor David Smith, All Souls' executive director of worship, sits at a two-tiered electronic keyboard on the chancel. Members of the New Dimensions Chorale gather behind him and begin to hum or sing along. Many members of the chorale, almost all African American, have sung together for decades, beginning at Bishop Carlton Pearson's Higher Dimensions Pentecostal congregation, then moving with the

218 | MISTAKES AND MIRACLES

bishop to New Dimensions as his theology became more Universalist. Now they bring their gifts to All Souls.

Electric guitarists sit in folding chairs below Pastor David and just in front of the pews. Beside these musicians, a flat-topped tent creates a small enclosure just big enough for the drummer and the drum set, with a clear Plexiglass panel in front and gray plush carpet covering the tent's walls and roof. Ever since the New Dimensions congregation merged with All Souls in 2008, worship leaders and technicians have worked to adjust the volume of the music for this service, finding the balance between loud enough to sweep congregants up in the spirit and not so loud that folks in the foyer can't hear each other speak. This enclosure is designed to muffle the drum set just enough. The description on All Souls' website makes sure that newcomers will choose this experience for exactly what it is: "The Contemporary Service has electric instruments and is electrifying. For those who want an energetic and embodied experience of God, it draws primarily from the Christian tradition and includes praise, as well as popular music."

On this particular Sunday, the spirit is strong in the room. About 130 people—a multiracial, multigenerational mix—stand in their places in the pews, most of them singing along, some waving their arms in the air, clapping, dancing, or swaying. "You are the source of my strength!" The chorale punctuates Richard Smallwood's modern gospel hymn with a pause at the end of each phrase.

Later, chorale and congregation sing Bishop Joseph McCargo's "Father Me," first with the original lyrics—"Father, wrap me in your arms and father me"—and then as "Mother, wrap me in your arms and mother me." Just as the volume is often readjusted, Pastor David Smith and the chorale keep adjusting the hymns' language to match this service's marriage of Pentecostal spirit with Universalist theology.

Once All Souls' leaders move The Point to 11:30, Marlin reflects, "The Contemporary Service has the opportunity to become everything we've wanted it to become." Enthusiasm infuses his voice as he describes the evolution. "Now it's for folks who really want that kind of Unicostal service within a free liberal religious Unitarian Universalist context."

The Contemporary Service, he explains, is "improv and worship all at the same time, a seventy-five- to ninety-minute container in which we are trying to create a deep transformative spiritual experience for folks, and we know what tools we have, and we're just going to get in there and see. With the praise music, David is testing: Is it alive? Is there something happening here? Is it ministering, is it healing? If the energy is not moving the way we want it to, he will move into the invocation and we'll keep trying until we find that energy, and then we'll go with it."

On this January Sunday, Pastor David senses the energy rising strong through the praise music. He allows it to go on for over half an hour, yet it doesn't feel that long. Then he calls Barbara forward to give a quick impromptu testimony about an upcoming event. In a side conversation, he and Marlin decide to drop an anthem and move Rev. Gerald's prayer to a different spot. Congregants go with the flow; there is no order of service binding the worship to a particular sequence.

When Caitlin Turner, chair of All Souls' youth group, offers the welcome and announcements, she too reflects the energy—what she calls the "fierce holiness"—she can feel in the room. Caitlin, who is white, tells the congregation that she likes to start a favorite hymn, "When Your Heart Is in a Holy Place," with a change to one word in the first chorus: instead of "holy," she sings, "when your heart is in a *lonely* place." So many people feel isolated and lonely as they first arrive for worship. But, she says, "the song still ends the same way. And I promise: You will leave here in a holy place!" The acknowledgment that folks arrive for this spirited service in all states of mind and heart provides a welcome for those not yet feeling "lifted up." Caitlin's promise that everyone attending will experience a transformation opens up that possibility for all.

When Marlin begins to preach, he perches on a high stool, wearing jeans and a gray print shirt. He knows his material and can speak without notes. He has preached a different version of this sermon at the Traditional Service the week before, but today he grounds the message in a biblical passage, the same one that Barbara has used earlier that morning. He gives it his own twist, titling his sermon "Is Jesus the *Only* Way, Truth, and Life?"

"Religion is supposed to bring us together, but it ends up breaking us apart," Marlin mourns. Differences in belief have served as excuses for wars and pogroms. Instead, he suggests, "how we deal with differences in belief is an indication of our capacity to love." The congregation recites its covenant every Sunday, which includes the promise "to seek the truth in love." Marlin spells out the meaning of this phrase: "Instead of going after the truth in ways that divide us, we go after it in love, because we know that love is more important than truth." This idea might cause more intellectually focused Unitarian Universalists to raise their eyebrows. But Marlin feels assured that those attending the Contemporary Service will remember that Jesus' whole ministry focuses on love, asking us to love one another, to love God, even to love our enemies.

And what does Jesus' instruction imply for how we are to live? "If we're ever going to understand God and truth, we not only have to come at it with our own experience, we need to be open to hearing other people's experiences," Marlin explains. Understanding people who see and interpret the world differently than we do is necessary for building our capacity for love itself.

Marlin invites the congregants to reach out to people with whom they have major religious differences. Talk with them, he urges, by asking not "what do you believe, but what do you *love?*" Ask them to share their experiences, and then listen in love.

He ends the sermon with a sincere "God bless you. I love you. Amen." The music swells again as worship draws to a close.

The main messages in both the Traditional and the Contemporary services feel directly applicable not just to each listener's personal life but also to a congregation that is trying to unite around so much diversity. Fall down, see the world from a fresh perspective, get up again. Be willing to risk making mistakes and to keep adapting as everyone learns from them. That's a Common Thread for building multicultural, antiracist Beloved Community. Another is to find a mission to which all can sign on, transcending individual beliefs. Marlin captures that Common Thread when he says that love is more important than belief.

Although it is held in the large formal sanctuary, the Contemporary Service feels intimate. Several times throughout its ninety minutes, worship leaders ask congregants to turn to each other and offer words of greeting and affirmation. The warmth and enthusiasm are palpable. The service draws not just former members of New Dimensions but also newer attendees at All Souls. Jim Cunningham and Brian Cordova, partners who are white and who come from different religious backgrounds, start showing up when they hear Bishop Carlton Pearson is going to preach. Now they wouldn't miss a Sunday. As Caitlin Turner predicts, congregants leave the Contemporary Service feeling the "fierce holiness" of that time and place.

The Same Message in Three Languages

When Rev. Fred Small, then senior minister at First Parish in Cambridge, first hears in 2013 about All Souls' three worship services, he asks how a congregation with three very different

222 | MISTAKES AND MIRACLES

worship styles can be a single community. "Isn't that like a family where everyone is in separate rooms watching a different TV show?" he asks.

"No," an All Souls staff member replies. "They're watching the *same* TV show in three different languages!"

We walk away from the three services on January 10, 2016, with just that feeling. Karin, the scientist-engineer, captures the experience in a metaphor close to her language of the soul. When she projects a three-dimensional image in two dimensions, the object's appearance depends on the angle of the projection. The viewer can only see a part of it at a time. "God, Mystery, Love is too big to be captured from only one angle," she says. "The truth lies in a higher dimension"—and together we burst out laughing at her unintentional pun.

Across the different sources and texts the ministers use on that Sunday morning, a complex commitment transcends the different angles on truth that they explore. All three services urge us listeners to search for our human truths in an uncertain world, to honor our individual differences, and to embody the unifying and transforming power of love.

At one point, All Souls' website amplifies its usual tag line, "Love Beyond Belief," with these words in bold block letters: "DIVERSE IN BELIEF, UNITED BY LOVE." Whether gathering in the sanctuary or in the social hall, congregants express a love for the community of All Souls and what they experience within it, and they demonstrate that love through the warmth of their welcome and outreach to strangers and congregants across a wide range of identities.

Still, the journey toward such unity is ongoing. When New Dimensions and All Souls first merge in 2008, some longtime All Souls members ask, "How could this 'Unicostalism' possibly be considered Unitarian Universalist?" It isn't just the form of worship—the clapping, moving, and handwaving to music louder

than usual—that concerns these folks, but the very language of
the service, with "God" and "Jesus" and "Spirit" showing up in
songs and sermons alike. Some members leave over these differences; others continue to puzzle over them.

Marlin, working with staff, takes a new approach to the conversation in a 2015 congregational survey. As in earlier such
surveys, congregants are asked to check boxes identifying their
theological beliefs; as always, they can check as many boxes as
apply. But this time, alongside "humanist," "Buddhist," "pagan,"
and many other affiliations, the survey includes the options of
"Unitarian Christian" and "Universalist Trinitarian Christian."

"Just having that box," Marlin says, "was like saying, 'You
belong. You can be a Trinitarian in this church. You're a Universalist? That's fine.' It told our Neo-Pentecostal members they
belong, and it told everyone else that's a legitimate category." The
survey itself is a helpful intervention for building an inclusive
multifaith congregation, "united in love."

"We need not worship alike to love alike." Indeed, the people
in all three services express their love for this place and its mission
and vision, and they demonstrate this common way of being in
their warm welcome to both familiar and unfamiliar faces that
morning. Yet the struggle to find ways to come together as one
body remains. What All Souls is trying to do flies in the face of
Tulsa's longstanding and intransigent segregation. We need some
understanding of that background in order to fathom the size of
the change that All Souls wants to embody.

THE TULSA RACE-RIOT MASSACRE
AND THE FOUNDING OF ALL SOULS

At the heart of the story of race in Tulsa lies a violent experience
that explodes and then gets silenced. All Souls' history is inti-
mately tied to this story.

On the evening of May 31, 1921, hundreds of white people from South Tulsa rage through the prosperous Greenwood district in North Tulsa, an area that Booker T. Washington dubbed the "Black Wall Street." Over the course of a night and a day, the mob kills as many as three hundred Black citizens, burning some of them alive. They loot and burn to the ground the neighborhood's businesses and homes, leaving some ten thousand people homeless. When the National Guard arrives, they imprison thousands of Black citizens while the white rioters escape arrest. The rampage is the worst race riot in the history of the United States. It is, in fact, a massacre.

What sparks the conflagration that day? Local news sources, including the *Tulsa Tribune*, owned by Unitarian Richard Lloyd Jones, report that a young African-American man has assaulted a seventeen-year-old white elevator operator in a downtown office building. "Nab Negro for Attacking Girl in Elevator," the *Tribune*'s headline trumpets. The charges are later proved false, but the rumor is enough to ignite the racial hatred simmering under the surface.

More than a year before the riot, Jones, son of prominent Unitarian minister Jenkin Lloyd Jones, has gathered likeminded liberal religious folks in his home. In March 1921, just weeks before the massacre, he signs the charter for All Souls Unitarian Church and begins fundraising for its first building.

Jones is a complicated figure. At this time, the Ku Klux Klan claims a wide membership in Tulsa. His newspaper neither endorses nor condemns the Klan, although on at least one occasion it publishes praise for the group: "The KKK of Tulsa has promised to do the American thing in the American way." Jones himself supports some liberal causes, helps to purchase Abraham Lincoln's birthplace in order to preserve it, and marries Georgia Hayden, a passionate advocate for women's suffrage and Planned Parenthood. Family lore claims that Richard and Georgia, like their neighbors, harbor endangered Black families in their home during the race riot itself. However, after its initial article (and, possibly, an editorial reporting a plan to lynch the young Black man), the *Tulsa Tribune* never mentions the matter again. It says nothing about the riot-massacre that follows or about the eventual clearing of the young man. Richard Jones's own grandson doesn't see that 1921 headline until almost ninety years later.

Indeed, an almost universal silence descends. The story of the riot-massacre is rarely told, not taught, and almost never publicly acknowledged; both white and Black people are reluctant to mention the event for decades. Some Black matriarchs tell their grandchildren, "We pretend it didn't happen."

Rev. Gerald Davis, who is African American, now serves as minister at the Church of the Restoration and affiliate minister at All Souls. In 1971, on the fiftieth anniversary of the 1921 race-riot massacre, he is enrolled at the University of Tulsa. For a paper on using primary sources, he decides to interview one of the riot's survivors. When we talk with him in 2015, he says that the survivor must have been expecting a white student to show up at her door. But "when this Black man shows up," he tells us, "she says, 'Baby, leave this alone. Don't you write about this.' She was worried about my safety," Gerald explains. "She wanted me to graduate unimpeded."

SILENCE AND CIVIL RIGHTS

When Rev. Dr. John Wolf arrives to serve as senior minister at All Souls in 1960, he too hears the prohibition against talking about the race riot. "Well," he laughs, "don't tell a Unitarian minister you can't talk about something!" John, who is white, reaches out to survivors of the massacre, records oral histories, and preaches on it. He breaks through the silence, at least within All Souls' walls.

He also focuses on building relationships with local clergy, Black and white. When in 1965 Rev. Dr. Martin Luther King Jr. invites faith leaders to join him for the march from Selma to Montgomery, Alabama, Tulsa clergy wonder how best to respond. John suggests that they should bring the Civil Rights Movement to Tulsa, instead of going farther south. "Why would we go there when Tulsa had the biggest race riot in the country?" he asks his colleagues.

They are in Tulsa when they learn of the brutal murder in Birmingham of Rev. James Reeb, a white Unitarian minister who has joined the Selma civil rights protesters and is beaten to death by white thugs after he dines in an African-American neighborhood. In response, All Souls hosts an interfaith worship service. Seventy clergy from different religions serve as ushers. A Baptist pastor and a Catholic priest offer the readings, and a rabbi preaches. "The whole town shows up," John exclaims. "Such a thing has never happened before in Tulsa!" After the service, participants march to city hall. Religious leaders, who remain largely silent after the 1921 massacre, are determined to be on the right side of history this time.

The multicultural, multiracial relationships that John builds during the Civil Rights Movement mark a turning point in All Souls' history and plant the seeds for the congregation's engagement with the wider community. During John's thirty-five-year tenure as senior minister, portions of All Souls' worship services show up on cable television almost every day. Its justice activities gain front-page newspaper coverage. All this attention demystifies Unitarian Universalism for the congregation's more conservative religious neighbors, as well as for Tulsans who had sometimes mistaken the liberal religion for a cult. The congregation becomes a powerful force in town, and it begins to develop some cross-racial relationships.

"WHITE ON THE OUTSIDE AND WHITE ON THE INSIDE"

At the same time, racial segregation remains a defining characteristic of Tulsa's demographics. John remembers the presence of some Persians and Arab Americans, along with a number of indigenous people, in the congregation in the 1960s, but "very very few Blacks." When he asks his friend Rev. Benjamin Harrison Hill, an African Methodist Episcopal (AME) minister, why All Souls fails to attract African Americans despite its clear solidarity, Rev. Hill famously replies, "John, that church is white on the outside *and* white on the inside."

John, knowing the importance of visible diverse leadership for building multiracial community, asks Benjamin, who is not then serving a congregation, to come help change All Souls. But the AME minister says simply, "I can't do it." If a Black person were to come to All Souls while still retaining professional connections or social ties on the city's predominantly Black north side, they would lose everything, no matter how successful their practice in medicine, law, or business. Such is the state of segregation in Tulsa in those days. Only recently have such divisions begun to blur.

Facing these entrenched separations, John and congregational leaders decide to bring Unitarian Universalism to North Tulsa. In 1987 they launch the Church of the Restoration in the Greenwood district. Since its inception, African-American ministers have served the Church of the Restoration, in covenant with All Souls.

Again, the power of relationships makes the establishment of this church a little easier. A Baptist church, with a largely African-American congregation, stands across the street from the building that the Church of the Restoration will use. John says to his African-American friend who pastors the Baptist church, "Here we come!" And John's friend replies warmly, "Come right ahead." For a while, the Baptists and the Unitarians share the Baptists' parking lot, greeting each other after their respective services. These small steps toward relationships, familiarity, and reconciliation mark All Souls' first intentional gestures toward multicultural ministries.

All of these historical events, then, form strands in All Souls' DNA:

- the longstanding racial tensions that erupt in white-on-Black violence in 1921 and the unclear role of a founding member of All Souls in those events
- the way the race-riot massacre becomes a taboo subject, hanging for decades like an unacknowledged cloud over the city
- Rev. Dr. John Wolf's determined leadership in breaking through racial and cultural barriers, disrupting the silence around the race-riot massacre, and forming interfaith coalitions that work for civil rights
- the intentional building of cross-racial relationships, inspiring congregants to take risks and to start a new congregation in North Tulsa with an African-American minister

These chapters in All Souls' history don't disrupt Tulsa's deep segregation, but they do begin to shift the culture of the congregation itself. It will take a tragedy at All Souls—an event both deeply personal and profoundly communal—to break hearts open throughout the city. This ragged broken-openheartedness, some congregants believe, is what ultimately makes the hard and heartfelt work of the merger possible.

A TRAGIC INITIATION INTO A FIERCE CONVERSATION WITH LIFE

Rev. Marlin Lavanhar arrives at All Souls in 2000, a young white man of thirty-one, called to serve as the new senior minister.

Marlin, his spouse Anitra, and their son Elias settle into Tulsa. In 2003, Anitra gives birth to their daughter Sienna, and the congregation shares the family's joy.

But just three years later, in a tragedy that rocks the whole city, Sienna dies suddenly from a virus that has been impossible to detect. Marlin tells the *Tulsa World* newspaper that the outpouring of love and support for his family from Tulsans of every faith and denomination has been comforting to them in the midst of their despair. "A tragedy like this touches all of us as human beings and transcends all differences of religion and theology," Marlin says. "It feels like a small town and as if the entire town is grieving with us."

All Souls' sanctuary is packed to overflowing for the celebration of Sienna's life. Every family in the congregation who has lost a child makes sure to be there.

Longtime All Souls member Jane Newman (she and her spouse Pat are both white) describes the impact of Sienna's death on the whole congregation: "It takes us *down to the ground* as a church. We go to a place like, oh my God, this is so painful, this is so real. It changes the church for anyone who was really in there."

Pat goes on, "I see everybody's face in a different way. If these are the terms [of life], then I want to be real, because I *have* to be real, and we *need* church."

The grief the congregation feels and the suffering they experience with their minister and his family break through some internal cultural barriers. White upper-middle-class liberal environments in the United States, even religious communities, often value looking as though everything is all right and not expressing a full range of feelings, especially pain. Most of the white folks in Unitarian Universalist communities no longer explicitly hold to the old British emphasis on maintaining a "stiff upper lip" in the face of adversity, but this cultural habit gets planted deep in the soil of the early white colonists, our Unitarian ancestors. It runs through the religion's DNA.

Such habits create a barrier for those who don't share the same background or temperament. Unitarian Universalists of color and those from working-class backgrounds have reported feeling put off or shut out by the "polished" or "perfect" appearance and manners of the white upper-middle-class people in their congregations. It can be tough for those in the dominant group to acknowledge this atmosphere, but newcomers from other groups may notice it right away.

In *Centering: Navigating Race, Authenticity, and Power in Ministry*, Rev. Natalie Maxwell Fenimore recalls how her earlier religious tradition invited members to "stand, in the midst of people, and speak your pain out loud. We call the pain into the room, and everybody in the room is called to attend to it. That is what unity is. That is what church is. . . . 'Church' is about building places where we can process pain and struggle as well as love and celebration."

Sienna's death breaks down the emotional and cultural barriers at All Souls. It brings a depth of pain and struggle into the heart of congregational life. Members wake up, Pat Newman says, to the fact that "we're all in this together, in this fierce conversation with life." After that, "being a middle-class gated community doesn't make any sense."

Jane adds, "I think that loss was some of the"—Pat offers the word *initiatory*—"the initiatory experience that creates the capacity to go into this journey [of building multicultural community] and to stay with it."

All Souls' prominence in the wider community, the web of relationships that its ministers have formed, Marlin's own broken-openheartedness in the face of this loss—all these elements help prepare the congregation for the great risky enterprise it will soon launch. Even more important, grief brings this congregation into deep communion with a sense of life's urgency and interconnectedness. As Pat Newman says, now they "*have* to be real, and we *need* church."

THE MERGER AND ITS
IMMEDIATE AFTERMATH

Bishop Carlton Pearson first comes to fame as an African-American Pentecostal minister serving Higher Dimensions Evangelistic Center, a multiracial megachurch of some six thousand members. Then, in 1996 while watching images from the Rwandan genocide on television, he has a vision of universal salvation and begins to preach what he calls the Gospel of Inclusion. Mentored in his youth by white evangelical leader Oral Roberts, who dubs him his "Black son," the bishop ends up being declared a heretic by the Joint College of African-American Pentecostal Bishops in 2004. As a result, Bishop Pearson loses thousands of congregants, along with the massive campus where they worshiped. NPR's *This American Life* devotes an entire hour to his story in 2005, and in 2018 the feature film *Come Sunday* dramatizes this part of the bishop's life.

Marlin reaches out to Bishop Pearson when he hears of the bishop's troubles, and they begin to build a friendship over monthly lunches. They realize how much they have in common theologically, for the bishop's Gospel of Inclusion is Universalism at its core. Years later, Bishop Pearson tells us how he had once assumed that All Souls harbored the devil. But as he gets to know Marlin, he comes to see the community as "very solid, very comfortable, very grounded in who they are: rebels but not radicals. Still, if it's going to be *All* Souls, that doesn't mean all *white* souls, or all *rich* souls, or all *non-Pentecostal* souls, or even all agnostics—it's just *all souls*. The word is *nefesh*, all living sentients, people that are alive and animated."

The bishop's observation reflects a reality. At the time that he and Marlin meet, All Souls is not living up to its name. In the spring of 2008, the All Souls staff conducts a survey among the congregation's members and friends, and more than 90 percent of respondents say they long for more multiculturalism and diversity in their church. They have no idea how to get there.

A few months later, in the summer of 2008, Rev. Lavanhar offers Bishop Pearson and New Dimensions, the bishop's new congregation of about two hundred people, the use of All Souls' sanctuary for free at 11:30 A.M. on Sundays. The lively Neo-Pentecostal service begins drawing All Souls' members too. "Why are they even interested?" the bishop wonders at first. Then he realizes that in those early days, among both the All Souls and the "New D" congregants, "there seem to be no blockages—just curiosity, openness, and intrigue on both sides."

Bishop Pearson, though, brings his own concerns. Interestingly, he is not worried about the multiracial mix; he looks at Rev. Wolf's civil rights activism and assumes that All Souls is ready to welcome an influx of Black people. Rather, he worries about All Souls' and New D's different cultures. Will the volume at that 11:30 A.M. worship service be too loud? Will the singing go on too long? Will the praise music keep people standing longer than is comfortable? These elements are central to New D's charismatic Pentecostal culture but foreign to All Souls.

"It's always a delicate balance when you care about the culture you're trying to *create*. Not *sustain*," he emphasizes; "we were trying to *create* a new thing. *Compromise* is the key word, which to me means co-promise—you promise to offend as little as possible, and I promise to become as little defensive as possible."

It's only natural that such worries underlie the initial enthusiasm and hope.

Before that summer, the second worship service on Sunday morning had been a repeat of the first. Many longtime congregants expect that it will return to that form after the summer ends—but it does not. It continues to feature the music of Pastor David Smith and the New D Chorale. Some All Souls members begin to murmur about their discomfort.

During that first year following the merger, Bishop Pearson and his family attend worship, and the bishop preaches occasionally at All Souls. Then, in 2009, he answers a call to a church in Chicago. For the next few years, until he returns and becomes a member of the staff, these two congregational cultures will strive to merge without him as a guide. For New D worshipers who have stuck with the bishop through thick and thin, his absence adds to the strain.

Nicole Ogundare, who has sung with the New Dimensions Chorale for decades and now serves on All Souls' staff as ministry and life events coordinator, remembers the magnitude of the change. All Souls has had a long history of working for the benefit of others in the wider community, but now the need for transformation has moved right into the building. "It's one thing for you to just put your dollars in or to do the justice-outreach thing," Nicole says, describing the congregation before the merger. "It's another when [those community members] bring their suitcase in, they put their clothes in your drawer, and they're not leaving!"

"It was very telling and revealing for me," she tells us later, "to have people say they supported racial justice and would talk about John Wolf protesting, marching, sitting at counters, etc., and then not have the ability to be tolerant of (let alone celebrate) Black folk and their culture under the roof of All Souls."

Bishop Pearson's recollection of those early days mirrors Marlin's and Nicole's:

> We *knew* we were invading. We were invited, but even the invitation was an invasion. And we were very aware of that. . . . David, who was our minister of music—well, he was key. I was just another speaker, and there wasn't a steady diet of me, but because David was there every week, it was a steady diet of his brand of worship presentation and the genre. He was trying to delicately keep the 120 or so of our people who came satisfied, yet not offend the hundreds who were already there.

He didn't want to become *more* invasive. He was between a rock and a hard place trying to satisfy everybody.

When we came, it was harder for some of the folks at All Souls than for us. Black folks are used to being rejected, so it didn't traumatize us or damage us. We didn't freak out: "I survived my job, so I'm gonna survive this church."

But we don't want to survive. We want to *arrive*, and we want to *thrive!* We want to go from *toleration* to *celebration!*

When we speak with Bishop Pearson in 2016, we can hear the passion in his voice as he lifts up these memories. The longing for the move "from toleration to celebration" and for thriving, not merely surviving, feels fresh and current in the ongoing story of race relations in the United States in the twenty-first century.

In truth, after the merger there is discomfort on both sides. Some longtime All Souls members, most of them white and some of them major contributors, withdraw their membership or withhold their pledges. Some longtime members of New Dimensions and Higher Dimensions leave too. It is only then, as Rev. Gerald Davis puts it, that this experiment moves "from possibility . . . to excitement . . . to *the work.*"

The unexpectedness of the merger makes the news at first. As Rev. Gerald says, most congregants feel excited and proud of the audaciousness of this move. But the honeymoon period quickly shifts into a much more complicated process of relationship testing. This is indeed when the real work of building multicultural, antiracist Beloved Community begins. Once more, All Souls, with its newest members from New Dimensions, finds itself in a "fierce conversation with life."

THREE CONGREGATIONS—AT LEAST

In the first three years of the merger, All Souls offers its three services at distinct times—the Humanist Hour at 8:30 A.M., the

Traditional Service at 10:00, and the Contemporary Service at 11:30. Whichever minister is preaching that day uses the same sermon for all three services.

"Some people, longtime members [of All Souls], would come out of services saying, 'All we ever hear about anymore is Jesus and the Bible. What's happening to our church?'" Marlin remembers. "Former New Directions folks would go, 'We never hear about Jesus anymore. We used to hear about the Bible all the time, but now we never hear it since we came to All Souls.' But it was the same exact sermon!"

People's discomfort with change can influence what they hear and see. The sense that they are not getting enough of what they already know and love is painful. Worship becomes a kind of "Rorschach test," as Marlin puts it, for people's expectations, theologies, and capacity to deal with change.

Rev. Dr. John Wolf says that there is always "more than one congregation" operating within a religious community of any size. The particular interests of different groups influence how the members of those groups engage, what they perceive, and how they tell the story of the congregation as a whole.

By the summer of 2009, a year into this experiment, All Souls contains at least three congregations, with different feelings about the merger with New Dimensions. One group—by far the majority—embraces All Souls' new identity, even with its awkwardnesses and discomforts.

A second group consists of those who have joined the congregation during that first year. Most of these new members have been drawn in by the lively spirit and celebratory nature of the Contemporary Service. They only know All Souls in this new incarnation, and they are enthusiastic participants.

And the third group comprises some longtime All Souls members—committed, influential, "foundational" members, Marlin calls them—who ask, "Are we done yet? Can we have our church back?" Some of these folks want to know, "Why are we making race such a big deal? The environment is a bigger deal." They wonder why All Souls is spending its congregational resources on trainings in issues of race and culture, and why the ministers prioritize getting people from different backgrounds into leadership positions on the Board and other committees.

Just as they interpret the worship services differently, so too congregants form their own stories about the larger direction of the congregation. The rumors swirl in conflicting directions. Marlin looks back on what he hears during this period with both wonder and humor. We can sense the pressure he experiences during these early stages of the work when, as he puts it, "we're into the fray and some of the conflict, *and* we're into the amazing beauty and life it brings to us." He goes on,

> Prior to the assent of people that this is the direction we're trying to take, it looked like it was just me, so it could feel like a takeover. "This is the senior minister who is trying to do this." There's a group of people who say, "Marlin's just doing this because in the Unitarian Universalist Association, this is like the Holy Grail, to have a multicultural church. Marlin's just doing this to make a name for himself nationally, and he's ruining the church."
>
> And other people are saying, "Marlin's trying to pull us *out* of the UUA; he's trying to build a megachurch. He doesn't even care about Unitarian Universalism, he just wants to build a big church for his own ego," or whatever reason they said I was doing it.
>
> On the other side, you had people who were like, "This church is a really wealthy church. It's just run by people who can give big money. Marlin's beholden to these people with a lot of money and that's why things aren't moving faster," versus "All Marlin cares about any more is bringing in, it seems like, a lot of poor people and people of color; that's where he

spends all his time and attention, he doesn't even care about us anymore."

It was ironic that different people were making completely opposite assumptions about what I was doing.

In Marlin's descriptions of those early days following the leap that All Souls has made, we hear his compassion for people struggling with their distress over unaccustomed change, even though that distress tends to lead them to target him. We hear the familiar story of people projecting responsibility for their discomfort onto the "leader's" moves and motives. The tenderness of this time—the range of hurt feelings and of sometimes-hurtful words—is fiercely poignant and oh-so-human.

Then, in the summer of 2009, Marlin calls a group of congregants together across the spectrum of these opinions. Some show up wanting the congregation to return to the way it was before the merger. They are pretty sure that theirs is the majority view. But when they see and hear most of the people in the room, including other longtime members, express their enthusiasm for All Souls' new identity, the first group realizes that there is no going back. They recognize that they need to "get busy." Marlin remembers this as a moment of conversion. These congregants, he says, feel "we better make this work, because if it doesn't work, this church is going to explode in a negative way." These members, who have felt such a sense of loss and discomfort, reconnect with all that they love about their congregation and determine to help it to thrive.

The discomfort that the merger causes could lead to a congregational split, or it could lead to renewed commitment. These longtime members opt for the latter. The heartbeat of this congregation, strengthened over years of engagement in the community and made tender by its proximity to tragedy—a heartbeat now mirrored in the faithfulness of its New D members—calls most of its people to stay and do the work.

THE POWER OF VISION 2021

Even so, the size of the change throws All Souls into a kind of identity crisis. The leaders call in a consultant, who suggests that what the congregation needs is a new shared vision. All Souls' Board and staff spend the second year after the merger gathering with groups of twenty to thirty congregants, asking each group the same questions in the same order and facilitating a conversation about what kind of community they want to create together. The facilitators hand over all the raw data to Marlin, and he, in consultation with the other leaders, drafts All Souls' 2021 Centennial Vision.

It begins:

> Our church is an embodiment and celebration of the world as we hope it will one day become. A climate of profound hospitality, love, and acceptance radiates from our campus and our members. Our sanctuary is bursting with people from a diversity of theologies, philosophies, ethnicities, cultures, colors, classes, abilities, generations, sexual orientations, and political persuasions, all dwelling together in peace, seeking the truth in love, and helping one another.

The document goes on to describe the specific goals that will help All Souls reach this vision by its hundredth birthday—the same year that Tulsa will acknowledge the hundredth anniversary of the race-riot massacre.

On Homecoming Sunday 2010, All Souls' leadership unveils Vision 2021. They print it on a huge poster and hang it in the sanctuary where everyone will see it as they walk in. During that Homecoming service, they invite congregants to sign the vision statement before they leave. Since then, as new members join, they too sign their names to Vision 2021.

The new vision guides All Souls' leaders and holds them accountable to its fulfillment. It also liberates and empowers them. "Any steps that we take," Marlin tells us, "as long as I can show that this is following the vision, no one can say, 'This isn't UU, this isn't All Souls.' No, we all agreed. This is how we're choosing to try to make this real. We can argue over strategy, but we can't argue over direction. This is the community we're trying to create: democratic, artistic, theologically free, covenant-based, inclusive, diverse, compassionate, loving, etc. If you're trying to create this kind of community, this kind of world, then you're in the right place. Stick around and help us do it."

Most people do stay after Vision 2021 sets the course. Long-time members resonate with its language, which Marlin sums up as "open and democratic and free." Those who want to build an "intercultural community that shares its resources and power among people with a true intention of not having a dominant culture" also see their aspirations spelled out.

Establishing a mission and vision that explicitly state the congregation's commitment to creating multicultural, antiracist Beloved Community is one of the Common Threads for this work. At All Souls, Vision 2021 communicates that, even though conflict over differences of opinion and desires will always exist, the congregation covenants to unite in working toward this shared goal. The vision sets free the energy that had been trapped by discontent. It funnels that energy into the work of personal and spiritual growth and into ever-evolving institutional experiments and adjustments on the journey. This is the power of an explicit statement of a congregation's intent.

The next sections offer a look at how this freed-up energy gets deployed. Here we see how other Common Threads show up in this story:

- **trainings in multicultural competencies and antiracism—** These transform staff as well as congregants. They make cross-racial relationships possible.

- **flexibility**—Leaders need to be willing to adapt the congregational structures that help to support and institutionalize this work. All Souls' willingness to shift its approaches as it learns from mistakes and responds to changing needs is a great gift.

- **tolerance for conflict**—Conflict is inevitable. Reconciliation is almost always a work in progress.

- **staying the course, recognizing that the work never ends, relishing the joy and life it brings alongside the difficulties**— These fundamental commitments create the culture shift that makes multicultural, antiracist Beloved Community possible.

Some of the details in these sections may inspire specific steps or adaptations in our readers' own communities. Taken as a whole, they demonstrate the value of persistence.

TRAINING AND TRANSFORMATION

Rev. Barbara Prose arrives at All Souls in 2011, a year after Vision 2021 is put in place. She has heard the dramatic stories about the merger with New Dimensions three years earlier, and she assumes that the congregation must be pretty far along in its antiracism work. But as she settles in, she begins to understand how new the work and the merged community still feel to leaders and congregants alike. She is in time to witness and participate in the intentional move toward deeper training and understandings. In fact, she experiences her own transformation in the process.

When we speak with Barbara in 2016, she identifies as a "white, cisgender, able-bodied woman." But she admits that she has only come to recognize the impact of her whiteness through the antiracism and intercultural journey she has taken with All

Souls. The daughter of Lithuanian Jews on her father's side and a French Catholic mother, she didn't feel American or Protestant enough in her surroundings—not compared to the WASP (white Anglo-Saxon Protestant) norms at her Boston high school. "I was definitely raised in a white bubble in the suburbs of Boston," Barbara remembers, "and I really didn't understand what it means to be a white person in America today. I was not taught to think about what being white meant on a personal, day-to-day level."

Now, Barbara says, "I have been transformed by being part of this community because of the multiracial, multicultural work that we do here together."

Early on, Barbara, along with a number of All Souls members, takes part in the Witnessing Whiteness group sponsored by Tulsa's YWCA. The group works its way through Shelly Tochluk's book *Witnessing Whiteness: The Need to Talk About Race and How to Do It*. The months-long experience gives Barbara and other white participants the chance "to name shame, guilt, confusion, and to just talk about things that have been off limits." The experience is healing, as well as painful, she says. "Identity work is important not just because of the call to racial justice, but for me as an individual, trying to make sense of my own cultural complexity. This work has been profoundly healing on so many levels. And it's really an intense journey."

She tells Marlin and the associate minister, Rev. Tamara Lebak, "I think we need to bring this work here," and they agree. On these next stages of the journey, All Souls' leaders will gradually implement a multilayered system for training and analysis around multiculturalism and antiracism. As in all the congregations we study, such trainings are not just thought exercises. Rather, they change hearts and behavior and make real relationships across differences possible.

BUILDING THE CAPACITY FOR
INTERRACIAL CONVERSATIONS

All Souls begins by establishing a multiyear process, based on the YWCA model. In the first year, participants join one of two racial identity groups: Mosaic (now called Shadz) for congregants of color and Rewire for white congregants. All Souls' website describes these groups:

> Shadz (formerly Mosaic) is a racial identity group for people of color which equips participants with tools to effectively challenge racism and develop allies across racial lines.
>
> Rewire is a racial identity group for white people to unlearn racism. Participants explore racial identity formation and learn how to be effective allies for racial justice.

In the beginning, the Rewire group reads Tochluk's *Witnessing Whiteness*; the Mosaic group works with Beverly Tatum's *"Why Are All the Black Kids Sitting Together in the Cafeteria?" and Other Conversations About Race*. The two groups ask their participants similar questions about their racialized experiences, especially at All Souls.

In the second year, participants continue in their identity groups and also move into multiracial groups, building the capacity to talk with each other about race and white supremacy culture.

Establishing racial identity groups, or caucuses, often raises anxieties in Unitarian Universalist congregations. Many white people and some people of color dislike the separation; it feels contrary to the congregation's unifying purpose and Unitarian Universalism's message of inclusiveness. But honest, respectful, complex cross-racial conversations about race and white supremacy culture remain taboo in most situations in U.S. life. Most of us need preparation and practice in order for these conversations to be authentic and productive. Those who haven't yet participated in antiracism work—including many white people and some people of color—first need to deepen their analysis of how systems of power and privilege impact their families, their lives, and their communities at home, at work, and at church. In the process, each group has different work to do.

White people need space where they can awaken to how systems of white supremacy and other oppressions have worked "below the radar" to offer them power and privilege in some areas and not in others. They need to call each other into awareness of their implicit bias and microaggressions, rather than unintentionally inflicting these hurts on congregants of color during cross-racial conversations.

People of color need space where they can examine internalized oppression and develop their own identities, a process that is sometimes thwarted by pressures to assimilate to the dominant culture. They need the chance to express the truths of their experiences of racism and white supremacy in the congregation without having to take care of white people who might feel defensive.

Imogene White, an African-American member of All Souls' Board, confirms the value of these racial identity groups. They are one way that "we, as a covenant, are actively working for our congregation to reflect our mission of true diversity." She goes on, "These racial identity groups help us, as individuals, come to a better understanding of ourselves and one another. True diversity is more than tolerance. It is understanding and accepting each other." The journey through Rewire and Mosaic into the multiracial groups builds that capacity in ever-widening circles.

A NEW STRUCTURE FOR SHARING POWER

In 2010, Marlin asks organizational development trainer Beth Zemsky to lead a workshop for All Souls leaders. Using the Intercultural Development Inventory (IDI), Beth helps participants understand their level of cultural competence. This tool awakens participants to the assumptions they carry about cultural differences, which overlap with racial and ethnic differences. It lays out a spectrum of developmental stages that moves from denial, through polarization, minimization, and acceptance, to adaptation. Then it provides a map for progress from wherever participants are in their development.

As often happens with this work, some white Unitarian Universalists and some UUs of color at All Souls are surprised and made uncomfortable by the results of their IDI assessment, which show them at an earlier developmental stage than they expected. Some of this discomfort leads to deeper conversations. Growing comfortable with discomfort opens pathways to growth.

After Beth Zemsky's workshop, All Souls leaders choose the term *intercultural*, rather than *multicultural*, to name their work of building antiracist Beloved Community. The website for the Spring Institute for Intercultural Learning describes the difference between the two terms:

> **Multicultural** refers to a society that contains several cultural or ethnic groups. People live alongside one another, but each cultural group does not necessarily have engaging interactions with each other.
>
> **Intercultural** describes communities in which there is a deep understanding and respect for all cultures. Intercultural communication focuses on the mutual exchange of ideas and cultural norms and the development of deep relationships. In an intercultural society, no one is left unchanged because everyone learns from one another and grows together.[5]

---

[5] We pick up this distinction in "Some Words about Language," and we explain that, in our usage in other chapters, *multicultural* and *multiculturally competent* communities demonstrate the kind of transformation that the Spring Institute reserves for *intercultural* ones.

These definitions lift up a crucial distinction, whatever language congregations use to describe it. Congregations that long to be "diverse" may succeed in creating a community in which folks with different racial, ethnic, and cultural identities "live alongside one another." But without intention, training, and practice, these congregations may not achieve the engagement and understanding that recognize systemic differences in power and that celebrate cultural differences as well as similarities. In other words, without that intention, training, and practice, congregations won't get to true *community*.

When congregations do the intentional work of building antiracist Beloved Community, they create a space where "no one is left unchanged because everyone learns from one another and grows together." The choice of which adjective to use— *multicultural* or *intercultural*—matters less than the commitment to an ongoing process of awakening, engagement, and relationship building.

Early on in their journey, with the encouragement of leaders from the Unitarian Universalist Association and their own growing understanding of the size of the task they have taken on, All Souls' leaders create the Intercultural Bridging Team, an intentionally multiracial leadership group. The team's participants are asked to help All Souls "bridge" the cultural chasms between the distinct groups that now gather as one congregation. Creating the team ensures that congregants of color have a powerful voice in the congregation's decision making around its intercultural, antiracist mission and vision.

Like the Antiracism Transformation Team at the Unitarian Universalist Church of Annapolis (UUCA), the Intercultural Bridging Team finds its most powerful and satisfying work to be the building of relationships among the members of the team. Sharing personal stories about the impact of race and ethnicity on their lives, offering vulnerable and honest assessments of how white supremacy and racism play out at All Souls itself, the team members feel a growing intimacy and friendship—a rare cross-racial experience, especially in Tulsa.

And, like UUCA's team, the Intercultural Bridging Team is sometimes seen by other congregants as an exclusive group. These congregants feel left out of the intense healing experiences the team members share. We wonder if these critical congregants, mostly white, also worry about a shift in power—away from themselves, where they have traditionally sensed it to rest, and toward this new multiracial team. We see this pattern in several of the congregations we study.

In truth, All Souls' leaders aim for power to be shared beyond the Intercultural Bridging Team. Racial diversity in lay leadership positions starts slowly, with one African-American member joining the Board in the year after the merger. But intentionality about diversity in leadership gathers steam in succeeding years. At the UUA General Assembly in 2015, Marlin speaks to the breadth of this intentionality. He says it's about "how we do worship, what we hang on the walls, who goes on the Board, what newspapers we advertise in for hiring. It's not about just putting people of color on a committee because of their color."

By early 2016, the staff, the Board, and every major committee at All Souls includes diversity in the areas of racial identity, gender, and sexual orientation. "That's become pretty systemic," Marlin tells us during our site visit.

Representation in these leadership positions does not automatically shift the power structure in a congregation. The assumptions and practices that underlie white supremacy culture are likely to continue without an equal intentionality about dismantling these norms. Ongoing attention, learning, and reflection are required if a congregation hopes to develop a new antioppressive culture in which no one culture dominates. And when All Souls both intentionally diversifies leadership groups and continues to emphasize antiracism training for congregants, real power sharing becomes possible.

SHIFTING NEEDS, MISTAKES MADE, LESSONS LEARNED

By 2015, and especially after the death of Eric Harris in Tulsa, the Black Lives Matter movement creates an agitating tension for All Souls. The congregation has a long history of engaging in community efforts for racial justice. Now it once again makes some innovative moves. During the 2015 Martin Luther King Day Parade, for instance, All Souls' float includes the New Dimensions Chorale rocking gospel tunes, alternating with moments of silence when congregants on the float put up their hoodies and lift their hands in the air to honor the "hands up, don't shoot" cry of the Black Lives Matter movement. As the parade progresses, the crowds lining the streets respond to the All Souls float by dropping into silence and raising their hands in the air too.

But the demands of working for racial justice beyond the congregation's walls feel beyond the scope and capacity of All Souls' current structures. Some members of the Intercultural Bridging Team want to focus on All Souls' role in these public protests; others want to stay focused on All Souls' internal transformation. This external/internal pull is a common struggle in congregations on this journey. At All Souls, some leaders of color on the Intercultural Bridging Team express both "curiosity and ambivalence about charging forward," Rev. David Ruffin reports. They ask, "Do we have the capacity for *everything*?"

"I can be very goal oriented," admits Barbara, reflecting on her impatience with the team's inward focus. As these tensions grow, she sees the need for including more members and friends in the work, for creating multiple bridging teams that offer the chance for multicultural holy conversations, and for building more connections between the Intercultural Bridging Team and the congregation. She also sees the need for a specific team that would oversee the congregation's racial justice work in the wider community. That team would become part of a network of social justice groups at All Souls. As the 2015–16 church year begins, the decision is made to disband the Intercultural Bridging Team.

By early 2016, when we interview her, Barbara wonders if the shift was a mistake. "I didn't understand how profound it was that we were just at the table together. It's huge—to sit at the table and listen to each other and share the hard stories." The fact that she didn't grasp the importance of those relationships and of the trust built by the Intercultural Bridging Team feels like an oversight related to being immersed in whiteness, she confesses. The focus on outcome and results reflects the primary values of the dominant white culture. The intercultural model requires an equal or greater focus on relationships and process.

Still, Kelli McLoud-Schingen agrees that by 2015 All Souls is ready for the shift away from the Intercultural Bridging Team. Kelli, an African-American consultant in intercultural work, first comes to All Souls to help resolve a conflict among the choirs. By 2016, she is on retainer for a certain amount of consulting work each month. For Kelli, the structural issue with the Intercultural Bridging Team is that it must remain relatively small and closed in order to maintain the intimacy of the small group ministry model. As more people come through the Rewire and Mosaic/Shadz trainings, more of them want access to the intercultural dialogue that the Bridging Team enjoys. "The work was getting bigger; it made sense to change the structure," Kelli says.

But the transition brings with it grief, loss, and confusion. Like Barbara, Kelli wonders how the change could have been communicated better, to make it less distressing for people. As some members of the team take on different responsibilities, their new roles seem unclear. Others don't have a specific place in the new structures, and they feel let down or left out.

Meanwhile, some members of color are simply exhausted or overstretched by the intercultural work they have been doing for the congregation. All Souls has a weekly Wednesday Connections event that includes dinner, a chapel worship service, and adult programming. At one point, Rev. David Ruffin asks an African-American member why more people of color don't attend these Wednesday gatherings, where social connections could deepen across race. "They're resting!" the person answers. Unless Wednesday Connections relates directly to intercultural work, many members of color don't come out for this midweek offering.

The lessons here? Perfection is not the goal. There is no one way to do this work "right." The needs of the world and of the congregation are going to keep shifting. Paying attention to missteps and missed opportunities, ensuring that there are spaces where feelings can be expressed and accountability upheld—these practices allow everyone to grow and relationships to deepen. Acknowledging limits in time, energy, and person-power can help congregations discover the structures and programming that will support their goals, no matter how large or small the congregation is.

Now, at All Souls, the Intercultural Bridging Team has evolved into the Racial Justice Team, also called Beyond Our Walls. This group oversees the congregation's work in the community and has a place on the Social Justice Council. The Intercultural Programming Team ensures that Shadz, Rewire, Cross-Racial Dialogue Groups, and other offerings—such as films, classes, and social events—continue to thrive within the congregation. Leadership development across the congregation includes taking the Intercultural Development Inventory. An Intercultural Executive Team, which includes Marlin as senior minister and Barbara as executive director of ministries, helps coordinate the many branches of work handled by all these different groups. All Souls keeps trying on new structures in order to keep both the inner and outer work moving forward.

CONVERSATIONS THAT GO DEEPER STILL

When David comes to All Souls as resident minister in August 2014, he arrives with glowing stereotypes about All Souls—a "perception from afar," he says, of "Disneyland exceptionalism." He has also heard that a number of former members of the New Dimensions congregation have left All Souls, and as he joins the congregation, he notices that these losses are greater than he expected. The racial identity groups, Rewire and Mosaic/Shadz, "offer foundational work," he says, "but I'm surprised to find myself in time for some of the most honest and deep interracial dialogue, precipitated in large measure by the death of Michael Brown and then Eric Harris here."

Encouraged by the Intercultural Bridging Team, David convenes two small group ministry experiences, called Soulful Circles. The first brings together graduates of the YWCA program and All Souls' own Mosaic and Rewire groups. The second is slightly larger, with invitations that reach into the wider congregation. Both, he says, are "so, so impactful and holy. People begin to show up in their vulnerability." Through the conjunction of what was going on in the congregation and in the world, "there was this call for 'no more talk, time to act.' But actually it was clear that we weren't really ready to act. So another way to answer that call was 'OK, if we're going to talk, let's talk real.' Let's talk about what it takes to become the actors that we want to be."

As a result, people of color have a place to protest, "Don't just put me on a panel to tell my story without things changing." Marlin confesses the mistakes he has made as his ego has become invested in creating this intercultural congregation. He admits that he doesn't know the way forward exactly. "I'm not getting this right," he acknowledges, "and I don't have to get it *right*—perfection isn't the goal." What matters, he says, is that "we're all in it."

Soulful Circles becomes an ongoing small group ministry program. Those initial groups mark a turning point toward deeper, more authentic conversations—more humility and patience among white leaders, more healthy boundaries set by members of color. Soulful Circles offer another location for the "fierce conversation with life" that now runs through All Souls' DNA.

In early 2016, when Gerald reflects on where All Souls is on the journey, he points to all this progress. On the Board and the staff, he sees multiracial leadership, "and we are *developing* leadership," he goes on. "We have caucuses specifically working on issues of race. And in working together, you really begin to see who the other person is. Sometimes you say, 'Have you *thought* about what you're saying?' The politeness is just about waning. People are starting to push back."

In contrast to the early days after the merger, the congregation's journey into intercultural, antiracist Beloved Community has now become a "sophisticated foray," Gerald says. "Before, we were working things out on the fly. Now it's a very sophisticated, organized operation." His tone conveys admiration, enthusiasm, and hope.

How does a congregation institutionalize its commitment to building multicultural, antiracist Beloved Community? The story of the structures and practices that All Souls has put in place to fulfill Centennial Vision 2021 shows how the process must be continually responsive—to congregants' needs and to events in the world. All Souls' leaders have sought examples from beyond their own walls, such as the YWCA program. They continually revise, expand, and deepen their structures. They make mistakes, hold themselves accountable, ask for help, and stay committed to the process. The size of the congregation makes certain resources available, such as a consultant on retainer, which most Unitarian Universalist congregations wouldn't be able to afford. Yet the emphasis on small group work and relationship building, on humility and flexibility, cuts across issues of resources. And the patience and persistence this work takes—especially when trying to reach large numbers of members—are Common Threads.

CONFLICT AND THE MOVEMENT TOWARD RECONCILIATION

No version of All Souls' story would be complete without a specific example of the kind of conflict that arises when two different cultures come together. We have already mentioned the struggle over music. In the first years after the merger, members of the New Dimensions Chorale know that some white members of the congregation linger in the parking lot after worship to complain about both the content (the language of "Jesus" and "Lord") and the volume of the music that New D and its band provide. Meanwhile, New D and its director Pastor David Smith strive to work within new constraints for their music. Almost no one really feels comfortable. For the most part, then, the New Dimensions Chorale and All Souls' adult choir sing at different services each Sunday, except when they join forces on special occasions like Christmas and Easter.

But this discomfort comes to a head on a particular Sunday in the summer of 2012, when All Souls hosts the Unitarian Universalist Musicians' Network annual conference. The adult choir, led by director Rick Fortner, sings a multilayered traditional hymn and then returns to their seats in the front rows. As the concert draws near its close, the New D Chorale takes the stage.

When New D lifts their voices, the audience rises to its feet, clapping, dancing, praising. The roof on the old white sanctuary seems to rise another few feet.

After the concert, though, rumors spread that some of the white members of the adult choir had put their fingers in their ears when New D was singing. For Nicole Ogundare, the gesture feels racist. The chorale gathers together to discuss it.

"Some said, 'I just deal with it,'" reports Nicole when she tells us the story. These New D members have already felt a number of slights. This event represents one more, and they are resigned to putting up with it. As Bishop Carlton Pearson says earlier in this chapter, they are used to the feeling of discomfort.

But Nicole has a different reaction. "We've just been learning to deal with it and push it under," she remembers about that time. "I said no." In those first four years of the merger, she has watched white congregants leave the congregation or stop pledging to protest the changes in worship. "We're not talking about baby stuff, we're talking about the vitality of the church. I was not willing to be fake." She writes a letter to the two choir directors, expressing her hurt and announcing that she cannot sing in joint appearances with the adult choir any longer.

Members of the adult choir, in turn, feel hurt by Nicole's letter. They haven't realized that New D was feeling unwelcome.

Instead of allowing the rift to fester and the story to become even more entrenched, All Souls' leaders bring in Kelli McLoud-Schingen to try to facilitate a reconciliation. When Kelli describes the process, we recognize some familiar patterns. Kelli tells us,

> I was given the background, the conflict, the letter that was written by Nicole. There was a deep desire to address Nicole's very heartfelt letter and to bring it to the fore, and there was also a lot of trepidation around it because people didn't understand why she was so offended.

So while it was a very difficult and uncomfortable time, and it would have been easy to sweep it under the rug, the church decided to do something about it. So I started with New D first. I went to their rehearsals. I did an Appreciative Inquiry sort of thing. There was a great deal of distrust. People said, "We can tell you everything you need to know, and it's going to be the same-old same-old."

And then when I went to talk to the traditional choir, their perspective was "What?" They were completely in the dark that anything could have been interpreted differently. It wasn't a cultural thing and certainly not a racial thing. Just some people in the choir have hearing issues that New D wasn't aware of. So the more elderly people with sensitive earpieces removed themselves from the situation, which was interpreted as "they walked out on them."

Then I brought the combined choirs and a few curious people, [along with] the leadership, into a cross-racial dialogue. There was a great deal of distrust from both sides about the ministers being there. I heard, "I'm not sure they need to be in the room because I can't speak freely," or "they aren't equipped to facilitate." I passed around a crystal globe as a talking stick and gave people a chance to say what they were thinking or feeling, but without cross-talk. After that was done, I do believe there were—baby steps, right?—I think there were some shifts. I don't think that fixed everything, but there was some shifting in perspective, which is all you can ask for.

Through the dialogue, members of the adult choir come to see how their actions could be interpreted as disrespectful and racist. Members of New D learn that physical issues, like hearing loss, can impact the older congregants' capacity to stay with their music. Understanding each other's experiences and needs lays the ground for a new trust to grow.

But even this misunderstanding has its roots in cultural differ- ence. In this case, we suspect that different groups have different levels of skill in dealing with discomfort. In white-dominant culture, people of color gain a good deal of experience with discomfort and often have well-developed strategies for dealing with it. White people, on the other hand, especially those from the middle and upper-middle classes, often feel a need to "fix," avoid, or suppress an uncomfortable experience, rather than sit with it and see what it has to teach.

It makes sense that folks in a dominant group, who have more control over many aspects of their lives than their nondominant kin do, would make a habit of rejecting or shying away from discomfort. In fact, one of the practices for building multicultural, antiracist Beloved Community involves learning to "be comfortable with discomfort." The conversations that Kelli facilitates among choir members help participants to move in that direction.

In October 2013, Al Letson, now the host of the podcast *Reveal*, devotes part of his radio program *State of the Re:Union* to the experience of the two choirs at All Souls. Toward the end of the broadcast, titled "Tulsa, OK: Reconciliation Way," he reflects on two definitions of *reconciliation*:

- the act of causing two people or groups to become friendly again after an argument or disagreement
- the process of finding a way to make two different ideas or facts exist or be true at the same time

Both of those definitions in practice are hard to do—bringing two different groups together in a city with as much hard history as Tulsa has is pretty tough, and making those two ideas, two sets of facts, line up . . . feels nearly impossible. And that is the hard truth behind reconciliation. Every space between each word of those definitions is filled with heartache, anger, history, and loss. In Tulsa, like the rest of America, like the rest of the world, sometimes you can find that perfect imperfect solution. Sometimes you can't.

The intimate sharing of feelings and experiences that Kelli encourages helps show the choirs that "two different ideas or facts [can] be true at the same time." When the differences—all true at the same time—are expressed, the new understandings can deepen people's respect for each other's worth and build a sense of common values and shared humanity. For the choir members, hanging in there with their discomfort and arriving at new understandings opens the possibility for new relationships to emerge.

When we speak with Nicole in 2016, she reflects on this earlier conflict with compassion. "Music is a big component here," she says. "And I guess it would be upsetting [for some of the long-time members of All Souls that] after every time we sing, people are jumping up, energetic. After every time we sing, they get up, clap, sing, shout. We in New D want to minister. We have a mission to break people's hearts open to hear the word of the man or woman of God. Highly intellectual people don't want to touch their feelings and emotions. They like to stay in their heads. To be able to open up and receive anything that would cause you to feel something—that's scary for people. So it's still a little bit of a barrier. We're still always assessing the volume in the sanctuary."

But she adds another definition of *reconciliation*. "Reconciliation," she says, "means heartfelt acknowledgment." By 2016, she sees how far the congregation has come. "I feel hopeful," she sums up. "We have more of a sense of community than we've ever had."

Bishop Carlton Pearson also finds hope in the congregation's intercultural growth. The bishop loves to tease out the etymology of a word and spin it into a fresh thought or resonance. He sees the great work of building *community*—"fellowship, communion, *koinonia*"—as the work of discovering and celebrating "what is *common* to us. Not necessarily what is familiar to us, but what are our commonalities? To me that's what Universalism is: the recognition and celebration of the commonalities. And the thing that is most common about us [at All Souls] is diversity—

our differences of opinion, of appraisal, of appreciation or depreciation."

The two choirs' rupture over their differences—of appreciation, appraisal, assumptions, comfort level, and culture—begins to transform into communion and community when all these differences are expressed, understood, and acknowledged from the heart. Members of each choir, in all their diversities, begin to feel a mutual sense of belonging.

"The Greek word for agreement," Bishop Pearson offers, "is *sumphóneó*—not to sound the same or sound alike but to sound *together*. I don't want the saxophone to sound like the viola. It's the harmony and the synchronicity—that's where true harmonic intercultural symphonic music occurs."

All Souls' choirs do not sound alike; they are not designed to create the same kinds of music. But through the honesty and the hard work of moving through conflict, hurt, and misunderstanding, the choirs can begin to "sound together" in an intercultural symphony of Love Beyond Belief. In fact, "Reconciliation Way," the name of Letson's radio broadcast, makes a good name for the road that All Souls has committed to follow.

TESTIMONIES OF TRANSFORMATION

"The work never ends." In Tulsa, as in all the congregations we study, this Common Thread runs strong. Mistakes and misgivings crop up and must be dealt with as directly as possible. All Souls, for all its larger-than-life story, remains a profoundly human institution. Yet we witness a sustained and fierce commitment to its vision, a willingness to experiment with new avenues for making this vision a reality, and a palpable aliveness and joy for those involved.

In 2011, the congregation votes to move their campus downtown to a plot of land that three All Souls families—the Duttons,

Tanners, and McElroys, all descendants of early members—donate. In April 2017, it votes to launch the capital campaign that will make the move possible. The new location will place All Souls just a few blocks south of the district where the 1921 race-riot massacre took place. The congregation hopes to form a physical and spiritual bridge between the still-segregated parts of Tulsa. True to its history, All Souls wants to use its new location to foster conversation, communion, and community among divided neighborhoods. The congregation would like to move into its new buildings in 2021—the hundredth anniversary of the race riots and of All Souls' own founding.

But we don't have to wait for the physical move in order to see the movement that All Souls' commitment to building antiracist, multicultural/intercultural Beloved Community has inspired. Rev. David Ruffin, for example, is surprised when he arrives in 2014 that All Souls isn't further along on its journey. But by 2016, he can offer a blazing affirmation of the rewards of this work. "For me personally," he tells us, "it's been [incredibly] meaningful and a huge, huge privilege. We're really doing it. We're really doing the work. It's spiritual, it's transformative. Always, always, it's changing us, it's changing me."

When Marlin remembers the first radical plunge that Bishop Carlton Pearson and All Souls' leadership took in 2008, he compares it to swinging for the fences in baseball. "You're either going to hit it out of the park or you're gonna strike out," he admits. "There were people who said, 'Don't swing for the fence. Take small steps, take small steps!' But we didn't, we swung for the fence, we went big."

Bishop Pearson echoes the importance of having the white ministers be willing to be bold. "If the minister is not adventurous," the bishop says, "if the visionary is not curious and adventurous and is not looking for an advent of something new to occur, then the conversation is not worth having. But both Dr.

Wolf and Marlin are curious," and this helps their congregants, especially those who are white, to find the curiosity, courage, and sense of adventure to encounter their own heritage of white supremacy culture and to change.

Marlin is quick to acknowledge that the congregation is still in the very heart of the work. "So far, so good," he assesses, "but it's tenuous and it's dangerous. It's risky. It's very, very exciting. It's the challenge of a lifetime. And I could go on and on about every story of connection and transformation and beauty that has happened alongside all the work."

We hear many of these stories. It feels right to let two of these congregants have the last word in this chapter.

BECOMING MORE FULLY HUMAN

Dan Piazzola identifies as white, straight, a husband, a father, a grandfather, and a seeker, semi-retired, and "becoming a senior citizen faster than I want to be" while still "trying to find out what I'm going to do when I grow up." Dan grows up in Montana and has a career in geophysics. He joins All Souls shortly after the merger with New Dimensions, partly because he reads about Bishop Pearson's conversion to Universalism. The process resonates with Dan. "Epiphany made sense to me," he tells us in 2016.

Rev. Tamara Lebak, then All Souls' associate minister, invites Dan to join a multiracial leadership-development class and then to take part in Witnessing Whiteness and Rewire. Dan has prided himself on being "open-minded, diversity accepting; I've argued with relatives when they made racist statements; I felt I was very antidiscriminatory." But when he sits down with Rev. Tamara to go over the results of his Intercultural Development Inventory assessment, he has a new awakening.

The assessment places him in what he calls "the self-congratulatory phase. It was like a shot in the heart, like, 'Whoa!'

I accepted what she was saying. I was, I guess, embarrassed and ashamed. I was so chagrined that I didn't want to stay there. Even in the process of sitting with Tamara and going through it, things started to open up. There's a clarity out there. You don't even know the right questions to ask, but if you stick with this course, the questions will come, and the answers will come. It was so clear to me after I was over that first threshold how much work I needed. So many people from where I come from—not just Montana, but white people—have no idea what it means to be an advocate."

As Dan participates in All Souls' intercultural trainings, serves on the Intercultural Bridging Team, and builds cross-racial friendships for the first time in his life, he feels more and more like a full human being. He finds it encouraging that more congregants want to participate in this process. But he also recognizes that some folks "feel like they're already where they need to be—they're open and caring, etc.—and you can't break that down unless you show them the other side of the veil. There's kind of a resistance," he admits.

On the other hand, when we ask Dan how the "experiment" is going—this building of Beloved Community at All Souls—he can't hold back his enthusiasm:

> Notwithstanding what I just said [about some people's resistance], I would call it an unqualified success! It has taken people who would have never done the work—from my perspective, I'm way too lazy to have gone through this by myself—it's taken people like me and given them a vehicle to see themselves, to see their relationship with the rest of the human race in a way they never would have. It's had a major impact on the life of the church.
>
> It's fatiguing in a way because you realize once you start into it, how much work there is left to do. But the beauty of this place is that you're surrounded by people.

We take Dan's last phrase to mean that he is surrounded by people who want to do the work with him. Surrounded by people who are willing, just as he is, to struggle with where they are in the process and where they want to be. Surrounded by people who are willing to stay the course, to stay in community with each other, and to become more complete human beings.

"TO HOLD YOU UNTIL YOU CAN GET THERE"

Dorothy Checotah is an African-American woman who grows up on Tulsa's north side, in the Black community. When she was about ten or eleven, she saw Rev. Dr. John Wolf on television. "I was fascinated by the man," she tells us. "I said to my father that I wanted to meet him. My father said that probably would never happen, just given that this was a white church 'outside and inside.'"

Dorothy's spiritual journey has taken her through a number of religious traditions, but she found Bishop Carlton Pearson and New Dimensions shortly after Pearson's conversion experience. When New D moved to All Souls and the bishop left for Chicago, some of her friends asked what she was going to do.

"I said, 'I'm *doing* it,'" Dorothy recalls. "I knew I had arrived on my journey. I'd been to Pentecostal services, Methodist, Episcopal, and I've always been able to get so much out of them. So when we came here, it was a combination of all of that. My big word is always 'the freedom to be who you are, as you are.' The freedom to reach out to others and love them the same. That's the gist of it for me."

When Rev. Marlin introduced her to Rev. Wolf, the minister who fascinated her as a child, her eyes filled with tears. "When I was in his presence, it was like the lion of winter. When he speaks, it's just like . . . Oh my goodness. He was so gracious."

Still, Dorothy remembers feeling like she didn't really know how to act or what to be—the same uncertainty that the bishop describes New D members feeling in those early days at All Souls. "There was already an established situation; you had to learn the protocols and procedures. I felt like *I* had to make the adjustments. I was kind of tired. You kind of felt like you couldn't be yourself, even something as simple as the services—no clapping, no speaking out. That was part of my upbringing as an African American; you're used to that. So you have to keep in mind what you're truly there for."

But by the time we meet Dorothy, she feels thoroughly at home and embraced. She loves each of the services for what they have to offer. "Every time I come into this building on a Sunday, I anticipate something good is going to happen," she enthuses, and by "good," she means that All Souls is "not afraid to approach a subject that some might want to shy away from. And there's always learning going on, and an opportunity to share with other people. I've attended all three services and enjoy all three. The humanist service, especially when jazz is being played, and people are talking about various subjects. Sometimes when I need to be more quiet, at the Traditional Service I feel a deep connection with people I'm sitting with. I might not even know their name, but just singing the hymns together. And then the Contemporary Service! To have that choice, I never thought there was that anywhere. I tell people, if you can't find it here, you're not going to find it."

When Dorothy imagines All Souls' future on its new campus downtown, she sees "a place kind of like Noah's Ark. You can bring every bit of who you are. I just see that. This will impact the world, because the world needs it. Just hold on, because what is to be is starting right here."

When we ask Dorothy, "If you could wish, or pray, for one thing for All Souls—for *all the souls* here—what might that be?" she replies,

Just to stay the course. To show Tulsa that it's for real, it's genuine. And I believe it's going to happen. It's going to happen.

People don't want to let go of what they know. Even though we've been taught to step out on faith, they don't know what that means. If it means that I have to hold your hand, to hold you until you can get there, I'm willing to do that too, just because I know, hey, [what we're creating here] is good for all of us. So I'm willing to take the risk.

At All Souls, we find a group of people "willing to take the risk" of building multicultural, antiracist Beloved Community because they experience it as "good for all of us." The tenderness and fragility of the project are ever-present. Historical divisions and the habits and power structures of white supremacy culture remain a part of the DNA in Tulsa, as they do throughout this country. But commitment and will, curiosity and courage, patience and persistence keep All Souls' leaders and congregants engaged in this "fierce conversation with life." Developing unexpected relationships, experiencing personal transformation, and savoring a community that, more often than not, embodies compassion and a love beyond belief—these are the gifts that fuel the journey. The congregation's Centennial Vision 2021 statement provides a North Star to guide it. Dorothy's words bring that vision down to earth:

You can bring every bit of who you are. I just see that. This will impact the world, because the world needs it. Just hold on, because what is to be is starting right here.

QUESTIONS FOR YOU AND
YOUR CONGREGATION

1. What is the most challenging aspect of All Souls' story for you and your congregation or faith community? What is the most exciting aspect? What elements of this unique story feel applicable to your context?

2. Are there elements of your congregation's or wider community's history that have been silenced or tucked away? What are they, and why are they difficult to examine and learn from? How can you help name these elements and begin the process of restoration?

3. All Souls discovers resources for deepening its cross-racial conversations and relationships through the local YWCA. To which organizations in your wider community can you turn for inspiration, accountability, and resources? What steps do you need to take to build your relationships with these community partners?

4. What practices for sharing differing experiences and hard truths has your congregation developed? How will All Souls' stories of conflict and reconciliation shift or deepen your own practices?

CHAPTER SIX

To Answer the Call of Love

KARIN'S JOURNEY WITH FIRST PARISH
CAMBRIDGE, MASSACHUSETTS

In covenant with one another
and all we hold sacred
we answer the call of love—
welcoming all people
into the celebration of life,
searching for truth and meaning,
and striving for justice and compassion,
to nourish and serve each other,
our community and our world.

—Covenant of First Parish in Cambridge,
adopted November 2003

WHEN I THINK BACK ON MY JOURNEY as a Unitarian Univer-salist over the past twelve years—a journey that is inextricably bound to my work toward an antiracist, multicultural future for our faith—I inevitably come away with a sense of bewilderment. Bewilderment that this work has become so central to my life, when I never went looking for it in the first place. It was never a conscious decision but was born of necessity. Perhaps none of us truly chooses to do this work; we are called to it. But in my case, it arises from a place of deep pain, from a desperation to find healing, from a determination to make a place for myself within Unitarian Universalism. It is the journey of one person of color among the many who are trying to find their way in this faith, some of whom sadly never will. My journey takes me over large distances both literally and figuratively, as I move across the country, embark on the long process of discovering my identity as a Unitarian Universalist, and learn to claim my voice.

My story is also that of First Parish in Cambridge, where I have found my spiritual home. It is a community that has nurtured me, held me, challenged me, and, above all, loved me. Its journey toward multiculturalism begins long before I enter the picture, but from the moment I join the congregation, its vision becomes my vision. I will travel with it through painful stumbles and moments of grace, as we claim our mission and hold it through the loss of our ministers and more.

MY ENTRY INTO UNITARIAN UNIVERSALISM

In the days after September 11, 2001, my husband Cade and I make the decision to walk into our first Unitarian Universalist congregation. In a northern California suburb, one of the most ethnically diverse areas in the nation, this congregation—like so many in our denomination—is nearly completely white. Until I see an older Japanese couple (who, I later discover, rarely attend themselves), I'm not sure I will return.

But I do. As a lifelong atheist, a Unitarian Universalist church is the only kind of church I'm willing to set foot in. I'm still apprehensive about the whole religion thing (although I am married to a liberal United Methodist), but this church can hardly be called a church. It meets in a day-care center where congregants arrive early to set up folding chairs and a lectern. The minister speaks of philosophical subjects like free will, with little use of the word

God. We get involved in church life. The congregation is there for us during the birth of our daughters in 2003 and 2005. In 2006, I am elected to the Board.

With the congregation having shown some confidence in my leadership and judgment, I decide it's time to examine a question I've pondered for some time: Why, in such a diverse community, is our congregation so overwhelmingly white? I am unaware of the conversation that has been unfolding for decades in the larger movement; my experience of Unitarian Universalism is still limited to my congregation. Little do I know that asking this question will cause me to face the deepest questions of identity and belonging, challenge some of my closest relationships, and change forever the direction of my faith journey.

At a Board meeting, I express my desire to see my congregation reflect the diversity of its surroundings. In my naïveté, I still think this is a matter of outreach, and I'm eager to apply my skills of organization and execution. To my great surprise, a white gentleman, one of the patriarchs of the church, challenges me with "How are you going to get buy-in from everyone?" I'm confused. Isn't this what it means to be a Unitarian Universalist, to create a community where everyone feels welcomed? I feel uneasy, but I am so new to these conversations that I do not detect the layers underneath his seemingly reasonable question, and I am unable to articulate all that this vision represents for me.

I continue to encourage conversations, and while some members are supportive, murmurs begin to stir. Gradually, it becomes clear to me that some individuals actively oppose any effort to make the congregation more diverse. I hear comments like "I'm the last white person in my neighborhood," or "I like coming to a place where most of the people are white." Later, I will hear of someone who states that they go to church to escape diversity.

There is a misconception, I think, that being a person of color automatically grants one the knowledge and perspective to speak articulately and with complete self-awareness on matters of race. But nothing in my life so far has prepared me for the onslaught of emotion that arises in these conversations. After all, I am trained as a scientist and engineer! I am a complete novice, unable to hear the fear that undergirds these statements that seem to disrespect my identity. I take each one of them personally, absorbing them like blows to my stomach.

My minister, a white man in his sixties, is unwilling or unable to facilitate conversations that might help us all bridge our differences, name our fears, and find redemption in vulnerability. He addresses my pain with urgency, but treats it as a personal pastoral matter. He encourages me to cut others some slack. "A lot of people find it difficult to be around those who are different than they are."

I react first with confusion. Sure, it's difficult, but isn't that what Unitarian Universalism is all about? The goal of world community? Justice and equity in human relations? "Well," he answers, "you can believe that everyone should get along but still prefer to be with people who are like you." I'm confused, because he seems to be describing a Unitarian Universalism that is different from what I have always imagined it to be. And yet—he's twice my age, and he has "Rev." in front of his name. I tell myself that he's got to know more about these things than I do. Maybe I *am* being oversensitive.

But my pain persists, and I begin looking elsewhere for understanding. I find allies in other congregations. I start reading books on antiracism, a term previously unknown to me. Through Beverly Tatum's book *"Why Are All the Black Kids Sitting Together in the Cafeteria?"* I learn of psychologist William Cross's theory of racial identity development, involving the stages of pre-encounter, encounter, immersion/emersion, internalization, and internalization-commitment. And I realize that I've been in the pre-encounter stage for most of my life, feeling that I was simply a flawed white person. My world turns upside down as I begin to grasp the depth of my internalized oppression. I am ready for liberation.

My transformation is rapid and life-changing. By this time, I am president of my congregation, but I can't help feeling like I'm leaving them behind as I grow into new understandings of myself and my faith. I demand more of my minister than he can give. At one point he tells me that it can cause more problems to call attention to racist remarks than to simply let them go. I tell him, "I don't want you to defuse my anger, I want you to share it!" Our conversations grow more heated. My congregation, once such a source of joy and validation, is no longer a haven.

And so I resign from my once beloved congregation, believing that my dream of a multicultural community will never be realized there. I fall into a deep depression; my performance at work suffers, and my job becomes one of the many casualties of the 2008 recession. I try other congregations farther from home, but nothing feels like a place where I can land. I ask myself the question that far too many Unitarian Universalists of color have considered: Is there really a place for me in this faith?

It is around this time that I become involved with DRUUMM—Diverse and Revolutionary Unitarian Universalist Multicultural Ministries, a national organization for Unitarian Universalists of color. I attend my first DRUUMM gathering at Starr King School for the Ministry, where I am warmly welcomed. Upon hearing my story, Rev. Danielle Di Bona tells me, "You know, every single person in this room has a story like yours. And what I tell myself is that I'm not going to let anyone else define my faith for me."

These words remain with me as I explore what it means to be a Unitarian Universalist without a congregation. I help to establish the Pacific Central District's Racial and Cultural Diversity Exploratory Task Force, along with Nancy and others. I end up on the Steering Committee of the Asian/Pacific Islander Caucus of DRUUMM.

Yet I long for a community where I can go week after week. Without a congregation, I am uncertain of my future in Unitarian Universalism.

HISTORY AT FIRST PARISH
IN CAMBRIDGE

On the other side of the country, unbeknownst to me, First Parish in Cambridge has been considering the issue of diversity as well. Established in 1636, the congregation has been a bastion of the elite, having hosted great thinkers for centuries. It is among the churches that created the Cambridge Platform in 1648, a document that defined congregational polity. Ralph Waldo Emerson delivered his "American Scholar" oration at the meetinghouse in 1837. Harvard commencement ceremonies are held in the church until 1873.

Yet First Parish in Cambridge is also located in one of the most progressive areas of the nation. Cambridge, Massachusetts, has been a Sanctuary city since 1985. It is the first city in the United States to issue marriage licenses for same-sex couples and the first city to have an openly lesbian African-American mayor. In this vibrant urban community, the congregation's desire to reflect the richness of its surroundings makes sense.

In October 2008, newly called minister Rev. Fred Small preaches a sermon entitled "Building the Beloved Community" in which he articulates the congregation's desire for greater diversity. "I invite you to join me in a vision of First Parish in Cambridge as a multiracial, multicultural, justice-making congregation," he says. "All we have to do is look around us at the faces in the pews and the pulpit to know we've got work to do. But it can be done. ¡Sí se puede!"

Fred is well aware of the magnitude of this endeavor.[6] His sermon goes on, "[Of] more than a thousand UU congregations, you know how many are multiracial? Five. Not 5 percent. Five *churches* . . . Five multiracial UU congregations in the entire country. We can be the sixth!" Applause breaks out.

For Fred too, this journey has deep personal meaning. "I really found my vocation to antiracism at First Parish," he explains. "Which is not to say that it didn't exist before, but in many ways it had lain latent—not entirely dormant, but latent—for many years. And looking back, I think there was this terrible hunger that I felt for racial justice and racial healing, but like many of us I had despaired of it. . . . It was a beautiful match between [First Parish's] need and my need."

After embarking on what he calls "a crash course on how to do this"—including workshops at General Assembly led by the UUA's Taquiena Boston and Rev. Alicia Forde—Fred lays out some specific steps for First Parish to fulfill this vision. As a white, male, heterosexual minister, he encourages the congregation to consider calling a minister of color, citing one of the core principles of building multiracial Beloved Community: diversity in leadership. In December 2008, the Transition Team—previously established to identify staffing needs after the departure of Rev. Jory Agate, minister of religious education—recommends that First Parish hire a three-quarter-time director of religious education, a part-time youth coordinator, and a full-time minister who is of color, Latino/a, or multiracial. (The gender-inclusive form "Latinx" is not commonly used at this time.)

Funding, however, is a concern. Having previously employed only two ministers, can the congregation really afford to add the equivalent of another nearly full-time employee? Eileen Sullivan,

---

[6] In this chapter we follow First Parish's custom of referring to ministers by their first names, without titles.

then vice-chair of the Standing Committee—First Parish's governing board—notes, "One of our biggest fears, I think, was getting over the financial aspects of it—that we could afford to do this. But hidden behind that, I think, were fears of, was this something we really wanted to do? Were we just saying we wanted to do it because it was the right thing to do, or was it really what was in our hearts? And as we went through the discussions, it became clear this was who we really wanted to be."

With the support of the Standing Committee, Fred and stewardship chair Gina LaRoche launch a special campaign to raise funds for the new ministry. Within months, the congregation has pledged $175,000, providing the Finance Committee and Standing Committee the assurance needed to endorse the new staffing. In February 2009, First Parish votes to call a minister of color through the Unitarian Universalist Association's Diversity of Ministry Initiative, the same program through which John Crestwell was called to the Unitarian Universalist Church of Annapolis.

FINDING MY WAY TO CAMBRIDGE

With this decision to call a minister of color, it is time for First Parish to become serious about the work of congregational transformation. In April 2009, Fred leads a team of five congregants to the UUA's "Now Is the Time" conference on multicultural congregations in Tulsa, Oklahoma. It is by far the largest delegation at the conference. I am there too, representing no congregation but hoping to find the support I so desperately need. During a moment of sharing, I describe in general terms the pain I have felt trying to be a member of this faith.

At the conference's finish, I share a car back to the Tulsa airport with five other people. One of them is Fred. As I say goodbye to him, he looks at me straight in the eye and asks, "Are you okay?" I answer that I'm going through a rough time, but I'll be all right. He responds, "Well, our flights don't leave for three hours, so if you'd like to talk to a minister. . . ." I'm surprised by the offer—I'm not this man's congregant, I don't help pay his salary—but I decide to take him up on it.

And so in a quiet corner of the Tulsa airport, I tell Fred about all that has happened in the past year and a half with me, my former minister, and my former congregation. He tells me that he's sorry. He says, "You are infinitely good. And—your minister is infinitely good." With this utterly Universalist sentiment, he goes on to add that my minister missed an opportunity to learn from a mistake but that I did not. In Fred's words, I find hope, forgiveness, and the beginning of what feels like healing. I know I will remember this conversation for the rest of my life.

Meeting Fred and other members of First Parish at the conference prompts me to visit the congregation's website when I return home. Its commitment to becoming a multiracial, multicultural community is evident. I listen to sermons, read the newsletter, and learn about the congregation's intent to call an associate minister of color. This sounds like the community I am looking for. Alas, I think, if only I lived in Cambridge.

As if hearing my lament, the universe responds. I have now been job hunting in California for months without results—and then, out of the blue, I am recruited for a position in the greater Boston area. The prospect of joining First Parish in Cambridge is now no longer a dream; it is a real possibility. I fly out a few days before my interview to worship there and talk to Fred, and the experience convinces me that First Parish could be my spiritual home. Cade and I, both graduates of MIT, discuss the idea of returning to the East Coast and decide it makes sense. Perhaps, I tell myself hopefully, the future of my Unitarian Universalism lies there.

I don't get the job I interviewed for, but the seed has been sown. I tell my career counselor that I'm moving my job search to

Boston. Within two months, I land a position as an aerospace scientist at MIT Lincoln Laboratory. Cade and our daughters will remain in California for a few more months to sell the house and wrap up existing commitments. In September 2009, I board a one-way flight from San Francisco to Boston, free and ready for a fresh start.

HEALING THROUGH SERVICE

I have landed in fertile soil for growing multicultural community, yet deep wounds accompany my excitement. I face the conundrum of desperately wanting connection while knowing that my depression and disillusionment can lead me to extreme emotions that may be difficult for others to deal with. Over the next several years, the congregation's unfailing ability to hold me in my pain while giving me the chance to serve will be crucial in helping me find my path again.

Fred knows I'm hungry to do the work of multicultural transformation, and within two weeks of my arrival he invites me to join the nascent Transformation Team. The Standing Committee has chartered this team to coordinate the congregation's efforts toward a multiracial, multicultural, justice-making future. Despite my very limited experience with the congregation thus far, the invitation doesn't feel like tokenism. Over the years I've amassed a multitude of resources on multiculturalism; I know I can help the team. The congregation's commitment to this journey is the entire reason I'm here. Serving on, and later chairing, this Transformation Team becomes a significant part of my healing process.

When I join the Transformation Team, it is led by Chris McElroy, a white woman in her fifties, a professional psychologist, and vice-chair of the Standing Committee. We become fast friends and close colleagues. Over the course of its first year, the

Transformation Team will hold a multitude of events to stimulate conversations on race. We screen PBS's three-part documentary *Race: The Power of an Illusion* and follow it with facilitated discussion. We explore *The Princess and the Frog*, Disney's first movie to feature a Black princess. As I witness and participate in dialogue after dialogue, hear others' stories and share my own, my mind and heart open wide to possibility. I grow stronger in my faith and more confident of my place here in this congregation and in the larger movement.

On the Transformation Team, I can use my organizational skills as I meet my need for healing. As an Asian-American woman, I've been socialized to serve, taught that my worth as a person is directly proportional to what I do for others. I cannot feel at home in a place where I am only receiving; I must give as well. The Transformation Team is my vehicle, and my fellow members become some of my closest friends in the congregation.

Creating opportunities for the congregation to engage with issues of race is rewarding, to be sure. But even more valuable to me is having this multicultural group of strong white allies and people of color whom I trust so completely. Whatever I encounter in the world or in the congregation at large, I know this is a safe place where I can share both my pain and my joy. This knowledge gives me the courage to make myself vulnerable and to speak my truth. Gradually, I discover the power of telling my story.

The members of the Transformation Team bond deeply through heartfelt sharing at our meetings and through attending workshops and events together. One of these is the Leading Edge Conference, an annual gathering focused on multicultural justice making hosted by Middle Collegiate Church in New York City. At the closing of one of the conference sessions, Rev. Jacqui Lewis, senior minister of Middle Collegiate, sings from *Sweeney Todd*: "Nothing's gonna harm you, not while I'm around. . . ." Tears stream down my face as I remember how alone I once felt, and how safe I feel now.

Later, sharing my reflections on the conference from the pulpit, I describe the burden of representation:

> As an only child with no extended family in the United States, as an Asian American growing up in Kansas, as a woman with three physics degrees, and as a Unitarian Universalist person of color, my life has been characterized by solitude. As anyone who's ever been in an extreme minority knows, that solitude is accompanied by the responsibility, often unwanted, of defining the stereotype. . . . For my entire life, nearly every action I've taken, every major decision I've made, has been influenced by the feeling that the world is watching, ready to form their beliefs about an entire group by who I am and what I do.

I describe what it feels like, in the multiracial environment of the conference, to be relieved of that burden, and my desire to find that same relief within Unitarian Universalism. I speak of the internal conflict between my love for this faith and my constant questioning whether there really is a place for me in it. After the service, many congregants thank me for sharing my story, and I realize once again how important feeling heard is for the healing process.

ELEMENTS OF TRUST

One of my earliest encounters with the congregation is at a meeting led by Mandy Neff, First Parish's director of religious education (RE). The meeting is designed for parents and caregivers of children who will be participating in RE, and I decide to attend, even though my daughters—then four and six—have not yet moved to Cambridge. As the subject turns to welcome, one of the other parents gushes about how warmly she has been received by the congregation. My experience has not been the same.

The truth is that in my first few weeks at First Parish, I haven't felt that welcomed at coffee hour and elsewhere. It isn't terrible, because I have the connections I've made before arriving at First Parish, but I've felt mostly ignored by the larger congregation. I want to share my experience too. I take a breath and say to the otherwise all-white group, "I actually haven't had that experience. I haven't felt very welcomed. And . . . I don't look like the rest of you."

It is a terrifying moment for me, bringing up the subject of race so early in my interactions with the congregation. Yet nothing bad happens. The room listens; some wonder with me whether race has been a factor, others claim that the congregation isn't all that good at welcoming in general, the other parent's experience notwithstanding. I hear no defensiveness or accusations of "playing the race card."

I will never really know whether it was race, or something else about me personally, or just the luck of the draw that caused me to be less warmly welcomed at first than the other woman. But that's not the point. The point is that we Unitarian Universalists have to be able to ask the question "Is this about race?" Sometimes it's not, but we must have these honest discussions. The next day, Mandy emails me to thank me for my courage in raising the topic. I feel heard, validated, and ever more convinced that everything will be okay.

This is not to say that First Parish is perfect or that microaggressions never happen. There is a white gentleman who tells me, "We're really enjoying our Asian granddaughters"—what am I supposed to say to that?—and who regularly greets any Asian newcomer with "ni hao!" ("hello" in Mandarin) even when they've explicitly said they're from a country other than China. I later have a bad experience in a covenant group when I propose alternate methods of facilitation to help ensure that everyone's voice will be heard.

But the difference between these experiences and those in my previous congregation lies in the *leadership*. The (mostly white) professional staff and lay leaders I meet all seem to "get it," so I can immediately find allies when I do experience something unpleasant. The active participation and education of such leaders is essential for a congregation to progress on the journey toward multiculturalism.

Conversations about multiculturalism in Unitarian Universalist settings frequently focus on worship style, particularly music. For me, however, the most salient issue has always been a difference in "power distance," the manner in which a culture distributes power and the degree to which people accept unequal distribution of power.[7] Asian cultures tend to be "High Power Distance" cultures, in which hierarchy is natural and expected. By contrast, the United States is a "Low Power Distance" culture, where power is distributed (or at least expected to be distributed) more equally. The dominant culture of Unitarian Universalism is also Low Power Distance, as manifested in our extreme individualism and distrust of authority. These two traits, along with exceptionalism, constitute the faith's "Trinity of Errors," as Rev. Fred Muir puts it in his essay in *Turning Point: Essays on a New Unitarian Universalism*.

For me, the consequence of being raised in a High Power Distance culture is that I place immense trust in authority. While this might seem foreign or distasteful to many Unitarian Universalists, I thrive in a well-defined hierarchy. I look to my elders to take care of me, and in return I offer respect and the presumption of correctness. I believe that my experience with my former

---

[7] In chapter 7, Nancy offers a more complete explanation of Rev. Dr. Eric Law's use of the concept of power distance.

minister was exacerbated by my utter trust in him, so that when I felt he was no longer on my side, it was a betrayal beyond understanding.

It is perhaps a mistake—albeit one I cannot help making—as well as a symptom of internalized racism and sexism, to grant so much power to an older, white, male minister. But at First Parish, it seems to work. With Fred at the helm, enthusiastically championing antiracism and multiculturalism, I feel protected and empowered. Much of what I am able to achieve is a direct result of the feeling of safety that his ministry provides.

MINISTERS OF COLOR

First Parish in Cambridge recognizes the importance of diversity in leadership—one of the Common Threads we describe in chapter 2. Over the next several years, we will call and hire a number of ministers and ministerial interns of color. Though the work of transformation belongs to us, we know these ministers will both challenge us and bring many gifts to help guide us on this journey.

In March 2010, the congregation votes to call Rev. Lilia Cuervo, a native of Colombia and former extension minister for the Spanish-Speaking Ministries (SSM) at the First Unitarian Church of San José, California. Her selection as the first Latin-American minister ever settled in the nearly four centuries of First Parish's history makes headlines in Boston newspapers.

I am elated. From my own experiences attending SSM as a resident of the San Francisco Bay Area, I know Lilia to be a deeply competent, warm, kind individual. I am excited to see what she will bring to her ministry at First Parish. And as a language lover and fluent Spanish speaker, I'm eager to explore multilingual congregational life.

When Lilia arrives in the fall, she is joined by new First Parish intern Elizabeth Nguyen, a queer Vietnamese American and lifelong Unitarian Universalist in her second year at Harvard Divinity School. The experience of having such a diverse ministry team is delicious. Seeing these different faces in the pulpit, tasting the multiplicity of cultural elements in worship—here is a multicultural Unitarian Universalism that I never could have imagined. It touches my soul in ways I have not expected.

Lilia brings to First Parish in Cambridge her warmth, scholarship, and passion for Unitarian Universalism, along with a culture different from that of most congregants. She leads the congregation in a celebration of the Mexican tradition of Día de los Muertos (Day of the Dead), where we transform our altar into an explosion of colorful *papel picado* and paper flowers surrounding photographs of loved ones who have passed. Congregant after congregant comes forward to share their memories and deliver tributes.

Spanish becomes a significant part of worship. Fred or Lilia greets newcomers with a bilingual welcome, and congregants sing the children to their classes in both English and Spanish. One hymn in every worship service is taken from *Las voces del camino*, the Spanish-language hymnal based on the work of Lilia and members of San José's Spanish-Speaking Ministries years ago. The congregation begins reciting the words of our congregational covenant in Spanish—translated by Lilia—as well as in English, every Sunday morning:

> In covenant with one another
> and all we hold sacred
> we answer the call of love—
> welcoming all people
> into the celebration of life,
> searching for truth and meaning,
> and striving for justice and compassion,
> to nourish and serve each other,
> our community and our world.

En convenio mutuo
y con todo lo que consideramos sagrado
respondiendo al llamado del amor—
invitamos a todos a la celebración de la vida,
buscamos la verdad y el sentido del ser,
y nos esforzamos para alcanzar la justicia y la compasión,
para apoyarnos y servirnos mutuamente,
a nuestra comunidad y a nuestro mundo.

While not everyone embraces these changes, for the most part people are willing to try and to learn.

The experience of hearing stories from the pulpit that resonate with my own, from people whose background recalls my own, is new and deeply meaningful. I have never worshiped in a congregation with a ministerial intern, never imagined seeing an Asian American in the pulpit. Elizabeth's presence at First Parish shatters my assumptions about ministry and the identities of people who enter it.

Asian Americans often struggle with not feeling "Asian enough," but being both Unitarian Universalist and Asian means I must navigate this insecurity in my church, as well as in the wider world. Because there are so few of us, I have felt like I have to be some archetype who speaks Mandarin, knows about Buddhism, and celebrates the Lunar New Year. In fact, I know very little about any established religion, and my best language other than English is Spanish. Yet sometimes I have felt that I will be accepted as a nonwhite person only if I conform to the Asian stereotype—only if I can provide European-American Unitarian Universalists with the "cultural experience" that lets them feel they are embracing diversity.

In 2010 at First Parish, Elizabeth begins her sermon on Lunar New Year by teaching us how to say "Happy New Year" in Vietnamese. "Chúc mùng nam moi!" she begins, and then she goes on, "Now here's the tricky bit: That's all the Vietnamese I know. Those four words. . . . And this is what is hard: that even to say Happy New Year requires a confession of assimilation on my part."

Hearing Elizabeth express the same sentiment I've struggled with my whole life brings tears to my eyes. With my less-than-perfect Taiwanese and Mandarin and my fragmentary knowledge of my heritage, I, too, wonder what I have lost through my efforts to fit in. I have never dreamed of hearing this experience articulated so clearly from a Unitarian Universalist pulpit.

There are challenges, too, that come with calling a minister of color. Some congregants find Lilia's accent difficult to understand, and race and culture complicate criticism of ministers who must already meet the demands of many. Carol Lewis, First Parish's congregational administrator, recalls, "The most uncomfortable things for me were some of the comments around 'I can't understand her when she preaches. She doesn't do this, she doesn't do that.' The comments were, as I perceived them, culturally or racially motivated."

Lilia and I also clash on the language that is used to describe the ongoing work of the congregation. While she is enthusiastic about multiculturalism, she is less keen on the word *antiracism*. For her, the word carries memories of conflict, of good white people being called racists and becoming alienated. Yet for me the word carries strength and connotes active resistance to injustice. I am unwilling to lose it, fearful that *multiculturalism* is not enough, that without a focus on antiracism the celebrations of different cultures will remain superficial. In one of my less faithful moments, I accuse Lilia of throwing people of color under the bus, to which she retorts that "some people" say I play the victim. I struggle with wanting to support my minister of color and yet needing her to understand the language I speak. We remain in covenant, but sometimes the chasm between us feels wide indeed.

Toward the end of Lilia's ministry at First Parish in December 2014, I ask her what she wishes she had known in 2010. She does not hesitate. "People expected me to be much more perfect than was realistic. Regardless of how long I've been doing this, how much I thought I understood about interactions, it's different when you are a congregant versus when you are a minister. As a minister, I didn't have as much room to make mistakes, make comments, share my own pain."

CHANGES IN WORSHIP

Gloria Korsman, former chair of the Standing Committee, describes a key principle that the congregation learned during the tenure of Rev. Anita Farber-Robertson, First Parish's interim minister before Fred's arrival. "We can't just keep doing the same worship service the way we always did. We had to be more willing to share cultural space and let the people who come participate in shaping what that looks like." If congregations seek more diversity in the pews, they must also examine whom their style of worship serves and whom it does not serve.

For Unitarian Universalist congregations, inclusive worship usually means moving away from our traditional Protestant-based liturgy to more embodied celebration, including music and arts from different cultures and new modes of expression. Gordon Dragt, former minister of Middle Collegiate, urges us to "transform the worship service into a worship celebration."

Fred and Lilia are up to the task. As a folk singer-songwriter, Fred brings song-leading skills to his ministry, and it quickly becomes a regular practice at First Parish to sing one song from outside our hymnal, often accompanied by clapping. Lilia introduces the practice of body prayer and encourages dancing in the aisles. Our worship leaders encourage us to hold hands during the benediction.

These changes are challenging for some, on both a personal and an institutional level. Some people will leave the church

284 I MISTAKES AND MIRACLES

because of them. For me, singing without instrumental accompaniment and with bodily expression brings back memories of being ridiculed as a child. Moreover, I am a classically trained musician with admittedly narrow musical tastes. But I know that multiculturalism means embracing forms of worship that may be uncomfortable for me but deeply meaningful to another person. It is my job to stretch too. In time, having practiced Sunday after Sunday for years, I have built confidence in my singing and clapping to the point that I no longer feel self-conscious about it—and this is a great gift.

Even as these changes become part of First Parish's new worship style, the ministers and Transformation Team are aware of the danger of cultural misappropriation: using the traditions of minority cultures without their consent, poorly, or disrespectfully. Fred tries different ways to avoid such misappropriation. When leading songs from the African-American spiritual tradition, for instance, he is always careful to contextualize them with an explanation of their history and meaning.

When the Music Committee plans to bring in Linda Brown-San Martin, a renowned gospel choir leader, to lead the choir and other interested participants in what has now become an annual Gospel Sunday, Charlene Galarneau—a white woman—raises the question of what it means for a largely white congregation to sing gospel music. The Transformation Team invites her into a conversation with members of the Music Committee to share her concerns. "For the most part, people were open, but there was one person there who, I felt, was fairly condescending, making fun of language I used. I used the language of cultural misappropriation and he said he didn't buy it. But Fred responded. He was really affirming. There is commitment, even if we stumble along the way." Charlene sings on Gospel Sunday and will later join the Transformation Team herself.

Peggy Kraft, a white woman in her mid-forties who loves Gospel Sunday, describes some of the challenges. "Some of it is that humanists don't want to hear 'Jesus' and 'God.' And some of it has the high potential of being caged in white New England: 'We don't clap, we don't move, this is not how we do church,' and therefore is a value judgment about the way other people do church. And it makes some people very uncomfortable. It bums me out, actually. . . . I'm proud of Gospel Sunday. I love Gospel Sunday. I like to feel the music inside. I'm glad we do it anyways."

Music and the arts are not the only elements of worship that change. The staff commits to diversity in all its worship leaders, both ministers and worship associates. Fred explains, "Mainly, I think that worshipers need to see consistent leadership of color, Latino/a, in worship. It could be, if you had a diverse team of worship associates. . . . And when I was in Cambridge we did our best to do that. . . . Hey, look, I'm a white guy, but my hunch is that if you're a person of color and you walk into the church and all you see is white folks up front, that's a very different experience from seeing people of color in leadership."

To that end, Fred, in consultation with Standing Committee chair Susan Shepherd, makes an explicit decision to hire only ministerial interns of color. After Elizabeth Nguyen's departure, First Parish will hire Kenny Wiley, who becomes a leader in Black Lives of Unitarian Universalism, and then Seanan Fong, a Chinese American. Rev. Mykal Slack, an African American, will also join the staff as worship leader and community life coordinator. The worship team makes an effort to recruit worship associates from a variety of backgrounds.

Seanan recalls his realization that all the interns at First Parish are people of color. "It did bother me at first. . . . I'm not really bothered by it now, because I kind of understand the mission and understand the importance of having ministers of color—that having ministers of color in the pulpit is really central to exemplifying [our mission]. It's hard to do that with a monocultural pulpit."

I have both committed and been a victim of tokenism. For those of us engaged in this work, sometimes our good intentions get ahead of us. Sometimes our desire to appear nonracist overshadows our knowledge that there are no shortcuts to the goal of Beloved Community. It is an easy trap to fall into, all the more because people's perceptions of any given situation can differ so widely.

For me, relationship and mission—two of our Common Threads—are the key to authentic invitation. When I'm asked by a worship leader to take a place in the pulpit, I know that together we are part of a larger goal, and I'm happy to bring what I can to the table. If seeing me in leadership can help others feel more welcome—as the Japanese couple did for me in my first congregation years ago—then it is a role I play with gratitude. I know that my identity is one aspect of who I am that provides value to my congregation.

MOVING FROM MINISTER-CENTERED TO MISSION-CENTERED

At the beginning of 2011, the Transformation Team turns to another important aspect of our journey, a revision of our mission statement. As in many congregations, our mission statement has stood for years without examination; few people even know what it is. And despite First Parish's long-stated desire for diversity and its visible steps in that direction, the congregation has never formally voted to make this goal a part of our identity. This is an opportunity to articulate our purpose within and outside our walls.

The Transformation Team convenes a series of workshops titled "Mission Matters." Participants look at dozens of photographs of congregational life and are asked to choose the ones most significant to them and explain why. The conversations are heartfelt, and sometimes unexpectedly emotional. Using these expressed priorities as a guide, the Transformation Team authors a draft that is then presented to the congregation for further input.

At our semiannual meeting in June 2011, First Parish votes to approve its new mission statement:

Awakened by worship,
nourished by tradition,
and united by love,
we strive to create
a multicultural, spirit-filled community
that works for justice,
fosters spiritual curiosity and faith formation,
shares joy, heals brokenness,
and celebrates the sacred in all.

We welcome people of all beliefs, ages, classes,
colors, ethnicities, abilities, sexual orientations,
and gender identities and expressions.

In this process I came across a picture of some congregants and me sitting behind a table for our Social Justice Council. While I have always been an activist on some level, landing at First Parish in Cambridge inspires me to focus on the issues most important to me, sharing energy, wisdom, and passion with others. Nowhere is this more evident than in my work with immigration, where I am a founding member of the Immigration Task Force. This group later changes its name to Beyond Borders–Sin Fronteras to avoid the militaristic overtones of the term *task force.*

The most valuable thing I have learned about social justice as a Unitarian Universalist is the need to be accountable to stakeholders—to follow the leadership of those most affected by the policies we seek to change. At First Parish, this manifests in a number of partnerships with community organizations like Centro Presente, an immigrant advocacy organization operated and led primarily by Central Americans. With them and with other First Parish congregants, I find myself demonstrating at the Massachusetts State House and calling legislators, reaching a level of commitment and empowerment I have not previously experienced.

While conversations about race and culture are commonplace when discussing immigration, my congregation makes a commitment to pay attention to these issues in other areas of its justice work too. Our Environmental Justice Task Force works with organizations such as Alternatives for Community and Environment (ACE), whose mission statement says that it "builds the power of communities of color and low-income communities in Massachusetts to eradicate environmental racism and classism, create healthy, sustainable communities, and achieve environmental justice." First Parish in Cambridge becomes a reliable presence at the Mother's Day March of the Louis D. Brown Peace Institute, which exists to support and heal families affected by homicide. Later, we join the Greater Boston Interfaith Organization, comprising dozens of congregations of diverse religions and cultures working together to promote the public good.

Laura Heath-Stout, a white young adult at First Parish who has also been active in Beyond Borders–Sin Fronteras and the Transformation Team, describes the value of having a community dedicated to antiracism and social justice: "I really feel that the relationships I've built with people in these groups strengthen me to do this work elsewhere. . . . I have this congregation to come to, people to ask for advice and support." I too find that being grounded at First Parish both inspires me and enables me to take greater risks in challenging myself and the world around me.

On July 29, 2010, I join four other members of First Parish, along with Unitarian Universalists across the country—including co-author Nancy—in traveling to Phoenix to protest SB 1070, the racist anti-immigrant bill. As we march in the streets, provide support to those arrested, and sing outside the Fourth Avenue jail, I feel a deepening of my faith, a more profound experience of what being a Unitarian Universalist calls me to do. The following year, I embark on an eye-opening, life-changing weeklong trip to the Arizona-Sonora border, where I walk through the desert and speak to migrants and Border Patrol officers. Through these transformative experiences, my home community of First Parish in Cambridge is there supporting me, thinking of me, and waiting to hear what I bring home. In 2012, our congregation sends a record number of people to Justice General Assembly in Phoenix.

Our mission of creating a spirit-filled, multicultural community that works for justice is realized both outside and within our walls. In 2011, the Transformation Team brings to the congregation the UUA antiracism curriculum "Building the World We Dream About," written by Dr. Mark Hicks. We invite as initial participants the ministers, the Standing Committee, the Social Justice Council, and members of the Transformation Team. When a whopping nineteen out of twenty-three busy leaders accept the invitation to participate in this yearlong, twice-monthly program, I realize with surprise and delight how widely this commitment to antiracism and multiculturalism is shared.

Mandy Neff, director of religious education, explains her role in working to realize First Parish's mission. In examining children's programming, she says, "one of the things I tried hard to do is make sure we have a diversity of voices in who tells the story and who the story is about. . . . The opportunity to tell the stories I want to tell is always coming up at First Parish, and so it's a wonderful place to be able to do this work—because it's not just me or some little team of teachers talking about it, it's the whole congregation thinking about how we constantly refresh this for ourselves."

Being an antiracist and multicultural congregation involves more than the racial makeup of the people in its pews, more than offering educational programming. At First Parish, we must also examine our congregational norms and expectations, recognizing that *process* can be as important as *task*. Two evolutions in congregational committee work signify this understanding. For years, I have had the Transformation Team do an extended, guided check-in—sometimes taking up as much as a third of the meeting. We pose such questions as "Which of your identities has felt particularly alive in the past month?" or "What is something for which you are particularly grateful today?" This practice of deep sharing and vulnerability engenders the trust that is absolutely necessary for the work of transformation. Over time, other committees, including the Standing Committee and Social Justice Council, adopt the practice as well.

Rev. Dr. Eric H. F. Law, an Episcopal priest and founder of the Kaleidoscope Institute, has written extensively on multiculturalism and spirituality. In his book *The Wolf Shall Dwell with the Lamb*, he describes a process called Mutual Invitation. In this process, the conversation facilitator invites someone to share first and then to invite by name another person to speak. That person may choose to speak or pass, but in either case, they will invite the next person to share. This process continues until everyone has been invited. The Kaleidoscope Institute's website explains,

> Because there will be participants with different perceptions of power, facilitation that exclusively uses the "volunteer style" of interaction that favors those from individualist cultures excludes those whose interactions favor a collectivistic cul-

ture. . . . It is important to remember that in some cultural settings, group members will not speak up in a discussion unless they have been invited. The reasons for this may be gender- or age-related or other traditions embedded deeply in one's culture.

There may be those who are uncomfortable singling a person out to share. For them it may feel like when they were a child and were being selected (or not selected) to play on a team. There are two safeguards built into the process that can assuage people's fears. One: each person invited has three options: share, pass for now (which means "I am not ready, please come back to me"), or pass (which means "I do not choose to share on this topic"). However, no matter which option is selected, the one invited has the privilege of inviting another person in the group by *name*. Two: Throughout the process, the invitation to speak passes back and forth, and no one is left out of the process.

First Parish uses Mutual Invitation from time to time, and I find it deeply empowering. I have grown up in a collectivistic culture where I have been taught to look out for others' wishes before my own and not to speak out for myself but rather to wait for others to invite my contributions. As a result, I often find myself silent in large groups when I am not in a designated leadership role. When I do speak, I am anxious about taking up too much time or space. While some find it challenging, Mutual Invitation gives me the permission I am always waiting for and often do not explicitly receive in other facilitation processes.

Under the sponsorship of the Transformation Team, in 2011 I begin a twice-monthly Spanish conversation group at First Parish. Both beginning speakers and native speakers attend. For non-native speakers like myself, it is an opportunity to hone our language skills, but I quickly realize that it is a spiritual practice as well. The ability to express oneself eloquently and effortlessly is a privilege that many take for granted. The struggle to articulate exactly what I mean in another language is an important reminder of the challenges that many immigrants face daily.

At the 2013 General Assembly in Louisville, members of the Spanish Conversation group, as well as Fred and Lilia, present an all-Spanish workshop entitled "Comunidades sin Fronteras." Toward the end of the workshop, a Latina comes to the microphone and explains, her voice choked with emotion, that although she has been attracted to Unitarian Universalism for its work on social justice, she has never experienced its spirituality until today. I am immensely proud to belong to a congregation that pushes the boundaries of what is possible in our faith.

In the summer of 2013, the acquittal of George Zimmerman for the murder of Trayvon Martin stuns the nation. The Transformation Team and Social Justice Council hold a healing session for congregants to share what is in their hearts. Since the subject is so sensitive, Marcia Hams, chair of the Social Justice Council, and I begin with Taizé music as people enter and then light a chalice and remind the congregation of our Covenant of Right Relations, adopted in 2010:

> In the spirit of right relations, we covenant to:
> - acknowledge and celebrate our differences
> - listen compassionately, speak respectfully, and take responsibility for our actions and feelings
> - speak from personal experience, use "I" statements, and avoid judgment, generalizations, and offering unsolicited advice
> - deal directly with others to resolve conflict
> - strive to stay in relationship through conflict
> - fulfill our commitments, complete our tasks, admit our mistakes, praise each other's successes, and say "thank you"
> - ask for help when needed and give help as able
> - assume the good intentions of others

We remind the group that everyone's experiences are different and deserve to be heard and to refrain from judgment, debate, or blame. At the conclusion of the conversation, we reiterate our commitment to justice and to each other. I believe that our abilities to listen deeply, to create and hold space for a range of emotions, and to recognize how events affect different groups of people differently mark important moves toward the transformation we seek.

TRANSITIONING OUT OF LEADERSHIP

By the end of 2013, I have chaired or co-chaired the Transformation Team for over three years. It has been a remarkable experience, though not without its challenges. With this work such a visible priority for the congregation, and our ministers and director of religious education so deeply involved in it, some congregants murmur that the Transformation Team is "too powerful." During the writing of this book, I discover that this sentiment is more common than I have realized. LeLaina Romero, a queer multiracial Latina who also serves on the team, points out that the Transformation Team is also the only committee of the congregation that is half people of color. Is this relevant to the accusations of being too powerful?

By 2013, I also start to feel that I need to rebalance my life. Since moving to Cambridge, I have dedicated so much of my time and energy to church and justice work, often at the expense of family and career. It has felt necessary as part of my healing process, but perhaps that is no longer true. While I am lucky to have a stay-at-home husband who ably cares for our young daughters, I feel that I've missed too much of their childhood. My career has taken a number of turns, including another layoff, but I've finally landed in the natural language processing field, a longtime desire of mine as it blends my technical and linguistic skills. Perhaps it's time to consider pulling back from congregational work.

I declare my intent to step down from all leadership roles by the spring of 2014. However, an incident occurs that causes me to leave earlier. Occasionally in the past several years, congregants both inside and outside the Transformation Team have raised the issue of other oppressions. What about LGBTQIA concerns? What about access and inclusion? Why doesn't the Transformation Team become an agent for education and change in these areas too?

At a meeting near the end of 2013, this conversation intensifies, and I handle it badly. The truth is that I am afraid. I'm afraid of losing our focus on antiracism. We are, after all, only a handful of people, and I fear we don't have the time to take on education in these other areas as well, especially since not all of us have expertise in them. I'm more afraid, though, of losing this group of tight-knit, trusted allies and people of color. Unintentionally, I have led this team to become not only a working committee but also a sort of covenant group, where deep sharing and listening have led to the kind of mutual trust so necessary for tackling issues as charged as race. I'm fearful of losing the one place where I feel totally safe to express my greatest joys and disappointments.

But it has never been all about me. One member says she feels silenced by our unwillingness to expand our scope. I'm panicked and defensive as the discussion heats up. By the end of the evening, raised voices and hurt feelings have dashed any hope of coming to agreement. Over the next several days, as I contemplate what appears to be a sea change in the Transformation Team's direction, I feel I can no longer be the one to lead it. I contact each of the members, apologize, and announce my intention to step down from the team.

My relationship with each individual is preserved, but I regret my handling of the situation and my inability to stay at the table. After a period of dormancy and several more conversations, the Transformation Team chooses not to expand its scope but to name the existence of other oppressions and acknowledge the need for intersectional analysis. Its new charter reads,

> First Parish has adopted in its mission the challenge of transforming into a multiracial, multicultural, justice-making congregation. Because we recognize the unique role and impact of racism in the histories and present situations of our country, of Cambridge, and of Unitarian Universalism, our Standing Committee has charged the Transformation Team with the role of facilitating this process.
>
> To that end, the Transformation Team creates space to challenge racism and to educate ourselves and our congregation about racism and multiculturalism. While this is our focus, we also recognize that racism intersects with other forms of oppression that many of us experience. . . .
>
> The work of transformation is bold, joyful, and deeply enriching. We acknowledge that all of us at First Parish are imperfect and often wounded. Yet we commit ourselves to this work, to continue to heal ourselves, each other, and our world. Although pain and discomfort may come up in the course of transformation, we maintain hope and joy in the process.

As these changes unfold, I realize that the mistake I made wasn't my point of view in itself but rather my failure to hear and validate others' opinions. I, too, have much to learn in this work. A few weeks later, Nancy invites me into partnership to write this book, and it is here that I continue my learning and contribute to the work of multiculturalism.

DEPARTURE OF OUR MINISTERS

The church year of 2014–15 sends First Parish into a time of enormous transition. In the fall, Rev. Lilia Cuervo announces her resignation as associate minister. Lilia's departure comes as a surprise and disappointment to me. Despite our conflicts, we have always loved each other, and she has brought so much to the congregation. Already involved in writing this book, I ask for an interview before we must begin the period of noncontact required when a minister leaves a congregation. She seems at peace: "I'm happy. Mistakes were made on both sides. But I think we ended up in a good place. I hope the next person is what you need to get to the next level."

Yet First Parish's finances suggest that there will be no next person. We have hoped that calling a minister of color would help us to grow enough that we could support the position with our regular operating budget after the special funding ran out. But while our congregation has grown substantially in some ways—maturing as an organization, deepening in mission—numerical growth and a corresponding increase in pledges are not among them. For now, First Parish will not be replacing its associate minister.

While this news is a disappointment, congregational life forges on. Under the leadership of Standing Committee chair Susan Shepherd, First Parish engages in a discernment process for a proposal by Harvard's Philips Brooks House to transform our basement—at that time rented by a local theater group—into a youth homeless shelter. After two years of laying the groundwork, the vote passes in the spring of 2015. First Parish has, once again, taken another large step toward living its mission.

Then, in mid-June, Rev. Fred Small abruptly announces his decision to resign at the end of September in order to pursue climate justice full time. I am shocked and devastated beyond words. For nearly six years, Fred has been one of the most significant figures in my life, serving as both pastor and colleague. I cannot imagine doing the work of congregational transformation without him; in fact, I can hardly contemplate being a Unitarian Universalist without him as my minister.

With my husband and daughters gone for most of the summer, I depend extensively on my relationships with other congregants to process my grief and disbelief. In fact, all of us depend on each other, gathering to process our feelings, doing the work that needs to be done for the congregational transition, reminding each other that the congregation is strong and that our identity does not depend on any individual minister. We rally around new Standing Committee chair Peggy Kraft, whose job is now very different from what she has imagined it would be. We are there with each other and for each other. By the time September arrives, I have achieved some measure of calm and optimism.

FORGING AHEAD

The Standing Committee hires as interim minister Rev. Clyde Grubbs, a highly experienced minister and founding member of DRUUMM with decades of experience in antiracism, multiculturalism, and antioppression. I have known Clyde for years, and I feel great relief at this news. Having Clyde as our minister gives me confidence that our work will continue even in the absence of Fred and Lilia. I feel I can finally relax into his leadership. Clyde, who identifies as Texas Cherokee, will be joined in his second year by Rev. Danielle Di Bona, of Wampanoag and Italian descent.

And the work continues. Clyde leads us in learning about the Doctrine of Discovery, by which Christian European nations justified the colonization of indigenous lands. The Doctrine of Discovery was repudiated by the UUA General Assembly in 2014.

Under the leadership of Marcia Hams, a white lesbian in her sixties, and Rashid Shaikh, who identifies as an Indian Muslim, the Transformation Team continues to provide opportunities for discussions about race, including screening the film *Cracking the Codes* and hosting a conversation with Black Lives Matter leaders as well as white allies. Attendance at these events is higher than ever.

I recall the words of a stewardship consultant who once said that leadership in congregations consists of groups in concentric circles, and that the more permeable the boundaries between the circles, the healthier the congregation. As I decide it's time to have a less visible role in the congregation's work toward antiracism and multiculturalism, I'm grateful that our mission has been so fully integrated into our identity that living it out depends on neither individual ministers nor individual laypeople.

Clyde leads First Parish through a number of organizational and governance changes that enable us to move forward more effectively. "For me, multicultural transformation is about becoming a democratic community that is inclusive. I had the impression that First Parish was not owning its democracy and empowering the leaders that it chose to be its leaders to help them make decisions," he explains. Our move toward new models of governance enables both the Board and staff to better act in service of our mission. When the Standing Committee wants to hang a large Black Lives Matter banner on the front of the church, it is empowered to make the decision after inviting congregational input rather than needing to call an entire meeting for a congregational vote.

Our understanding of congregational transformation has evolved too. We talk less about being more diverse (which is sometimes called "browning the pews") and more about being antiracist and antioppressive. Rashid describes his own evolution: "Some of what I have realized is that for a while I had a very naïve notion of transformation—that transformation would reflect itself with how many brown bodies we had in the pews. I have now appreciated, I hope very deeply, that that's not the way to think about transformation. What we mean by transformation is something much much broader . . . a lot more active engagement with the communities around us, working with the communities, working with ourselves, which is working *within* ourselves." Diversity may be a byproduct of our progress, but it should not be the end goal in itself.

We also continue expanding our understanding of multiculturalism and antioppression beyond race and ethnicity to include gender, sexual orientation, and ability. It is now common to share gender pronouns during introductions in groups, and there are more conversations on welcoming those living with mental illness and physical disabilities. Though we have further to go in some of these areas, we are now better able to recognize and speak about intersectionality.

LOOKING TO THE FUTURE

Throughout the course of our interviews with other congregations, Nancy and I have often asked the question, "Is your multicultural mission minister-led or congregation-led? If your minister left tomorrow, would the work continue?" At First Parish in Cambridge, we are living our answer to these questions.

In the spring of 2016, we co-authors ask a few members at First Parish to describe where the congregation is now. Gloria Korsman responds, "It's like we're climbing a mountain. We hit a bit of a plateau for a while, and I think this next settled ministry will be really important for going forward. I really do think that we've had some disappointment and some setbacks, but we're still on the path."

Peggy Kraft, after serving as chair of the Standing Committee through Fred's departure and the arrival of Clyde, says,

I think I would have said something different a year ago than now. I would have been a lot more concerned. . . . Certainly going into the interim, it was a question of whether First Parish would own the mission. In the work I've done so far, the people I'm talking to, there's no hesitation. There's no "Why are we still doing this? It was Fred's thing." It's "Who do we need next?" There are a lot of unanswered questions about what we need in a minister, but the sense that the new minister will help us continue in this mission seems to be solid. We haven't had to call a meeting to say, "What is our mission?"

I co-chair the Search Committee for our next called minister. In the packet of information that our congregation puts together for candidates to review, Clyde includes a letter that offers this affirmation:

I have served 12 Unitarian Universalist congregations in a professional capacity. First Parish is the most mission-centered congregation I have worked with as a minister. . . . The mission guides the work of the Standing Committee, and has empowered its ongoing longtime work of antiracist, antioppressive, and multicultural transformation over several years.

Throughout the fall and winter of 2016, the Search Committee hosts several conversations with groups within the congregation, as well as with the congregation at large, asking what we congregants are seeking in our new minister. Members articulate a desire for someone who will help us build community, preach inspirational sermons, provide pastoral care, lead our organization effectively, and help us fulfill our mission to become a multicultural, justice-making congregation.

We find our candidate in Adam Lawrence Dyer, originally of nearby Framingham and currently living in California. A Black gay man, Adam has vast experience teaching about and working for equity, particularly around issues of race, class, and culture. He is a poet, singer, and blogger. His 2016 book of meditations, *Love Beyond God*, is published as part of Skinner House Books' inSpirit series. We are impressed by his warmth, talent, pastoral nature, and ability to communicate with a wide range of people.

The final stages of the search process, in the spring of 2017, occur amid the unfolding conversation in Unitarian Universalism around hiring practices and white supremacy culture. Religious educators, including Christina Rivera, Aisha Hauser, and our former intern Kenny Wiley, call for congregations to participate in a "UU White Supremacy Teach-in" in late April or early May. The two suggested Sundays overlap Candidating Week at First Parish, when the full congregation first gets to meet Adam, and he rises to the opportunity. His sermon on April 30, "We Are Jazz," speaks frankly about his own experiences around race and the role of discomfort in collective liberation. At the end, he receives a standing ovation. The following Sunday, First Parish in Cambridge votes unanimously to call Adam as our next settled minister. He responds,

> It is an incredibly humbling honor to have the opportunity to serve as the next Lead Minister at First Parish, Cambridge. I am truly inspired by this loving congregation and its mission to cultivate a multicultural and diverse community. I look forward to being a part of what promises to be a bright future for the church as we continue to be deeply engaged in social justice, excited about conserving and promoting the rich history of the community, and invested in creating a uniquely spiritual space where all are truly welcome.

Over the next year, we continue to deepen our understanding and our commitment through Adam's sermons, a workshop series on resisting white supremacy, and a caucus for people of color. A new chapter in the long history of this congregation begins.

THE JOY OF THE JOURNEY

As I look back on how far First Parish and I have come in the past nine years, I recall a conversation with Fred very soon after my arrival. In it, he describes the journey toward multicultural community as "fun." I challenge him on the use of that word, saying, "I think for something to be fun, it has to be optional. This isn't optional for me."

Some years later, I share this conversation with Victor Lee Lewis, a nationally recognized African-American social justice educator well known for his work in the groundbreaking 1994 race-relations documentary *The Color of Fear*. Victor agrees, "'Fun' is too glib. But this work, it can be described as—joyful."

As Nancy and I complete our work on this book, we decide that our original title, *The Joy of the Journey*, is far too simplistic to describe what we are learning. Still, *joyful* is a word that resonates with me. Through both the tears I have shed and the laughter I've shared with my many companions on the journey, there has been great joy as we all seek to build the Beloved Community, to live fully into our humanity, and—above all—to answer the call of love. Even as I know there is no final destination, no paved path to follow, it is in the striving that I have come to know myself and others so deeply and to understand that living my faith brings both great challenges and great rewards. It is a privilege to do this work.

QUESTIONS FOR YOU AND
YOUR CONGREGATION

1. Does your congregation have a formal commitment to antiracism and/or multiculturalism in the form of a mission or vision statement? How does the presence or absence of this formal commitment affect your work?

2. To what extent does the journey toward multiculturalism depend on the efforts of specific individuals, either ministers or laypeople? How can you approach a "tipping point" of engaged participants in this work and avoid burnout of those who have been its primary leaders?

3. What support systems, either formal or informal, exist for people of color in your congregation?

4. How do you approach issues of intersectionality? Do your efforts toward greater inclusion include consideration of age, ability, class, sexual orientation, and gender identity and expression, as well as race and ethnicity?

CHAPTER SEVEN

Loves, Losses, and Shifting Paradigms

NANCY'S JOURNEY WITH FIRST UNITARIAN CHURCH
SAN JOSÉ, CALIFORNIA

> One mistake we often make is trying to lead with our
> strengths rather than our heartbreak.
>
> —Rev. Marlin Lavanhar

> We need to counter the culture of purity and perfection
> with a Universalist theyology of love and with new prac-
> tices that teach us we will not be rejected but can find our
> way back when we fail.
>
> —Rev. Sean Parker Dennison

"CAMINANTE, NO HAY CAMINO, se hace camino al andar."
("Traveler, there is no road; we make the road as we go.") Spanish poet Antonio Machado's lines describe what it feels like for
any congregation trying to find its way as it builds multicultural,
antiracist Beloved Community. The commitment to this journey
simply doesn't come with a roadmap. As the stories in this book
show, every congregation discovers and creates pathways that
loop-de-loop and circle back, that branch and almost dead-end.
Yet with intention, patience, humility, and persistence, congregants

and leaders inch forward together, experiencing joys as well as trials along the way.

When I look back on my own journey toward multiculturalism, Machado's words feel spot on for me too. That journey began in my early childhood in the rich racial and ethnic mix of San Antonio, Texas, and has continued through multiple cross-country moves. Along the way, teachers, guides, and companions have shown up with suggestions and signposts for which way to go next. I could never do this work alone.

But it's when I look at my growth as a minister since arriving at the First Unitarian Church of San José (FUCSJ) in 2005 that I really see the shape of this unpredictable journey. Searching, risky, sorrowful, challenging, celebratory, and even miraculous elements show up in rhythmic measure. I bumble and stumble. The congregants and I try out new approaches. We lose one path and create another. We learn, and grieve, and increase our capacity to love. Through it all, we inch forward together. And that feels like a miracle in itself.

Rev. Sean Parker Dennison, in his 2015 Berry Street Lecture, quotes a sermon delivered by Rev. Marlin Lavanhar years before. Even these references loop-de-loop, weaving relationship to relationship. Rev. Marlin says, "One mistake we often make is trying to lead with our strengths rather than our heartbreak." Rev. Sean goes on to urge us faith leaders to "lead with our heartbreak, even with our failure. We need to counter the culture of purity and perfection with a Universalist theyology[8] of love and with new practices that teach us we will not be rejected but can find our way back when we fail."

---

[8] Rev. Sean's word *theyology*, he explains, "decenters the masculine root *theos*" and "disrupts the gender binary." For me, its ambiguity between singular and plural also points to the broad network of theological roots at the source of our faith.

Marlin's and Sean's words encourage us travelers to disrupt white supremacy culture by rejecting the pressure to do this work "the right way"—as though there is just one right way. They urge us to accept our own and each other's failings and limitations along with our strengths and achievements. They ask us to live "broken-openheartedly," as I like to put it—with hearts broken open by pain and thus able to grow larger still.

This chapter offers the story of my own love and heartbreak, failures and rediscoveries as I have traveled with the First Unitarian Church of San José. It traces the way the congregation's story and my own weave together. It hints at what it feels like to be a white minister, called to the work of antiracism and multiculturalism, serving a congregation that also claims a multicultural mission and vision, in the midst of one of the most racially, ethnically, and economically diverse cities in the United States. Where are the mistakes, misgivings, and miracles along the way—for me and for the people I serve? What gives us pause, and what keeps us going?

Most of all, what happens when just one model of building multicultural Beloved Community becomes identified with the whole project? And what happens when that model must change? This is the story of loving and losing a ministry precious to the congregation and to me and of the work we are doing together now to shift paradigms and to take our mission deeper still.

ORIGIN STORIES

The congregation's story begins in the early 1860s, with a determined, progressive couple—Laura J. and B. F. Watkins—who long for a Unitarian presence at the southern end of San Francisco Bay. They put their remarkable organizing skills to work, and in the fall of 1865, they gather about a hundred people to hear Rev. Charles Gordon Ames speak. As the era's church-planting

Unitarian "missionary" in Northern California, he is quite a catch to help launch the new congregation. On that first Sunday, he preaches about his recent visit to the Civil War–torn South. He cries out for the freedom and dignity of all people, including those who have just been freed from slavery. At First Unitarian, whenever we tell folks who we are, we still brag about these beginnings.

By 1892, the congregation has built its own building in the heart of downtown. It develops the habit of taking unpopular stands for freedom, dignity, and justice. It works for affordable housing and jobs for the unemployed as early as 1910. It opposes the internment of Japanese-Americans in World War II. Congregants bring the detainees coffee, blankets, and sack lunches at the railroad station as a way of saying, "We see you, we honor you, we know this is wrong." In the McCarthy era of the 1950s, First Unitarian refuses to sign the required loyalty oath and, as a consequence, loses its tax-exempt status. (A Supreme Court decision restores it six years later.) In the 1960s, it serves daily meals to the unhoused. The congregation builds a sturdy identity in the region as an action-oriented, justice-seeking community. Congregants develop an ethos of showing up when they see a need.

But there's a flip side to the history of FUCSJ's first hundred years. Recurring financial near-disasters, a rapid turnover in ministers, and wildly fluctuating membership numbers build anxiety into the congregation's identity too.

By the mid-1980s, FUCSJ is so small that it is on the verge of closing its doors. Congregants' collective self-esteem is at an all-time low.

This is when the Unitarian Universalist Association's Office of Extension Ministry suggests that recently ordained Rev. Lindi Ramsden might be a match for the struggling congregation. If First Unitarian hires Rev. Lindi, she will be one of the first out lesbian ministers to serve as solo pastor in any mainstream congregation in California. She has been searching for almost a year for a congregation ready to make that leap.

When Lindi and her family pay an exploratory visit to First Unitarian on a Sunday morning in the spring of 1985, only a dozen of its thirty members attend worship that day. Even so, the congregation "doesn't seem that broken to me," Lindi remembers later. "They have a beautiful building—it needs some structural work, but it's gorgeous. They have wonderful people, they can throw an amazing potluck, they care about their kids, and they have great music. There are people with serious mental health challenges in the congregation, and others with almost no income, but the congregation is really generous in finding ways for all different kinds of people to participate. Yeah, there are broken parts in the system—and then there are these gems of capacity and willingness."

First Unitarian and Rev. Lindi agree that they are a match, and she takes up her ministry there that summer.

"Gems of capacity and willingness"—when Lindi says these words to Karin and me in 2015, my heart soars. Great people and potlucks, the love of children and music, the beautiful building, the warm, wide, deep inclusiveness—these gems of capacity and willingness still form the core of FUCSJ's identity. They hint at why I fall in love with them too.

THE BIRTH OF MULTICULTURAL MINISTRIES AT FUCSJ

In the first months of Rev. Lindi's settlement in San José, she leans into her passion for building a multicultural, multiracial community at First Unitarian. This part of the story begins when the congregation engages with the Central American refugee crisis of the 1980s. First Unitarian votes almost unanimously to join the

Sanctuary Movement, and the vote marks a culture shift in the conflict-averse congregation. Rev. Lindi and other congregants host refugees in their homes. The congregation receives threatening phone calls from Salvadoran right-wingers, and cars with dark-tinted windows park outside Rev. Lindi's home. But the congregants and their minister carry on.

Then in 1993, one of those refugees, Edgar Cruz, by then a member of the staff, asks a seemingly simple question: "Why don't we offer services in Spanish, like that Episcopal cathedral around the corner? People like me respect what the church is doing; we share the same spiritual journey, and we want to learn more about Unitarian Universalism."

The program that grows out of Edgar's question forms the heart of First Unitarian's multicultural work for almost twenty years. Originally called Unitarios Universalistas de Habla Hispana (UUHH)—Spanish-Speaking Unitarian Universalists—and then Spanish-Speaking Ministries (SSM), this program brings national attention to FUCSJ, and it catches my heart during my ministerial search process. A few scenes from its early years capture the hope, the drama, and the Common Threads that run through its beginnings.

SEEDED WITH HOPE

The group that conceives of UUHH first gathers over a potluck meal in First Unitarian's basement in late spring of 1993. Some participants are Spanish-speaking or bilingual Latinos/as; some are bilingual European Americans. Some are members of local Latinx lesbian and gay groups that meet in the church building. Mexicans, Salvadorans and other Central Americans, Protestants, Catholics, pagans, atheists, agnostics, and more crowd around the table that day—each one finding in Unitarian Universalism a spiritual home that finally makes sense for them.

Ervin Barrios, who emigrated with his family from Mexico as a young man, remembers the group's mood: "Because there was a good group of us who spoke Spanish or were bilingual, we thought creating worship in Spanish would be extremely easy. We didn't come into it with fear. We just thought it was a positive next step, so let's do it!"

The food, the lively conversation in Spanish, the hope, the joy, the vision—these are the seeds for this multicultural ministry. They propel the staggering amount of work it actually takes to bring this vision to life. The group finds, creates, and translates readings for worship. They draw on memories of childhood hymns in Spanish, and they translate Unitarian Universalist favorites. By that winter, the small group has pieced together enough worship materials to launch full-length services in Spanish, even if they have to sing the same ten hymns over and over for the first year.

"Every time I am translating all this material," Ervin remembers, "I am thinking, this is going to have international repercussions. Think of how many people can benefit from it, anywhere they speak Spanish." Ervin's enthusiasm and expertise will draw him into the coordinator role for the program more than once.

Indeed, as word of the new program spreads, requests for these resources begin to trickle in from around the world. Eventually, the small spiral notebook of hymns in Spanish that First Unitarian collects becomes the foundation for the Unitarian Universalist Association's Spanish hymnal *Las voces del camino*, published in 2009.

The early days of UUHH also allow longtime congregants to see Unitarian Universalism "from the margins." Lisa Heller, a white European-American member who is bilingual, offers a Unitarian Universalist history class in Spanish for the new Latinx members. When she gets to the story of Michael Servetus, Edgar Cruz, a Central American refugee himself, exclaims, "That's a *refugee story* about a Unitarian founding father!" Servetus, declared a heretic in the sixteenth century for questioning the doctrine of the Trinity, flees for his life from his native Spain, seeking freedom to speak and live in ways faithful to his beliefs. Some four hundred years later, the new immigrants see themselves in this Unitarian ancestor.

"I had never thought of the story in that way," Rev. Lindi marvels. These new Unitarian Universalists teach her how to read this foundational story from the margins. When I hear this story years later, my heart breaks open too.

EARLY DISSENT

Alongside the energy and enthusiasm, the program also sparks dissent in the wider congregation. "Conflict is inevitable," as our Common Threads predict. Rev. Lindi holds congregation-wide conversations to discuss the new program before it begins, but opponents still feel that the leaders have "forced" this new vision on them. At one point, when Lindi invites the congregation at the English-language service to recite its affirmation in both English and Spanish, a white member storms out. Congregants in the sanctuary can hear him shouting from the narthex that he has grown up in this religion and doesn't need to "go through this in order to prove I am a good Unitarian!" The disruption causes ripples of discomfort in a congregation still tender about its earlier history with conflict.

A few prominent members leave First Unitarian when the program begins. Others stay but worry about how FUCSJ will pay for UUHH's coordinator, accompanist, and other costs once the initial grants run out. Some wonder whether that's where the congregation's resources should go at all. Money often becomes the focus of fights when a multicultural mission and vision are made explicit. I will inherit this struggle when I arrive in 2005.

How much attention should a congregation give to early protests when a dream is first coming into being? How can leaders stay in relationship with dissenters, allowing those critiques to make a multicultural program stronger? Or should congregants accept the losses in membership and support that usually accompany change, without letting those losses distract from the vision?

Both/and—this concept runs throughout our Common Threads. Congregational leaders must discern, case by case, when to engage and when to let go, without diluting the overarching goal. Despite the uncertainties and challenges at First Unitarian, the new vision's passionate champions forge ahead. They decide, as Rev. Lindi says, to "pay attention to the health and build on it."

THE FIRE

In the early 1990s, new staff and student ministers bring fresh energy to the congregation. In the spring of 1994, Rev. Geoff Rimositis's call to serve as associate minister for religious education affirms that families and youth remain at the heart of First Unitarian's identity, at least for the predominantly white part of the congregation. Meanwhile, students at Starr King School for the Ministry in Berkeley, including Peter Morales and Lilia Cuervo, lend their skills to preaching and translating for the Spanish services.

Then, on the night of October 16, 1995, the church almost burns down. The day before, FUCSJ has ordained Unitarian Universalism's first Latina minister, Rev. Patricia Jimenez, a community minister called to hospital chaplaincy. The next night, a small spark left by contractors repairing the roof turns into a six-alarm fire, devouring the roof of the social hall and part of the sanctuary roof.

The fire, which causes millions of dollars' worth of damage, challenges every dream First Unitarian has been building. The congregation goes into exile, worshiping in the cafeteria of the senior center across the street. For the next few years, Rev. Lindi spends the majority of her time writing grants, building relationships in the wider community to help fund the church's reconstruction, and leading three capital campaigns in a row. Congregants dig deep, giving and giving again of their time and money, supervising reconstruction, designing new offices in the basement, painting every wall.

During this recovery time, leaders experiment with different ways to keep the UUHH ministry going. First they try offering the Spanish service in an office down the street. Then they try holding a semi-shared service, in which everyone initially gathers together in the community center, and worship leaders deliver the opening words and the story for all ages in both English and Spanish. When the children are sung out for their classes, the Spanish speakers leave too and hold the rest of their service in Spanish in another room.

"Everyone *hated* it," Lindi remembers. "It was an experiment that didn't work."

But FUCSJ continues experilearning—another Common Thread. "We had all sorts of activities in Spanish," Ervin Barrios recalls: "worship services, workshops, conversations, gatherings, etc. We even hired a Spanish theater director for a community project. There were two consecutive UUHH coordinators during that time."

Overall, though, the congregation is shell-shocked and stretched to its limits. Under such stresses, keeping UUHH going at all is something of a miracle.

On the other hand, another aspect of First Unitarian's multi-cultural vision gains momentum during the recovery, fueled by city grants. In 1997, FUCSJ launches the Third Street Community Center (TSCC) to serve its Spanish-speaking neighbors. Congregants serve as some of TSCC's first volunteer teachers in the children's after-school programs as well as in the computer and English-as-a-second-language classes offered for adults. Once again, First Unitarian is throwing open its doors to the community, as Rev. Gordon Dragt recommends.

When the congregation returns to its beautifully restored building in 1998, the dream of the full-fledged Spanish-language worship service rises again. Ervin Barrios returns to the coordinator role. The congregation hires and ordains Rev. Lilia Cuervo as its extension minister. And once UUHH has its own Latina minister, it enters into what Ervin calls its "peak period."

REV. LILIA'S MINISTRY

Rev. Lilia deepens and expands the UUHH program. She leads spiritual retreats and classes on Unitarian Universalism in Spanish. She sets up parties—*convivios*—in her and others' homes where Spanish and English speakers mingle. She stays late in the office for those who want pastoral care after their shifts end. She builds the leadership skills of Latinx worship associates, some of whom serve in both the Spanish and the English services. The name of the program is changed to Spanish-Speaking Ministries (SSM) to reflect its expansion.

Attendance at the Spanish service on Sunday mornings, though, is spotty. Some Sundays, the front pews of the round sanctuary hold forty people or more. On other Sundays, Rev. Lilia is still standing at the front door when it's time for worship to begin, wondering whether more than a handful of people will show up.

On the other hand, after the fire some English speakers begin attending the SSM service regularly. During the recovery, the congregation has added an interpreter's booth on the balcony level, and a handful of bilingual congregants volunteer to take turns murmuring the English translation into headsets for those who need it.

Everyone who shows up for these services cherishes SSM. They keep their hope for its continuance and growth cupped in their hearts, like a carefully tended flame.

BIG TRANSITIONS

Any major trauma, with its aftermath, enters into the DNA of a community and gets passed along from generation to generation. For First Unitarian, the story of the fire includes not just the shock of destruction but also the fierce resilience of the congregation's recovery. FUCSJ gains a new sense of itself as strong and resourceful.

Then in 2003, Rev. Lindi accepts the call to create the Unitarian Universalist Legislative Ministries—California, a group that will advocate for Unitarian Universalist values with state legislators in Sacramento. She has served FUCSJ for seventeen years, through periods of great growth and experimentation and through the defining crisis of the fire. She has broken through the congregation's old pattern of short-term ministries and its boom-and-bust waves of membership and crises of confidence. At the time of her leaving, First Unitarian is a warm, spiritually healthy, fun-loving, midsized program church, with a famous innovative ministry in Spanish and a growing Third Street Community Center sharing the building.

But money is still an issue. The congregation must decide during the interim period whether it will continue to support its multicultural mission in general and Spanish-Speaking Ministries in particular. For the monthly newsletter, Rev. Lilia writes a five-part history of FUCSJ's multicultural engagement. By the time she reaches part 3, the congregation's anxiety about its resources has reached a peak.

On the one hand, she writes, non-Latinx members who are worried about SSM's survival are asking, "Are we . . . doing everything possible to make the Latinos feel welcome here? Are we somehow precluding them from the empowerment of belonging to the Board and from participating in every aspect of our church?" There have already been Latinx Board members, but in such times of stress, the distance between the Spanish-speaking members and most of the other congregants becomes more apparent.

On the other hand, Rev. Lilia notes the growing voices of dissent and fear from those who question the validity of the SSM project. She writes,

> I have perceived some anxiety on the part of those who believe that numbers are the main indicator of success, and perhaps a sense of failure on the part of those who expected that by now the SSM should be able to pay for all the expenses of a full-time, full-range ministry.
>
> The more I think about these and other issues, the more I feel like saying: "Relax, look back and count your blessings. Learn to appreciate all the good that has been done as a church and individually. Try to remember who are the Latinos in this church, and how much they have already received, as well as given and participated in: from belonging to the Board, to leading services both in English and Spanish, and a lot in between. Try to learn firsthand, by talking to them (even if you need to do it through an interpreter), how much this faith and this church mean to them and how their lives have been transformed since they have been coming here. And foremost, please try not to judge results based on the American non-Latino culture, which in general measures success or failure with a somewhat linear, homogeneous yardstick that in most cases doesn't apply to us."

When I read this account years later, my heart aches at the subtext. Cross-cultural relationships have clearly proved daunting for some congregants, especially in the face of language barriers. Some English speakers don't have a strong sense of Latinx members' contributions to the congregation, let alone the power of Unitarian Universalism in the Spanish speakers' lives. The "linear, homogeneous yardstick," characteristic of white supremacy culture, uses numbers and dollars as the measure of success and overlooks the transformative power of the faith. Rev. Lilia urges a multicultural perspective and a glass-half-full vision of what FUCSJ has accomplished so far on its journey. Her buoyancy and affirmation model another way to approach this tense interim time.

In the first five years of my ministry with FUCSJ, I strike many of the same notes that Rev. Lilia sounds in this history. With SSM's passionate champions, I look for ways to establish and deepen cross-cultural relationships. With FUCSJ's leadership, we explore different cultural styles and standards. And we too are worried about the tough decisions to come.

But the resource issues at FUCSJ are also real. During the interim between senior ministers in 2003–05, First Unitarian must face the fact that, with fewer than three hundred members, it has seriously stretched itself to support three full-time ministers (Rev. Lindi, Rev. Geoff, and Rev. Lilia) along with part-time staff, including the coordinators of the Spanish-Speaking Ministries and Social Justice programs. By receiving generous grants and by falling behind the UUA's fair compensation standards, FUCSJ has kept this large staff afloat. With no in-house funds available to replace the grants, lay leaders realize that they will have to reduce the ministerial staff to two. They choose to keep an associate minister for religious education (Geoff) because of the centrality of children and youth to the congregation. They also want to call a new senior minister. Congregational leaders ask the Search Committee to find a candidate for senior minister who will share FUCSJ's commitment to building a multicultural Beloved Community, one who can serve both the English and Spanish speakers.

Over the course of Rev. Lilia's ministry with First Unitarian, lay leaders ask her twice if she would like to be installed, rather than continue year to year as a contract minister—a step that would represent an even deeper commitment between congregation and minister. "They look at alternatives for saving money in order to pay my salary," Lilia tells us co-authors. The will to keep her on staff has been strong, she wants us to understand. Even so, now the congregation will have to say goodbye to her.

When congregations on the road to multiculturalism feel they must release staff members of color, they often cite budget limitations as the defining factor in the decision. (I will face the same dilemma a few years later.) But budgeting always tells a story about a congregation's commitments and priorities. Diminishing funding for staff and programs focused on communities of color inevitably communicates that a lesser priority is placed on serving and including those marginalized communities. At best, this experience represents a case of intention versus impact.

Could First Unitarian have made a different choice, and what could that other choice have been? I'm not sure about the answer to either question, especially at this point in the congregation's journey. Instead, the leadership sincerely hopes that this change in staffing will help to bridge the gap between what seem like two congregations. For a long time, the passionate champions of the multicultural mission have maintained a vision of "one congregation in two languages." Maybe the new staffing structure will help move that vision forward.

These, then, are the elements in place when First Unitarian's *camino* and my own journey intersect.

ON THE WAY TO SAN JOSÉ

In 2003, as FUCSJ moves into its interim period, I am a year out of divinity school and have finished my parish internship on the

East Coast. I can now enter into search for a settled ministerial position in a congregation. Looking back, I am struck by how much, in my first applications, I soft-pedal my commitment to the work of multiculturalism and antiracism, even though I have spent the previous five years focused on my own awakening and on what I, as a white minister, can bring to the work of undoing racism in my faith.

My first year of search fails to produce a match; no congregation calls me. When I start again the next year, I dig deeper for the courage to be authentic. That second year, my applications emphasize that I am looking for a congregation ready to travel along the road to multiculturalism and antiracism. I promise to meet congregants where they are and to move forward together. This is exactly what the First Unitarian Church of San José is looking for.

FUCSJ catches my heart from my first glance at its search packet. Creativity, resilience, determination, and warmth—these qualities are the threads of gold that shine through the congregation's story. Its people are clearly willing to take risks and to show up for justice; at the same time, they value having fun. In those days, the word *fun* even shows up in the first sentence of their paragraph-long mission statement. They have an active hiking group, and they also serve meals at a shelter for unhoused folks living with mental illness. They have survived the fire, and their Spanish-Speaking Ministries program shines like a jewel, unique in our Unitarian Universalist movement. In fact, their commitment to SSM is so bold that it doesn't even occur to me to ask whether this is the only expression of multiculturalism and antiracism at FUCSJ. Surely it is enough! If only I can be so lucky as to be called to this plucky, adventurous congregation!

I make it to Candidating Week, which is the point in the ministerial search process when a search committee presents its choice to the whole congregation. By midweek, I have led worship at

both services on one Sunday, preaching my sermon in Spanish at
9:30 A.M. and then again in English at 11:00. That Tuesday evening, the members of the Spanish-Speaking Ministries and I sit
down to dinner. This gathering—our first real engagement with
each other—encapsulates some of the joys and the worries that
will arise in my first few years at FUCSJ.

FIRST ENCOUNTERS

Long tables form a large rectangle crowding the congregation's
Ramsden Fireside Room. I look out at the faces of about twenty
SSM members, almost all Latinx, along with the chair of the
Search Committee, Steve Stein, who is white.

The language question is tender for all of us that evening. My
Spanish facility is intermediate at best, and my lack of fluency
already has me wondering if I am worthy of this call. Rev. Lilia
has offered the Spanish-speaking congregants a multilayered
ministry for the past seven years. Now, the contrast between Lilia,
a native Colombian and an experienced minister fluent in both
Spanish and English, and me, a white European American and a
new minister with limited Spanish, feels stark. The whole point
of Spanish-Speaking Ministries is to offer an expression of Unitarian Universalism in the language of the soul for those who take
part. Will these congregants and I be able to meet soul to soul?

Our first discussion is about how we will handle this question of language throughout the evening. We decide to try an
experiment: The congregants will speak in Spanish, and I will
respond in English. Whenever any of us gets stuck understanding each other, Ervin Barrios will jump in with a translation. I
hope to face the challenge with a sense of adventure, curiosity,
and humility, but of course I also feel a little terror. Let's just see
how well I can do.

We begin the conversation with smiles all around.

The congregants' warmth and eagerness to make me feel welcome and at ease are palpable right away. Our conversation tackles serious issues, but always with a ready sense of humor. Congregants ask me why building multicultural, antiracist community is so central to my ministerial call. I tell them we can't really live our faith without it, and my whole life has led me to this call. They want to know how familiar I am with immigration issues. Though such issues are in my bones from growing up in San Antonio, I admit that I have everything to learn about life for immigrants in the United States in the twenty-first century. They ask how I will manage the language issues. Well, I already have learned a second language (French), and I have a base in Spanish, so I promise to work incredibly hard at becoming fluent. By the end of the evening, I have two tutors—Ervin Barrios and Smitty Smith—with whom I will study weekly for the next two years.

For me, twentieth-century theologian Henry Nelson Wieman's understanding of God as "creative interchange" captures what happens that evening. The encounter that the SSM members and I share changes me, pointing me in new directions for growth. All of us in the room experience the beginnings of soul connections, grounded in humor and compassion, even without a shared fluency in a common language. I am buoyed by hope as I walk out the door.

Looking back, I also see in that evening's gathering some of the main themes that will run through the first chapter of my ministry with San José:

- **my insecurity and sense of unworthiness**—Perfectionism, one of the characteristics of white supremacy culture, sometimes manifests in feelings of insecurity and unworthiness, like the ones I feel that night. When this kind of perfectionism becomes a habit of overwhelming self-criticism, as it often has in me, it can keep us too focused on ourselves and hinder cross-cultural understanding and connection. In my perennial struggles with self-criticism, I see the intersections of white supremacy culture with regional, generational, and gender conditioning. Learning how to dance from self-conscious insecurity to healthy humility is one of the gifts that my journey with FUCSJ will offer.

- **my deep-seated longing for a specific kind of multiculturalism**— I yearn to see people of color and white people sit side by side around a table, as they do at this gathering. I don't realize it at the time, but underneath this longing lies a particular—and limited—vision of multiculturalism for congregations, sometimes called the "browning of the pews." In this view, only congregations with a sufficient demographic mix can be called multicultural. If I stay focused simply on growing the number of Latinx participants in SSM, I will miss the other diversities present in the congregation. I may also ignore First Unitarian's longstanding call to engage and build solidarity with the wider community. My dawning realizations about the many forms that multiculturalism can take are among the gifts of this call.

- **the thrill to my ego of leading a congregation with a famous, innovative, cross-cultural ministry**—Ministers, who hold power through our position and yet are called to serve, must pay particular attention to the places where our ego tantalizes us with the promise of personal recognition or "specialness." If I feel pride in the fame of Spanish-Speaking Ministries, then I will probably get attached to the outward form of this program rather than staying laser-focused on its underlying mission. Like the rest of humankind, I will never entirely overcome my ego. This makes "staying woke" even more important!

- **my pride at being able to learn another language**—Can I become fluent, or at least nearly so, in Spanish? And even if I do, what will I be missing? There's so much more to cross-cultural understanding than just sharing a spoken language!

• **my growing passion for these people and this program**—This is the burning coal at the heart of our story for the next few years. Love keeps all of us in the work of building multicultural, antiracist Beloved Community. "Relationships, relationships, relationships" is the Common Thread that sustains me in the work's joys and sorrows.

The next Sunday, after an English-language worship service that offers simultaneous translation for Spanish speakers, First Unitarian votes to call me as its next senior minister. Amid the hearty hugs afterward, I feel a whoosh of transcendent homecoming and grace. We have said yes to each other. The next stage of the journey begins.

EARLY SUPPORT AND SOME RED FLAGS

Almost nothing (except perhaps a major fire) will test a congregation's essential character like calling a new minister to her first settled position. In the summer and fall of 2005, I am awash in the tsunami of responsibilities that inundate an incoming senior minister: understanding the new policy governance system, creating worship with a team new to me, responding to national disasters like Hurricane Katrina, and figuring out my role in areas that aren't my strength. Through it all, the vast majority of First Unitarian leaders and congregants show up with an eager, open, forgiving spirit.

I preach in the Spanish service at first monthly and later twice each month. Spanish-speaking congregants greet my sermons with love and generosity. I have to adjust my sermon-writing schedule so that my text can go to Ervin for translation by Thursday or Friday. I use the same message in both the English and Spanish service rather than trying to adapt to the congregants' differing circumstances. Latinx and other bilingual congregants help lead the remaining elements of the Spanish service, and they design the entire service on those Sundays when I am not preaching. We try meeting regularly for worship planning, but these congregants are already stretched thin from having covered Spanish-Speaking Ministries on their own after Rev. Lilia's departure. The meetings peter out within a few months. Do I not know how to partner with them across differences in language and culture? This question lingers in my mind and heart.

When we hire congregant Roberto Padilla as half-time coordinator of Spanish-Speaking Ministries that fall, we all feel relieved. Roberto was a medical doctor in Mexico until he fled for his life after antigay violence killed one of his friends. In the early years of my ministry, he supplements his FUCSJ income by waiting tables at a nearby restaurant. But his heart is with First Unitarian. Though without ministerial training, he is a keen observer of life and an avid fan of Rev. Lilia's preaching. He offers sermons two or three times a month. He tackles translating our website into Spanish. In the first couple of years, Roberto offers translation when Latinx congregants ask me for pastoral care; eventually, some come to see him as another pastor whom they can consult. Despite our best intentions, Roberto often works more than his allotted twenty hours a week.

Looking back now, it is easy to see the red flags waving: the dependence of Spanish-Speaking Ministries on lay and underpaid leaders of color; my lack of deep intercultural understanding with this small, diverse part of the congregation; my overwhelm as a new minister in a very busy congregation; my increasing realization that FUCSJ's commitment to multiculturalism is focused almost exclusively on the Spanish-Speaking Ministries. The pressure to make this program work—in my own heart as well as in the majority of congregants' minds—is oversized.

"THIS OTHER CONGREGATION"

Longtime congregant Cheri Goodman, who is white, captures part of the difficulty when she reflects on her own attitudes toward SSM. As a new congregant in the early 1990s, she is drawn to First Unitarian because of the congregation's "social consciousness." She remembers thinking it is "cool" that the congregation has been part of the Sanctuary Movement, but all she can personally offer the multicultural mission is her "benign and disinterested blessing." It is "very easy for me as a middle-class white person focused on having children and family to ignore the fact that we have this other congregation."

"This other congregation." Despite Rev. Lilia's much-appreciated efforts to bring people together across language, race, ethnicity, and culture, the majority of non-Latinx members never participate in these gatherings. When I arrive, I quickly see that I am serving two congregations: a small family-sized group that worships in Spanish and loves Unitarian Universalism and a mid-sized congregation that worships in English and has its fingers in dozens of pies. Every Sunday we worship leaders continue to call out our aspiration to live as "one congregation in two languages." In my first years with FUCSJ, transforming that aspiration into a reality becomes one of my main goals.

SPARKLING MOMENTS AND NATIONAL ATTENTION

What keeps us going are the sparkling moments when we embody this vision. On one Sunday morning less than two years after my arrival, we welcome ten congregants into membership. Some are recent attendees, others longtime friends of the church who finally want to "make it official." Exactly half of this new-member cohort is primarily Spanish-speaking, the other half primarily

English-speaking. Some twenty congregational leaders join the new members for an early breakfast before the two services. The Fireside Room is crowded with tables, just like that night during my Candidating Week when I had dinner with SSM members. A babble of Spanish and English fills the air. And I am so proud. The numbers aren't huge, but they are *equal*. It feels like an enormous success, a symbol of what we are creating.

During the half-decade between 2005 and 2010, we receive increased national attention. At General Assembly in June 2006, Julia Rodríguez, a longtime FUCSJ congregant just beginning to see herself as Latina, introduces an Action of Immediate Witness (AIW) about immigrants' rights. FUCSJ's delegates, including me, their still-new senior minister, leap to support her, and the Assembly passes the resolution.

At another General Assembly a few years later, Roberto Padilla and I lead opening worship for the Multicultural track and later present a workshop on our program. The attention feels supportive and affirming.

In 2008, the SSM worship team brings tears to the eyes of the multicultural "Now Is the Time" conferees, who visit our sanctuary on a Sunday morning. Rev. Wendy Pantoja, who is Latina, mentions how powerful it is to experience Unitarian Universalism in her native language for the first time.

That same year, FUCSJ receives grant money from the Fund for Unitarian Universalism for the JUUNTOS/Together Project. The grant pays for more translation, for bilingual signage on the front of the building, and for appearances by Latinx bands in both worship services. I am disappointed when congregants don't call for more of this rousing music, but at least we are trying out new styles.

The JUUNTOS grant also supports creative multicultural workshops led by member Rodrigo García. The workshops, called Conociéndonos/Getting to Know Each Other, reach about thirty people, a multiracial, multiethnic group that is again half Spanish-speaking and half English-speaking. Rodrigo introduces us to theater games borrowed from participatory theater and Theater of the Oppressed, designed to help build trust across differences in culture. Participants laugh, improvise, and make art together. The experience is intensely emotional and delightfully fun. On these workshop days, the congregants' openheartedness shines; they are willing to plunge in, to take risks, to go deep. As actor, minister, and passionate champion for multicultural Beloved Community, I am in my element. Such activities knit members of the "two congregations" together in new ways.

But as with most of these initiatives, after the buoyant moment of the workshops, the question "What next?" hangs in the air. Folks who participate experience a transformation, but the connections don't lead overall to more intimate socializing, such as invitations to each other's homes. And home hospitality is a key cultural element for our Latinx members.

Instead, FUCSJ's leaders, most of us white, are immediately on to the next urgent demand. While some of us relish the growing warmth in our cross-cultural connections, the Common Thread of "relationships, relationships, relationships" hasn't yet entered the whole congregation's bloodstream as the path to the multicultural, antiracist Beloved Community that we claim we want.

RESISTANCE AND REACTION

Some people in the "English-speaking congregation" don't experience the rewards of these deepening cross-cultural connections. They grow bolder in their objections to the amount of money we spend on Spanish-Speaking Ministries. They point to the diminishing number of people who show up for the Spanish worship service on Sundays.

In response, I grow increasingly defensive. "Not on my watch will Spanish-Speaking Ministries die!" I say hotly within the safe space of a ministers' retreat during my first year. A few years later, I blurt something similar to congregational leaders.

My colleagues try to warn me about the dangers of such an either/or proclamation by a minister. But I can't hear their good advice at that stage of my journey. My love for the people, staff, and process of the Spanish-Speaking Ministries is commensurate with the amount of work it takes to keep it up and running. Like its other passionate champions in the congregation, I hold in my heart only one vision of how our multicultural, antiracist Beloved Community should look.

EVERY SUNDAY SOMETHING HOLY HAPPENS

When I arrive in 2005, there are about thirty people on the SSM rolls. Worship attendance usually ranges from a dozen to twenty, and each year it shrinks a bit more. Early in my ministry, Roberto repeats the same reassurances to me that he once offered to Rev. Lilia when the sanctuary is empty when it's time to begin: "Don't worry. They're coming."

The early morning hour of the service plays a role in the small attendance, but the rest of the congregation is unwilling to consider rescheduling the English service. Roberto also reminds me that Latinx and European-American cultures have different senses of time. In *People of the Dream,* Michael Emerson offers an explanation: Many white European Americans think it's rude *not* to show up on time or even early for an event. Latinx people may feel that showing up on time could signal that they think *they* are the most important participants—and that too seems rude. When I show Roberto this description, he exclaims, "Exactly!"

Rev. Lilia believes that First Unitarian's reputation as an LGBTQIA-friendly congregation, flying the rainbow flag every Sunday, also keeps some Latinx people away. "We were known as the 'gay church,'" she says, "and there's homophobia in the Latino community."

Still, every Sunday, by the time the hugs are passed around—a ritual that follows our saying the affirmation in Spanish and English—and certainly by the time the sermon begins, a handful or more of faithful people have gathered in the chairs set up on the labyrinth to draw the congregation close. Then, every Sunday, something holy happens.

What do I mean by "holy"? At both of First Unitarian's services, worship brings people together across vast differences—different countries and classes, different employment statuses and income levels, different skin colors, sexual orientations, gender identities and expressions, abilities, and ages. This bridging of differences feels holy. Hearing diverse expressions of our faith's message of universal love, interconnectedness, and commitment to building a more just world feels holy too. And witnessing one another growing into a life guided by this vision—that feels holiest of all.

But perhaps the 9:30 service seems even more sacred to me because, in spite of its small numbers, it manages to be both amazingly diverse and deeply Unitarian Universalist. The intimacy of a family-sized congregation—gay and straight, young and old together—combined with the warmth of Latinx culture and the gratitude that this time and place exist where we can share this unusual faith in what is for most participants the language of the soul, brings tears to my eyes every week. I continue to feel unworthy to be their minister: I can't ad lib in Spanish during a sermon in order to speak to the moment. I can't address my message to the specifics of these listeners' lives. I can't understand every heartfelt word that folks say to me after the service, though I can grasp the essence and offer expressions of love in return. Yet the warmth, compassion, and sense of inclusion are palpable in the room. Looking back, I see clearly why I would blurt, "Not on my watch will this ministry die!"

The English-speaking congregants who make a point of attending both the 9:30 and 11:00 A.M. services capture what makes the early service so compelling. Bob Miess, a white congregant who serves as congregational president in the early years of my ministry, makes a commitment to show up for the 9:30 service almost every Sunday, even before simultaneous translation is available. Not a Spanish speaker, he does the things that don't require language—handing out hymnals, playing the guitar, lighting a candle in silence. When asked to speak, he offers a few words in English. He places his focus "not so much on the language as on the tone of voices, the faces, the warm hugs every Sunday," he says. "At the SSM service, I feel a combination of extreme isolation and a sense of being welcomed into the community even though I'm not like everyone else." He imagines that the Spanish speakers have similar feelings in other parts of their lives.

In "Ten Essential Strategies to Grow a Multiracial, Multicultural Congregation," Rev. Jacqui Lewis talks about the importance of working with "another cultural language" in order to grow our compassion. "Becoming conversant in another language stretches us and makes us empathic listeners," she writes. Bob and other English speakers experience this spiritual growth through participating in the Spanish service.

Then, as Bob moves from those first feelings of isolation into a sense of inclusion and belonging, he senses how this experience represents a larger truth: "We all find ourselves in these places of being different, of not being a part of what is going on, yet sometimes the miraculous happens and we are part of it anyway. That miracle is at the core of multicultural ministry. If we move away from worrying about the language and just enter into the experience, we can be touched, and we can touch. And we can weave together community across the language barrier."

If only more English speakers could share this barrier-shattering experience, Bob and I both dream.

Marla Scharf, a lifelong Unitarian Universalist who is biracial, finds another kind of sacredness at the 9:30 service. As a member of FUCSJ's Board, she makes a commitment to attend regularly, and she finds it the perfect place for healing. She calls attending the SSM service a "significant turning point in my life. I realize how much it means to me to be in that community of tanner-skinned people from a nondominant culture." Even with differences in language and country of origin, she can relate to SSM's lay-led services where leaders "talk about people having survival issues every day." For Marla, there is a richness simply in "being among brown faces." Like caucusing, Spanish-Speaking Ministries offers a space where people of color hold the center.

Those of us English speakers who attend the Spanish service share our enthusiasm with others in the congregation who have never tasted it. We urge everyone to give it a try. Though some do, the service remains small and intimate. How can I, then, as senior minister, help spark the movements that might weave the two congregations together?

One of the theories that I have held since I began my own antiracism training is that we all need to start by looking at the roots of what keeps us apart. We white congregants and leaders need to become conscious of how white privilege works in the social systems in which we swim. We need to dive deep into the history that continues to create divisions based on race, skin color, and ethnicity. All of us, white folks and people of color, need to develop a common language for talking about the forbidden topics of race, whiteness, and white supremacy culture. This is foundational work on the journey to creating multicultural, antiracist Beloved Community, and it's part of my focus, at first tentatively and then with increasing momentum, when I get to San José.

THE FIRST SERIES OF TRAININGS

There is no one-size-fits-all approach to trainings on antiracism and multicultural competencies, as the stories from all our congregations show. Creativity, flexibility, a willingness to try many paths, discernment about where folks in the congregation are on this journey, and the courage to stretch and to lean in even when resistance arises—all these qualities are key. The first series of trainings that we try in San José trace my own learning curve, as well as the congregation's.

Midway through my first year with FUCSJ, congregant Frances Schwab—a white woman then in a mixed-race marriage—asks how and when I will urge the congregation to engage in antiracism training. I'm thrilled to hear her use the word *antiracism*. In that first year as a settled minister, I have grown cautious again about using this term.

I am also a little at sea about how to apply my own antiracism training in this new context. On the East Coast in the early 2000s, these trainings have focused almost exclusively on the Black-white dynamic. New to San José, I don't yet understand how, in a white-dominant culture, the history of the enslavement of African peoples affects Latinx and Asian communities too. I have not yet begun to grasp the nuances of colonialism and postcolonialism that lie at the heart of California history. I don't yet discern how these distinct threads are woven finely into a web that includes all this history: the U.S. acquisition of the West; the colonization of indigenous peoples, the immigration of Latinx and Asian peoples, and the conversion and forced labor of them all; and the foundational fact of the enslavement of people of African descent. This understanding comes later; in fact, it continues to grow to this day.

Frances and I invite all who are interested in "undoing oppression" to gather. At the group's first meeting, the long tables in the conference room are full to overflowing. People are hungry to do the work.

Because our invitation has cast a wide net, participants want to talk about all the oppressions, especially those they experience themselves. Sexism, homophobia, transphobia, ableism, and classism join racism as areas people long to lift up. Some congregants feel that so much attention goes toward the Spanish-Speaking Ministries that we have lost ground on dismantling other systemic oppressions. We don't yet have the language of *intersectionality*, which names the ways in which various oppressions overlap and sometimes even contradict each other within and among our various identities.

Over a series of meetings, a team forms and names itself the Inclusion Group. It's a tepid descriptor, I feel. But even though I explain to the group why it's important to name explicitly what we are trying to dismantle, using words like *antiracism*, the majority of participants object to such "anti-" words as "too negative." They worry that these words will turn off others in the congregation.

Still, it's a start!

Adapting an older Unitarian Universalist curriculum, Jacqui James's "Weaving the Fabric of Diversity," subsets of people from the larger group help me lead a yearlong series of worship services, one on each of the named areas of oppression, each service followed by a workshop that takes the conversation deeper. Though the services are offered in Spanish and English, and congregants at both services are diverse in gender and sexual orientation, the workshops (in English, with Roberto translating) draw just the English speakers. The experience confirms what I have already been learning: All oppressions are important and need our faith's attention, but when each of us jockeys to keep our own issue central, the work on each one is diluted. Too often this jockeying keeps us from getting serious about issues of race and white supremacy.

The Inclusion Group represents baby steps on the journey, awkward and stumbling. But at least the work of this new era has begun.

Then, in 2007, Dr. Mark Hicks invites First Unitarian to serve as one of the pilot congregations for his new curriculum "Building the World We Dream About." Like the other congregations in our study who use this curriculum, First Unitarian experiences a sea change over the course of our thirteen-month involvement. Many participants move from being on the fence to becoming passionate champions of the congregation's multicultural vision. White participants' moments of discovery and realization bear out my gut feeling that congregations can't get anywhere in building multicultural, antiracist Beloved Community until they understand how the concept of white privilege is at work in their lives and in their institution. White participants' lives are changed forever by this awakening.

The class launches with almost thirty people attending, a mixture of races and ethnicities. But by the end of the long curriculum, almost all of the Latinx participants have dropped out, and we are lucky to have ten to fifteen white members show up for the last class sessions, along with co-facilitator Marla Scharf, who is African American and white, and Julia Rodríguez, who now identifies as mixed Latina and white.

For a Sunday in November 2008, participants design and lead both the Spanish and English services. The people of color who offer testimony that morning go to depths in their truth telling that have never before been reached at First Unitarian.

Martha Barahona, for example, speaks in Spanish of her own struggle to name her identity. As the class begins, she feels mostly "different" because she is mestiza—indigenous and European—

and because, though many people assume she is Mexican whenever she speaks Spanish, she is actually Salvadoran. "But this doesn't bother me," she adds quickly, for now she has another dilemma: she has become a U.S. citizen. What will she call herself now? "Building the World We Dream About" leads her to a new place on this journey of discovery:

> Las clases me enseñaron que lo más importante es ser yo misma y aprender a ver a los demás como los seres que también luchan por ser ellos mismos también. (The classes taught me that the most important thing is to be myself and to learn to see others as beings who also struggle to be themselves too.)

Co-facilitator Marla Scharf begins her reflection by acknowledging the courage it takes to speak: "I'm going to risk telling my story. My experience was painful." The sessions on white identity were particularly difficult for her: "I was so not prepared for the struggles I witnessed when people worked to *not* define their identity. People tried to define white identity by defining what was Black, or what was Latino, or what was Asian. People who identify as white defining white identity as *not being* . . . not being one with curly hair, not being one with dark skin, etc." She goes on,

> I felt shocked at how deep down racism and racial concepts are; how deeply embedded and invisible they are to the person holding them. I learned how deep the white racial identity wounds are, especially the wounds inflicted by "learning to be white." I felt if my UU people, my UU people whom I know and love and who are *for* love, if my UU people are this way, what hope is there? I felt despair.
>
> My experience taught me how extremely tough it is for a person of color to engage in antiracism anti-oppression work. I started dreading "Building the World We Dream About" Sundays. I discovered I needed to consistently, every week,

work to recover and heal myself. I learned how necessary it was for me to be held and supported by another seminarian of color [who was also a] co-facilitator. And I learned the parameters of my own strength, in myself being the supporter, the holder, of a younger person of color who was facilitating the "Building the World" class at yet another congregation.

In its original form, "Building the World We Dream About," like many antiracism curricula, encourages using a cross-racial pair of facilitators. I remember how both Marla and I enter into co-facilitating with energy and hope. But the pain and retraumatization that Marla experiences over the course of those thirteen months show how risky it is for folks of color to take on the teaching role in white-dominant congregations.

Marla also reflects on what she and the class gain from the experience. "I hold a deeper, more visceral experience of how race, racism, oppression, and white identity have hurt, and still hurt, *whites*. I have deep, deep respect for each and every class member who undertook this journey," she tells the congregation during that worship service in 2008.

Participants arrive in the first classes ready to receive a step-by-step "action plan" for diversifying the congregation's demographics, Marla remembers. But "as the challenges increase, especially the challenge of white identity, they learn that the first action—and I would say continuous action—must be *inner* action, inner action in a safe community context." Understanding the structures of white supremacy culture, waking up to how these oppressive systems restrict all our lives and destroy some—these are necessary moves for any congregation that wants to build multicultural, antiracist Beloved Community.

Marla closes her reflection with a call to action for white folks awakening to these truths—a call that still rings clear more than a decade later:

I ask you to take time and space and energy to consider how your experience informs and challenges your personal theology. The Universalism of Unitarian Universalism means all are saved, and yet what has this class taught you about how people, how white people, really are not saved . . . not saved when so many are asleep to whiteness and white identity, not saved when we live in a world of interconnectedness and in a world that works hard to put those who have woken up—a bit—to their white identity back to sleep? I ask you to keep working, keep waking up, and keep sharing the work.

When I rediscover the text of this worship service years later, with so much more congregational life under the bridge, I am struck by the turning point it represents—in my ministry and in the life of FUCSJ. I can't speak for the years of worship that have preceded my time in this congregation, but in my era, this service is the moment when a new intentionality and a greater truth telling begin. Congregants of color—along with white folks who find new meaning and purpose as they face the truths of their white privilege—begin to make a profound shift in congregational culture. My commitment to this journey helps provide the platform, but it takes building a critical mass of passionate champions for the work to gain traction.

THE HEARTBREAK OF ENDING

That worship service takes place in late 2008. The Great Recession has hit San José hard across all but the very wealthiest social classes. The congregation feels the impact of the recession over several years. We painfully nip and tuck at our budget with each fiscal cycle. We ministers and staff, hoping to preserve all our programs, refuse increases to our salaries and take cuts in our benefits. Some staff positions are discontinued, like the part-time social justice coordinator, who has helped create social justice activities linking the Spanish-Speaking Ministries, Third Street Community Center, and FUCSJ's children's programs.

We also lose the Spanish-Speaking Ministries accompanist. Roberto and I reassure each other that the SSM congregants "can sing a cappella; we'll use recorded music; we'll find volunteers!" But in truth, the 9:30 services lose life and polish without Gildardo Suárez's passionate playing, and we don't have enough lay leadership to fill in the gaps. Surely this new loss, like the earlier loss of Rev. Lilia, sends a further message to SSM members about where this ministry sits in the congregation's priorities. Now even fewer members show up on Sunday mornings for the Spanish service.

Despite these cuts, FUCSJ is still living beyond its means. Where will the necessary major cuts—tens of thousands of dollars—come from now?

Finally, in the spring of 2010, the Program and Operations Council—the Executive Team of the congregation, which includes the ministers—faces a hard fact: The 2010–11 budget will have to sunset the Spanish-Speaking Ministries coordinator position at the end of December 2010. The Council affirms that the multicultural mission remains a priority, but the future of Spanish-Speaking Ministries itself is now in doubt.

With heartbreak but with as much clarity as I can muster, I agree that this is the move we need to make. In truth, this way of building a multicultural congregation, now in process for almost twenty years, has not brought us to where we want to go: into one community, built on diverse relationships and a deep mutual understanding of what multiculturalism and antiracism require of us all.

Among congregants, the decision sparks all kinds of responses: from grief to relief, from an "I told you so" satisfaction to a sense of betrayal, from shame and despair to a foggy uncertainty, and much more in between. Will we actually let go of the program that has made us famous in the Unitarian Universalist world?

Does this mean we are giving up on the multicultural mission for which we have worked so hard?

Many people have more than one of these responses simultaneously, and there isn't much time or space to process all these feelings. The sunsetting of the SSM coordinator position exactly coincides with the beginning of my first sabbatical. I will be away for six months. Making matters still more complicated for me personally, my spouse and I will use my sabbatical to help him move across the country to another ministry. Our marriage has struggled during our years in San José; I am hoping the sabbatical will give us a fresh start in a bicoastal relationship.

My heart and mind are pulled in many directions. The situation points out just how complicated ministry—both professional and lay—can be. Stresses and heartbreaks sometimes converge from all directions. White supremacy culture drives us forward with a nagging sense of urgency. Creating more spaciousness for compassion, healing, and integration of our life experiences is countercultural but a necessary move for Beloved Community.

In 2010, all these circumstances mean that both Roberto and I, SSM's two professional leaders, will be gone at the same time. With six months to plan for these departures, the question of how First Unitarian will now move its multicultural mission forward becomes an issue for the whole congregation rather than the active concern of just those who have supported SSM or participated in "Building the World We Dream About."

In response, FUCSJ's leaders bring in Rev. Alicia Forde as a facilitator from the UUA staff. She leads a weekend-long conversation that October about FUCSJ's multicultural vision, and it draws over eighty people, diverse in every way. It is clear that First Unitarian has reached the tipping point; a critical proportion of the congregation are now committed to its multicultural mission and vision. It's not clear what the next steps will be to fulfill that vision, but as Bob Miess, then the congregation's president, says, the vision "is in our DNA." This is the good news that comes out of the crisis.

Meanwhile, congregational leaders host potluck parties for SSM participants to ensure that those most affected have a say in what happens next. There haven't been many *convivios* since Rev. Lilia left. These new parties remind folks, even those who haven't been coming to worship, of the deep sense of community they share.

Still, no realistic plans arise. The handful of Latinx lay leaders, already so stretched by their personal and work lives that they cannot make attendance on Sunday mornings a priority, want worship services to continue. But they can't hold them on their own. And it's clear that I can't create and lead both Spanish and English services without a lot of support.

Ultimately, FUCSJ's elected leaders, supported by Roberto and me, decide to sunset the 9:30 Spanish service and to transition to a half-hour bilingual circle-worship service called Alabanzas (Praises). Alabanzas, modeled on the deep listening and sharing of our thriving small group ministry program, will take place in a cozier space than the sanctuary. It will require almost no weekly preparation, and the worshipful circle will hold whoever facilitates it—minister, staff person, or lay member.

Nevertheless, despite all the conversations, the workshops, the parties, and the processing, the decision to discontinue the Spanish service comes across as imposed from the top. Have we leaders reinscribed the dominant power structure, with mostly non-Latinx folks deciding the fate of a program that serves Spanish speakers? How could we have moved through this moment differently?

I still don't have clear answers to these questions. In the rush to handle a hundred different tasks before I go on sabbatical, I don't think to create a ritual that would honor the passing from one form of "congregational life" to another. Some folks surely need more opportunities to express their range of feelings. The spoken and written explanations that we offer don't satisfy those who are most disappointed.

My own tendency to keep rushing onward, quickly reframing a loss into a gift, cheerleading for the new way instead of sitting with the pain of losing the old, also discourages us from providing a healthy period of grieving. Instead, we leaders lift up a hopeful narrative to the congregation, framing the loss of Spanish-Speaking Ministries as a natural evolution in FUCSJ's journey toward multiculturalism. The SSM program has had a good run of almost twenty years. Nothing will be lost from this grand experiment! Let us move forward with pride and renewed energy!

These exhortations are true, but they hold only one piece of the truth.

In *Centering: Navigating Race, Authenticity, and Power in Ministry*, Rev. Natalie Fenimore writes that "Unitarian Universalism does Easter without Good Friday." She remembers how the church of her upbringing would offer a place where people can "process pain and struggle as well as love and celebration. This is a 'Strength-in-the-Valley' theology," she explains. In contrast, "Unitarian Universalism has a 'Mountaintop' theology. But you cannot really get to the mountaintop until you've been in the valley. You can't just skip over the struggle."

When I look back at the sunsetting of Spanish-Speaking Ministries, I see myself embodying and encouraging the institutional tendency to skip the pain and rush to the celebration. I see this avoidance of pain as part of white supremacy culture, where "mastery" and "perfection" are so highly valued that heartbreak and failure are often hidden away. At First Unitarian in 2010, we don't yet have the wisdom of Rev. Marlin's and Rev. Sean's words about leading with our heartbreak and trusting that in a Beloved Community, we can find our way back from failure.

So I tuck away my personal heartbreak about this ending. I barely acknowledge my fear that I am actually the cause of SSM's "failure." After all, I know that I can't be the sole cause of anything in community—that would be an egocentric idea indeed. But I also sense that I haven't been able to minister with deep effectiveness to both congregations. At the time, in the midst of disruption in my personal life, I can't quite bear to process my professional shortcomings too.

All these mistakes are clues to a bigger picture. It has taken me years and the writing of this book to come to new insights about this passage in FUCSJ's and my ministries together. These new understandings may help all of us who are on the road to building multicultural, antiracist Beloved Community.

REFLECTIONS ON POWER AND CULTURE

In *The Wolf Shall Dwell with the Lamb*, Rev. Dr. Eric H. F. Law writes that leaders who want to help build multicultural communities "must learn to do power analysis on a given situation. Based on this analysis, the leader will determine [their] style of leadership, theological emphasis, and spirituality." In other words, we leaders—ministers and lay leaders alike—need to learn and develop the style, message, and practice most relevant to our specific context. Many ministers learn the importance of local context early on in their ministries, but Rev. Law's understanding of cultural differences in relationship to power takes this need for adaptability even farther.

Law uses the concept of "power distance" (which Karin mentioned in chapter 6) to describe these differing relationships. Cultures that historically or currently have hierarchical governmental and religious structures tend to have "High Power Distance." These cultures recognize that societal systems keep the distribution of power unequal. People with High Power Distance expect recognized leaders to hold authority and to make responsible decisions. In everyday congregational life, folks with High Power Distance may be reluctant to speak up in a group if they aren't the facilitator or don't hold a position of authority themselves. They may need to be explicitly invited to contribute to the conversation. This is what motivates Law's practice of Mutual Invitation.

People from cultures with "Low Power Distance" tend to believe that everyone not only should be equal but also *can* be equal, given enough individual effort and will. In the United States, with its cultural emphasis on democracy and its myth of "pulling oneself up by one's own bootstraps," folks in dominant groups—such as white, straight, cisgender, able-bodied, and middle- to upper-class people—often assume that everyone comes to the table with equal access to power and authority. Even when currently established leaders have the best of intentions, this cultural bias, if unrecognized, can reinscribe systems of inequality. In a congregational setting, for example, people with Low Power Distance may expect that anyone who wants to contribute will naturally speak up. Those who remain silent must be choosing not to speak, so the established leaders shouldn't push to have those voices heard. These assumptions miss all kinds of systemic reasons that marginalized folks may not feel empowered to join the conversation as equal partners.

I have read Eric Law's books early in my ministry with FUCSJ. But this understanding of power distance doesn't really sink in until after we have sunsetted the Spanish-Speaking Ministries. As I reread *The Wolf Shall Dwell with the Lamb*, it hits me with a thunderclap how my Low Power Distance assumptions have influenced my interpretations in SSM group meetings. In those early years, I didn't know how to move fully into the authority that comes with the senior minister position. I didn't know how much the community *needed* me to move into that role. And

I didn't know how to use that authority skillfully to ensure that all voices feel heard.

It's a humbling realization.

In *Centering*, Rev. Lilia Cuervo remembers Catholic Latinxs coming to FUCSJ and asking for the priest. "Why don't you bring a man to the pulpit so people will know there's authority here?" she hears. Similarly, some Spanish-speaking attendees assume that I will take on the final decision-making role. After all, surely the senior minister is equivalent to a priest. But others question my authority because of my gender, and they wonder about Roberto's authority because he is not ordained. A whole lot of intersectionality is at play.

If we leaders know enough about cultural differences, then we can adapt our leadership styles in ways that meet folks where they are and center the relationships themselves. In High Power Distance cultures, for instance, the leader with recognized authority becomes even more of a symbol for the whole institution. This representative aspect of the role may be obvious when we ministers show up in the public square. But within the congregation, we need to sense how our ordination and our leadership style bear different weight depending on our congregants' cultural expectations.

When I am called to FUCSJ in 2005, the majority of the congregation wants a minister who will model shared ministry. That's what I want too. But I wonder if the Spanish-Speaking Ministries needed something a little different: a minister who would take charge of all the administrative logistics of the program and exercise her decision-making power with clarity and ease. Under that kind of leadership, worship and other gatherings could once again focus on the healing message of the faith and on how to get through this troublesome life rather than on how to run a program. I wasn't there yet.

All this leads to another question: Do the messages I offer meet congregants' needs? I have been preaching roughly the same sermon at both the 9:30 and 11:00 services; only the language in which I deliver it changes. But can the same message really meet people where they are in their lives when the social hierarchies of this country's culture make our life experiences so different? Despite my best intentions, has my own identity as a white person limited my capacity to match the healing messages of Unitarian Universalism to the two very different "congregations" I've been serving?

When Karin and I interview Roberto Padilla in 2015, he captures the impact of my sermons for SSM with compassion:

Nancy hace muy bonitos sermones, muy inspiradores, pero no me tocan. No terminan por llenarme. ¿Que hago? . . . Practicamente me voy a mi casa con la mitad, probablemente, o menos, de lo que Nancy hubiera querido proyectar. . . . Porque no va dirigido a gente latina. No va dirigido a la cultura latina.

¿Qué sucedió con toda la gente en español . . . ? Porque no les interesa venir a oír un sermón, aunque la mayoría era bilingüe. Pero son sermones para americanos. No para latinos. Y allí donde, en una forma personal de pensar, se rompe el multiculturalismo. . . .

Y no es culpa de Nancy. . . . Como reverenda, la quiero muchísimo y la respeto y he aprendido mucho de Nancy. . . . La falta es que, por mucho que Nancy quiera, no lo puede entender que es ser latino. O que es ser hindú, por ejemplo. . . . Y no es culpa de Nancy. Ella no pidió ser americana. . . . Ella no pidió ser blanca. ¡Yo no pedí ser brown!

(Nancy gives very beautiful, very inspiring sermons, but they don't touch me. They don't end up grabbing me. What's going on? . . . I actually go back to my house with half, probably, or less of what Nancy wanted to project. . . . Because it doesn't get directed at Latinx people. It's not directed at Latinx culture.

What happened with all the people in Spanish ...? Because it doesn't interest them to come hear a sermon, even though the majority were bilingual. But her sermons were for Americans—not for Latinos. And that's where, in my personal way of thinking, multiculturalism broke down.

And it's not Nancy's fault. . . . I love her a lot as a minister, and I respect her and I've learned a lot from Nancy. . . . The problem is that, as much as Nancy would like, she can't understand what it means to be Latino. Or what it means to be Hindu, for example. . . . And it's not her fault. She didn't ask to be American. . . . She didn't ask to be white. I didn't ask to be brown!)

When I read Roberto's words now, I am more excited than discouraged. My cultural entrainment as a white person runs deep. But what mitigates this cultural entrainment is *awakening to what it means to be white.* My early sermons did not acknowledge our cultural differences, and I did not take my research and relationships deep enough to be able to speak to the pressing issues of that smaller congregation. In the language of the Intercultural Development Inventory, my sermons—unconsciously, unintentionally—were minimizing the differences between the majority Latinx members at the Spanish service and the majority white attendees at the English service. It's a relief to see this now, because I know there is a path for growth—and because I can see how the congregation and I have indeed grown in the years since we sunsetted the Spanish-Speaking Ministries.

I finally understand at least one of the ways in which I fell short as the white minister of that small multicultural congregation. I expected that congregation to run like our predominantly white congregations: highly individualistic and self-starting rather than deeply familial. SSM members wanted and needed a strong and very present ordained leader, even if I wasn't fluent in Spanish. Roberto Padilla did amazing work as SSM's coordinator and lead preacher, but the program also needed a deeper engagement from its senior minister.

I'm not saying that, had I known then what I know now, we could have saved the program, or even should have saved it. I still believe that the Spanish-Speaking Ministries constitute just one of the early legs of our journey. But I am saying that despite my best intentions and biggest love, I looked at our version of multiculturalism through the lens of my own whiteness.

Had I been farther along in my intercultural development then—willing to own the authority of my role and also to own my ignorance of the lived experience of this small but crucial part of the congregation—I would have shifted my leadership style and my message. I would have worked with staff like Roberto differently. I would have worked harder and faster on building multicultural competencies in the wider congregation. Granted, I would have needed near-miraculous skills at balancing all the competing demands for the senior minister's time in a midsized congregation. Yet this more nuanced understanding of multicultural leadership would have helped me—and the whole congregation—discern how best to use our time and energies to build a Beloved Community appropriate for that era.

It is good to pause to reflect on all this now—without shame or blame but with humility and a willingness to grow.

This leads me to one more angle on my early reluctance to inhabit the full authority of the senior minister role in this multicultural setting. When I work at the UUA in the late 1990s, researching literature on whiteness for the Faith in Action department, I read about how white people—especially white women—have a habit of adopting a position of incompetence when working with colleagues of color. This habit is spelled out in an essay titled "The White Girl in Me, the Colored Girl in You, and the Lesbian in Us: Crossing Boundaries," by Medria L. Connolly, who is Black, and Debra A. Noumair, who is white. The essay appears in *Off White: Readings on Race, Power, and Society*, published in 1997.

Connolly describes the dynamic that develops between the two authors as they write the essay together. Noumair grows increasingly anxious about their project, doubting her own skills. At the same time, Connolly finds herself "getting loaded [by Noumair] with more powerful, idealized attributes, which of course runs quite contrary to the reality of my experience as a Black woman where I feel devalued in relation to White women, not idealized."

Until these two authors look at this pattern deeply and work it through, Noumair's abdication of her own competencies, alongside Connolly's acceptance of Noumair's idealization of her, actually robs both of them of the truth: Like all human beings, they are each a mixity of vulnerability and power. In her insecurity, and masked by it, Noumair is sidestepping her responsibility to use her power and skills to help repair the damage done by white supremacy culture. Until these two women confront and name this pattern, they cannot meet as full human beings, each gifted with unique talents and perspectives, each harmed by racism, sexism, and homophobia, and together capable of great creativity.

I have seen this defense mechanism in myself. It's another way of asking people of color to do the "spiritual domestic labor" for us white folks. Early on in my own journey, it shows up in my stumbling inarticulateness when I try to enter into conversations about race. Such uncertainty diminishes what I have to offer and deflects my own responsibility. In working with members of Spanish-Speaking Ministries in those early years, I sometimes feel helpless and incompetent. I almost throw up my hands: "Who am I to suggest what we need to do?"

Instead, I could have mined the skills I do have in order to encounter folks with curiosity, humility, and a strength born of genuine vulnerability. I could have taken a hard, honest look at whatever prejudices were still running through my bloodstream, impeding deeper, truer relationships. And, just as I asked Roberto about different cultural attitudes toward time, I could have asked better questions about authority and power and how we could reach each other across our differences and our fears.

What a dance cross-cultural, cross-racial relationships are in a culture wrecked by white supremacy! Now I can see more clearly how I stumbled, especially at the intersections of race and gender.

Yet true humility, curiosity, and willingness to move forward in accountable relationships were also present among us. Combined with love, humor, respect, and generosity, these attributes made space for the creative interchanges that transformed a small program into a brightly shining jewel. Throughout its twenty-year history, the adventurous experiment that was UUHH and SSM had its beauties and its flaws, its gifts and its failings. All of these are to be cherished, learned from, and woven into the fabric of First Unitarian's long history.

By 2011, then, it is clear that FUCSJ and I need to shift paradigms for building a multicultural, antiracist Beloved Community. The loss of Spanish-Speaking Ministries gives us a chance to start again, building on what we have learned.

A NEW BROKEN-OPENHEARTEDNESS

Love at first sight, joy in the holy moments, more than a little overwhelm, and some life-changing heartbreak—such highs and lows mark the first chapters of my ministry with the First Unitarian Church of San José. When I return from sabbatical in midsummer 2011, the congregation and I are ready to go deeper. I come back seasoned with grief—my marriage will end within the year—but also clearer about my strengths and my limits. I return with a new set of questions too, which continue to evolve over succeeding years:

- What looks and feels different about the congregation in this era that follows the years of focus on Spanish-Speaking Ministries? What do we notice, and what do the changes teach us?
- How can the congregation and I share leadership around our multicultural mission and vision? Has my own passion for this work restricted the power that must reside in congregants themselves to make changes and help us to grow into a multicultural, antiracist Beloved Community?
- How does our work on multicultural competencies impact the way we engage with the diverse city and county in which we live, and how has this engagement changed us as individuals and as a community?
- How do we bring multicultural, antiracist values and practices into the preparation and offering of worship? And how do these practices transform all our relationships, so that worship becomes an expression of who we are becoming, rather than simply an aspiration?
- How do we face directly into the pain of loss and change—in our congregation, in our personal lives, and in our world—and remain grounded in a sustaining faith? How do we live with renewed broken-openheartedness in the face of suffering and sorrow?

The following sections offer glimpses of how First Unitarian and I have explored these questions.

NOTICING THE CHANGES

In 2011, I come home to a congregation that is different from the one that called me six years earlier. Most of the Spanish speakers who have attended the 9:30 worship service are no longer in church on Sunday mornings. Some have chosen to support non–Unitarian Universalist family members by attending their churches;

some find their time too full; others just don't feel the same sense of homecoming at the 11:00 A.M. service in English. Some will continue to return a few times a year, especially when they receive a personal invitation or when our annual Día de los Muertos celebration comes around.

Familiar faces, dear to those of us English speakers who have championed the Spanish service and who have come to know each other's beautiful, idiosyncratic selves, are no longer among us. I reach out to some by phone or email, I hear about their new life circumstances, and we express our warmth and care. But the hoped-for integration of the "two congregations" as a result of sunsetting SSM doesn't happen.

On the other hand, shifting away from Spanish-Speaking Ministries allows many of us to notice truths in our congregation that have been overlooked or invisible because we have been focused so intently on just one version of multicultural ministry. In 2011, for example, Tamara Payne-Alex, then program officer at FUCSJ and herself biracial African American and white, notes that non-Latinx people of color—longtime members as well as new attendees—seem more visible in worship services and congregational life now. During the years of pouring our energy into the Spanish-Speaking Ministries, other racial, ethnic, and cultural diversities at FUCSJ have sometimes been ignored. Have these voices been unintentionally suppressed? Have other differences been minimized, other riches lost, as a result?

It strikes me now that this act of noticing is an essential spiritual practice for building multicultural, antiracist Beloved Community. Noticing the changes; noticing what has been missing and is still missing; noticing what is true in the present moment—such noticing calls us to use all our faculties of mind, heart, and body. It calls on all our senses as well as our capacity to analyze what we perceive. It requires us to pause for reflection and to make space for new input. This aspect of waking up to the present moment helps us, especially white people, awaken to the presence of white supremacy culture among us.

More and more I sense how this awakening asks those of us in the dominant culture to adopt a new, deeper sense of time. This sense of time has a longer arc than U.S. culture promotes, one that allows us to witness the centuries-long history of oppression still driving our present actions. It has a slower, more spacious pace, emphasizing process over product—both the outward process of relationship building and the "*inner* action" of self-reflection that Marla Scharf calls for in her "Building the World We Dream About" homily.

I realize that this kind of slowing down is a privilege not available to all. For those engaged in a very real and urgent struggle for survival, slowing down the process of change can cause more deaths. But for those of us for whom white supremacy culture's sense of urgency is a habit rather than a life-saving necessity, slowing down is essential. In this case, slowing down becomes a sign not of resistance to change but rather of a willingness to root the change deeply in new ways of being.

INSTITUTIONALIZING SHARED LEADERSHIP OF THE MULTICULTURAL MISSION

Ministers and lay members have shared the work of building multicultural Beloved Community at FUCSJ since the beginnings of this commitment. The 1980s Sanctuary Church movement, in which First Unitarian congregants accompanied those in danger of deportation, and the basement breakfast out of which the Spanish-Speaking Ministries were born serve as vivid examples. In the years since 2011, I have seen this shared leadership take root more deeply. With lay leaders helping to set the mission and vision, new ways of being are changing our congregational culture.

For instance, while I am on that first sabbatical, the Board takes the lead in creating a new, shorter mission statement:

Bound together by our commitment to making Love visible, we gather to deepen our spirits, to work for justice, and to create one sacred family.

Our Common Thread of intentionality emphasizes that congregations on the road to multicultural, antiracist Beloved Community all need an overarching goal or mission. The overarching goal, tied to the faith's core message, inspires and unites congregants to do the work that makes such Beloved Community possible.

First Unitarian's new mission statement is exactly this kind of goal. Every phrase requires us to do the work of multiculturalism and antiracism. Making Love visible, deepening our spirits, working for justice, creating one sacred family—none of these is possible without a fierce commitment to the well-being of all creatures and existence bound together in the "inextricable web of mutuality," as Dr. King puts it. At FUCSJ, we can only fulfill this commitment through persistent work to understand and dismantle the barriers that keep us human beings apart. We have to dig into an understanding and an undoing of the white supremacy culture in our midst in order to fulfill this mission. We have to learn how to build real relationships across many diversities in order to bring this mission to life.

Over the next few years, the congregation and I allow the new mission to become the boss, as Rev. Jacqui Lewis urges in *The Power of Stories*. We leaders boil down this short statement into an easily remembered phrase: We are here to "Make Love Visible in all that we say and do." Repeating this phrase every Sunday morning, we go from a congregation that can't recite and rarely refers to its long, juicy, but complex earlier mission statement to one that can call out the new phrase with gusto when prompted. Congregants begin to use it in their daily lives. It becomes a spiritual practice and a new measure for our lives as we ask, "How are we Making Love Visible in this meeting at church or in that interaction on the street today?" The words take on muscle and flesh as they help us leaders decide where we will put our energies, resources, and focus, and as we witness the results. The loss of a beautiful, innovative, but time-consuming program clears the way for a deeper and more cohesive mission.

Similarly, during my second sabbatical in 2017, the Board drafts a Moral Position on Racial and Ethnic Equity and presents it to the congregation, which, after some discussion and wordsmithing, adopts it. First Unitarian's Moral Positions—authorized by a 2013 change in our bylaws—apply Unitarian Universalist Principles to a general area of public life. Once the congregation adopts a Moral Position, congregants can submit specific statements in support of it, and the Board can then approve these statements by an online or in-person vote, allowing them to be publicly expressed as official statements of the church. The nimbleness of this system lets us respond more quickly to pressing issues while still speaking with one voice as a congregation.

For example, in April 2017, FUCSJ'S new Sanctuary Support Team drafts a statement in support of the Moral Position on Racial and Ethnic Equity. Quickly approved by the Board, the statement allows us to join the network of congregations in the South Bay offering sanctuary and accompaniment for immigrants at risk of deportation. Dozens of congregants join the Rapid Response Network, ready to show up when we get a text about ICE activity. A small group of white and Latinx congregants become the accompaniment team for a mother and child taking physical sanctuary in a nearby church. The golden threads from our history in the 1980s shine again in this renewed commitment, and our deepening understanding of the social forces at work make the relationships more authentic and equitable. Congregants are Making Love Visible indeed.

I'm equally moved by the way multicultural, antiracist best practices are now integrated into congregational life. I'm often the one who introduces these practices, but congregants' willingness to try them on and adopt them is what brings about real change. For instance, the Board and the Program and Operations Council now use process observation at the end of each meeting. This practice asks us to reflect on how the team has sought and attended to the voices of people in traditionally marginalized groups. In the everyday work of the congregation, questions like "Can we afford to replace the boiler?" and "What safety policies need to be in place?" take up a lot of meeting time. Process observation keeps in front of us another question: Does each meeting help to advance our multicultural, antiracist vision of Beloved Community? Just making time at the end of a two-hour evening meeting for this question to be named helps to keep our mission in mind.

Similarly, Eric Law's practice of Mutual Invitation brings the sharing of power, the warmth of invitation, the riches of deep listening, and the acknowledgment of different cultural and personal styles of communication into all the circles where we use it. Not everyone at FUCSJ loves Mutual Invitation as much as I do, but I can see how it has changed the tenor of gatherings as varied as our agenda-packed leadership meetings, on the one hand, and the small, worshipful Alabanzas services on Sunday mornings, on the other. We have vastly fewer intellectual debates in our congregation now and many more connections heart to heart, including when we disagree. Our communal emotional literacy is growing, and that feels like a countercultural move in itself.

GLASS HALF EMPTY AND GLASS HALF FULL

Bringing the next set of multicultural antiracism trainings to the congregation plays a big role in helping to create these new ways of being. For the first rounds of Dr. Mark Hicks's curriculum "Beloved Conversations: A Congregation Meditates on Race and Ethnicity," we specifically invite major decision makers to take part. The groups include elected leaders and other volunteers who help manage our main areas of ministry. Not yet ready to lean back from my own leadership in this work, I co-facilitate our early offerings of Beloved Conversations, first with Gautam Biswas, who is Indian American, and then with seminarian and field-education student Nikira Hernandez, who is Latina, Native American, Asian, and white. Like those of "Building the World We Dream About," this program's small group sessions develop everyone's capacity for cross-racial conversation, and they help us to see the water of the culture in which we swim.

These trainings have a mixed impact. Gautam remembers how he is changed by one African-American congregant's testimony. She mentions that she always makes sure to have her driver's license and some money with her, in case she gets stopped or stranded. "That has stayed with me," Gautam says. "I did not use to carry that with me always, but now I explicitly have it in the driver's pocket." There's no question for him but that "hearing those personal testimonials and being able to offer mine" are powerful, and that overall the class "gets it."

But the times when we are able to create the "container that's really necessary for the crucible of transformation, where the idea and the emotion all come together and people really feel it deeply," don't happen often enough for Gautam in that first round of "Beloved Conversations." During the class sessions themselves, the pace of change can feel slow for both of us. Yet out of that class come congregational presidents and other Board members who help lead the institutionalizing of our mission and vision. I'm learning to trust the process.

Similarly, Julia Rodríguez turns her learnings from the second "Beloved Conversations" class into even more intentionality about the content that she and a group of lay leaders produce for our small group ministry program. I am moved by their courage, straightforwardness, and compassion as they invite participants to speak from the heart in such sessions as "People of Color and White Allies" (2016) and "White Fragility" (2017). Since about half of our congregants participate in small group ministry, meeting once or twice a month, this intentionality ensures that First Unitarian's conversations about the impact of race and racism, of white supremacy culture, and of white privilege on our own lives and on our society reach a wider audience even than those present in the sanctuary on Sunday mornings.

But these small group ministry sessions also surface conflict. Some of the white participants who haven't experienced any of our multiculturalism and antiracism trainings object to the topics and stay away from such sessions. Some people of color feel they can't risk showing up to their group when white members may express microaggressions or worse. Some small group leaders with less experience in multicultural competencies struggle to handle the range of feelings in their group, and our systems for dealing with such conflict are clunky and incomplete. I strive to show up pastorally for the people most troubled on all sides, suggesting new perspectives to those who haven't participated in antiracism trainings. I also discover the strengths of the small group leaders and members who lean in to witness with those most hurt by such interactions. It's not all up to me, as minister, to listen and teach. The web of care isn't perfectly woven—how quickly that word *perfect* still springs to my mind!—but it is stronger than ever before.

Some of my ministerial colleagues, along with the social justice teams in the congregations they serve, ensure that antiracism trainings like "Beloved Conversations" happen annually or biannually. In this way, the trainings reach an ever larger percentage of their congregations, and more and more congregants understand and embrace the language and perspectives of this work. But I fall behind in scheduling these trainings. Working on this book and participating in our multiracial community-organizing activities occupy every spare moment in my ministry for several years. As Karin and I visit the other congregations included in this project, I notice how the consistent trainings, offered year after year, create a powerful forward momentum. I notice how easy it is for that momentum to slide when our intention falters. "The work never ends," our Common Threads remind us.

Still, I notice how multicultural competencies and antiracism awareness have entered more and more into the congregation's bloodstream in San José. Rev. Geoff Rimositis, for example, adapts our children's religious education programs so that each Sunday they support building multicultural, antiracist Beloved Community. He also comes back from one of his sabbaticals trained to administer the Intercultural Development Inventory (IDI), and all our elected and appointed leaders on the Board and the Program and Operations Council take it. When our results come back, Rev. Geoff consults with each of us individually, as well as in a group.

Unless people develop intercultural competency, systems of oppression are likely to remain the status quo. But there is no value judgment attached to the different stages identified by the IDI; we are where we are, often as a result of influences beyond our control. And we all have the capacity to grow. Once we know where we are in our intercultural development, the IDI offers suggestions for how to grow into the next stage.

The IDI reveals that lay and ordained leaders at FUCSJ are at stages ranging from polarization to adaptation. As a group, we land, as do most Unitarian Universalists, at minimization, the stage where people know that there are differences among cultural groups but emphasize that the similarities are far more important. Given our strong Universalist roots, which proclaim that we are all beloved, this stage makes sense. Yet the minimization stage can keep us leaders stuck, ignoring cultural differences, much as my early sermons ignored differences between the Latinx and non-Latinx cultures at FUCSJ. Folks on the margins who remain at minimization, where they may "go along to get along," also lose out on the full expression of their humanity, which is enriched by but not limited to the influences of their many identities.

Having our leadership take the IDI and discuss it feels like a huge move forward to me, and I am thrilled with the possibilities that this model offers for directing our intentional growth. But we haven't yet figured out how to incorporate regular IDI-inspired practices that might increase our self-understanding and further shift our ways of fulfilling our multicultural, antiracist mission. Rev. Geoff retires in July 2018, before he can help lead us in this exploration. Will the IDI resurface as a guide in the years to come? I hope so. But our dip into the IDI is a great example of how different aspects of this journey can leap forward and then stall or slip back. We are building the road as we go.

Through all of these examples, I can choose to see the glass of our work as half empty or half full. Admittedly, it is hard to track the positive changes when we are in the midst of the daily pressures of life. In recent years, the congregation and I have reeled from local blows, including the deaths of beloved community members, and from national ones, such as the harm being done to our democracy, to civil rights, to the planet, and to all of life. It's easy to get discouraged and to feel that nothing we do will ever be enough. But this book's Common Threads urge us to take a both/and perspective. Pausing to notice and to celebrate our new ways of being helps us to build resilience and to discern how to be more effective agents for change. I need this strength-building practice too. The next sections, then, dive into two crucial areas where the shifting paradigm of our multicultural work—moving from Spanish-Speaking Ministries to more congregation-wide engagement—is changing how we live and work together. These areas—community organizing and worship style—have played a big role in my own journey in recent years.

ENGAGING IN BELOVED COMMUNITY BEYOND OUR WALLS

The First Unitarian Church of San José has belonged to People Acting in Community Together (PACT) since a few years before I arrive in 2005. PACT is the Santa Clara Valley affiliate of the national Faith in Action community-organizing network (formerly called the PICO National Network). With PACT, FUCSJ has taken up issues of health care, education, affordable housing, immigration reform, sanctuary, police accountability and transparency, and more.

In the early years of my ministry, swamped with new-minister learnings and obligations, I struggle to show up for many of PACT's interfaith clergy and community meetings. I often make an appearance at their public actions, knowing how important it is for clergy to be present as symbols of our faith. I sometimes have a speaking or singing role, especially as my Spanish facility improves. But mostly I feel curious about these brilliant, passionate people from across the spectra of race, ethnicity, religion, and class. How in the world do they find time to show up at a moment's notice, when protests, press conferences, and meetings with public officials on an urgent issue are announced at the last minute? The demands seem huge and never ending.

After I return from my first sabbatical, I begin to understand. By then, my friendships with religious leaders from other faiths have deepened, and my availability to FUCSJ's lay social justice leaders has increased. They convince me that my priorities need to shift.

Relationships, relationships, relationships—this Common Thread runs through every aspect of building multicultural, antiracist Beloved Community. After FUCSJ sunsets the Spanish-Speaking Ministries program, I have a growing hunch that, if we do the inner work of antiracism in our congregation well, then the healthy, accountable relationships we build with our kin throughout our county will become a powerful expression of our multicultural mission. We will Make Love Visible by becoming dependable allies, accomplices, and partners, both followers and leaders in the work of transforming this valley. Such engagement is, after all, in FUCSJ's DNA. Now we have a chance to take it further, with more consciousness of the ways in which white privilege and white supremacy culture affect us all.

But what I don't realize in 2011 is how much this part of my journey will challenge, confront, and change me. At that time I'm only beginning to glimpse how this ever-widening web of relationships will take hold of my heart. I don't really grasp yet how the hard, detailed work of organizing to change even a small part of public policy embodies people's struggle for their very lives. In many ways, faith-based community organizing is where my own intercultural development gets real.

A couple of scenes can trace the arc of my growth.

In July 2011, I show up for a meeting with the PACT immigration team. About twenty lay leaders from a number of local

Catholic congregations, along with a smattering of folks from FUCSJ, gather around the tables in the library of Westminster Presbyterian Church. I am one of just two or three non-Latinx people present.

The team is planning a prayer vigil to take place outside San José's city hall a few evenings later, in response to the San José Police Department's recent agreement to cooperate with ICE as it targets transnational gang members. The local immigrant community's worries about gang violence are only exacerbated by the possibility that ICE, with its history of unjust deportations, will increase its presence on the streets.

The conversation that evening is mostly in Spanish, and I can mostly follow along. I haven't been part of earlier planning sessions, so the team kindly brings me up-to-date. I know most of the people in the room from our earlier work together on immigration reform.

But as we begin to brainstorm a structure for the prayer vigil, I grow anxious. I happen to be the only ordained clergyperson there that night, and I feel frustrated that the early draft of the vigil doesn't have much of a liturgical or spiritual feel to it. Instead, the team is following the usual format for a community-organizing "action"—testimonies and speeches, reports and demands.

If we want to touch hearts, I argue, we can't just cite all the facts and figures you have gathered in your research. We can't have so many words (there's an irony: *me* calling for succinctness). We need to center the vigil around ritual, I insist.

The other folks in the room take up my suggestions with care, and we launch into a lively conversation. But eventually a PACT staff person gently asks us to make space for those who haven't yet spoken, those who might be most affected by the issue.

As I see and hear the power shift, as I notice who hasn't been speaking and who has, I realize what I have done: I have set myself up as an "expert." I have grabbed a lot of airspace. I have centered my perspectives, even though I have not shown up for most of the earlier meetings. I haven't earned my place yet as part of the "us" in charge of the vigil. I haven't taken the time to sense my appropriate role; I haven't tended to these relationships. My intentions are good, and my training in worship planning has merit. But when I slow down, I can see the impact of my clumsy barging in: When I take up so much space, I undermine the actual leaders and silence those most affected. I have unconsciously, almost in spite of myself, exerted my white privilege.

At an appropriate moment, I apologize in Spanish to the group. Then I sit back, flooded with shame. I have had years of antiracism training by then. Shouldn't I have known better? Why didn't I catch myself before that drive to "contribute," to set things on a path that I considered right and effective, took me over?

This is the power of white supremacy culture. I need a lot more practice decentering myself, a lot more time just showing up at the table, a lot more waking up to our different perspectives and experiences, a lot more awareness of how my deepest assumptions about trust and power, intersectionality and solidarity, were driving me before I can be a really good co-conspirator with my colleagues of color.

That night, the immigration team meets my apology with compassion and forgiveness; they welcome me into collaboration. The vigil ends up a both/and blend of powerful organizing action and transformative ritual. I play a small role in it. Quiet and humbled, I witness the beauty and bravery of community members' leadership, especially as they pray over the chief of police, who shows up for the vigil and who holds the fate of their loved ones in his hands.

My experiences in that planning meeting and at the vigil mark a turning point in my personal journey.

In late 2014, the PACT clergy caucus responds to the non-indictment of Darren Wilson in the killing of Michael Brown by launching what we call the Beloved Community Movement in Santa Clara County. This multiracial, multigenerational coalition of faith leaders brings together law enforcement command staff, elected officials, and hundreds of community members for dialogues about building trust between the police and community in order to save lives. We research best practices from around the country. We meet with the mayor, the police chief, city council members, and other decision makers. We help revise policies to increase police accountability and transparency. Through this long, hard, sustained work, the frustrations of people long denied agency in their sense of safety, opportunity, and well-being in our community become integrated into my own heart.

Still, we clergy, including those of color, realize that our roles offer us some protection from the worst pain that community members experience. Privilege comes with our status. So we invite more laypeople into leadership of the Beloved Community Movement. Young people of color, those most affected by implicit bias and lack of trust in law enforcement, become the leaders, and the tone of the work shifts. Now my intercultural understandings and my capacity to notice the working of white supremacy culture in myself must grow even more. Gradually, I develop a better understanding of how to show up. I learn when to acknowledge how limited my white perspective is ("look, I'm the white person here . . .") and when such acknowledgment sounds like overapologizing, undermining the strength of the relationships we have built. I figure out when to use the power I have in order to build bridges with decision makers. I get better at speaking multiple "cultural languages." I keep learning when to lean back or lean out altogether. I begin to be able to notice and to quiet my own anxieties, and this makes all the difference in my ability to relinquish my need to speak at certain times and to know how to use my voice appropriately at others. I'm a work in progress, but this soul work brings joy and a depth in cross-racial relationships that I have longed for all my life.

What's equally gratifying is how many FUCSJ congregants also find a calling to this movement, also experience changes to their ways of being through these relationships forged across race, ethnicity, class, and power. Our congregation's inner work on dismantling white supremacy culture in ourselves makes these relationships possible. Minimization—the IDI developmental stage of our leadership groups—becomes impossible as this multiracial, multiethnic, multireligious group, the Beloved Community Movement's leadership team, shares the truths of our stories, researches the impacts of systemic injustices, and lobbies hard for institutional change.

The distance that persisted between most of the English-speaking congregants and most of the Latinx congregants at FUCSJ throughout the era of Spanish-Speaking Ministries has melted away in this new paradigm of our partnerships in the community. Those of us involved experience a mutual love and respect built on honesty, companionship, and humor in the midst of struggle. Our new friends won't be joining First Unitarian, though my Baptist, Methodist, Catholic, and Jewish clergy colleagues from PACT sometimes lead worship in our sanctuary. But the Common Thread of "relationships, relationships, relationships" runs through our congregational life whether or not the demographics of our membership change dramatically.

WORSHIP AS AN EXPRESSION OF WHO WE ARE BECOMING

At the same time, worship at First Unitarian still bears the powerful, positive mark of the Spanish-Speaking Ministries. The intimacy of the Alabanzas service, held in our tiny circular library, offers the same dance of hugs among all who attend that the old 9:30 service in Spanish did. At Alabanzas, we still sing and recite the liturgy in Spanish, even though the sharing of personal stories has shifted to English. In the primary worship service at 11:00 A.M., we continue to recite our affirmation in English and Spanish and sing the children off in both languages when they go to their programs after the story for all ages.

But the paradigm shift has made us more mindful about integrating best practices for building multicultural, antiracist Beloved Community into worship every week. All of the worship associates (more than a dozen) and I watch, and rewatch, the UUA's 2017 "Decentering Whiteness in Worship" webinars. In worship, choir director John Ector offers brief reflections that set the context for our increasingly diverse musical offerings and that open all of us up to "deeper relationships with the life and the life blood behind the music," as Dr. Glen Thomas Rideout calls for in "UUs, Music, and Appropriation," an episode of *The VUU*, the Church of the Larger Fellowship's weekly podcast. I keep experimenting and encouraging our worship teams to try new styles. Worship has grown livelier and more engaged, less word-driven and more relational. I'll probably never be completely satisfied, but the seeking is our sacrament, as our affirmation says.

What moves me most is witnessing congregants taking the lead on embodying this multicultural approach in worship. For instance, in 2013, I invite congregants of Indian descent to help create an annual Diwali service. It has now become another High Holy Day at FUCSJ, not yet as elaborate as Día de los Muertos but still anticipated and relished.

We know that simply honoring holidays and holy days from a variety of cultures can amount to tokenism. Gautam Biswas, a congregant born in India, admits that these celebrations are "always a little tricky, because sometimes I feel, it's that old feeling of exoticization, of Unitarians thinking, 'Oh, aren't Hindus

368 | MISTAKES AND MIRACLES

interesting?' But it's also a chance for me to celebrate and show off the culture. There are some aspects of Indian culture that I just love." It's both/and—the risk of tokenism but also the power of making visible a cultural thread that has been present at FUCSJ for a long time.

When Sundar Mudupalli, another congregant originally from India, launches into his reflection in the Diwali service in 2017, he names the questions that the worship team takes up as part of their preparation: *Why* are we celebrating Diwali in our congregation? "Are we being cultural voyeurs? Is this another aspect of white supremacy benevolently accommodating other cultures when convenient?" The very fact that these questions are being asked shows how far we have come on our journey!

Then Sundar goes on:

> What I see is not voyeurism, but a wholeness that comes from incorporating aspects from other cultures that speak better to me than my own. For example, in the spiritual practice of my birth, I don't have a way of honoring the dead. I find that the Day of the Dead celebration, which we will honor next week, incorporates my desire to respect and honor my ancestors.
>
> So, too, from Diwali, we can incorporate the long view presented in the *Ramayana* into our spiritual practice.

The epic *Ramayana* tells a complicated story of exile and struggle, desperate plot twists, unexpected sources of strength, stubborn persistence, unlikely allies, and eventual homecoming. This story of the "long view"—years of trial followed by a return home—runs counter to the U.S. culture of instant gratification and resistance to discomfort. Sundar, by weaving together wisdom from the Hindu tradition and from his own direct, multinational experience, embodies a uniquely Unitarian Universalist message of hope in hard times. As the white senior minister, I know now that a big part of my job is to make space for such voices to be heard in worship and throughout our communal life. An even bigger part of my calling is to model integrating this diverse, multicultural wisdom into my own life.

THE POWER OF PERSISTENCE AND BROKEN-OPENHEARTEDNESS

When I look back at my journey so far with the First Unitarian Church of San José, I can see how I have grown and changed. From that new, eager, stumbling, but hopeful minister who arrives in 2005, I am becoming a humbler, more resilient "leader-learner"—a role that my late beloved mentor Rev. Marjorie Bowens-Wheatley modeled for me early in my formation. I still stumble plenty, but I have experienced the courage and persistence of the long view, with its promise of homecoming after great struggle, even after failure. I know how transformative it is when a community chooses to live with broken-openheartedness, facing into pain and self-awareness, into cultural distress and communal failures, and growing more large-hearted, compassionate, and forgiving as a result.

In a conversation that Karin and I have in 2016 with Rev. Abhi Janamanchi, whom we consider one of the prime mentors for this book, I put it this way. My words are a little clumsy; I am feeling my way forward, making the road as I go, but arriving home at last:

> I'm just wondering whether actually feeling called to ministry, and maybe to parish ministry in particular, has something to do with the capacity to *stay in it*, even when the reality is not— [*I can't find the word, so I hurry on.*] There's something about having a community within which we are moving and working and trying, and we see the human stories, and we see their struggles, and we see—I see *myself* fall and rise and fall and rise, and I hit a wall that I didn't know was there, and I turn

and hit the other wall, etc., and yet I *know* I'm growing through that, I know I am being blessed, it will not let me go until it blesses me—or I will not let it go until it blesses me—and seeing that happen again and again with my people, even when I get so frustrated or impatient, being *in it*, in the actual work of trying to create this Beloved Community on a small scale . . . It just makes it worth it. I would rather be spending my life that way than not. I can't imagine what else I could do that would offer me so much hope.

QUESTIONS FOR YOU AND
YOUR CONGREGATION

1. Where do you see yourself or your community narrowing the focus of your work toward multicultural, antiracist Beloved Community because you have limited your vision of what this community might look and feel like? What are the costs of such narrowing? What gifts does your particular focus offer? What other paradigms for multicultural community could you explore that are appropriate in your context?

2. If you are reading this book with a group, do the responses to this chapter differ depending on group members' identities—especially those identities related to race, ethnicity, and gender? What kinds of conversations do these different perspectives spark?

3. What losses and "failures" have you and your congregation experienced on the road to multiculturalism? How do you weave the story of these losses, mistakes, and misgivings into your congregation's narrative? Which of your stories show how pain and vulnerability can become strengths that lead to resiliency, hope, humility, and joy?

CHAPTER EIGHT

The Journey Continues

I like to invite folks to spend some time thinking about
what the heart of Unitarian Universalism really is. . . .
Where is the faithfulness for you? . . . Where is interwoven community and relationality for you? What are
the things that can never be set down? What's inherent
to us?

—Rev. Sofía Betancourt

WHEN, IN JANUARY 2014, we tiptoe into envisioning this project, we have no idea of the size and scope of the task we are taking
on. Published examples of this type of work are daunting enough.
We have studied the earlier literature about multiracial congregations, where charts and tables spell out statistics alongside the
descriptions. We know in our bones how hard it was to create the
consultation, convened by Rev. Marjorie Bowens-Wheatley and
the UUA's then-president John Buehrens, which became the 2003
book *Soul Work*. We know, because we are among them, that the
authors of chapters intended for the *Mosaic* book have poured
time and energy into their creations. We feel accountable to all
these predecessors.

Gradually, our dream swims into focus: We want to tell congregational stories in rich detail. We want to share stories that
will humanize the challenging and sometimes mysterious work

of building multicultural, antiracist Beloved Community: stories that will draw whole communities of people together, stories in which people of many different identities can see themselves. And we want to tell these stories in a single joint voice rather than as an edited collection of chapters. We want to invite our readers to join us on this journey of discovery and to offer ourselves as their companions.

We are friends before we set out on this project. Having worked together first on the Pacific Central District's Racial and Cultural Diversity Task Force in 2008–09, we have already established a strong foundation of mutual trust and respect. But we cannot imagine how, and how much, our relationship will deepen through living, traveling, laughing, crying, pondering, questioning, writing, editing, and talking (and talking and talking) together over the course of five years.

Tending to our relationship becomes a major way in which we are accountable to each other and to the work. Over and over we pause to examine how we are showing up for each other, as well as how our relationship affects which stories we tell and how we tell them. We don't want to reinscribe white supremacy culture, yet we also know that our individual identities and personalities inevitably show up in our writing.

We realize that Nancy's voice is more prominent throughout this book, both in the chapters that we create together and in the fact that chapter 7, in which she tells her individual story, is longer than chapter 6, in which Karin tells hers. We decide from the beginning that Nancy will be the primary author because as an experienced writer and editor, she is more comfortable with the written word, and as a minister, she is also more embedded in congregational life—including the work of antiracism and multiculturalism—than Karin is.

But Nancy, with an ever-growing awareness of how her whiteness impacts the way she sees the world, worries that "my perspective, no matter how hard I try, bleeds through. And that means that, for some readers, this will feel too much like a book 'written for white people.' Not that such a book is a bad thing. As happens with caucusing, there's work that we white folks need to do on our own. But that's not the book that you and I—Karin and Nancy—want to produce. We long for there to be space in these pages for everyone's story to be heard and felt, as much as possible. Just like we want each of *us* to show up in these pages."

Wrestling with this balance throughout our journey, we discover better and better ways to show up as full partners. During the interviews with our conversation partners, we both pose questions, with Karin naturally taking a larger role when we speak with people of color. After our site visits, we highlight each other's notes; we trade off making transcripts of our interviews; we go back and forth over the outline of each chapter. In weekly and sometimes daily bicoastal conversations, we comb through our insights and analyses until the words on these pages represent our common thoughts. The final editing of this manuscript feels like a partnered dance in which we relish the sense of rhythm and flow.

Accountability and trust, honesty and risk taking, compassion and kindness—these become our own Common Threads.

DIFFICULT PASSAGES

When we walk into the sanctuary at the Unitarian Universalist Congregation of Phoenix on the Sunday of our site visit, early in our research, we have already been in town for a few days, meeting congregants, conducting interviews, and getting to know the area. We enjoy the warm welcome at the door and greet people we have come to know as we take our seats. Nancy feels a sense of comfort in this space. Always the extrovert, she turns to say hello to her neighbor and then turns back to open the familiar gray hymnal to the opening hymn.

Karin, though, is having a different experience. After a few moments, she leans over to Nancy and murmurs, "I meant to wear my nametag from First Parish. It has my name in both English and Mandarin. But now I'm so glad I don't have it with me. I just don't want anything else identifying me as 'other.'"

This difference in our experiences comes up again and again. Nancy remembers having some of the classic white responses to Karin's remark: surprise, frustration, disappointment, shame that she couldn't see things from Karin's point of view. As we finish this project, Nancy looks back and understands more clearly what made it so hard:

In those moments when your experience was so radically different from mine—like walking into the Phoenix sanctuary and you're not feeling comfortable while I could walk in feeling open and curious and at home—I wasn't keyed in to what you were seeing and feeling. It was humbling. It opened the gap, the distance between your experience and my experience. That was always hard for me. I love intimacy and I love a sense of closeness—that's probably my lifeblood, one-on-one closeness, so when it would become clear that there was just this gap in life experience and in experience of the world that felt unbridgeable—that was scary to me. And sometimes I just didn't want it to happen, I didn't want to have to turn toward the pain. That seems like a combination of my personality, my personal history, and the influence of being white in this culture.

For Karin, the feeling that she may not be accepted or welcomed in Unitarian Universalist spaces is familiar:

I can't remember who said that as a person of color, you're always one foot in and one foot out. That's how it feels to me. The only place I feel fully *in* is when I'm at a DRUUMM gathering or some other gathering with UUs of color. Mostly I feel like I'm here, but still not completely. I'm still not fully a member of this faith—if that even makes sense, because is the faith the belief system and how you choose to live your life, or is it the reality of the institutions and communities? My congregation is my spiritual home. In Unitarian Universalism at large—I don't know. . . .

Her voice trails away.

Because of these differences in our experiences and expectations, our site visits almost always carry some strain. This strain comes to a head for both of us when, in May 2016, we visit the Unitarian Universalist Church of Annapolis for the second time. The congregation has recently experienced a major conflict, described in chapter 3 ("Conflict Is Inevitable and It's Messy"). The hurt and anger felt by our conversation partners are still raw. The beauty, energy, and hope that they had expressed during our visit the year before now feel fragile, at best.

When we get back to our rental car after a set of these painful conversations, Karin begins to cry. She wonders whether she can stay in Unitarian Universalism.

This moment is a crucible for us both. On the basis of our first visit and our later phone conversations with ministers and congregants, we had been holding a glowing view of UUCA's progress toward building Beloved Community. Now, as we hear about the seeming rapidity with which the conflict has erupted and about the harsh words that have been said in the midst of it, our hearts sink. Both of us feel discouraged. What stories will we have to tell, if even this congregation is struggling? More important, what hope can we hold for Unitarian Universalism if this work is just so damn hard? We both wonder about the validity of this book project. We both wonder about the prospects for our faith.

We sit in sorrow, fear, and frustration for some time. Gradually, we decide to "keep on moving forward," as Pat Humphries' song says.

Looking back as we near the completion of this book, we can see the larger context of that crucible moment more clearly. Nancy realizes why Karin's uncertainty about being able to stay in Unitarian Universalism feels so terrifying: "I'm giving my life to this vocation. My whole life is tied up in this religion and consequently also in this book. But—this faith is more built for me. We just can't get past that, really."

There's compassion in this realization—compassion for herself but also for other white people who grow fearful or defensive when Unitarian Universalism is criticized for the ways in which it remains trapped in white supremacy culture. But for Nancy, the ever-deepening realization that "this faith is more built for me" also provides motivation and energy for helping the faith to change. The possibility that her friend Karin might leave Unitarian Universalism refuels her commitment to the work that this book is all about.

Karin looks back on that moment of crisis in Annapolis, and she, too, has a larger perspective on it. "I feel like the grounding of my faith is so strong," she says, "but sometimes when I'm faced with the reality of it, it feels like, 'I don't know if I can do this.' I have to keep in mind what Rev. Abhi said so beautifully about what a lot of people of color do: We look at the aspirations of our faith rather than the realities of our faith." Coming home again to her congregation in Cambridge, witnessing the persistence of both lay and ordained leadership and their commitment to staying on the journey, and experiencing the warmth and passion of her white allies and accomplices, Karin too chooses to stay in this work, even when she feels vulnerable and exposed.

For both of us, the disappointment that we feel when we arrive for our second visit to Annapolis, and then the hopeful developments that have taken place since, become the heart of what we learn: None of us can do this work without conflict. What matters is *what happens* with that conflict. In Annapolis, we watch congregants and ministers try to deal with the conflict; we witness them take small steps toward healing, toward new ways of being. In each of the congregations we study, redemption may be incomplete; it may be partial, in every sense. But turning to face the trouble offers hope every time.

WHAT WE LOVE BEST

Relationships, relationships, relationships! Without question, the sparkliest moments of our journey happen whenever we make connections with our conversation partners, whether on our site visits, through emails and phone calls, in hallway conversations and over meals at General Assembly, or at home in our own congregations. The courage and generosity of spirit that our conversation partners have offered us leave us in awe. To be trusted with their stories—to be allowed to witness to their joy, their pain, their confusion, and their hope—has been a great gift. We are so grateful, and we hope we have proved ourselves worthy.

These truths shine: People want to tell their stories about this journey toward multicultural, antiracist Beloved Community. Even the conversation partners who have ambivalent relationships with their congregations or with Unitarian Universalism are hungry to speak and to be heard, to work through their experiences out loud. It matters that we co-authors—and now our readers—*listen*. Over and over we witness this human longing to find a place of meaning making and belonging; over and over we witness the willingness to wrestle with the realities of a place when it falls short of its aspirations. We love this.

But what we love most is the way in which our own relationship has deepened and grown. Just as we put the finishing touches on the manuscript, we marvel at these changes:

KARIN: We'd already known each other for years, but working on the book has taken our trust and understanding to a new level. I am so grateful for the closeness we've developed across our different identities and for the ways this friendship enriches my life.

NANCY: We've shared *so much life*—job changes, heartbreaks, troubles, and worries. We created this container where we could bring all of that. Sometimes in our weekly conversations we wouldn't even get around to talking about the book. We knew when the personal stuff needed to take precedence over everything.

KARIN: It's like the book was the vehicle for us working together and getting to know each other, but the relationship was the top priority.

NANCY: Yes! And then there are all these different layers to who each of us is. Some of them are related to all those differences between us that we talk about, including race and ethnicity, but there's also this ineffable other thing. I mean, what an amazing contrast and complement we are! I know what it is: It's *intimacy*; it's our hanging in there. Ultimately that becomes part of the beauty of the whole thing. Because the book has taken twice as long as we expected and we've had to hang in for so long, it's been the vehicle that's kept us together so that the whole relationship could really bloom—Oh, wait: That's what you just said, isn't it!

And we laugh. We know each other's idiosyncrasies so well, and the container of friendship that we've created holds them all, our gifts and our challenges, with love, humor, and compassion.

HOW THIS BOOK HAS CHANGED US

Everything we've shared here hints at the many ways in which this project has changed us. Here are a few more, in our individual voices:

FROM KARIN: Telling my own story was (and is!) terrifying. Who was it who said that the thing you're most scared of is what you have to write about? But the vast majority of times I've decided to go ahead and be that vulnerable, it's worked out well because that's the kind of thing that draws people—the very human stories that we have. So one thing I've learned in doing the work of multiculturalism and antiracism is how having the courage to be vulnerable and telling my truth is what changes lives—both mine and those of the people who listen to me.

Still, it's one thing to do that in the safe place of my congregation, where relationships are strong and trust is deep. It's quite another to share some of my most tender moments with strangers who don't know me and will judge me only by my words. I'm learning to take greater risks.

I also think more expansively about the journey toward multicultural, antiracist Beloved Community now. At the beginning of my time at First Parish, I was so wounded that my work had a sort of urgent, panicky feel to it. Out of my pain, I would think, "There's only one way to do this, and it has to happen *now.*"

I don't feel any less convinced of the importance of this goal, but now I've internalized the fact that institutional change takes a lot of time. There's not this simple road. Looking at the journeys of other congregations, I really see how the road winds and turns back on itself and takes detours. I don't get as upset about individual setbacks in the work because I've seen that this is the way it happens. I have a maturity about doing this work that I didn't have before.

FROM NANCY: I've struggled a lot with my inner critic throughout this process. Linebacker Girl (my inner critic has a name) thought I surely couldn't write this book without her constant nagging. I've learned to reassign her to another job so that the creativity can flow. Now I can take leaps and make mistakes on the page knowing that you and I, Karin, will find them and fix them as best we can. I've let go of some of that addiction to perfectionism that's part of white supremacy culture—and, oh God, it is so liberating.

But the biggest way I've been changed is that I have more capacity to sit with pain, to sit with unresolved, potentially irredeemable situations. To sit in the messiness of it, and the sorrow, the disappointment, and still know that there are also bright spots and sparkling spots and that there's hope and there's joy. The process of writing this book has mirrored the work we're writing about—messy, hard, with lots of detours, filled with mistakes *and* miracles. But I think I've actually learned how to be comfortable with the discomfort! To hang in there when the process gets hard, because we made ourselves a promise and we have an accountability to each other and to the people who have trusted us with their stories.

All of this—the small growing freedom from perfectionism, the comfort with discomfort, the hanging in there with the pain, and knowing that joy and hope still exist—all of this makes me feel more alive.

NO STORY IS COMPLETE

The work of building multicultural, antiracist Beloved Community work never ends. It is not about arriving at a specific destination or achieving a particular outcome. Rather, it is about creating new ways of being and institutionalizing the systems that support these new ways of being. Relationships form the heart, the focus, and the call of the work.

Over and over in these pages we have repeated these Common Threads. Over and over the congregational stories we share bring these Common Threads—the generalizations we risk making—into the gritty, complicated truths of lived experience.

Yet these stories, no matter how detailed, can never be complete, for congregational life is constantly evolving. During the years we give to this book, four of our five congregations see shifts in ministerial leadership. In 2017, Rev. Fred Muir retires as senior minister of the Unitarian Universalist Church of Annapolis, and the congregation's faith development minister, Rev. Christina Leone Tracy, accepts a call to serve as senior minister of the Fox Valley Unitarian Universalist Fellowship in Appleton, Wisconsin. Rev. Susan Frederick-Gray is elected president of the Unitarian Universalist Association and now worships at First Parish in Cambridge, and First Parish experiences its own ministerial transition, as Karin describes in chapter 6. And at the First Unitarian Church of San José, long-serving associate minister Rev. Geoff Rimositis retires in July 2018, and interim director of religious education Susie Idzik comes on board to help lead a visioning process for the future. The congregation faces new challenges and opportunities for how it staffs for whole-church faith formation and multicultural, antiracist Beloved Community.

Sadly, some of our conversation partners do not live to hold this book in their hands. In 2017 alone, Michael Willis of Annapolis passes away after a long illness. Celso Salinas-Mireles, the DREAMer we interview for the Phoenix chapter, is tragically killed in a motorcycle accident. And Rev. Dr. John Wolf, minister emeritus at All Souls in Tulsa, dies at the age of ninety-two.

These lists of transitions and losses only catch a part of the story. Each of the congregations we study is living into its next chapters, even as their chapters in this book go to press. This constant movement is especially true for congregations striving to build multicultural Beloved Community. The habits of the heart so necessary to this work—adaptability and entrepreneurship; a willingness to take risks and to feel uncomfortable; patience, perseverance, courage, and humility; and a pulsing sense of aliveness and love—drive these congregations forward.

OUR HOPES FOR WHAT'S TO COME

As we lift our eyes from these pages and turn our hearts and minds toward what's to come, we still hear the voices of our companions, mentors, and conversation partners on this journey ringing in our ears.

Rev. Sofía Betancourt's charge to the gathered throng at Justice General Assembly 2017 feels crucial:

> I like to invite folks to spend some time thinking about what the heart of Unitarian Universalism really is. Not what it looks like, not the old familiar comforting expression of it, but what *is* Unitarian Universalism to you? What are the central values, not necessarily the messages of how they're expressed? Where is the faithfulness for you? Where is spiritual practice for you? Where is interwoven community and relationality for you? What are the things that can never be set down? What's inherent to us?

Sharing Rev. Sofía's questions and listening to the diverse answers, feeling our way toward consensus about who we Unitarian Universalists are, anchoring ourselves in the call of our faith—these practices may seem countercultural. They take time; they cause dissent; they may seem mired in thought rather than leaping forth into action. They resist the sense of urgency that white supremacy culture pushes on us all—an urgency that can seem like the only responsible reaction to desperate times.

But weaving these practices of reflection into our hectic lives, and in this way deepening our connection to the heart of Unitarian Universalism, grounds our faithful action in a way that can sustain and unite us. We co-authors see how this praxis—action and reflection finely woven together—strengthens the congregations we study. We hope it becomes widespread.

Finally, our own journey and its lessons bring us back around to the struggle and the blessing of this work. In one of our many heartfelt conversations with Rev. Abhi Janamanchi, he uses a story from the Hebrew scriptures to capture the mix of holiness and messiness that striving for multicultural, antiracist Beloved Community will always bring. In the story of Jacob wrestling with the stranger through the night (Gen. 32:22–32), Jacob has, as Rev. Abhi says, a "wounding experience. It's not a fun experience!" We passionate champions for Beloved Community mustn't expect this work to be fun.

Then Abhi continues the story:

> Jacob prevails but he doesn't *win*, and he's wounded in the process. And the stranger blesses him and renames him Israel, which means the one who has striven with God.
>
> That's a powerful metaphor for what we are called to be in this world as Unitarian Universalists. It calls for us to be open to the spiritual discomfort of engaging with "the other": to be present in that way, and to know that we will come out of that experience transformed and even renamed. Part of our spiritual task is to develop the muscle, the spiritual muscle, to be present to that discomfort and pain. This is where I think we have growing up to do. Being by nature conflict averse, we want quickly to move to the resolution phase, where we can just be renamed and we carry on!

Abhi laughs at the familiarity of this longing for the quick fix, the easy redemption.

But to obtain the blessing of multicultural community, we Unitarian Universalists must risk the wounding and the pain; we must welcome proximity to the unknown. If we do, we will emerge transformed, recipients of new life, which is what Jacob's renaming represents.

We co-authors feel the power of this story. We see its themes running through the stories we have shared here. Most of all, we have experienced it ourselves, in the wrestling, and the blessing, and the new life of this journey. Mistakes and miracles, indeed.

And now, the journey continues. . . .

Resources for the Journey

BOOKS, ARTICLES, AND TALKS

Ajayie, Luvvie. "Get Comfortable with Being Uncomfortable." Video of a talk given at the TEDWomen conference, New Orleans, LA, November 2017. www.ted.com/talks/luvvie_ajayi_get_comfortable_with_being_uncomfortable.

Alexander, Michelle. *The New Jim Crow: Mass Incarceration in the Age of Colorblindness*. New York, NY: New Press, 2012.

Bellevance-Grace, Karen. "Full Week Faith." Presented at the LREDA Conference in St. Paul, MN, October 2013. fullweekfaith.weebly.com.

Coates, Ta-Nehisi. *Between the World and Me*. New York, NY: Spiegel & Grau, 2015.

Connolly, Medria L., and Debra A. Noumair. "The White Girl in Me, the Colored Girl in You, and the Lesbian in Us: Crossing Boundaries." In *Off White: Readings on Race, Power, and Society*, edited by Michelle Fine, Lois Weis, Linda C. Powell, and L. Mun Wong, 322–32. New York, NY: Routledge, 1997.

Crestwell, John. *The Charge of the Chalice: The Davies Memorial Unitarian Universalist Church Growth and Diversity Story*. Camp Springs, MD: Movement Ministries, 2007.

DeYmaz, Mark. *Building a Healthy Multi-ethnic Church*. San Francisco, CA: Jossey-Bass, 2007.

DeYoung, Curtiss Paul, Michael O. Emerson, George Yancey, and Karen Chai Kim. *United by Faith: The Multiracial Congregation as an Answer to the Problem of Race*. Oxford, UK: Oxford University Press, 2004.

DiAngelo, Robin. *What Does It Mean to Be White? Developing White Racial Literacy*. New York, NY: Peter Lang, 2012.

DiAngelo, Robin. *White Fragility: Why It's So Hard for White People to Talk about Racism*. Boston, MA: Beacon Press, 2018.

Dragt, Gordon R. "Gordon Dragt's 16 Tips for Turning Your Church Around." In *One Foot Planted in the Center, the Other Dangling off the Edge: How Intentional Leadership Can Transform Your Church*, vii–viii. Salt Lake City, UT: Millennial Mind Publishing, 2009.

Emerson, Michael O., with Rodney Woo. *People of the Dream: Multiracial Congregations in the United States*. Princeton, NJ: Princeton University Press, 2008.

Fine, Michelle, Lois Weis, Linda C. Powell, and L. Mun Wong, eds. *Off White: Readings on Race, Power, and Society*. New York, NY: Routledge, 1997.

Jones, Kenneth, and Tema Okun. "White Supremacy Culture." https://alliesforracialequity.wildapricot.org/cwsc

Law, Eric H. F. *The Wolf Shall Dwell with the Lamb*. St. Louis, MO: Chalice Press, 1993.

Lewis, Jacqueline J. "Ten Essential Strategies to Grow a Multiracial, Multicultural Congregation." www.jacquijlewis.com/books.

Lewis, Jacqueline J. *The Power of Stories: A Guide for Leading Multiracial and Multicultural Congregations*. Nashville, TN: Abingdon Press, 2008.

Lewis, Jacqueline J., and John Janka. *The Pentecost Paradigm: Ten Strategies for Becoming a Multiracial Congregation*. Louisville, KY: Westminster John Knox Press, 2018.

Muir, Fredric, ed. *Turning Point: Essays on a New Unitarian Universalism*. Boston, MA: Skinner House Books, 2016.

Oluo, Ijeoma. *So You Want to Talk about Race*. Berkeley, CA: Seal Press, 2018.

Ortiz, Manuel. *One New People: Models for Developing a Multiethnic Church*. Downers Grove, IL: InterVarsity Press, 1996.

Paul, Jon. "I Need an Accomplice, Not an Ally." http://efniks.com/the-deep-dive-features/2017/9/6/i-need-an-accomplice-not-an-ally.

Rahnema, Mitra, ed. *Centering: Navigating Race, Authenticity, and Power in Ministry*. Boston, MA: Skinner House Books, 2017.

Regan, Margaret. *The Death of Josseline: Immigration Stories from the Arizona-Mexico Borderlands*. Boston, MA: Beacon Press, 2010.

Stevenson, Bryan. *Just Mercy: A Story of Justice and Redemption*. New York, NY: Spiegel & Grau, 2015.

Tatum, Beverly. *"Why Are All the Black Kids Sitting Together in the Cafeteria?" and Other Conversations about Race*. New York, NY: Basic Books, 1997.

Thurman, Howard. *Footprints of a Dream: The Story of the Church for the Fellowship of All Peoples*. New York, NY: Harper and Brothers, 1959.

Tochluk, Shelly. *Witnessing Whiteness: The Need to Talk about Race and How to Do It*. Lanham, MD: Rowman & Littlefield Education, 2010.

"UUs, Music, and Appropriation, with DeReau K. Farrar and Dr. Glen Thomas Rideout." Episode 196 of *The VUU*, a podcast of the Church of the Larger Fellowship, October 26, 2017. youtube.com/watch?v=vW8kiCkbA-8.

Yamamoto, Raven. "Takeaways from 'I need an accomplice, not an ally.'" laloyolan.com/social_justice/takeaways-from-i-need-an-accomplice-not-an-ally/article_c32b76d7-2194-5d94-92f1-d52a911e775d.html.

Yamamoto, Yuri, Chandra Snell, and Tim Hanami, eds. *Unitarian Universalists of Color: Stories of Struggle, Courage, Love, and Faith*. Self-published, Lulu, 2017. uuofcolorstoryproject.com.

Yancey, George. *One Body, One Spirit: Principles of Successful Multiracial Churches*. Downers Grove, IL: InterVarsity Press, 2003.

FROM THE UUA

"Building the World We Dream About." An antiracism multicultural program. uua.org/re/tapestry/adults/btwwda.

"Decentering Whiteness in Worship." A webinar recorded on June 1, 2017, by Rev. Erika Hewitt, Dr. Glen Thomas Rideout, and Julica Hermann de la Fuente; and a follow-up conversation recorded on September 12, 2017, among Julica Hermann de la Fuente, Dr. Glen Thomas Rideout, Christina Rivera, and Rev. Erika Hewitt. uua.org/worship/words/decentering-whiteness-worship-webinar.

Justice General Assembly, New Orleans, LA, 2017. Video, audio, transcripts, and workshop materials. uua.org/ga/past/2017.

Fortification. A podcast about the spiritual lives and spiritual sustenance of leaders in social justice movements. uua.org/action/love/fortification-podcast.

Las voces del camino: Un complemento de "Singing the living tradition." Boston, MA: Unitarian Universalist Association. 2009.

"Racial and Cultural Diversity in Unitarian Universalism." Resolution of Immediate Witness, General Assembly, Calgary, AB, 1992. uua.org/action/statements/racial-and-cultural-diversity-unitarian-universalism.

"Toward an Anti-racist Unitarian Universalist Association." Business Resolution, General Assembly, Phoenix, AZ, 1997. uua.org/action/statements/toward-anti-racist-unitarian-universalist-association.

UUA Common Read. Past and present selections offer starting points for community-wide conversations that support building multicultural, antiracist Beloved Community. uua.org/books/read.

OTHER EDUCATIONAL TOOLS AND CURRICULA

"Beloved Conversations: Meditations on Race and Ethnicity." A curriculum for exploring the role of race/ethnicity in individual and congregational lives, offered by Meadville Lombard Theological School. meadville.edu/fahs-collaborative/fahs-curriculum-catalogue/beloved-conversations/.

BLUUBox Spiritual Subscription. A monthly service from Black Lives of Unitarian Universalism, offering Black-led spiritual content and analysis. blacklivesuu.com/bluuboxhomepage/.

Eighth Principle of Unitarian Universalism. 8thprincipleuu.org/.

"Implementing Small Group Social Change Ministry." A guide written by Kelly Dignan and Kierstin Homblette Allen, with a video talk by Rev. Howell Lind on small group justice ministry. mdduua.org/ministries/building-beloved-community/small-group-ministry-for-social-change/.

Intercultural Development Inventory. A tool for assessing and improving intercultural competence. idiinventory.com.

Small group ministry sessions developed at the First Unitarian Church of San José. sanjoseuu.org/FUSJC_SGM/sgm_sessionLists.htm. See especially the general sessions "G342—People of Color and White Allies" and "G379—White Fragility."

"UU White Supremacy Teach-ins." Offers readings, stories, sample sermons, and more, as resources originally intended for the teach-ins held by Unitarian Universalist congregations in April and October 2017. uuteachin.org.

DOCUMENTARIES

The Color of Fear. Directed by Lee Mun Wah. 1994. Available on DVD and as streaming video from Stirfry Seminars & Consulting, diversitytrainingfilms.com.

Cracking the Codes: The System of Racial Inequity. Directed by Shakti Butler. 2014. crackingthecodes.org.

Middle Collegiate Church. YouTube channel with worship services and other videos. youtube.com/user/MiddleNYC.

Traces of the Trade: A Story from the Deep North. Directed by Katrina Browne, Alla Kovgan, and Jude Ray. 2008. tracesofthetrade.org. Discussion guide available at uua.org/racial-justice/discuss/movies.

PODCAST SERIES

Brown, Autumn, and adrienne marie brown. *How to Survive the End of the World.* endoftheworldshow.org.

Fortification. See "From the UUA" above.

Letson, Al. *Reveal.* www.revealnews.org.
Mathews, Rev. Michael-Ray. *Prophetic Resistance.* propheticresistance podcast.libsyn.com.
Wilmore, Larry. *Black on the Air.* art19.com/shows/larry-wilmore.

FICTIONAL AND FICTIONALIZED FILMS

BlacKkKlansman. Directed by Spike Lee. Focus Features, 2018.
Black Panther. Directed by Ryan Coogler. Walt Disney Studios, 2018.
Mi familia. Directed by Gregory Nava. New Line Cinema, 1995. Discussion guide available at uua.org/racial-justice/discuss/movies.
Smoke Signals. Directed by Chris Eyre. Miramax, 1998. Discussion guide available at uua.org/racial-justice/discuss/movies.

ORGANIZATIONS

Allies for Racial Equity (ARE). Antiracist movement among white Unitarian Universalists. alliesforracialequity.wildapricot.org.
Black Lives of Unitarian Universalism (BLUU). Provides information, resources, and support for Black Unitarian Universalists and works to expand the role and visibility of Black UUs within the faith. www.blacklivesuu.com.
Diverse and Revolutionary Unitarian Universalist Multicultural Ministries (DRUUMM). National organization for Unitarian Universalists of color. druumm.onefireplace.org.
Kaleidoscope Institute. Offers information on the practice of Mutual Invitation, as well as much else, in pursuit of its mission to provide resources to equip church leaders to create sustainable churches and communities. kscopeinstitute.org.
King Center. Offers information about the Beloved Community and other aspects of Dr. Martin Luther King Jr.'s legacy and philosophy. thekingcenter.org.

Acknowledgments:
Villages to Thank

FROM BOTH OF US: We truly have whole villages of people to thank for their support and their contributions to the writing of this book. We can only list a small percentage of them by name here. We hope that all who have played a role will feel their spirits shining through these pages and know that we carry you always in our hearts.

Dr. Janice Marie Johnson, co-director of Ministries and Faith Development with the Unitarian Universalist Association (formerly the UUA's multicultural ministries and leadership director), launched this project in December 2013 when she asked if Nancy would respond to a request for proposals to Skinner House Books for books on multiculturalism and antiracism in our Unitarian Universalist movement. Nancy asked Karin to become her partner on the project within the month, and we co-authors spent nine months crafting that proposal. From that initial invitation, Janice Marie set us free to find our focus and our voice, meeting with us at General Assembly each year and waiting with abundant patience for the manuscript to reach completion. We consider her the godmother of this book, and we are grateful!

Mary Benard, editorial director of Skinner House Books and UUA Publications, has supported us and urged us on from the beginning too. Her belief in us helped us to embrace our new identities as co-authors. Her respect, her questions and suggestions, and her feedback have built our trust in our instincts about the direction of the project—an immeasurable gift, especially when our own confidence flagged and our inner critics threatened to shut down the creative flow. Thank you, Mary, for being coach and doula for this book.

Shoshanna Green has brought a graceful touch, a fine eye for detail, and a complex and wide-ranging understanding of the Unitarian Universalist world to the copyedit of this book. Kathryn Sky-Peck and Jeff Miller, in their work on the cover and design, have brought beauty to these pages. We are so lucky that all three of these artists are part of the Skinner House team.

At Mary Benard's suggestion, we applied for and received two grants from the Fund for Unitarian Universalism. These grants made possible our site visits to the congregations studied here. Without the generosity and vision of the grant panel, there truly would be no book, for these in-person experiences allowed us to enter into these stories with nuance and depth.

Well before we started work on this project, we were passionate fans of the Rev. Dr. Jacqui Lewis, senior minister of Middle Collegiate Church in New York City, and Middle Collegiate's annual Leading Edge Conference (now the Revolutionary Love Conference) had inspired and provoked our growth. Once our work on this book began, however, these conferences and Rev. Jacqui's personal encouragement provided just the fuel we needed when our own tanks were running dry.

The sheer volume of our thanks to all our conversation partners could overflow oceans. The ministers, members, and friends of the congregations we studied, and other colleagues and friends for whom the work of building multicultural, antiracist Beloved Community is a sacred call, have shared their time, their thoughts, their hearts, and their stories with us with remarkable honesty and vulnerability. You have taught us what it means to be on this journey for good. You have shown us the rich intersectional truths of individual personalities and life experiences woven into larger communities striving to dismantle oppressive systems.

We include among our conversation partners the authors we have read, the speakers we have listened to, the artists who have inspired us, and the activists who have shown us ways to keep on moving forward. Most of these people will never know how much they have influenced and guided us. We hope they know how much good they do in the world.

We want to lift up two more people by name who have served as spiritual guides for this project: Rev. Abhi Janamanchi and religious educator Aisha Hauser. Their friendship, their words of wisdom, and their insights have stretched and enlivened us each time we have met, talked, or corresponded. Early in the project, we began to schedule semiannual meetings with Rev. Abhi. Each of these holy conversations has grounded us in the real hope and purpose of this work. We have come to see Rev. Abhi as our minister for this project.

Similarly, Aisha has been our teacher. Meeting her for coffee, sharing rapid-fire conversations whenever we are in the same state, and paying attention to her passionate perspectives on white supremacy culture and its impact on our institutions have deepened our own perceptions. Her love of life and generous friendship have brought us joy. Her courage and leadership in our faith have served as models to which we aspire. Aisha also served as first reader on this book, and her comments have made it infinitely better.

Thank you, Aisha and Rev. Abhi, for all that you are and all that you do. We know that you, in turn, are surrounded by a cloud of witnesses and partners in your work, and our gratitude extends to this wider circle too.

FROM NANCY: Karin, how could we have known that our nascent friendship and early work together in California would provide such a sturdy launch pad for the journey we have taken with this project? It seems a kind of miracle that we could take this leap together and discover just how compatible we are for this intimate work! From that January phone call when I surprised you with the proposal to work together on this book, through the long slog and many doubts and fears we have weathered together, to the wee-hours happy dance we shared when we sent the manuscript off to Skinner House, your courageous "yes" to all of this experience has taught me so much about risk and endurance, wisdom, self-awareness, and love. Thanks to you and to your beautiful family for adding this calling into an already full life. I look forward to all the ways in which our friendship will continue to grow.

To my far-flung and ever-close Framily—you simply make my living and loving possible. I cherish every visit, every phone call, every story shared and life experience mined for all it's worth. Terry Ross, Deb Norton and Chris Nottoli, JP Stephenson and Rusty Kelly, Helen Zelon and all my Brooklyn family, Douglas Leach and Scott Cunningham, Susan Letteer, Alisa Genovese, Revs. Beth Banks, Alicia Forde, and Leslie Takahashi, Vail Weller, and other beloved Unitarian Universalist colleagues, my housemates of Atlantis (Hannah and Graham, Leslie and Girish, Missy and Phillip, Kasey and Joel, and the children), and the Hallelujah Sisters in San José, Revs. Dana Bainbridge and Jennifer Goto—your companionship, not just during the writing of this book but throughout the ages and stages of my life, has offered a home of the soul and helped me to clarify my thinking and tap into my feelings so that I could find the words to put on the page.

To everyone and every place that provided shelter and a place to write, I give my thanks: from libraries and coffeehouses across the country, to the homes of old friends opened to me after decades apart, to my sweet "second homes" with the good folks listed in the previous paragraph. Patty Strong and Granny's Kitchen in Julian, California, and the crew at the Starbucks on Coleman in San José deserve special mention. You all are awesome, generous participants in this project.

My teachers form another long list of those whose words and lives are woven into this book. Many of them I have the honor to also call my friends and Framily. Everett Fly, from elementary school in San Antonio; Revs. Mel Hoover and Bill Gardner, from the UUA's old Faith in Action Department; Dr. Mark A. Hicks; Paula Cole Jones; Akemi Flynn and the members of People Acting in Community Together's Beloved Community Team—thank you for helping me to shift my way of being in order to join in the work of building multicultural, antiracist Beloved Community.

Finally, my heartfelt thanks go to the members, friends, and staff of the First Unitarian Church of San José, including my dear colleague, now minister emeritus, Rev. Geoff Rimositis. Your patience and support as this project stretched over many years testify to your capacity to Make Love Visible in all you say and do. And Susie Idzik, interim director of religious education, you arrived in time to witness the final stages of the project's labor and delivery. With your speaking truth and cheering on both the congregation and me, we made it through the trials of my holding two more than full-time jobs.

FUCSJ, I am so grateful for all the ways that we are growing together.

FROM KARIN: There are two ministers without whom I would not be a Unitarian Universalist today. The first of these is my co-author Nancy. During a time when I was disillusioned with Unitarian Universalism, all but ready to walk away, Nancy's listening ear and unfailing commitment to the work of antiracism and multiculturalism enabled me to hold on long enough to find a new spiritual home. I am so honored to write this book with her and proud to call her my friend. Nancy has taught me much about relationship, trust, and faith, and I am deeply grateful that she is in my life.

The second minister to whom I am indebted is Rev. Fred Small, former senior minister at First Parish in Cambridge. His generosity of ministry and unflagging support for my leadership were essential in my journey of healing, and his articulation and demonstration of Unitarian Universalist values have both strengthened and deepened my faith. I will carry the lessons he imparted to me for a lifetime.

I have immense gratitude for DRUUMM (Diverse and Revolutionary Unitarian Universalist Multicultural Ministries), and its Asian/Pacific Islander Caucus, for providing support and spiritual nourishment to me and so many other Unitarian Universalists of color.

I thank all the ministers, staff, and congregants from First Parish in Cambridge who have supported me throughout this project and who continue to create communities that celebrate the sacred in all. Revs. Lilia Cuervo, Danielle Di Bona, Clyde Grubbs, Elizabeth Nguyen, and Mykal Slack have been especially significant in my journey. I am grateful to past and present members of the Transformation Team and Racial Equity Team, with whom I have shared tears and laughter, difficult conversations, and life-changing revelations. Of particular note from these teams are Charlene Galarneau, Marcia Hams,

Gloria Korsman, Chris McElroy, LeLaina Romero, Susan Shepherd, Rashid Shaikh, Rev. María Cristina Vlassidis Burgoa, and Marcia Yousik.

Finally, I thank my husband, Cade Murray, who has always encouraged me to follow my dreams, and our daughters, Kiera and Kyla, who inspire me every day to work for a better world.